Unity with diversity in the European economy: the Community's Southern frontier

Centre for Economic Policy Research

The Centre for Economic Policy Research is a network of 130 Research Fellows, based primarily in European universities. The Centre coordinates its Fellows' research activities, providing central administrative services and communicating research to the public and private sectors. CEPR is an entrepreneur, developing research initiatives with the producers, consumers and sponsors of research. Established in 1983, CEPR is already a European economics research organization with uniquely wide-ranging scope and activities.

CEPR is a registered educational charity. Grants from the Leverhulme Trust, the Esmée Fairbairn Charitable Trust, the Baring Foundation, the Bank of England and Citibank provide institutional finance. The ESRC supports the Centre's dissemination programme and, with the Nuffield Foundation, its programme of research workshops, while the Alfred P. Sloan and Ford Foundations support the Centre's programme of research in International Macroeconomics. None of these organizations gives prior review to the Centre's publications nor do they necessarily endorse the views expressed therein.

The Centre is pluralist and non-partisan, bringing economic research to bear on the analysis of medium- and long-run policy questions. The research that it disseminates may include views on policy, but the Board of Governors of the Centre does not give prior review to such publications and the Centre itself takes no institutional policy positions. The opinions expressed in this volume are those of the authors and not those of the Centre for Economic Policy Research.

Officers

Director
Professor Richard Portes

Assistant Director
Stephen Yeo

Director of Finance and Research Administration
Wendy Thompson

31 January 1990

Unity with diversity in the European economy: the Community's Southern frontier

Edited by
CHRISTOPHER BLISS
and
JORGE BRAGA DE MACEDO

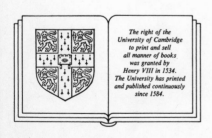

The right of the
University of Cambridge
to print and sell
all manner of books
was granted by
Henry VIII in 1534.
The University has printed
and published continuously
since 1584.

CAMBRIDGE UNIVERSITY PRESS
Cambridge
New York   Port Chester
Melbourne   Sydney

Published by the Press Syndicate of the University of Cambridge
The Pitt Building, Trumpington Street, Cambridge CB2 1RP
40 West 20th Street, New York, NY 10011, USA
10 Stamford Road, Oakleigh, Melbourne 3166, Australia

First published 1990

Printed in Great Britain at the University Press, Cambridge

British Library cataloguing in publication data
Unity with diversity in the European economy:
the Community's southern frontier.
1. European Community countries. Economic integration
I. Bliss, C. J. (Christopher John), 1940–
II. Macedo, Jorge Braga de
337.142

Library of Congress cataloguing in publication data applied for

ISBN 0 521 39520 8

CE

Contents

Figures

Tables

Preface

This volume contains the proceedings of the concluding conference of a research project on 'Economic Integration in the Enlarged European Community', conducted under the auspices of the Centre for Economic Policy Research. The conference was hosted by the European Cultural Center at Delphi on 26–27 October 1989. Our thanks are due to Pericles Nearhou for making available the facilities of the European Cultural Center, and to Litsa Florentis at the Center and Ann Shearlock at CEPR for their work in organizing the conference.

Financial support for the project was provided by the Commission of the European Communities, the German Marshall Fund of the United States, the Secretaría de Estado de Comercio of the Spanish Ministerio de Economía y Hacienda, the Fundación Banco Exterior de España, and the Instituto do Comercio Externo de Portugal, whose support we gratefully acknowledge.

Paul Compton and Sarah Wellburn at CEPR have been responsible for guiding this volume to press rapidly and efficiently, keeping contributors and editors to a very tight production schedule. Our thanks are due to them and to John Black of the University of Exeter, whose work as Production Editor has been invaluable.

Christopher Bliss
Nuffield College, Oxford
and Centre for Economic Policy Research

Jorge Braga de Macedo
Commission of the European Communities
Universidade Nova de Lisboa
and Centre for Economic Policy Research

15 January 1990

Conference participants

Christopher Bliss *Nuffield College, Oxford, and CEPR*
William Branson *Princeton University and CEPR*
Christina Corado *Universidade Nova de Lisboa*
Michael Emerson *Commission of the European Communities and CEPR*
Nicholas Floros *University of Athens*
Vitor Gaspar *Universidade Nova de Lisboa and Ministry of Finance, Lisbon*
Konstantine Gatsios *Fitzwilliam College, Cambridge, and CEPR*
Nicholas Glytsos *Centre of Planning and Economic Research, Athens*
Jordi Gual *Instituto de Estudios Superiores de la Empresa, Barcelona, and CEPR*
Alexis Jacquemin *Commission of the European Communities*
Nicholas Karavitis *University of Athens*
Louka Katseli *University of Athens and CEPR*
Nickolina Kosteletou *University of Athens*
Leslie Lipschitz *International Monetary Fund*
Jorge Braga de Macedo *Commission of the European Communities, Universidade Nova de Lisboa and CEPR*
Luis Mañas *Repsol SA*
Carmela Martín *Universidad de Madrid*
Jackie Morin *Commission of the European Communities*
David Newbery *Churchill College, Cambridge, and CEPR*
Joan Pearce *Commission of the European Communities*
Richard Portes *CEPR and Birkbeck College, London*
Dani Rodrik *Harvard University and CEPR*
André Sapir *Université Libre de Bruxelles and CEPR*
Alexander Sarris *University of Athens*
Alasdair Smith *University of Sussex and CEPR*
Anthony Venables *University of Southampton and CEPR*
José Viñals *Banco de España and CEPR*
Stavros Zographakis *University of Athens*

Foreword

MICHAEL EMERSON and
RICHARD PORTES

Territorial enlargement versus deepening of the integration process: the European Community has been persistently concerned, if not at times tormented by this dialectic. It was true of the first enlargement in the 1970s. So also in the 1980s, as the Community decided more ambitiously than in the previous decade to enlarge and deepen both at the same time. Greece joined in 1981, and Portugal and Spain in 1986. Thus the second enlargement saw the Community's divergences in terms of level of development widen considerably. Notwithstanding, 1985 saw the Commission advocate a new push to complete the Single Market in the eight years to follow.

Already by 1988 the agenda lengthened further, with renewed consideration being given to monetary union. Spain then joined the European Monetary System in 1989. Also in the late 1980s the issue of further enlargement was being posed again, this time by Turkey in 1987 and Austria in 1989; and the broader question of EC–EFTA ties became prominent. At the close of the decade the Community's future relationship with Eastern Europe came explosively to the top of its priorities.

The present study has attempted to throw light on the economics of this dialectic between widening and deepening. The questions of concern to the politicians have been quite clear. Put in a neutral way, could the relatively weak economies of the new, geographically peripheral Member States withstand the double shock of accession and completion of the Single Market? Worse, might their economies be driven into relative depression, as was seen in the Mezzogiorno after Italian unification? Or better, might the double shock enable these countries to accelerate their modernization? Do economic principles point to a pre-determined outcome? If not, what are the conditions for securing the better outcome? What should be the responsibilities of national and Community authorities in this process?

At the outset of the research programme reported here, there was no self-evident answer to these questions. Economists were variously able to point both to divergence as well as convergence theorems. On the right, Adam Smith optimists presumed that the invisible hand would secure advantage for all. On the left, Kaldorian pessimists feared for the progressive immiserization of the weak and peripheral regions. The fundamental issue was quite open.

It is for the editors, Christopher Bliss and Jorge Braga de Macedo, to draw together the conclusions of the various studies in a comprehensive manner. For our part, we draw attention selectively to some of the main points that emerged at the programme's concluding conference in Delphi in October 1989.

One fundamental conclusion is that in fact no simple paradigm, be it that of the Adam Smith optimists or the Kaldorian pessimists, prevailed. It all depends. This may sound like banal agnosticism or the well-known story of the two-handed economist. But the conclusions are in fact a good deal more dramatic.

The degree of indeterminacy in the likely outcome is not a small margin surrounding a neutral centre point. Rather, several arguments point to a wide possible range of positive or negative impacts. Since these can accumulate, the range of overall possible outcomes may indeed be between brilliant achievement and big difficulties. Four examples of this type – the arguments that can go either way – may be picked out.

First comes an argument from the analysis of industrial organization and the location of investment, as set out by Paul Krugman and Anthony Venables. A small, peripheral and previously protected economy stands to make particularly large gains in economic welfare as a result of integrating with a large, efficient economy. The relatively low wage may also then attract investment from the core. On the other hand, there will be some tendency for industry to concentrate nearer to the core region, partly because of the higher amount of protection relinquished by the peripheral economy. It seems difficult to know *a priori* on which side the balance of advantages will fall.

Second is an argument well known in the literature about the sequencing and design of programmes of measures to remove market distortions. A first-best solution is usually seen as coming from a comprehensive improvement of product and factor markets. If instead only partial reforms are undertaken while other pronounced market distortions remain, then the size of the likely gains may be highly uncertain, and the partial reforms might even bring overall losses.

In the case of EC enlargement and completion of the internal market, the accent is on the liberalization of the markets for tradable goods and services and internationally mobile capital. Labour markets are little affected: external mobility is assured, but internal rigidities are not directly attacked. In addition, public goods and services and many aspects of financial market regulation are not directly affected. Thus the externally imposed reforms are indeed only partial. The country studies for Greece, Portugal and Spain analyse the extent to which these countries are so far succeeding or failing with their internal measures to assure overall coherence of their policies addressed to product and factor markets.

Third is a related argument which has a more institutional character. The issue is whether the Member States can secure support from the Community institutions in the pursuit of national policy objectives. Comments at the conference by Konstantine Gatsios used the example of competition policy, where the Commission has an independent capacity to rule national subsidies illegal. If national governments and the Commission pursue consistent objectives, for example to secure higher efficiency in enterprises earlier benefiting from state support, the Member State can derive enhanced credibility for its own policy. But if the Member State and the Commission are working at cross purposes, the confusion perceived by the private sector can be very costly for the economy.

Fourth is an argument relating to the structural funds, which is set out in the paper by Christopher Bliss. Widely differing impacts are possible. In the worst case the beneficiary, whether government or private sector interests, is induced to pursue rent-seeking strategies rather than advances in productivity to complement the funds' contribution to improving infrastructure or the stock of labour skills. In the best case the beneficiary pursues these complementarities, and more broadly the nation is encouraged to raise its level of ambition in responding to the challenges of integration into the EC and modernization.

The accumulation of these four arguments points out both opportunity and risk. If all four factors can be turned positively, their combination can become not just a set of policy improvements, but rather a comprehensive and credible regime change, so perceptions of the economic attractiveness and prospects of a country may be quite transformed. Synergies are created. In the contrary case, there may be a failure in the processes of competition, with severe costs and delays before the resources of non-viable enterprises are redeployed more efficiently. The three country studies portray Spain as coming closer to the former model, Greece closer to the latter, with Portugal occupying a somewhat ambiguous position in between.

These were major themes at the conference. There were also several issues that might have been expected to emerge strongly, but did not in fact do so. These instances of 'the dog that did not bark' may offer clues that will help in identifying the key determinants of success or failure in the integration process. Here we give five important examples.

First, participants did not call for massive expansion of the structural funds. As suggested above, it is quality that will be decisive, at the already planned substantial quantity. Efforts should focus on proper targeting and implementation of structural fund policies and complementary measures at national level.

Second, although at the onset of the research we had expected cross-border labour migration in the Community to be a prominent theme, in the event it played a relatively minor role in the studies and the conference. There was considerable discussion of the problems of national labour markets, but international mobility of labour between the South and North of the existing Community drew much less attention than the integration of goods and capital markets.

Third, although the Brussels compromise of February 1988 has surely not resolved the Community's problems with the Common Agricultural Policy – if only because of its effects outside the EC – the CAP went virtually unmentioned in the conference papers and discussions. It is clearly of major significance for the economic structures of the recent entrants, and for intra-EC resource transfers, but it may perhaps be taken in its current form as a datum in assessing how the integration process will work over the next several years.

Fourth, the often acrimonious disputes over 'harmonization' and Brussels-imposed uniformity in the approach to 1992 also did not feature in our meeting. These issues – the details of taxes, standards and regulations – are perhaps more significant to the more developed countries in the Community. They will have relatively little bearing on the success or failure of the integration process for Greece, Portugal and Spain.

Finally, we heard little of the arguments over fiscal rules and macroeconomic policy coordination that have become so important since the Delors Committee Report. Of course policy choices with regard to the EMS, particularly for Greece and Portugal, were major future themes, as was the progressive loss of monetary policy autonomy, but there was much more attention to the domestic constraints on and problems of fiscal policy than to any rules that might be prescribed centrally.

These are the lessons we drew from the conferences and the research programme it summarized. Their importance is much enhanced by current developments in Eastern Europe. The work presented here illuminates the key issues underlying the interplay between widening and deepening in the existing European Community. It suggests the relevant questions in examining possible forms of association with the Eastern countries, as well as others that have indicated their desire for closer attachment to the Community. The experience of Greece, Portugal and Spain may also help to interpret and guide the development policy choices of the Eastern countries.

Moreover, there is little doubt that beyond the widening-deepening dialectic there lies ahead for the Community a similar and fundamental tension between North–South and East–West integration. We may hope that the research reported in this volume will contribute to understanding and perhaps to resolving these tensions. We commend it to the reader.

1 Introduction

CHRISTOPHER BLISS and
JORGE BRAGA de MACEDO

1 Enlargement and integration

The enlargement of the European Community (EC) is the expansion which brought in Greece in 1981 and Spain and Portugal in 1986. For want of a better term, we shall refer to the three recently added members of the Community as 'the newly integrating countries' (NICs) of the EC. The integration of the NICs is made more complex by the fact that the EC and its European environment are changing so fast. Thus the problem of transition includes the effects on the NICs and on the rest of the EC of the mutual desire to achieve an integrated European economy.

On the internal front, the single market initiative embodied in the Single European Act of 1985 will abolish by January 1993 a wide range of barriers to trade within the Community, including customs procedures, local quality regulations, and many similar constraints. Deepening and broadening the existing European Monetary System (EMS) will amplify the single-market effects and may induce an even greater growth momentum than was observed in the past eight years. By raising the standards of convergence of performance and policies among heterogeneous countries, however, the objective of a single currency will also raise the risks of divergence of living standards across the European economies.

On the external front, the attractiveness of the Community as a whole has been dramatically illustrated by the requests for assistance following the rebirth of democracy in central and Eastern Europe. Further enlargements or deeper forms of association with neighbouring countries are therefore likely. These will affect the degree of divergence among the current members, but in which direction it is hard to predict. Pessimists will claim that the re-emerging Central European division of labour will threaten cohesion among the Twelve. Optimists will argue that a broader market will bring the NICs closer to the EC core.

Uncertainty attaches to the question of what changes will be brought

1

about by the single market. The road to the single currency, let alone the objective, remain controversial for some EC member states. Excessive state intervention and regulation, protected and inefficient industry, obsolete and stagnant financial systems, low wages and low productivity; these are not invariable features of the NICs. Yet they are found even in Spain, the least 'southern' of the NICs. The optimists and the pessimists alike will look to the NICs for an indication of what a single market and currency might bring. In those countries both the greatest benefits of the reforms and the most awkward transition problems may be encountered.

For this reason, an examination of these countries can illuminate the general issue of what full membership of the single-market Community en route for economic and monetary union will entail. This will in turn shed light on possible future enlargements – Austria and Turkey – as well as on the upgrading of relations with the European Free Trade Association (EFTA) – the creation of the European Economic Space – and last but not least the prospect of a Common European Home.

2   Unity with diversity

Unification raises many issues and it would be a mistake to attempt a comprehensive list. The issue of convergence versus divergence often arises, however, and may help to focus the enlargement and integration discussion. Of course both tendencies will assert themselves and policy will often be addressed to influencing the consequences of unification in this regard. Unification will necessarily imply a considerable convergence of goods prices and of the environment of regulations and institutions within which producers and factors will operate. We shall call this regime convergence, and unity in the title has that connotation. It does not follow that regime convergence will cause the regions of the Community, or particular member countries, or like groups, such as industrial workers, to experience convergence in the sense of the constituent economies of the Community tending to become more alike. On the contrary, divergence may be the outcome.

The theme of this book is that both convergence and divergence are likely to result. Indeed, diversity is what we observe in the experience of the three NICs. While we would take their diversity to be fundamental in their European heritage – and indeed in what is sometimes called European culture – an enduring disparity of living standards among the twelve member countries would threaten mutual political responsiveness. In time the disparity of living standards across the Common European Home will be questioned along similar lines. Hence diversity and unity interact on the internal and external fronts.

Regime convergence will not always lead to uniformity of local situations. For example, Community-wide codes and regulations for banking and finance may not eliminate the local market effect on conditions experienced by borrowers, just as national codes have not eliminated local financial markets. Also, greater regime unification may result in actual conditions moving further apart. Countries and regions may increase the extent of their specialization when the market is enlarged. This suggests that convergence and divergence coexist and that whether convergence or divergence dominates depends on the particular situation: initial conditions, national and worldwide developments and policy responses at the regional, national and international level.

Standard trade theory teaches that international exchange will often tend to make countries more alike with regard to standards of living and more unlike with regard to production activities. The arguments pointing to that type of outcome are powerful and should not be lightly dismissed. But taking scale economies and imperfect competition into account, as has been increasingly done over the last ten years, substantially qualifies these long-accepted presumptions.

The finding that freeing trade will tend to make for a divergence in the pattern of production specialization turns out to be more robust than the conclusion that living standards will tend to converge, or even to improve everywhere. It is possible for an enlarged market to exhibit a strong centripetal tendency and for the peripheral regions or countries to suffer an absolute decline.

Three factors which counter that tendency need to be taken into account:

(1) As long as the periphery remains a source of cheap labour, it will compete for mobile, and especially labour-intensive, activity;

(2) Labour migration out of the disadvantaged regions should raise the standard of living, at least of the migrants, and ideally of those who remain behind; and,

(3) Policy directed towards raising income in the periphery may offset what would otherwise be net losses. The policies might take the form of direct transfers, might involve the partial subsidy of investment, or might consist of assistance to adjust through, for example, retraining.

The picture has been painted with a very broad brush. To obtain a clearer view one has to look at the particular, which is what the following chapters do. The chapters divide according to how they select their specific approach. The issues of structural interventions, trade and financial liberalization, complemented by a supra-national view of the

European car market, are addressed by the first collection of papers. Building on the issue papers, three country studies describe the present state of the newly integrating national economies and point up implications for their further integration into the European economy.

3   Adjustment and compensation

What can economic theory teach us concerning such radical economic reforms as the single market initiative or the 1988 decision to use the new Community structural funds to enhance economic and social cohesion? Christopher Bliss offers the twin concepts of identification and addressing to illuminate the problem of helping groups adversely affected by reforms. The former concerns the selection of the groups to be assisted, the latter the choice of the mechanism for delivering assistance. The two need to be considered together because a process of self-selection frequently operates.

With regard to identification, losses that are due to reform and losses, or relative disadvantage, that are due to unrelated causes stand side by side, for there is no good reason to differentiate strongly between them in the way that the Pareto compensation principle does. The ideal mechanism is the lump-sum transfer, a once-for-all pay-off of the minimum cost of a loss. Only unanticipated compensation schemes are lump-sum and non-distorting.

Although self-selection is a good principle to aim for, it may be that no scheme that achieves what is wanted will also meet this requirement. An appealing idea is that parties should be compensated for the cost of adjusting. It is argued, however, that subsidy for adjustment is only an ideal mechanism where paternalistic considerations or externalities bulk large. Questions of dynamics and future responses raise substantial problems. Once-for-all payments for the costs of reform and a refusal to pay more later may not be a credible strategy.

The Community is concerned with the reduction of inequality as well as with compensation for the cost of change. It proposes a loosely specified application of its structural funds to achieve these ends. The concept is correct. In some versions, however, this programme could prove to be extremely expensive. Otherwise the coverage may have to be disappointingly narrow. Focusing on accelerated adjustment will not necessarily narrow the scope and control the cost. If rapid adjustment generates external economies, then it should in principle be subsidized. Yet the gains may be private or the externalities negative. Some formula will be needed, but this one seems questionable. Confounding aid for adjustment with assistance for the unfortunate may lead to ineffective unfocused intervention. The Community's problem is similar to those addressed by various national regional policy programmes. These have often disappointed, and the Community should seek to learn from these experiences.

Bliss also emphasizes the need to maintain adherence to the principle of openness and expanded trade with the outside world. Internal reform and external trade relations interact in complex, even obscure, ways. There is a danger that the commitment to openness will amount to little more than the avoidance of extreme injuries from trade, and that trade policy will become a mechanism for alleviating internal stresses within the Community, including the problems which the structural funds were meant to obviate but to which they may in practice prove unequal.

In his comment, Michael Emerson argues for a more precise description of the objectives of the structural funds. Specifically, equalizing resource endowment and securing regime change are as much central concerns in the application of Community policy as are the regional issues emphasized by Bliss. Equalizing resource endowment involves ensuring that all regions have the infrastructure to permit them to 'accept the full force of EC competition'. Regime change is a similar concept with a still broader reach. The structural funds are a sweetener which may help to persuade the weaker EC members to risk the perilous switch away from 'protectionist state corporatism'.

4   Trade liberalization and catching up: another U curve?

The effects of reducing trade barriers between national units which vary in market size and wage level are examined by Paul Krugman and Anthony Venables. In the context of the popular constant-returns-to-scale perfect-competition trade models, the size of the domestic market is unimportant, and, provided that factor availability does not differ excessively, trade allows the periphery to find employment for its labour at the same level of wages as is paid at the centre.

Krugman and Venables show that these conclusions are profoundly altered when increasing returns to scale and an imperfectly competitive sector are introduced. There are clear implications here for the European Community. The addition of new members and the 1992 single market reforms both constitute reductions in barriers to trade, and the importance of increasing returns, and of imperfect competition and oligopoly, are generally conceded.

The country is not the natural unit to consider. Rather the centre will be a densely populated region with a high wage level, corresponding in Europe to the North–West industrial region centred on Belgium. The periphery may be thought of as Ireland and Southern Europe, including the three NICs. The advantage of the periphery is its low wage level. The disadvantage is the small size of its market.

The choice of industrial location may show a U-shaped response to a lowering of barriers to trade. If barriers are huge, production has to be located close to individual markets. The periphery attracts some manufacturing production, but its low labour costs do not suffice to attract industrial production destined for the centre. With moderate barriers to trade, economies of scale dominate and production is concentrated at one point, which will then be the centre with its large market. Finally, when there are very low barriers to trade, production is pulled to the low-cost production point, and the periphery becomes the manufacturing producer.

Whether lowering barriers to trade will help or harm peripheral industry involves a genuine ambiguity. It is important to note that the welfare issue is by no means identical with the location issue. Even when location is unaffected the small country benefits from a reduction in trade barriers because of increased competition among sellers in its home market. The model indicates that these welfare benefits are large.

In his comment, André Sapir stresses the unusual nature of the message that location matters. Drawing an analogy with Korea, which 'remains badly located', he sides with the optimists: 'neither Greece nor Portugal will remain in the periphery if they succeed like Spain in building a sufficient infrastructure'.

5   The European car market: a specific case of adjustment

The results of a computable model of the European car market are presented by Alasdair Smith in a modified version of his and Venables' well-known model. As is often the case with an exercise of this kind, as much interest attaches to the input of assumptions and the special considerations that have to be taken into account as to the conclusions.

The European car market is modelled as an imperfectly competitive environment, with access by outsiders, especially Japanese exporters, importantly restricted by voluntary export restraints (VERs). As in the Krugman and Venables model discussed above, a quantitatively important effect on welfare is the lowering of prices in regions in which the enlargement of the market strengthens competition.

When markets are merged, their individual VERs have to be consolidated into a Community-wide VER. It is shown that the outcome, say for welfare levels, is highly sensitive to the level at which the overall VER is set. A VER of given size is more costly in an integrated market than with segmented markets. The analysis is oriented towards computing short-run effects with a fixed number of firms. The authors note, however, that some of the effects modelled are so large that substantial long-run restructuring is no doubt implied.

6 Financial liberalization and integration

When the 1992 legislation on financial markets removes all formal restriction on capital movements, it will not be possible for a country which pegs its exchange rate to the EMS grid to pursue an independent monetary policy. Even a country which is outside the EMS but targets its exchange rate on the EMS, say by the stabilization of the real exchange rate with the EMS, will forfeit an independent monetary policy. Monetary policy cannot be applied both to stabilizing the exchange rate and to stabilizing the domestic economy against real shocks.

This seems to be a striking example of convergence, in this case of macroeconomic policies. If, however, macroeconomic policy must converge and disturbances to individual countries are separated and distinct in their timing and scale, convergence of policy will be associated with a divergence of individual instability, against which the authorities will be powerless to act.

William Branson argues that the above simple and familiar conclusion needs substantial qualification when local financial intermediaries enjoy an advantage in assessing and monitoring local borrowers. This is an instance of the well-known conclusion that imperfections of information importantly affect how the capital market operates.

The local intermediary enjoys a partial monopoly power, purchased with the overhead outlays necessary to gain the information and expertise with which to assess and monitor local borrowers. A two-tier interest rate system results, with a higher rate being paid by the small local borrower. The local intermediary and its depositors earn a surplus which is the difference between the high local lending rate and the common international rate of interest paid by the usually large internationally creditworthy borrower.

The existence of a two-tier market does not allow the domestic monetary authority to regulate the local rate of interest by altering its own money supply. Monetary policy as such remains constrained by the requirements of a fixed exchange rate. Other instruments which regulate local lending, however, such as credit ceilings, and especially the deposit rate paid by the intermediary, will affect the cost of credit to small borrowers in the domestic economy independently of the level of the international rate of interest.

An extra degree of freedom for the domestic monetary authority follows from its ability to regulate the local financial intermediary, and with that freedom comes the possibility of applying a domestic stabilization policy even when the exchange rate is fixed. A clear implication of this line of argument is the idea that national governments should aim to maintain control over the financial intermediaries that operate within their borders.

Another point emphasized by Branson is the radical consequences for the NICs' financial sectors implied by the structural reforms which follow the opening up of banking to international competition and the imposition of common regulatory principles. In Greece and Portugal (and also in Turkey) administered interest rates and credit rationing have favoured public enterprises and large capital-intensive private businesses. The consequence has been a kind of dualism, with costs of borrowing and marginal returns to investment differing markedly between the favoured entities and small-scale private business. Also, the balance sheets of some financial institutions are burdened with a mass of non-performing debt. Hence an abrupt liberalization could be followed by business failures, public deficits and unemployment.

Where fiscal policy is concerned, Branson argues that because stability of incomes increases factor mobility, there is a complementarity between an integrated fiscal system, such as that provided by the Federal Government in the USA, which stabilizes incomes against local fluctuations, and the factor mobility which aids adjustment in the face of fluctuations in demand.

Paul Krugman's note on macroeconomic adjustment and entry to the EC models a policy dilemma well-advertised by the example of Spain, but equally applicable to Portugal, Greece, or any country outside the narrow band of the EMS. A country which chooses to enter the exchange rate mechanism, or even to align its exchange rate informally with the EMS, has to take an important decision as to what level of its exchange rate to select. Moreover, argues Krugman, there is an essential asymmetry in the costs to the policy-maker of aiming too high or too low. Rolling back the real consequences of an undervalued exchange rate by creating a bit of extra inflation is less costly than repairing the consequences of an over-valued exchange rate by contractionary policies.

This asymmetry encourages the policymaker to aim low. Capital markets, however, always aim for the centre, as a systematic bias reduces profitability. The resulting conflict between the exchange rate which the policy-maker would like to start out with and the exchange rate which capital markets regard as right is the macroeconomic policy dilemma.

A characteristic outcome will result when the government tries to use monetary policy to hold down the exchange rate below the level which the capital market would otherwise think appropriate. This in turn leads to an expansion of the economy and to inflation. The inflation which the government wanted to keep in hand, in case its estimate of the right level for the exchange rate should turn out to be too low, is forced on it at the outset. In a version of the IS–LM model discussed by Branson, the author shows that a combination of looser monetary policy and tighter fiscal policy would provide a solution to the macroeconomic policy dilemma. Whether such a policy combination would be feasible depends on the particular case. For Spain a rough calculation suggests that a very severe fiscal tightening would be required.

Vitor Gaspar's joint comment on Branson and Krugman is concerned to refine those authors' arguments rather than to refute them. For Krugman's model he proposes that expectations about future exchange rates should be endogenous. Employing the strong assumptions of fixed long-run output and purchasing power parity, Gaspar derives an expression for the steady-state equilibrium exchange rate. It follows, for instance, that financial integration, by lowering the risk premium and transactions costs, will tend to lower the real exchange rate. Also, encouraging domestic saving emerges as an alternative to Krugman's fiscal tightness.

In response to Branson's paper Gaspar considers the question of the sustainability of public sector budget deficits. Not surprisingly his conclusions are quite similar to the conditions relating to the feasibility of debt service that have been applied to the case of debt-burdened countries.

7   Spain: the least 'Southern' country

In a synthetic paper José Viñals examines how 'Southern' the Spanish economy was when it joined the EC in 1986, and again today. He sees the adjustment process as involving the opening up of trade, the opening up of the capital account, and the liberalization of banking and financial services. In this context he asks which specific characteristics of goods, factor and financial markets make for difficult adjustment problems, and how far automatic market mechanisms can be relied upon to mitigate these problems. Finally he raises the issue of which Community-wide policies are both desirable in themselves and would facilitate the successful integration of Spain.

Among the four relatively poor members (Greece, Ireland, Spain and Portugal), Spain has by far the highest per capita income. Spain's inflation rate, public finances and external debt are closer to those of an average EC member than to the other three. Spanish unemployment is much higher, however, and this seems to go beyond differences in the measurement and meaning of unemployment in the various countries.

In the period before Spain joined the EC, trade deficits persisted and were only partly offset by surpluses on the services account, especially from tourism and remittances. The rising cost of energy imports contributed to the problem. There was a rapid expansion in international trade, and the current and trade account deficits shrank. Even so, Spain was relatively less open than other late entrants to the Community, because of its high nominal and effective protection.

Spain's exports included a large component of manufactures (78% on the eve of entry), but their composition was strongly biased towards moderate- and weak-demand products. Trade is seen to consist to a great extent of intra-industry exchange with the versions of products sold abroad being inferior to those imported. A careful comparison of the labour and capital inputs to exports and to domestic demand shows that Spain exports relatively labour-intensive goods to other OECD countries, while exporting relatively capital-intensive goods to non-OECD countries.

An examination of the size of Spanish manufacturing plants reveals that they are mostly small (only 0.2% employ more than 500 workers) and particularly they are smaller than comparable plants in Germany, France or Britain. This may help to explain the failure to develop new technology and new products, which in turn may account for the bias towards the production of weak-demand goods. The financial structure of Spanish industry exhibits the heavy reliance on bank debt to be found in several other EC countries.

Spain is often thought to be a country of cheap labour. The relevant comparison, however, is of unit labour costs evaluated at current exchange rates in a common currency. Spanish labour had a considerable advantage in 1970 which it lost by 1979 and largely regained by 1985 (when it is estimated as a 43% advantage). Will Spain retain this comparative advantage in cheap labour following the 'EC cum 1992' shock?

Spain has made extensive use of capital controls, both on short and long-term transactions, since 1939. Only recently has the process of dismantling these controls begun, and much remains to be done. Eventually, however, in a single-market Community, they must all go. The effect of controls on short-term capital movements is revealed by covered interest arbitrage differentials. Although these have been small, the reason is that the authorities intervened regularly in the forward market. None the less, the abolition of short-term capital controls is unlikely to produce a large shock to the economy.

The Spanish banking system is characterized as costly, and also profitable by virtue of a high degree of concentration and a consequent weakness of competitive pressures. Other financial markets are sometimes perilously thin, including the long-term bond market and the stock market. There are fears that after 1992 the stock market might be swept away as business moved to a larger centre such as London. More likely the Spanish stock exchange would continue to operate as a local exchange taking advantage of local expertise, much as regional stock markets operate in Britain or the US. In that case there would have to be an improvement in the efficiency and promptness of settlement.

The most difficult adjustment problems for the Spanish economy will come from the real trade side and from the need to maintain the advantage of cheap labour while improving the functioning of the labour market. Patterns of production and international trade will need to adapt to reduced protection against imports and to the need for efficient production with reasonable scale economies. Trade adjustment may be classified under the familiar headings of trade creation (expanded Spanish trade with the EC) and trade diversion (substitution of higher cost EC import sources for non-EC sources). Since Spain must reduce its tariffs against the outside world to conform to the common external tariff, it seems likely that gains from trade creation will exceed any losses from trade diversion and that the changes will increase general welfare. The usual caveat that particular groups may be adversely affected will apply.

A detailed examination of the effects of Spanish membership in the 1986–88 period shows that, while comparative advantage explains much of the change which resulted, specialization within the intra-industry category seems also to have increased.

Where the capital account is concerned, short-term controls have been oriented more to discouraging the inflow of 'hot money' than to keeping capital in the country. In one perspective of 1992 it is noted that with the peseta shadowing the EMS, as it already does, and with free capital mobility, monetary policy will become less effective than fiscal policy. The Spanish study echoes Branson's point that local financial intermediation may be robust against international competition, observing that the entry barriers produced by the extensive existing Spanish banking network may protect it for some time. The point does not detract from the need for reform and reorganization of the Spanish financial system.

Perhaps the most interesting feature of the Spanish experience from the perspective of other countries is that Spain has proceeded to adapt to openness 'the wrong way round' in terms of the standard model of adaptation. Specifically, Spain liberalized capital flows before it liberalized trade in goods, and did so with apparent success. The analysis and digestion of this experience will be a priority not only for students of the EC but also for all students of structural reform.

8   Greece: the most 'Eastern' country

The existing structural characteristics of the Greek economy, which will determine the short- and medium-term effects of integration with the rest of the EC, are addressed by Louka Katseli. This forms the basis for an analysis of the likely path of structural adjustment which the economy will follow and for the consideration of policy proposals to lessen the costs of structural adjustment.

Following its Treaty of Association in 1962, Greece largely eliminated tariffs and quotas against imports from the Community. Nevertheless, there was 'active use of domestic policy instruments for the selective protection of industrial activity'. Where 1992 is concerned, Greek industry attaches much greater importance to administrative barriers and frontier delays than to technical specifications, which affect it less since its production is generally low-tech. Similarly restrictions on the capital market and exchange controls rank relatively low in Greece compared with, say, Spain or Portugal. Also Greek industrialists take a far more pessimistic view of the effects of the single market on their own industries than do their Spanish or Portuguese counterparts.

The Greek economy is described as 'state corporatism'. This implies that industry is regulated by a complex interlocking oligarchy consisting of the state, financial institutions and industrial families. Consequently the line between private and public is blurred. While the government 'interferes' directly and indirectly in the running of private industry, industry makes its influence felt on government. A dirigiste and bureaucratic control of credit by public sector banks is an important means of applying public influence to the private sector.

Data are presented which show that over time the nominal effective protection rate, defined to include taxes, subsidies, and border taxes, as well as tariffs, has increased, while nominal rates of protection have declined. This effect is especially marked for intermediate goods, whose prices may therefore be expected to decline under the single-market arrangements.

These measures take no account of selective protection through the control of credit, which is shown to be of great importance. An extreme case is the 'soft budget' enjoyed by a company taken into bank ownership as a result of its financial difficulties. Households are also protected from the harshness of a market economy and its fluctuations by countercyclical state-provided employment and countercyclical wage levels. As Greece becomes more integrated into the world economy, the whole elaborate structure of interlocking interests and feather-bedded production and employment is threatened.

Meanwhile the state has been operating with something like a soft budget on account of its heavy recourse to deficits and borrowing, with the deficit increasingly financed from abroad. The paper details the numerous rigidities that characterize an economy with a dual system, in which the amount of flexibility and information varies greatly between the two segments of the economy. The protection of feeble producers and subsidized credit lead to excess capacity and excessive capital-intensity. The banking system falls victim to the same rigidities and exhibits over-manning and an excessive concentration in traditional and undemanding activities, such as the marketing of government bonds. At present, Greek banks fall foul of the EC's Second Directive, concerning the asset structure that banks are permitted.

With employment concentrated in agriculture and the public sector, the industrial labour force plays a lesser role than elsewhere in Europe. The labour market is highly segmented between rural and urban, and between public and private. The public sector takes the lead in fixing private wage levels.

With the increasing integration of the world economy, Greek production has been subject to greater competition from foreign producers both at home and in third markets. Price competitiveness has been defended by repeated devaluations of the currency, resulting in the period 1981–87 in a small depreciation of the real exchange rate. Even so, overall trade competitiveness has declined and the trade deficit has risen.

The Greek study provides the starting point for an essential and important debate concerning the question how an inward-looking and distorted economy such as that of Greece will adapt to more openness and greater uniformity with its European partners with regard to economic institutions and arrangements. The lazy answer would be that integration will blow away Greek singularity and any economic activity that may shelter behind it. That is the unity of the title. Diversity will also feature, however, in the actual outcome.

9   Portugal: where East meets West

The notion of an 'ambiguous' policy response to the EC is chosen by Jorge Braga de Macedo as a central focus for his study of the Portuguese experience. The westernmost country in Europe turns out to share more features with East European economies than would be expected from the brief rule of the 'revolutionary captains' of 1974–75. Public response to

European integration has been ambiguous ever since the late 1940s when Portugal accepted Marshall aid and so took on the challenge of catching up with the rest of Europe. Until the revolution the domestic objective constraining external liberalization was establishing a single market with the colonies, or 'national integration'. The 1976 constitution brought another constraining domestic objective, which survived until after accession: the commitment of the state to transform Portugal into a 'classless society'. To help the transformation, firms in protected sectors, especially financial conglomerates, were nationalized, and these nationalizations were enshrined as 'irreversible conquests of the working classes'. Until it was overturned by the second amendment to the constitution in 1989, the irreversibility of the nationalizations basically froze the public sector.

This ambiguous response brings about inconsistency between the political objectives of the revolution and the economic objective of external liberalization. This consequence is evident in the labour market. A law passed in 1976 restricted lay-offs to the most extreme cases. To preserve their capacity to adjust the workforce in response to changes in economic activity, employers have resorted extensively to renewable short-term contracts (usually 6 months). Such contracts accounted on average for 12% of total employment during 1983–88; and their existence makes the market much more segmented than rigid.

Segmentation and rivalry among trade unions have generated a flexible real wage in Portugal and the lowest unemployment rate in the Community (except for Luxembourg). Also contributing to this situation was the high rate of migration to the rest of the EC, especially the rich Northern countries, during the 1960s.

The divergence between the political aims of the revolution and the economic aim of closer integration with the European economy emerges also in Portugal's industrial sector. The political resilience of state-owned enterprises remained long after their external competitiveness had been overtaken by private exporters. This segmented structure appears in different guises throughout the period. Manufacturing industry is dominated by textiles and oil-refining, each a prime example of the dual structure of industry: the first segment is labour-intensive and oriented towards exports and the domestic market; the second is more capital-intensive and import-substituting, and includes firms nationalized after the revolution.

The major restructuring of Portuguese industry has probably yet to take place. Some of the opportunities of EC membership have been exploited, but fundamental changes have been postponed. They cannot, however, be postponed indefinitely: eventually an improved domestic environment will be needed to contend with the effects of continued trade liberalization. The difficulty is that the changes may be delayed until a time when the external environment, and in particular the common external tariff, is less favourable.

Excessive financial regulation in Portugal in the 1960s led to the creation of industrial groups which were able to provide their own finance, each group associated with its own commercial bank. After the nationalizations of 1975 the managers of the commercial banks probably viewed the nationalized sector as one very large group, a perception reinforced by the closing down of the stock market shortly after the revolution. Urged by the politicians to put banks 'at the service of the people', the managers saw the abnormally high level of gold and foreign exchange reserves as collateral against which the nationalized industries were borrowing. Accordingly they took on riskier borrowers and projects, but at the same time rationed credit. Over the next decade arrears and bad debts accumulated, and by 1986 the system was effectively bankrupt.

In the previous year, 1985, the government had authorized new entrants, domestic and foreign, in the banking sector. The new banks avoided holding public debt instruments, other than Treasury bills, and were also reluctant to lend to state-owned enterprises. Instead of attacking the debt overhang of the nationalized banks, the government decided to regulate the new banks further. The only long-term solution, however, must be the purification of tainted banks rather than the contagion of 'clean' ones. Once more, in the light of the single market objective, the process of catching up needs to be coupled with economic restructuring. The banking sector, through privatization or other means, will have to absorb the overhang of inefficiency. As with trade and industry, the pressure for financial readjustment is coming more and more from outside. Against the slow evolution of Portuguese nationalized banks, financial restructuring in Spain began several years ago and continues, in the form of mergers among large banks, often encouraged by the monetary authorities.

A frozen public sector that includes banks also constrains fiscal adjustment. In July 1989 the government approved a revised version of the Programme to Correct External Imbalances and Unemployment. The plans to reduce consumption and transfers, to increase taxes and to privatize public enterprises, including banks, should generate primary surpluses sufficient to stabilize the total debt to GDP ratio before 1992. The problem is more serious than it appears, however, partly because of the lack of reliable data on public finance but more significantly because of disguised fiscal policy. The existence of implicit taxes and hidden deficits is central to the pattern of macroeconomic adjustment observed in

Portugal since the revolution. The adjustment process has largely spared public expenditure.

In the present economic situation the government is unwilling to make Portugal a full member of the EMS. To the extent that monetary policy is tied to a passive crawling peg which cannot improve competitiveness, the benefit of waiting is dubious. The pressure is there, however, particularly since Spain decided from June 1989 to bring the peseta within the wider band of the EMS. For the time being the most appropriate solution is probably a policy of shadowing the Deutschmark. Although this too entails elements of ambiguity, it would generate the right signals by demonstrating a commitment to disencumber the economy of the burden of a frozen public sector.

The conclusion of the study reinforces the view that options for internal policies are restricted but not eliminated by enlargement. The author argues that to embark on external financial liberalization requires not only external trade liberalization – which has to a large extent already been achieved – but also domestic trade and financial liberalization, which have been sorely lacking because of the overhang of the 1975 nationalizations. This seems contrary to the tenor of the Spanish study, but upholds the precedence of internal over external liberalization.

10   Soft budgets revisited

The first aspect of increased European integration pertains to its effects on markets, say for labour or capital. These may be less important ultimately, argues Dani Rodrik, than 'the impact on established modes of public sector behaviour and state–society relations', because the latter will determine the setting in which markets operate.

In all three NICs the public sector is large and interrelated with the private sector in numerous and complex ways, and something akin to 'soft-budgetism' appears common. Rodrik questions, however, whether the concept of a soft budget really pinpoints the essential feature. The state is budgetarily too relaxed because it is engaged in a kind of game with private agents in the outcome of which a loose budget emerges. The dynamic inconsistency of industrial governments is a parallel case. Soft budgets are an outcome emerging from a particular national situation, not a parameter of the economic environment. Rodrik demonstrates how the behaviour of individual agents within a system differs sharply according to whether they find themselves in a hard- or a soft-budget regime. For the whole system, however, the budget is always hard. Hence a soft-budget outcome typically means that the burdens of adjustment fall disproportionately on weak sectors of the economy or society. That leaves many problems, listed by Rodrik, which cannot plausibly be blamed on soft-budgetism.

Integration may have contradictory effects. On the one hand, EC rules and directives may make it easier for politicians and administrators to say 'no'. On the other hand, the provision of central funds to assist transfers could lead to a magnification of soft-budgetism.

11 Unity, diversity and the policy domain

The various chapters reviewed above look at the EC in its movement towards the single market and the full integration of the NICs from widely different perspectives. There can be no question, therefore, of encapsulating the arguments in a summary overarching conclusion. The conclusion is that these are big and complex changes, and they will not have uniform implications good for all cases or for all countries.

From the last observation it follows that a more unified EC will not be one that can deal exclusively in generalities and confine its attention to getting the regulatory framework correct at the centre. This point is already understood. The danger may be that the general and the very particular will find themselves uncomfortably married. The administration of the structural funds, which seems on the face of things to be very much a question of the particular and the specific, might benefit from the application of tighter Community-wide principles. Banking regulations, which seem on the face of things to be very much a question of general principles, might be more beneficial to all if they allowed scope for national flexibility. Other examples treated in this volume show that most policy domains present elements of both unity and diversity. Could this be specific to the Community's Southern Frontier or is it rather a characteristic of the European economy? The research described in this volume seems to point in this direction.

2 Adjustment, compensation and factor mobility in integrated markets

CHRISTOPHER BLISS

1 Introduction and outline

The meaning of the terms adjustment, compensation and factor mobility will be clear. The term 'integrated markets' should be taken to cover all the problems which confront the European Economic Communities (henceforth often called the Community or the EC), as it enlarges by adding, and fully integrating, new members, and as it implements the 1992 single internal market initiatives. These reforms are intended to establish a single market among the Community members by the 1st of January, 1993.

If at all successful, the single market reforms will constitute an outstanding experiment in market integration and may well be the most important question to consider in connection with the future of the Community. The question of enlargement of the EC by the addition of new member countries, on the other hand, might appear to be a less pressing and topical question. Although the absorption of the latest recruits, Spain and Portugal, is definitely incomplete, the timetable and the nature of the transition are already settled questions. The decision whether to include Turkey remains to be taken but everyone agrees that it will require a long, complex, and to a great extent a political process to determine the answer.

I have chosen to treat the question of the internal market and the question of enlargement together for two reasons.[1] First, the two cases raise numerous similar conceptual problems. Secondly, the manner in which I treated enlargement in previous work (Bliss, 1990) strongly emphasizes the relations of the enlarging Community with the outside world. It is salutary to carry some of the same emphasis over to the discussion of the internal market. To this end I shall employ the term 'reform' to cover either an enlargement of the Community, or a change which makes the internal market function more efficiently, whenever the distinction between these two types of development is unnecessary for my point.

The 1992 movement, like any other reform, may be considered according

18

to how the undoubted gains are distributed between nations and groups inside and outside the Community, and according to who the losers may be, again inside or outside the Community. Of course this exercise has more than a simply forensic interest. If a general gain is the objective, then one needs to ask how some of the gains might be redirected in favour of those who would otherwise lose. Also, losers form political blocs and engage in counter-activity. Examples would range from farmers pouring milk on to Brussels streets, through governments of member nations withholding real compliance, to outside trading blocs initiating trade wars. The design and evaluation of reforms has to take account of such messy political considerations.

These observations might be regarded as platitudes. In documents on the implications of the reforms the Commission already advertises its concern for the issue of how the benefits of reform are to be directed so as to achieve 'the strengthening of the Community's economic and social cohesion and, in particular, to reduce the gap between its different regions and the backwardness of the least favoured regions.' (EC Commission, 1987c). This is different from, and in some respects more ambitious than, the 'paying off the losers' criterion which is the standby of the economic theory of trade and market reform.

The Commission also takes pains to assure the outside world that enlargement and the single market will not be the vehicle for benefiting the EC at the expense of the rest of the world. Where enlargement is concerned the point is hardly disputed. As the joining countries are required to align their external tariffs with the common external tariff (CET) of the Community, and as existing external tariffs of the joining countries are typically higher than the Community's CET, the outside world has nothing to fear from enlargement as such. This assumes that treaties of association take care of agricultural goods, which has been broadly the case, but see below for the case of US agricultural exports.

With the single market the case is less clear. Quality regulations can and have been used to protect home markets. With the establishment of the single market the structure of protection will be radically overhauled. For example, individual country quotas will have to be replaced by Community-wide quotas. It can be argued quite plausibly that this will tend to blunt the force of protection, because the centre will be more restrained in practice than individual governments would be. Yet, even if the Commission were less inclined to protect than national governments – and many North Americans are not ready to believe that – single market reform brings new opportunities for underhand protection.

It is almost a definition that, provided side-payments are allowed to compensate groups which would otherwise lose, greater efficiency permits all parties to benefit. Moreover, the fruits of greater efficiency can in principle be applied to the reduction of inequality between well-off and badly-off parties, say regions. The mechanism, if no other means suffice, will be subsidies from central funds.

The Commission is adopting an approach which can be traced back to the start of the Community of six, and which was supposed to be embodied above all in the Common Agricultural Policy (CAP). The approach might be summarized as modernization and increased growth in combination with a catching up for the poorest regions or groups. In directing attention to the ambitious nature of the Commission's programme I do not intend to discredit its intentions, which seem to me admirable. Equally, the reference to the philosophy behind the CAP is not malicious, although it does draw attention to a history now generally recognized to have been, in some respects at least, unfortunate. The intentions were excellent, and even the economist must allow that the successful implementation of difficult political changes is not just a question of balancing a double-entry account. It demands excitement and enthusiasm, and even some bravado. Also, a programme need not be seen in all-or-nothing terms and counted a failure if it does not achieve all that it proposes to achieve.

After allowing the above points, I remain impressed by how ambitious is the announced programme, especially when it is noted that the instruments which will be employed to achieve the designated ends are limited. As well as the finiteness of the resources at the Commission's disposal, the complexities of the political processes within the EC must be taken into account, a point to which I shall return below.

In my work on enlargement and the common external tariff I drew heavily on a way of looking at customs union formation – and hence of looking at customs union enlargement and/or internal market development – which I designated Kemp–Wan (KW) after the authors of the neatest and most elegant statement of the idea. (See Kemp and Wan, 1976, and further references in Bliss, 1990). The Kemp–Wan result shows how the benefits of a customs union, in their case, or the enlargement of an existing customs union, may in principle be realised without any consequent harm to the rest of the world. The method is to adjust the structure of common external tariffs so that trade flows with the outside world are maintained at a constant level while the community of insiders will enjoy the benefit of free trade with each other.

This is a typical economist's result. On the positive side it cuts through a great deal of complexity to get to the essential point that gains in efficiency should be realizable in a world run by intelligent people and inhabited by rational actors. On the other hand, it misleads by supposing that even intelligent and well-motivated leaders will have ideal instruments of policy at their disposal – specifically non-distorting taxes and transfer payments.

The result may mislead again in assuming that the outside world would react in the manner which the model deems to be rational, namely accepting passively changes which do it no harm. In a world in which international relations are conducted by governments, which in turn react to numerous and disparate internal pressures, and in which, furthermore, the conduct of trade is supposedly subject to legalistic formulae, such as the GATT rules, the economist's concept of 'no harm' – that is not making worse off than an assumed clear-cut initial reference point – may not ensure passive acquiescence.

The whole question of what it is to make no worse off is a complicated, partly because inescapably dynamic, issue. This problem arises as much in the internal political transactions of the Community, or another bloc or nation, as when we consider the Community's relations with the outside world. For example industries commonly claim to have been harmed by competition from imports when arguably they have been harmed as much, or even mainly, by other developments, such as technical stagnation in combination with a rise in the general level of wages.

The economist's non-distorting transfer payment is an admitted ideal. In fact no such instruments exist. However the ideal still serves to define an absolute bound which real-world instruments can never achieve. It also directs us to look for and at the distortions and misallocations which will always accompany actual concrete interventions. As the Commission's programme for disbursing its Structural Funds proposes clear objectives and means of intervention, we are in a position to evaluate to some extent the distortions which are likely to arise, and even to compare their costs with the benefits which will flow from extending assistance to disadvantaged regions and groups.

Section 2 examines the question of how reform, and especially the establishment of the single market, is likely to affect identifiable groups within member countries and outside the Community. The argument will be mainly theoretical but I take care to keep the theory within ear-shot of measurement and application. The discussion notes how the conclusions are affected by different ways of modeling economic change and by the presence or absence of factor mobility.

Section 3 first looks at the criteria proposed by the Commission for expending the Structural Funds. It will be argued that the intended scheme is not the same as compensation but that many of the same problems and principles as are raised by compensation will still be encountered. The claim is that all schemes for assisting transition, which is a more general notion than simple compensation, encounter two characteristic problems,

denoted respectively *identification* and *addressing*. To put it briefly, the
first problem concerns deciding which groups or interests need to be
assisted. The second problem concerns the design of policies that will in
fact reach and assist the groups concerned. For example, the Commission's view that the unemployed young especially merit assistance is an
identification. A set of schemes to help the young unemployed obtain jobs
would be well or badly addressed, according to how effective it turned out
to be in assisting the particular group for which it was designed.

Section 4 examines the twin problems of identification and addressing
in more depth. It briefly considers some questions of natural justice and
equity which broadly take the form: who deserves to be helped? It also
examines the problems for identification and addressing which spring
from the fact that the effects of a policy extend over time. This gives rise to
important dynamic issues and also to some characteristic problems of
strategy and expectations.

Section 5 looks again at relations with the outside world. In principle
the outside world is only a separate group, or collection of groupings (e.g.
non-EC industrial, developing countries of various kinds, etc.), which
needs to be compensated or assisted to adjust much like an internal
grouping. In fact the manner in which these considerations work themselves out is very different where the outside world is the group to be taken
into account.

Section 6 looks at factor mobility. In the models of much received trade
theory, free and uninhibited exchange substitutes for the mobility of
factors. In reality the two will have different roles to play, especially when
there are differences in technology and efficiency which cannot be reduced
to the local availability or non-availability of certain factors, or when
increasing returns to scale are important. As there is no scope in the
Community for massive migration on a Nineteenth Century scale, migration will tend to operate as a safety valve, allowing particular groups to
better themselves by moving. It also operates as a selective or filter process
and this may amount to an external diseconomy of migration.

Section 7 notes some general conclusions. Although much of the
analysis is rather general and even abstract, it is important to draw out the
concrete policy implications of the analysis and these are presented in this
concluding section.

2   The effects of reform and redistribution

This section first examines the question of how reform, and specially the
establishment of the single market, is likely to affect the Community, on
the one hand, and the outside world, on the other. This is a large question

which can only be answered effectively from detailed empirical studies. Other chapters of this volume throw a good deal of light on the answer to the question; for particular industries and for the conduct of policy; for the joining countries from the work by the country teams. However it is clear that exercises of this type can never be easy or the results at all certain. Despite these challenging problems, some general principles may be discerned.

Emerson *et al.* (1988) provides an excellent and wide-ranging discussion of the implications of the single market (see also Padoa-Schioppa, 1987). The emphasis of the Emerson study, generally speaking, is directed to the size of the efficiency gains that might be realised, with possible negative consequences of the structural changes which will be required – including costs to identified groups – receiving a secondary emphasis. Nevertheless, a view emerges as to the nature of those costs, the relative importance of different kinds of costs, and the strategy that should be employed to deal with the most important.

These points are well-illustrated by Part D, Section 8.3, entitled 'Accompanying microeconomic policies'. The argument notes that:

> After a time lag, the increased dynamicism of the competitive process will also promote new investment, prompt the restructuring and multi-nationalization of companies, lead to relocation, disengagement and "creative destruction" (sic) . . . Although these effects are generally favourable, they are likely to create a climate of increased uncertainty for those involved in the economic process. (p. 138)

Particular problems to which attention is drawn include, first, concentration and a diminution of competition. This is a natural consideration in view of the emphasis which the argument has placed on increasing returns to scale. However the authors are not unduly concerned by this issue, as they feel that it can be taken care of by means of suitable regulations. A second matter involves the '. . . expectations concerning the distribution of benefits between factors of production, sectors and regions' (p. 138). These are classic issues of trade theory, but they are viewed in a different light from the one with which the student of international trade will be familiar. To put it simply, the problems are viewed as questions of adjustment, to be taken care of by 'transitional arrangements'.

How far is it correct to see the problems which will be created by reform as transitional? And even granted the assumption, by what mechanisms will the Community actively intervene so as to promote adjustment and ease transition, and will those mechanisms prove adequate? There are several mechanisms at issue. Indeed if the implications of the reforms are as radical as we are encouraged to expect, then hardly any major aspect of

EC policy-making will be able to stand aloof from the questions of adjustment and compensation for the costs of reform. That would probably be an insidious and undesirable tendency in practice, and if the lesson is that it needs to be reined in, then it is an important lesson. However it will not be easy to do so, for reasons which are partly practical and political, and in part theoretical.

The discussion of these issues needs to be developed in some detail and will largely be postponed until later sections. However the fundamental point is quite simple and is indeed familiar from, for example, the problems of administering unemployment benefit, or anti-poverty programmes, within member states. Such schemes work most smoothly and economically if they can be reduced to clear-cut and simple formulae which induce the minimum of rearrangement of their actions and affairs in those who might benefit from the programmes. Unfortunately these ideals are often in conflict with another consideration, namely that the programme should to a great extent achieve its objectives. Specifically it should assist those parties who need or merit assistance, and in the manner intended, to adjust not to stagnate, for example, and so forth. If these problems are large and inescapable within national programmes, they are not easy or unimportant where Community-wide programmes are concerned.

How does the Commission intend to proceed? The main route relevant to the present argument is the reform of the Structural Funds (see EC Commission 1987c). This initiative shows a clear awareness of the danger of a programme designed to aid transition and compensate for costs of adjustment becoming bogged down in a mass of detail, conflicting claims and pressures, and generating a bureaucratic explosion. It proposes concentrating on specific objectives and it nominates several of these. Described more briefly than in the document, and no doubt less precisely, the objectives are:

(1) The promotion of investment and productivity growth in less developed regions;
(2) The reintegration of areas hard hit by adjustment (e.g. coal or ship-building regions) back into the developing economy;
(3) Combating long-term unemployment and assisting the integration of the young into the labour market; and;
(4) The adjustment of agriculture and the development of rural areas.

This programme is described as a 'concentration of Community structural action', and the need for 'demanding eligibility criteria' is underlined. The philosophy is sound. Yet the programme is not narrowly focused. It is hard to see how it could be, given the wide scope of the difficulties which a huge and radical reform may be expected to engender. The Commission is not given to shrugging off difficulties and it reveals here its characteristic optimism concerning the fruitfulness of well intended and carefully planned intervention. Which particular problems are likely to cause the most acute difficulties to this approach is an issue to which I shall return.

For the remainder of this section I propose two questions. How does the philosophy for dealing with trade and structural adjustment which is developed in the Commission's publications compare with the one that economists are used to applying? This comparison involves not only the concepts that economists employ, but also includes those features of their discussions which spring from the way that they tend to specify and construct their models. Secondly, how do the interests and possible reactions of the outside world need to be taken into account, and can an external policy for the reformed Community be inferred from taking that point into account? The two questions raise similar considerations in a manner which I hope to clarify.

A standard method of modeling reform which economists employ is first to identify changes which will increase efficiency and then to investigate methods of implementing those changes that will make each and every individual better, or at least no worse, off than he or she would have been without the changes. Despite its artificiality, this Pareto improvement approach has been extraordinarily effective in throwing light on the design of good economic policy.[2] One reason is that the types of policy which are selected by the Pareto test are just the same as those that could be selected by the maximization of some weighted objective. Indeed the method would appeal to an administrator interested only in greater economic efficiency, without regard to the distribution of losses and benefits, at least to the extent that it would select the right type of policy. The most popular mechanism for implementing efficiency-improving reforms, and the one from which the most well-known and influential findings flow, is the method of lump-sum compensation (LSC). The idea is that resources are transferred to compensate those who would otherwise suffer losses. The transfers or compensation payments are lump-sum in the sense that they are once-for-all pay-outs related only to the losses which individuals would unavoidably suffer. They cannot be related to any feature of behaviour – as a negative income tax is – in a way which would alter the behaviour of those concerned.

There are more instances certainly in which the case for greater economic efficiency can be defended despite the problem of distribution and the presence of losers. For example, Diamond and Mirrlees (1971) demonstrate an approach to welfare recommendations and the design of reforms which does not require, indeed it prohibits, lump-sum compensation. However, without going into details here (see again Corden, 1984 for an introduction), the result requires both some possibly doubtful assumptions, and more importantly for our present purpose, the use of tax instruments in the form of discriminatory indirect taxes and subsidies which would be inconsistent with the basic aims of the single market reforms.

Before returning to the Commission's approach, it is worth pausing to ask whether anything usable for real-world policy can be extracted from the standard economics approach (which I shall call the economics approach for short). I think that a lot can be made of it but that there are formidable difficulties in applying it at all exactly. The most important messages of the theory are two in number. First it invites us to consider compensating losers. Only the familiarity of this idea makes it seem obvious and trivial. But second, and this is certainly not trivial, it provides essential guidance on how compensation is to be calculated and administered if the cost is not to be inflated by wasteful changes in economic behaviour induced by the compensation itself. Unfortunately, the strict conclusion is that the ideal, completely non-distorting LSC is an impossibility. No planners or administrators have the information available to calculate just how much a specific individual will unavoidably gain or lose from the single market and even if they did, and taxed or subsidized that individual appropriately, the European Court would not uphold tax demands not computed from a publicly available formula.

These difficulties might be finessed if not-very-distorting formula-based compensation schemes could be devised. For example paying all coal miners over 45 a retirement bonus may seem to be an extremely poor approximation to the theoretical ideal of paying lump-sum compensations to those whose names appear on a designated list, and who all happen to be 45-year-old coal miners. However in practice the two schemes may not produce very different results. A much more serious problem for the economics approach is that it is too static. Simple full-information models make it seem obvious who are the gainers and the losers from reform. Indeed the gains and losses relative to the pre-reform starting point can be precisely computed and displayed. This is not the case in reality and many real-life policies run foul of this difficulty. I consider this problem again in Sections 3 and 4 below.

The approach of the Community,[3] exposed in its publications and in its proposals for action, is halfway between the simple liberal (in the European sense of that term) view that change which promotes efficiency is a good thing in itself, and the economic theorist's notion that change can only be recommended if all losers can be protected and compensated – in other words that there should be no strict losers. Commission publications indicate that efficiency should be promoted but in conjunction with steps to ensure that not only badly-hit losers, but also those parties which could be left out of the benefits of the reforms, should be compensated. The favoured form of compensation is assistance to adjust. Beyond that there is a clear aim to promote equality between regions and groups within the enlarged and market-unified Community.

How will the outside world be affected by the reforms and how, and by what means, should the Community take the interest of the outside world into account? This is a lively political issue at the present time. The rest of the world, especially the United States, expresses fears of a 'fortress Europe'. Spokesmen for Europe vigorously deny any such intention. To arbitrate on these issues one has to overcome just the kind of difficulty discussed above, in connection with the static nature of economic models, and the difficulty of identifying harm or gain unambiguously.

Were Europe to complete its integration and then proceed to erect large tariff barriers, it would clearly be fortress Europe, and harm to the rest of the world would hardly be in doubt. However nothing like that will conceivably happen. Rather changes over time will make some exporters into the EC, certainly, find that the European market is less accessible to their sales than used to be the case.

There will be numerous reasons for these developments. Perhaps Europe will have made changes of a protectionist character, or changes seen by the affected parties to be protectionist in intent, as the ban on the import of hormone-treated beef was seen by the US. On the other hand, the single market by itself could be the explanation for increased resistance to imports. For example, greater economies of scale might make European producers more competitive in their home markets and in selling abroad.

In my own discussion of enlargement, building on the KW approach, I demonstrated how complicated the calculations might have to be which would arrive at the tariff changes that would leave trade flows with the rest of the world unchanged following an enlargement. The same point applies with equal force to the formation of a single market. Those were questions of abstract modeling. However the lively political questions are neither easier to solve, nor are they even wholly different in character from the problem posed by the KW approach. True, it is not necessary to leave trade flows unaffected, but only to avoid harm to the rest of the world. However what does, or does not, harm the rest of the world would be extremely difficult to calculate, even for a disinterested arbitrator. When the issue must be determined in a sometimes emotive exchange between the participants themselves, then the outbreak of trade warfare is a very real danger. Of course we must not resign ourselves to such a drastic outcome. To avoid it, an awareness of the complexity of the problem should help. Formal statements of a belief in the benefits of free trade, or legalistic claims to be on the right side of the rules, are a less than adequate response to a delicate and dangerous situation.

3   Principles for allocating the Structural Funds

We have seen that the philosophy of the European Community, as embodied in the pronouncements of its Commission, is far from being a simple laissez-faire approach. Neither is it argued that increases in efficiency are simply a good thing, and that if they bring harm to some groups, or even if they leave out some parties, that is unfortunate, but no reason to hold back progress. Nor is it even claimed that attempts to intervene so as to influence the consequences and course of reform might in principle be a good idea, and might in theory serve to mitigate the harshness of change, but would in practice do more harm than good – a typical conservative argument against intervention. No, the Commission recognizes that there will be losers, and even looks beyond strict losers to include groups or regions that might remain 'backward' while the remainder of the Community progressed, and it proposes not to ignore the issue, but rather to intervene with direct action to assist deserving cases. The chief means of intervention is to be the direction of the structural funds.

I first examine the criteria proposed by the Commission for expending the Structural Funds. I will argue that the intended scheme is not at all the same as the economic theorist's compensation but that many of the same problems and principles as are raised by that compensation will again be encountered. Indeed all schemes for compensating those who lose by a reform, or to redistribute the benefits of reform, encounter two character-istic problems. These problems are denoted respectively identification and addressing. Recall that the first problem concerns deciding which groups or interests need to be assisted, while the second concerns the design of policies that will in fact reach and assist the groups concerned.

The Commission's view that the unemployed young especially merit assistance is an identification. The addressing will consist of specific schemes to help the young unemployed obtain jobs. How well such a scheme is addressed is determined by how precisely and effectively it assists the intended group without excessive costs or unintended benefits to third parties.

Probably the Community would insist that it does not want to compen-sate, like an insurance company paying out for fire losses. It might argue that there is no essential and unavoidable long-term loss to any party from promoting efficiency and market integration, an issue to which I shall return. However there plainly are short-term losses. The only question that would divide observers concerns, as usual, how long is the long run and how short the short run. Whatever the answer, and the answer must vary to some extent from case to case, the Community sees its role as assisting transition. Making the short run shorter would encapsulate the idea in a phrase.

Assisting transition is a different notion from simple compensation, and to an extent it is more general. For instance, a straight lump-sum payment might be reasonably seen as assistance for transition, say in the case of a fixed payment for the loss of a job. The firm, or society, tells the worker in effect: sorry about your misfortune, but here is some cash to see you through until you can put yourself back on your feet again. The payment simply makes good the lack of income during a transition period. Yet not all cases of assistance for transition can be equated with straight compensation. Suppose, for example, that re-training courses to improve the income and employment prospects of those whose employment has been creatively destroyed are paid for entirely by the Community.

Consider two individuals, called Paulo and Pedro. Paulo would have paid for retraining from his own savings had it not been subsidized, and he would have paid for exactly the type and amount of retraining that he will undertake when it is subsidized. For Paulo the subsidy is equivalent to a lump-sum payment or a once-for-all income transfer. Pedro, on the other hand, would not have purchased retraining, not even if he had received a lump-sum in the form of a lottery prize exactly large enough to pay for the retraining. However as he did not win a lottery prize, and as the training is available to him without charge, he will take the retraining. For Pedro the scheme turns out to be an inducement to retrain.

The argument can be developed at length. Let the cost of retraining be 1,000, expressed in terms of a suitable currency unit. Then Paulo has certainly received a lump-sum payment of 1,000. What has Pedro received? Certainly not 1,000, as he would prefer 1,000 in cash to an entrance ticket to a subsidized retraining course, and one cannot prefer the equivalent of a thing to the thing itself. However what if Pedro would have been exactly in the position of Paulo – he would have taken the same course and paid for it from his own pocket – had the cost been 800? Then Pedro has received a lump-sum payment of 800, by logic parallel to the case of Paulo, and a further 200 has induced him to adjust in a different manner from the one that he would have chosen by himself.

With this kind of example in mind, how are we to maintain a quantifiable distinction between LSC and the subsidy of adjustment? Is indeed subsidy of adjustment the right concept for analysing the Commission's programme for the Structural Funds? Imagine, for instance, that the method adopted to help, say, the young unemployed in a certain region is to encourage investment in new activities in that region. As the most plausible means to the direction of investment available to the Commission is grant aid, let it be grant aid that promotes investment in the region concerned. As a consequence of this aid, industry expands and more young people obtain employment.

In certain respects this case turns out to be no different in kind from the example of a retraining course already described. However there are important additional complications. The retraining course was supposedly a service which individuals could in principle purchase privately and the social costing of which raised no conceptually awkward issues.

None of that applies with the redirection of investment. True we can imagine a willingness to pay test. If a typical inhabitant of a certain region would be indifferent between receiving 5,000 in cash and having a particular plant located in that region, we may include in the consequences of locating the plant there an implicit LSC of 5,000 per household. However it is far from obvious how the sums concerned would be measured. Moreover, even if such willingness-to-pay experiments could be undertaken, it is not clear how much credibility could be attached to the responses. Consider that economists find it difficult to assess the full implications of the location of large-scale investment – how important are the external economies, what their nature is, etc. It is not clear that ordinary people, even on the spot, are in a much better position to make such assessments.

Perhaps none of this matters. Indeed the whole exercise could be the pursuit of a spurious precision which is not in fact required. It may suffice to identify certain groups or regions which should be aided, and to aid them. It might not matter if Region A receives 10% more than it truly merits and Region B 15% less. It depends upon what is the ultimate aim of the programme. If the idea is to help the weak or the harmed in amounts judged in a rough and ready manner to be commensurate with the loss suffered or the need for help, then the help can be provided and there it is. However if it is held that suitable aid and encouragement to adjustment will put an end to anxieties about backward regions, disadvantaged groups, or the problems of creatively destroyed communities, then there is a simple empirical question: will the programme do this?

Again, it is impossible to ignore the example of the CAP. In part the CAP was designed from its inception as a scheme to aid the adjustment of the backward in combination with price changes which would make them better off during the, presumed to be temporary, transition. I am certainly not claiming that none of this worked out as intended, but surely the

Community did not foresee how what it was doing would work out, and would probably have modified the scheme considerably had it foreseen the results.

An issue which is well typified by the history of the CAP is the question of time-span. Specifically, are the benefits of reform eventually disseminated throughout the system? If they are in due course generally disseminated how long does this process require? Very little economic analysis has been applied to these issues, although the problem has certainly interested students of economic development. The field of economics which would seem to be most relevant is international economics, because the evaluation of the implications of reform has always been a central concern of that field. However there is little work on which one may draw directly.[4]

Consider two alternative views, each expressed starkly to underline the difference between them. According to the first view, individuals or families are identified with factors of production, of a specific or a general character, and these associations persist over many years, if not for many generations. According to the second view, the association between families, or social units, and factors is a transitory matter. For example, labour can learn new skills and adapt to changed market conditions. Or it can get up and migrate to where it is better paid, or to where the opportunities exist for making a good living. Capital can also migrate and furthermore the ownership of capital, like the possession of skills, is something to which families can and will migrate if conditions favour that change.

Of course expressed so crudely these views are both nonsense but they do indicate two directions of emphasis. Moreover, these directions correspond roughly to the one adopted by most received economic theory, on the one hand, and by the Commission and fairly expressly by Emerson *et al.* (1988). One may rehearse some obvious arguments for or against each side. For instance historical experience provides numerous instances of regions or peoples seemingly locked into the economic consequences of shocks long since past. Dore (1982) provides a fascinating case-study of this type. Yet there are also examples of the total transformation of entire countries, so much so that the extent to which old income distributions or divisions of labour can explain present patterns is small indeed. Taiwan seems to be such a case, and it is not alone in apparently owing part of its success to the disruptive effect of war on its social structure.

The European planners will argue that which type of outcome will tend to arise depends upon the policy regime, and that they intend to establish one which will make Europe flexible and adaptable. In this case what is needed is not the economist's side-payments and monetary compensations for any losses that may flow from reform. Rather what is required is assistance to make the required transition rapid and not unduly difficult for the adversely affected parties. If the approach will be dirigiste, it might be added, there are respectable grounds for favouring administrative intervention when external economies and diseconomies are as omnipresent as they are likely to be in this case.

To assess this type of argument, which notice is my interpretation of a position which goes beyond the position itself, one needs to have some general idea of what kinds of losses and inequalities are likely to be generated by, or to persist following, the completion of the enlargement process and the internal market programme. To begin with the inequalities, as these are somewhat easier to assess, those that exist today between different regions and countries of the enlarged Community are, or course, considerable. According to EC Commission (1987b), p. 1, 'around one fifth of the population lives in such regions, where income levels, measured in terms of GDP per head of population, trail behind the Community average by up to 60% or more.' If this situation seems daunting, then that is what it is. However no one imagines that the problem will be overcome quickly or soon disappear. It is a matter of 'helping the disadvantaged regions to catch up', to borrow a Commission phrase, rather than eliminating inequalities. It is hard to see how considerable regional inequalities will not persist within the Community well into the next century.

These problems are similar to those with which many national governments have had to contend for a long time, but now written on a larger map and with gradients and obstacles even greater than those which most national governments have faced. It is a matter of the greatest importance that the Community should allow these experiences to inform its plans, as for the most part they seem not to have done.

Almost every country could contribute experiences from which valuable lessons can be extracted. The experience of Italy seems to be especially relevant, as that country has lived with a sharp North–South divide which has to a considerable extent persisted despite large and expensive programmes, not very different in spirit from those now proposed by the Commission.[5] Of course every national example will be replete with special factors which will suggest that generalization from it would be perilous. Certainly the case of the Italian South includes particular features not closely replicated elsewhere. Even so, outcomes from regional policies which disappointed the hopes and expectations of their authors can be reported not just from Italy, but from the United Kingdom and from several other countries.

As a non-specialist, I hesitate to offer a view as to what are the central and important reasons why regional policy has often disappointed the expectations that attached themselves to it. If forced to offer an opinion, I would suggest that the programmes have often lacked a clear view of the nature of the problem that they are supposed to resolve and a clear determination of objectives and means.

To cite one instance, the United Kingdom in the 1960s and 1970s, the policy was intended to help disadvantaged regions, and at one time it targeted investment into those regions as the variable to be influenced by policy. This was surely not the right variable to target, as net new employment corresponded more closely to what was desired, and in any case, even investment was badly measured and monitored. Firms relocated across administrative boundaries, or relocated temporarily to enjoy tax advantages. Much of this was fairly obvious with the advantage of hind-sight because the funding committed could not have been expected to move massive objects. As some costs, e.g. employees' housing, are cheaper in depressed regions, private firms must have good reasons for not being there in the first place. In a few cases the decision will have been marginal and small inducements will have tipped the balance the other way. However in most cases large inducements will be required and it soon becomes expensive. In principle sufficient external economies could bring it about that following the movement of numerous firms they will all find that producing in their new location is so successful that no continuing inducement is needed. However well-attested stories with that happy ending seem to be quite rare. The reason may be that governments prove unwilling to finance a big push towards a region on a sufficient scale to arrive at the virtuous outcome.

How does all this relate to the economic theory of interregional trade? Much of that theory is fairly complacent concerning the problem of backward regions. The basic and most popular neoclassical model leads to the conclusion that market forces and individual initiative will tend to iron out regional differences. The combined assumptions of constant returns to scale and free mobility of factors guarantee that there can be no persistent regional inequalities in the returns to any factor. However the neoclassical approach can readily be adapted to throw a good deal of light on real-life regional problems, and when its usual assumptions are modified, further insights become available.

For an insight available from within the neoclassical framework, notice that the concept of a factor of production is an ambiguous and adaptable idea. Textbook treatments often concentrate on highly aggregated general categories, such as labour and capital. However the disaggregation of these categories may show up important explanations for income differences. For instance, the quality of the labour force in a depressed region tends to be low and to deteriorate over time as a consequence of the depressed nature of the region's economy. A mass of unskilled inexperienced young workers with only 5 years of poor quality secondary schooling behind them may constitute a regional problem if they all inhabit a certain region. However they may earn no less or live no worse than comparable workers in the most economically dynamic and prosperous region. They lack an incentive to migrate unless they can command the resources and the impetus to improve the marketability of their labour services.

A common neoclassical view is that migration is unnecessary in many cases. A regional division of production specialization, which should arise naturally, will tend to equalize the returns to factors in different places – the factor price equalization result. This conclusion however depends upon assumptions the validity of which is questionable in applications to actual cases of interregional income differentials. With many distinct factors and goods the factor price equalization mechanism is uncertain, Ethier (1984).[6] If factors have adapted to specific locations or activities, inequalities may persist over long periods, Neary (1978). When factors are immobile and regions specialise income differentials can persist indefinitely, Bhagwati (1984). With increasing returns to scale, or with imperfect competition, inequalities may again persist in the absence of free migration of factors, Helpman and Krugman (1985), Kaldor (1970), and with non-traded goods, Faini (1984). With external economies present, a region which starts with a slight capital-labour ratio advantage may enjoy a cumulative advantage which leaves its factors much better remunerated than those of a region which started slightly behind, Krugman (1981). And so on.

Of course if labour, which is the factor most liable to suffer location-based or correlated inequality, is freely mobile between regions and can easily metamorphose itself into the most suitable type for any situation, then no inequalities can endure. Even without metamorphosis, free mobility would equalize the net advantages for each grade or skill of labour between different regions. These obvious points partly serve to underline how imperfect is the actual mobility of labour. Again the example of North and South Italy, which have seen long-term inequalities persisting in the face of considerable migration, is instructive.

I now attempt to draw together the argument of this section. Economic principles do suggest that the passage of time will tend to moderate the effects of shocks to standards of living that may follow from reform, and may even iron out inequalities between regions and groups. They do not suggest however that this process will be either rapid or certain. The Commission's philosophy, on the other hand, emphasizes carefully targeted assistance with demanding eligibility criteria, with the aim of helping the affected parties to adjust. I have shown that it is difficult to draw a clear line between assistance to adjust and simple lump-sum compensation. However the difficulties are not only conceptual. These points are further developed in the following section.

The Commission envisages a full-scale employment-creating and regional policy. This approach mirrors that adopted by several national governments in the past, usually with somewhat disappointing results. The lesson may be that the whole approach is misconceived, or it may be that there are important lessons to be learnt from previous experiences which need to be taken into account when the policy direction, which until now is general in character, is translated into detailed decisions. These are again questions which are further examined in the following section.

4   Identification and addressing

This section considers the problems of identification and addressing in more detail. The terminology expresses similar ideas to those proposed by the Commission when it employs the terms 'priority objectives' and 'demanding eligibility criteria' (EC Commission, 1987c). However, a subtle difference of view is reflected in my own preferred terminology. To me priority objectives too readily suggests a list of outcomes which the administration, in this case the Commission, would like to see happen. We all have such lists but I doubt that formulating and refining them is a good way to go about economic planning. My own usage concentrates on a narrower approach. To illustrate the point, more rapid economic development in the backward regions of the Community may be an objective, but it identifies the group to be affected too widely and vaguely, and nominates no intervention to address the groups concerned.

In fact identification and addressing are different aspects of the same problem and need to be considered together. This is because a process of self-selection frequently operates, so that which parties are helped, and how they are helped, will depend upon the mechanism for assistance established. Suppose a backward region with many unemployed young. It is decided that improved training and employment opportunities are needed and funding is made available, particularly for training, with free courses, etc. Here policy has identified a group, deemed to merit help; a need from which that group is felt to suffer, lack of education; and an intervention, provision of education, judged to take care of the problem.

This might all work very well but notice that exactly what will happen will depend upon the responses of all affected parties to the new situation. For example, the courses provided may not be what the young unemployed would ideally like, but because they are available and free they may be taken. If places on training courses are scarce they may go to those judged to be most likely to benefit from them, who could well not be those in greatest need. Once trained the young may decide to migrate. If helping them specifically was the objective, then no matter. But perhaps helping their region was also an objective, in which case it may be unfortunate that the scheme has resulted in the purchase of one-way railway tickets by the able young.

The Commission's documents frequently show an awareness of the very same difficulties which my own approach is designed to illuminate. However it is not surprising that there is a lack of explicit reference to the crucial issue of the political process through which these interventions have to be mediated. Although it is natural that such a delicate issue should be underplayed, it is nonetheless of central importance.

I first consider identification in greater detail. Recall the conclusions of the background discussion of Section 3. A reform which leads to an increase in general economic efficiency will probably, although this cannot be proved, help all groups, or regions, or factors, however sub-sets of parties are described, in a long-enough run. However this long run may be surprisingly long, and absolute gain is consistent with marked relative loss. To hope that initial inequalities will tend to get ironed out is to ask for even more than a basic all-gain-at-least-something test.

In national politics a presumption that the general good should be sovereign is usually moderated by the principle that sufficiently acute individual costs deserve to be compensated. If the growth of tourism spoils the calm of a quiet sea-side resort, spoils it, that is, for the inhabitants who want it to be quiet and calm, we tend to feel sorry for those whose way of life has been upset but to expect them to move and to pay any financial penalties themselves. However if a new airport produces shattering noise levels over a previously-quiet area, the harm is often seen to be too concentrated and inequitable to be passed over, and official compensation is advocated and sometimes paid.

These rough and ready principles, supported by no more than a couple of examples, do not always translate to EC reform. Airport noise is a simple fact which can be measured by noise meters and its origin and causes are not in serious doubt. Even in that case the measurement of the costs is not a simple exercise, although the loss of market value to the housing stock has been defended. Consider two factories in Spain which close down during the process of Spain's full integration into the EC, leaving their towns without a major employer. In one case Spain's EC membership is clearly instrumental in bringing about the factory's closure; in the second case other forces, say a technical innovation, account for the failure of the business.

There are complex issues of natural justice and equity here, some of which economists have taken care to side-step, although they have often re-asserted their existence in discussions of welfare economics and redistributive justice. With the economist's Pareto improvement method the idea is that a reform should be so managed that no party or group shall suffer. The easiest way to ensure that result is lump-sum monetary compensation of the losers, but even without that mechanism an all round benefit can sometimes be organized by the manipulation of policy parameters. For some detail, see Diamond (1982) and references therein.

The Commission's philosophy is simpler than the Pareto-improvement approach. The aim is to ensure that the relatively badly off will be assisted, especially to adjust, regardless of the actual cause of their need. The latter approach seems on the face of things to be so evidently better and more just that it is important that its possible drawbacks should be noted. The original aim of identifying losers and compensating them once-and-for-all was motivated by the consideration that this type of intervention is fully neutral: it does not induce any undesirable response in the behaviour of present or future generations. This is a property of an incomplete compensation scheme so long as it is unanticipated. If those who do not need compensation do not get it, because for example they are too rich to merit it, then the compensation is still lump-sum and non-distorting. Once, however, formulae start to be applied, and their effects foreseen and taken into account, however demanding the eligibility criteria, then two new principles will apply.

First, private agents will respond to the shape of the formulae. For instance the investment plans of private firms, governments and local authorities, will be geared to attracting grant aid.[7] Secondly the political process will try to operate on the determination of the formulae. For example governments and groups will try to get criteria for assistance established which will in the outcome rebound favourably on their own constituencies. I do not propose to say much about this last issue, largely because there is not much to say at a general level that has not already been discussed. In the specific context of the Community, evaluating the scope for the 'gerrymandering' of regulations depends upon an understanding of the internal politics of the Commission and its interaction with the European Parliament and with national governments.

These are complex questions concerning which it would be presumptuous of me to offer opinions. Even if one had the answers for today, they are likely to change over time. However the issue is bound to be important. It always has been when rules are supposed to govern the allocation of large quantities of resources. A parallel problem is encountered when cost-benefit analysis systems are applied, supposedly to take such questions out of the political arena. Political players soon learn to play their side of the net according to the cost-benefit analysis rules.

As the ideal non-distorting interventions of economic theory will not be available, one needs to ask how closely it will be possible to approximate them in practice. Two approaches are possibly useful here. The first is already part of the Commission's approach. If the identification of need is precise and narrow, there will be less scope for shifting into the coverage of the policy. If large declining cities are identified as a problem area, then grant aid specifically targeted at cities passing clear and objective tests may capture the intended category. Such demarcations create anomalies but these may be worth enduring if the alternative is a system the complexity of which creates endless scope for manoeuvering. The argument is analogous to the issue of tax-system design. In theory simple systems, say of income taxation, are too imperfect and complicated intricate rules are superior. In practice the opposite may be the case, precisely because simple systems create less scope for costly strategies of tax minimization.

I attach more importance however to the second principle, what I shall call the principle of self-selection. This idea is already familiar from the theory and practice of help to the impoverished and the principles may be applied to grant aid. To illustrate the point, consider the following marginal but illuminating example. Certain charitable organizations offer free meals on Christmas Day at various not-too-smart locations. These organizations need hardly concern themselves at all over the problem that people who do not need the help will turn up to enjoy it. Almost anyone who presents himself or herself for a free Christmas dinner in a shabby location needs it. The intended recipients identify themselves.

As this idea is seductive, let us note its immovable limitations. Schemes for which the ideal subjects select themselves must be limited in scope. The broader the scope the more likely they are to attract non-intended adherents. A less marginal example of appropriate self-selection than the free Christmas dinner might be subsidized training for relatively modestly remunerated skills. The provision of such training in the depressed regions of the Community to all the qualified who present themselves might pick out some of those whom the Commission would like to target. There is no point in taking a course like that unless one is needy. Moreover the intervention may be superior to job-creation schemes which operate through the subsidy of investment or employment without reference to a precise need.

The free provision of training is not the ideal of lump-sum compensation. Our hypothetical Paulo and Pedro of Section 3 remind us that even if all who attend these courses are precisely those to whom help should have been directed, the help is of less value to them than its resource cost –

except in the unlikely instance of an individual who would have spent all the cost on the training had he received a cash grant. This type of example raises two issues which need to be considered carefully and separately.

First, is getting training, or more generally adjusting, a matter concerning which private decisions are likely to be socially optimal, or are there externalities, or other reasons, why the authorities may wish to induce a different outcome from the one which the individuals would choose if they were to be given sufficient money to adjust to the extent that they chose? Secondly, is a subsidy to adjust a non-distorting intervention? These questions are interconnected and both raise complex issues of the dynamics over time of the response by the individual decision-making unit and the counter-response by the authorities, the discussion of which will be postponed until the end of the section. Even there it will only illustrate the possibilities.

Aside from dynamics, the main reasons why letting the individual unit decide how rapidly to adjust might not be the best policy are what might be called 'paternalism' and 'externalities'. With paternalism the authorities know better than the individual unit what the benefits of adjusting will be, in which case a financial inducement to adjust more than would otherwise be chosen makes sense. Although this type of view appears patronizing to the individual unit, whether it be a person, a family or a local authority, it has a certain plausibility where education is concerned. We academics like to argue that only by going to school does one put oneself in a position to properly judge whether going to school is a good idea. However conceding to this point the respect which it surely deserves, it is doubtful whether a considerable role should be allowed to paternalistic considerations.

External economies are a weightier problem. The argument would be that the rate of adjustment selected by the individual agent affects not only that agent but also others, in which case a subsidy, or conceivably a financial disincentive, might be appropriate.[8] In practice this point is likely to amount to a version of the old argument that regional growth and development aids further growth and development by the generation of numerous economies, both pecuniary and non-pecuniary, in the region. For an enthusiastic advocacy of this case, see Kaldor (1970).

These are serious arguments, but it is important that they should not be allowed to establish a general presumption that subsidies for change or adjustment or development can be justified on theoretical grounds. In many cases these subsidies are at best unnecessary and at worst highly distorting. They have even generated external diseconomies, as in the case of the EC subsidies for agricultural drainage schemes.

Next we need to consider the problems for identification and addressing which spring from the fact that the effects of a policy extend over time. This gives rise to important dynamic issues and also to some characteristic problems of strategy and expectations. We begin by considering again the economist's ideal compensation for loss due to reform. Take a specific individual unit and suppose that the authorities command perfect information concerning that unit and indeed the whole economy. Of course this is an absurd assumption, but I want to examine some difficulties which persist even when we accept the assumptions on which the method depends.

Exactly how much compensation should be paid to leave the unit no worse off? In a simple case in which the unit is passive the answer may be determined by computing the monetary value of the loss. However more usually the extent of the loss will depend upon the subsequent behaviour of the unit. Suppose, for instance, that N loses his job as a result of the single market reforms. His loss will be huge if he never works again, but if he searches for a new job, and perhaps retrains, he could be employed again after a relatively short period. The right compensation is the minimum consequent loss. Hence, if adjustment makes the eventual cost of change smaller, then adjustment should be assumed in the compensation scheme. This is not a case where adjustment has to be subsidized. It will be in the agent's interest to adjust provided that the terms on which compensation is paid do not deter adjustment.

This last proviso is vital and in reality is frequently not satisfied. For example unemployment benefit is paid until a new position is acquired. Single mothers are supported until they marry or cohabit, etc. An obvious reason for such schemes is that information on the true long-term net discounted cost of misfortune is hardly ever available. Then it makes sense to allow subsequent history to determine what the cost has been. However subsequent history is an unreliable witness. If future compensation payments depend functionally on how the unit behaves, or even on what happens to it, if what happens to it is not independent of decisions and behaviour, then the compensation eventually paid will not equal the true long-term net discounted cost.

The ideal lump-sum payment seems to avoid this problem because it is paid at the outset and there supposedly the matter finishes. It is as if the system could dispose once and for all of the problem by paying a suitable sum and telling the affected party to go away and never return again. 'This will be sufficient compensation if you adjust optimally', the agent is told, 'and, therefore, no further compensation will ever be paid.' The trouble is that this announcement is not credible. It is rather like a mother whose son has ruined a pair of his school trousers telling the boy that she will buy one new pair of trousers for him to learn to look after them (adjust) and that if

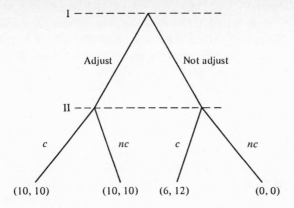

Figure 2.1 The adjustment game

he subsequently ruins that pair, he can go to school in rags. Mothers make such threats and children learn that they cannot be put into effect.

The situation is modeled simply in the Adjustment Game of Figure 2.1. There are two players called B and C. B is a backward unit or group and C is the Commission. Before the game starts B has already been paid an appropriate payment for his misfortune in being or becoming backward, part of which may be the costs of adjusting. The game proceeds as follows. B moves first, at level I, and chooses between adjusting, which is a troublesome business, and not adjusting. Then C moves at level II and chooses between paying further compensation, as necessary, or not doing so. If B chooses adjust at the first stage then C's decision at the second stage is vacuous. However it is represented as a branching decision with identical outcomes to maintain symmetry.

The pay-offs to the two players are represented at the ends of the branches, with C's pay-off first. If B adjusts he enjoys a benefit 10 and C enjoys a similar benefit, in his case from seeing B do well and from having disposed of an awkward problem. If B does not adjust and further compensation 'c' is paid, then this is much worse for C who only gets a pay-off of 6, but is better for B, who avoids the unpleasant work of adjusting and receives further compensation. Very bad for both is the outcome in which B does not adjust and no further compensation is paid, 'nc'. This case gives both parties 0, which represents the worst type of outcome. Although it has cost C nothing to choose nc, he suffers psychic and political pain because the problem of B's backwardness goes on, and without further compensation has become more acute.

The only plausible solution to this game is the (6,12) end-point. Why? If B at I chooses the move adjust he will certainly get a pay-off of 10.

Suppose that he chooses the move not adjust. Then C will have to move at the right-hand node at level II. However this faces C with choice of voting himself 6 or voting himself 0, and he will plainly choose the first, and play c. Then B will get 12. So if B chooses adjust he gets 10 and if he chooses not adjust he gets 12, and not adjust is clearly superior. C cannot resist this logic but he will not like the conclusion. What he would like to do is to precommit himself to play *nc* regardless of what B chooses. This corresponds to making the original compensation once-for-all. In that case B will find himself choosing between a move that would give him 10 and a move that would give him 0, and will prefer the former – adjust.

Konstantine Gatsios has pointed out that this simple game could be developed in directions which reveal more of the structure of the typical situation. It would pay C for instance to create uncertainty as to his tastes. Once the calculation of what C will do at a node becomes uncertain taking the game to that node must be less attractive. Similarly, C might act to reveal false tastes to establish a reputation which will reward him in future games.

If this argument seems abstract and fanciful, recall that several depressed regions inside nations have been given what purported to be, in part at least, adjustment assistance, repeatedly over periods decades long. Cannot C 'stand on principle' and refuse further aid? A popular axiom of game theory prohibits him from doing so, but the axiom may be more popular with game theorists than with the public.

In any case, there is one respect in which the simple game makes the non-adjust solution less likely than will be the case with real-life games. In the game of Figure 2.1 there is full information and transparency. Hence B's defiant choice of non-adjust is a clear provocation to C. 'I am not going to look after by trousers, because I know that you cannot bear to see me go to school in rags and will always buy me a new pair!' However in reality there is always uncertainty and a lack of clarity to the situation, so that it may be far from clear in practice whether B was defiant and non-responsive, or whether he suffered further misfortune.

The chief points to emerge from our lengthy discussion of Identification and Addressing are the following:

(i)   Identification and addressing need to be considered simultaneously because a process of self-selection frequently operates;

(ii)   Losses due to reform and losses or relative disadvantage for independent reasons need to be considered beside each other;

(iii) Only unanticipated compensation schemes are lump-sum and non-distorting. Once formulae start to be applied, and their effects foreseen, then behaviour will respond;

(iv) Self-selection is a good principle to aim for in schemes but it may be that no scheme that achieves what is wanted will satisfy this property;

 (v) Strict subsidy for adjustment is only desirable for paternalistic reasons or with externalities, and otherwise a subsidy for adjustment is inferior to straight cash compensation; and,

(vi) Once-for-all payments for the costs of reform and a refusal to pay more later, may not be a credible strategy.

5   Relations with the outside world

So far our argument could have concerned a Community consisting of the whole world, as if the entire world had come together to form a Community and was about to establish a single market. We have seen that the interests of different groups and regions within the Community may diverge. However no such group is outside in an institutional sense. All can participate in policy formation, at least in theory, and the interests of all would be represented, again in principle at least, in the Commission's objective function.

The world outside the EC is in a different position. It is like the other country of simple trade models. Its interests do not need to be taken into account, except in so far as the treatment that it receives may induce it to adopt policies which harm the home country, say by starting a trade war.

Yet the outside world may expect to be affected by enlargement and by the formation of the single market as much as many Community members will be affected. In my earlier paper, Bliss (1990), I argued that there is no reason in principle why the new developments in the Community have to harm or threaten the outside world. This sounds familiar: it is what Community spokesmen have been saying to the world for some time. However my way of looking at the problem is different from the official view. The latter often amounts to a claim that the Community will 'play by the rules' e.g. not raising tariff levels or using regulations or quotas to close off its markets to non-EC imports.

This raises two questions. First, is it true? Secondly, is it enough? The first issue is notoriously complex and it is too early to form a clear view of whether the Community will work to produce the open trading area that it claims to want. Verreydt and Waelbroeck (1982), although it needs up-dating, provides an excellent explanation of why it is difficult to read the Community's intentions from isolated actions, especially when they are undertaken by member states. Many of the indications in recent times which might be read as discouraging have involved the issue of whether policy neutrality, say unchanged tariffs, is enough in a changing union.

The conclusion of my own argument is that policy neutrality, however defined, is not an adequate response to the problem that enlargement and the single market may be trade diverting in themselves.

This is obvious with enlargement, although because the recently joining members are not large, especially as international traders, the issue is not as generally important as it might have been. Even so, at the level of individual products, large trade flows and their diversion have been involved. A notable example is imports of US feed grains into Spain, famous because it generated trade-war rumbles. An application of the Kemp–Wan model produces the conclusion that the Community has to be active if it is to avoid harming the rest of the world. The outcome could be realised accidentally by neutral policies, but neutral policies are no guarantee of the outcome, and the reasonable presumption is that in general they will not achieve it.

The Kemp–Wan approach assumes that tariff levels can be altered at will by the union. In fact GATT regulations prohibit tariff increases. However if the Community wants to secure the interests of the rest of the world, either because it believes that the benefits of its reforms should not be at the expense of the outside world, or because it wants to avoid provoking retaliation and a trade war, it can probably achieve that end and still enjoy gains from its own increased unification by only cutting tariffs.

It is of the greatest importance that the Community's external policy should be actively and effectively trade promoting. The Community is a large actor in world international trade. It is therefore in a position to influence the tone of international trade policy in the 1990s. If the Community is seen to have 'gone protectionist', other trading blocs may soon follow it.

What will be the character of the trade diversion losses for the outside world if they are not offset? Some of them will be the perfectly familiar examples of customs union theory. Internal barriers to trade between A and B come down, and now B can compete with imports from C in A's market. It only depends upon the costs of production of A, B and C, and upon the change in the tariff structure consequent upon enlargement. This framework was exploited in my previous paper, Bliss (1990), and I develop it no further here. Diversion of this type is not unrealistic, indeed the diversion of feed grain exports into Spain from the US to the rest of the Community, although it actually involved quotas and their adjustment, is basically of that pattern.

There is another type of trade diversion, which I think is likely to be important in the future, and which is capable of causing hard feelings at least, if not of starting trade wars. It is not only because tariffs and other restraints on free exchange are removed that trade is diverted from one country or bloc to another. The size of the unified market area will itself be a factor, if, as we must reasonably assume, economies of scale are important.

Imagine again our three country world in which A and B form a customs union. A and B are somewhat different, but C, the outsider, is still more different. At the start the union is a lazy union. Formal tariff barriers are removed but, as with pre-1993 Europe, there are many costs to trade between A and B. C exports motor vehicles which are also produced in A. B may import C's motor vehicles because in equilibrium A cannot satisfy all of its own and B's demand, or because love of variety means that it prefers to mix the two types of motor vehicle if their prices are not too different. Now, with no change in external tariffs, A and B form a unified market. This gives A's motor vehicle producers an added advantage in exporting to B. They expand production and their costs come down. Their new trading advantage is further reinforced, and so on. The formal model would be the same as Krugman (1984), but the boost to A's industry would come from market unification, not from protection.

The final outcome of this process is that the establishment of a single market, without any formal change in external policy, has diverted exports from C to A. This example justifies my earlier remarks to the effect that in practice 'fortress Europe' is not an outcome that need have labels all over it. The whole question of what constitutes a constant degree of openness in an enlarging union is difficult to determine and administer. The answer offered by the Kemp–Wan approach is that constant trade flows with the rest of the world is a basic minimum of openness. However in a changing developing world this base-line loses its precision and appeal.

A major area of concern is encountered when this argument is re-connected with earlier discussions concerning compensation and adjustment. Above I discussed this topic as though the only mechanisms for compensation would be budgetary allocations under the structural funds scheme. However, as I point out in Bliss (1990), trade restrictions are a ready, and budgetarily economical, manner of providing compensation. There lies a great danger. For example, if enlargement or the single market put pressure on high-cost producers within the Community, then extra protection helps them a bit. That protection cannot always take the form of higher tariffs, but it often does not need to do so in our world of quotas, regulations and managed trade.

6   Factor mobility and the regions in an enlarged Single Market

In the argument of Section 3 we already encountered the idea that the free and uninhibited exchange of goods and services between countries and regions may substitute for the mobility of factors. Yet even in the Nineteenth Century context with the export of wheat and meat from land-rich new countries to land-poor Europe, the trade was accompanied by large-scale migration of labour to the same land-rich new worlds. The explanation of that migration is complex and includes political influences as well as economic. However the motives for migration are typically complicated.

One reason why Europe exported population in the Nineteenth Century is that its own internal barriers to movement were high. Prior to 1914 these did not usually take the form of immigration restrictions at international borders. However in long-settled regions language, religious and cultural barriers could be just as deterrent as formal restrictions. Some of these barriers remain in Europe, with the consequence that Europe is unlikely to witness internal population movements of the kind that the US has experienced since the Second World War, even after 1992 reforms have removed particular inhibitions to the free mobility of labour.

In the Nineteenth Century instance the land could certainly not move to the labour. Today land scarcity and abundance are less crucial, especially as new agricultural technology has made land effectively abundant even in land-starved Europe. If we think of factors in terms of broad categories, then capital will be the natural candidate to be the other factor. In attaching as much importance to the free movement of capital and labour as to the free movement of goods, the single market initiative recognizes that these are not alternatives or substitutes, but that both will be required.

Even if a somewhat secondary role is to be expected of labour mobility, the simultaneous liberalization of the flow of goods and services and of capital markets signals a radical reform the eventual implications of which are difficult to predict. That efficiency in a global sense will be promoted seems extraordinarily probable. Strictly speaking, appeals to the economic argument that free markets promote efficiency are out of order, because the welfare economics of a complex locational model with increasing returns and local external economies of various kinds will support no simple and unambiguous efficiency result. Further, even if there will be, as seems overwhelmingly clear, an increase in overall efficiency, this is quite consistent with distributive consequences unfavourable to certain parties.

For our purposes the important question is what the scope will be for benign intervention, especially through structural funds disbursement, following the far-reaching shake-up of economic activity and its location which the reforms may bring about. Some of the trends will push in opposite directions. For example an economy like Spain's has and will come under increased competitive pressure in its home market as the penetration of foreign products increases. However the rapidly disappearing imperfections in the Spanish capital market have surely increased the cost of capital to Spanish producers in the past. Greater freedom of goods movements may pull activity away from Spain, cheaper capital will pull it towards Spain.

The United States is sometimes proposed as an example of what a unified market can achieve. It is an instructive example with many suggestive features. One would be that a unified market of huge physical and economic dimensions will contain several and even conflicting solutions to the locational problem. A high degree of specialization combined with a large market may produce a great concentration of activity, on the one hand, or multiple poles and centres, on the other.

In 1920 the number of US motor vehicle manufacturers was counted in hundreds. Today the fingers of two hands would number producers responsible for 95% of total national production. The chief reason for the shift was the production line but mass production in one locality depended crucially upon the creation of dealer networks which made it possible for the local buyer of a Detroit-produced vehicle to deal with a local seller.

The economies of mass motor vehicle production are traditional scale and pecuniary economies. These remain important but the proportion of national product accounted for by products for which they are a crucial consideration has declined steadily over time. In their place have arisen new and different economies of location. Service industries often have to be close to their market. Footloose industries, high value added and low bulk of inputs and outputs, can even locate where the labour would like to be – the sunbelt effect. Most interestingly, some activities generate powerful local external economies for like activity – the silicon valley effect. This effect sometimes amounts to simple scale economies in specialist suppliers whose output or service is effectively non-tradeable, the case discussed by Faini (1984).

If the US unified market suggests exciting and rich possibilities, then it also sounds some warnings. First, the US economy taken as a whole is not particularly successful, not on the test of productivity growth and dynamicism, although it is certainly rich in per capita and absolute terms. Secondly, clear successes for the unified US market stand beside serious regional problems, problems which have proved to be as recalcitrant to what the authorities felt to be adequate responses, and as enduring over time, as some of the comparable problems in Europe. Inner city decay and social stagnation in some of the old urban areas coexist with explosive growth in some of the new. Rural areas flourish in California but form pockets of acute deprivation in the Appalachian region.

A closer comparison of the US and Europe would show that regional diversity has declined more in the US since the Second World War than it has done in Europe. Thus, while the US has been stagnant where productivity growth is concerned, it has proved dynamic and flexible with regard to regional adaptation. Against the discouraging experience of the Appalachian region must be set an impressive record of progress and catching up in the Southern states.

Perhaps Europe will turn out to be a late arriver where adjustment through integration is concerned, much as it was a late arriver in modernizing industry after the Second World War. However the case of the US is importantly different because it possesses a common language and a broadly similar, if far from uniform, culture.

The policy of the Community with regard to regional problems promises to be more interventionist than US policy has attempted to be, at least since the New Deal, and there is every reason to expect that this more active approach will meet with some successes. However the sheer scale of the problem, especially when regions are in or will reach the position in which decline and out-migration result in a vicious circle effect, will ensure that there will be problem regions within the Community for a long time to come.

Here the issue of addressing is again relevant. If structural fund payments go into such regions, as they will, they must avoid compounding the problem for the long run by encouraging the growth of a rent-seeking grant economy. The comparative advantage of a difficult region too readily turns out to be the attraction and control of assistance. The right central administration operating with the right formulae should in principle keep this problem under control. If there is a great scarcity of historical examples of success in this enterprise that only serves to underline how difficult the problem really is. Finally, we may note again that time limits on assistance and help are neither necessarily appropriate, as central administrators surely will not command the information to set such limits correctly, nor are such limits, as the adjustment game illustrated, workable or credible.

7   Conclusions and policy

The argument of this chapter has been based upon a traditional approach which has been reformulated and extended somewhat to take into account specific problems which arise in the context of the development of the EC and its institutions, especially by enlargement and the establishment of the single market. The basis of the approach is the understanding that greater efficiency and universal gain do not always, or even typically, go hand in hand, especially not if the time horizon is measured in decades rather than centuries. When the Community's concern for the reduction of inequality is taken into account, there is even less reason to suppose that these problems will take care of themselves.

The Community recognizes the point and proposes a loosely specified system of intervention, on a scale which may or may not prove adequate to make a large impact on the problem, through the allocation of its structural funds. My concern has been to clarify the problems which a programme of that type will encounter and to demonstrate some principles which it ought to respect. I have explained these principles in terms of the twin ideas of identification and addressing. The first has to do with the selection of groups to receive assistance, the second to do with mechanisms for the disbursement of assistance, and with agents' reactions to the presence of assistance.

The chief lessons for policy which emerge are the following. First, compensating the relatively unfortunate for being relatively unfortunate is a different exercise from assisting groups or people to adjust so as to improve their fortunes. The former is expensive and should ideally take the form of once-for-all unconditional grants. As this is infeasible in practice, schemes which happen to catch the unfortunate will be employed. Schemes for which the right parties self-select themselves would be ideal, but may not exist or have a sufficiently broad coverage.

Secondly, the idea that the subsidy of accelerated adjustment is generally an ideal intervention must be questioned. If rapid adjustment generates external economies, then it should in principle be subsidized. However the gains may be private or the externalities negative. Even if adjustment assistance is disguised compensation it might do well in our imperfect world with limitations on the information and instruments available to the authorities. For instance, a subsidized retraining scheme might self-select just the badly off unemployed young who should be given unconditional grants. However the programmes need to be designed with a clear sense of the different objectives, motives and mechanisms that may operate. Confounding aid for adjustment with assistance for the unfortunate from the start of the exercise will tend to produce a muddled unfocused intervention.

The third broad conclusion was illustrated by the adjustment game of Section 4. That example can usefully be placed in the context of a more general framework with a more general conclusion.

The Commission does not exist as something wholly independent of the parties who it aids and influences. It enters into a complex inter-temporal relationship with those parties: a game in which it does not hold all the cards. The grant-seeking units need funds, the Commission needs success for its policies. It is difficult to know what policy conclusions to draw from this point. If the argument points to a hands-off approach with fairly rigid time-limited formulae applied to structural fund allocation, then the case for more flexibility would soon seem compelling. There is an inescapable dilemma here, familiar from the experience of the industry regulation field. Those too close can be captured by those they are supposed to regulate; those too distant can make silly mistakes.

My last reference was to experience, and experience, and learning from it, is my fourth general point. The programme for intervention through the allocation of the structural funds exhibits design features remarkably similar to various national regional policy programmes that presently exist, or that have existed in the past. Yet the Commission seems not concerned to learn from these, often disappointing, experiences. In this it must be mistaken.

My fifth, and last, conclusion concerns the need to maintain a lively adherence to the principle of openness and expanded trade with the outside world. Internal reform and external trade relations interact in ways that I have shown may be complex, even obscure. The two dangers in these circumstances are: first, that the commitment to openness will become purely formal, amounting only to the avoidance of clear and provocative trade insults; and, secondly, that trade policy will become a mechanism for alleviating internal stresses within the Community, including the problems which the structural funds were meant to take care of, and for which they may be insufficient in scale.

My list of warnings and cautions inevitably sounds a negative note. Although the reasons for excitement and enthusiasm are evident, and some of the grounds for caution are subtle, the consequent allocation of space to the two should not be mistaken for a weighting of their relative importance. The enlargement and market reform of the Community promise huge economic gains and forms a background against which working to ensure that all will eventually share in those gains is a thoroughly worthwhile and sensible undertaking.

NOTES

Support from the Commission of the European Economic Communities is gratefully acknowledged.
1 The close connection between the problems posed by enlargement and those posed by the single market is recognized in the opening of the Commission document, *Making a Success of the Single Act*, EC Commission (1987a).
2 For the application of the method to trade policy and for many references, see Corden (1984).
3 The reader will notice that I oscillate between referring to the Commission as the moving force in the Community, and the Community itself, which should

mean the European Parliament. I recognize that there is a subtle political structure at work and that formally the Commission only proposes ideas. However the Commission publishes its ideas extensively and when we are concerned with the philosophy behind reform it is natural to refer to the Commission's ideas as if they were the same as those of the Community.

4 A notable exception is the 1980 NBER conference, the proceedings of which are to be found in Bhagwati (1982). However many of the authors of these excellent papers neglect the distribution issues posed by adjustment and response. Most of the work builds – valuably without question – on the static factor-based trade model, although factor mobility, which is one of the ways in which factors avoid long-term unfavourable effects, does get an airing. Further relevant work concerns the so-called 'specific-factors model', on which see Jones and Neary (1984).

5 For an excellent summary of why intervention to improve the economic situation of the Italian Mezzogiorno has produced disappointing results, see Padoa-Schioppa (1988).

6 In fact the factor–price equalization mechanism may fail even with just two goods and two factors and no specialization. This is the famous case of factor-intensity reversals. The plausibility of factor-intensity reversals across international comparisons was argued by Minhas (1963). Regardless of the plausibility of this case, many goods and factors certainly provides an expanded scope for the mechanism to fail.

7 My own Oxford College became involved in precisely this process when it allowed the existence of EC funding to influence its decision not to write off its long moribund heat pump but instead to resurrect it.

8 It may seem odd that adjustment could ever be too rapid and the practical importance of the possibility is questionable. However Neary in Bhagwati, ed. (1982), shows how in a distorted economy, in which some parties adjust slowly, it is not necessarily good that others should adjust as rapidly as possible.

REFERENCES

Bhagwati, J.N. (ed.) (1982). *Import Competition and Response*, Chicago: University of Chicago Press.

(1984). 'Why are services cheaper in poorer countries?', *Economic Journal* **94**, 279–86.

Bliss, C. (1990). 'The Optimal External Tariff in an Enlarging Customs Union', CEPR Discussion Paper, No. 368.

Corden, W.M. (1984). 'Normative theory of international trade', Ch. 2 in R.W. Jones and P.B. Kenen, (eds.), *Handbook of International Economics*, Amsterdam: North-Holland.

Diamond, P.A. (1982). 'Protection, Trade Adjustment Assistance and Income Distribution', in J.N. Bhagwati, (ed.), *Import Competition and Response*, Chicago: University of Chicago Press.

Diamond, P.A. and J.A. Mirrlees (1971). 'Optimal taxation and public production', *American Economic Review* **61**, 8–27, 261–78.

Dore, R.P. (1982). 'Adjustment Process: A Lancashire Town', in J.N. Bhagwati, (ed.), *Import Competition and Response*, Chicago: University of Chicago Press.

EC Commission (1987a). *Making a Success of the Single Act: A New Frontier for Europe*, Commission of the European Economic Community, Communication 87 (100).

(1987b). *Economic Situation and Development of the Regions of the Community*, Commission of the European Economic Community, Communication 87 (230).

(1987c). *Reform of the Structural Funds*, Commission of the European Economic Community, Communication 87 (376).

Emerson, M. *et al.* (1988). *The Economics of 1992*, (Study directed by M. Emerson assisted by M. Aujean, M. Catinat, P. Goybet and A. Jacquemin), Brussels: Commission of the European Communities.

Ethier, W. (1984). 'Higher dimensional issues in trade theory', Ch. 3 in R.W. Jones and P.B. Kenen, (eds.), *Handbook of International Economics*, Amsterdam: North-Holland.

Faini, R. (1984). 'Increasing returns, non-traded inputs and regional economic development', *Economic Journal* **94**, 308–23.

Helpman, E. and P. Krugman (1985). *Increasing Returns, Imperfect Competition and the International Economy*, Cambridge, MA: MIT Press.

Jones, R.W. and J.P. Neary (1984). 'Positive theory of international trade', Ch. 1 in R.W. Jones and P.B. Kenen, (eds.), *Handbook of International Economics*, Amsterdam: North-Holland.

Kaldor, N. (1970). 'The case for regional policies', *Scottish Journal of Political Economy* **17**, 337–48.

Kemp, M.C. and Wan, H.Y. (1976). 'An elementary proposition concerning the formation of customs unions', *Journal of International Economics* **6**, 95–97.

Krugman, P. (1981). 'Trade, accumulation and uneven development', *Journal of Development Economics* **8**, 149–162.

(1984). 'Import protection as export promotion: International competition in the presence of oligopolies and economies of scale', in H. Kierzkowski, (ed.), *Monopolistic Competition and International Trade*, Oxford University Press.

Minhas, B.S. (1963). *An International Comparison of Factor Cost and Factor Use*, Amsterdam: North-Holland.

Neary, J.P. (1978). 'Short-run capital specificity and the pure theory of international trade', *Economic Journal* **88**, 488–510.

(1982). 'Intersectoral capital mobility, wage stickiness and the case for Adjustment Assistance', in J.N. Bhagwati, (ed.), *Import Competition and Response*, Chicago: University of Chicago Press.

Padoa-Schioppa, T. *et al.* (1987). *Efficiency, Stability and Equity: A Strategy for the Evolution of the Economic System of the European Economic Community*, Oxford University Press.

(1988). Address to the European Parliament – Liberal, Democratic and Reformist Group Conference on the Mezzogiorno of Italy and 1992, Naples, December 19, 1988.

Verreydt, E. and J. Waelbroeck (1982). 'European Community Protection against Manufactured Imports from Developing Countries', in J.N. Bhagwati, (ed.), *Import Competition and Response*, Chicago: University of Chicago Press.

Discussion

MICHAEL EMERSON

Christopher Bliss analyses two distinct but tangential aspects of the EC's southern enlargement: the role of the structural funds and the adaptation of the common external trade policy. While his paper excels in setting out the economic principles in question and does not try to be empirical, it is nonetheless much more than a purely academic exercise. The author reveals a perceptive understanding of the real policy issues, in some cases dilemmas, that confront policy-makers in the EC institutions and the Member States.

The first two words of the Bliss paper 'Adjustment and Compensation' correctly identify the two-sided character of the structural funds. The politicians' willing use of value-loaded and only semi-technical terms like convergence and cohesion to envelop this policy domain underlines the need for rigorous economic analysis. Bliss is quite aware of this. He observes the institutional factors at work: 'The Commission does not exist as something wholly independent of the parties who it aids and influences. It enters into a complex inter-temporal relationship with those parties: a game in which it does not hold all the cards'. Amen.

Bliss quite appropriately gives some space to describing the theoretical properties, but practical irrelevance of the economist's first-best technique of compensation. The argument proceeds as follows.

Market integration generates aggregate welfare gain. But some parties may lose out. The efficient solution is based on the Pareto-optimal principle. A lump-sum payment is made to bring the losers up to the point of indifference, so they do not block the market integration policy. Lump-sum compensation has the excellent quality that it introduces no distortion of economic incentives.

Unfortunately life is not so simple. Can we really identify quantitatively the losses of the losers, distinguishing between various causes of a country or region's disappointing economic results? Can the institutions credibly offer one-time lump-sum compensation, when the payer and beneficiary are wedded together in a permanent and deep politico-economic relationship? Bliss notes that the answers are no.

Where do we go from there? Bliss advocates a meticulous process of 'identification and addressing'. The political institutions are invited to identify precisely what the problem is that they wish the structural funds to fix, and then to define the operating rules of the instrument of intervention to address this problem. Again, amen.

In this spirit I identify three interpretations of the objectives of the structural funds, and shall comment on each in turn. These are (i) the objective of equalizing resource endowment, (ii) the objective of securing regime change and (iii) the regional policy objective.

The first two points are less clearly identified and addressed by Bliss than in the real actions of the Community institutions.

By equalizing resource endowment is meant the task of raising the quality of public economic infrastructure in the weak regions (transport systems, telecommunications etc.) and the level of human capital endowment in vocational skills to the point that the regions in question are no longer disqualified on these scores from progressing to a high level of economic development. The structural funds may be viewed as aiming to do just this. The political contract between the EC and its weaker economic regions is thus structured along the following lines: (a) the weak regions accept the full force of EC competition, (b) the EC offers finance to raise the level of basic economic resource endowment (other than its natural features) to usual Community standards, and (c) beyond that the regions are left to their own devices to determine how they fare in the competitive process. This may be considered a fair and clear deal. The structural funds cannot guarantee success, but they help assure that a pre-requisite of success is not absent.

By securing regime change is meant a still broader operation of political economy. The regime change in question is the transition from the totalitarian, protectionist state-corporatism of the early post-war decades in much of Southern Europe to their new regime of democracy and open market economics. The Community now accentuates this regime change with 1992 and the prospect of economic and monetary union. This transition is, at the level of many enterprises and workers, a painful one. Many enterprises can fail. Many people can become unemployed, as Spain knows well. The economist may say: if these countries believe that the new regime offers a better deal, then why is it necessary to subsidize them into it? The answer is about the probabilities of success and the severity of the adjustment problems in the transition. The chances of success may be uncertain, especially if the difficulties of transition are so severe as to risk undermining the capacity of the political majority to hold to the strategy. Budgetary help at that time eases the problems in several ways: In improving infrastructure and manpower training it increases the attractiveness of the economy for investment, and so helps secure growth from the supply side. The financing of such expenditures by the Community may mean that the investment climate can thus be improved without requiring severe cuts in current public services or increases in taxes.

Finally, on the regional problem Bliss observes that traditional regional aids have not been successful, and criticises the structural funds for perpetuating these mistakes. In fact the recent reform of the structural funds has seen steps in the direction that Bliss may favour. In particular the rules have required that regional authorities prepare plans at a decentralised level, with the idea of creating incentives for local authorities to prepare development or reconversion strategies. The emphasis has already moved away from the automatic subsidisation of private investment, which often seems to have led to instances of inefficient capital deepening.

3 Integration and the competitiveness of peripheral industry

PAUL R. KRUGMAN and ANTHONY J.
VENABLES

As the Southern European countries enter the European Community, a key question is how that entry will affect the competitiveness of their manufacturing sectors. Optimists believe that the mutual opening of markets, reinforced by 1992, will make manufacturing in Southern Europe highly attractive; they thus expect that manufacturing sectors in the entering countries will expand, and that manufacturing wages in the Southern entrants will converge over time towards Northern European levels. Pessimists worry that in spite of lower wages, Southern industry will have difficulty competing with Northern, and that there will have to be both a shrinkage of manufacturing and a reduction in relative manufacturing wages.

This dispute is immediately crucial for macroeconomic and exchange-rate policy. If the pessimistic view is right, then the new entrants ought to be trying to keep their exchange rates somewhat undervalued in order to start out with a cost advantage that will ease their adjustment. Even if the pessimistic view only *might* be correct, the countries might want to err on the side of undervaluation, as argued in Krugman (1990). As the case of Spain has recently shown, however, financial markets are currently inclined to be optimistic rather than pessimistic, which can make an attempt to follow a prudent exchange-rate policy difficult.

The dispute is also important for structural policy, especially regional policy. The size and kinds of assistance that will be needed will depend on the effect of the enlargement on industrial competitiveness. Also, understanding the mechanisms of the change in competitiveness may give clues to which kinds of policies will help the adjustment and which may actually make the problem more difficult.

The purpose of this paper is to focus on one particular source of ambiguity regarding the effects of integration on the manufacturing competitiveness of the entrant nations: the role of comparative market access.

56

Type of region	GDP per capita (Europe = 100)
Central	122
Intermediate	105
Inner periphery	89
Outer periphery	64

Table 3.1. Peripherality and per capita GDP

The paper is in seven parts. The first section sets out some general considerations regarding the role of market size in assessing the effects of trade liberalization. Section 2 sets out a formal model that can be used to address some of these effects. Sections 3 and 4 look at the effects of increased integration on manufacturing output for given wage rates, while Sections 5 and 6 look at the effects on wage rates themselves. A final section draws some conclusions.

1 Market access and manufacturing competitiveness: defining the issue

A glance at the economic geography of Europe reveals that the richest regions in per capita terms are also, by and large, the most densely populated. Furthermore, the wealthy regions are clustered close together, in the northwestern part of the continent. Exactly why this should be so is a matter of some dispute – how much represents cultural contagion, how much the cumulative processes that result from economies of agglomeration? – but it has the definite implication that the high-wage regions are also the regions with the best access to markets.

The European Commission has developed a simple index of 'peripherality' based upon distance from purchasing power, and used it to classify regions into a number of categories. There is a striking gradient in per capita income, and thus presumably also in wages, as one moves away from the central areas toward the peripheral ones (Table 3.1).

Why should peripheral areas pay lower wages? At least in part the answer must be that their peripheral location makes them less attractive, other things equal, as a site for production than the central regions. Thus in order to attract firms the peripheral regions must offer a compensating wage differential.

Now what both entry into the EC and the effect of 1992 on the working of the Community should do is make mutual market access easier and cheaper. Carried to its limit, this process would eliminate any advantage to a central location, and thus work to the advantage of production in the peripheral areas. One might therefore suppose that a step in that direction will necessarily have the same effect – that the reduction in barriers to trade due to EC enlargement and 1992 will tend to increase manufacturing production and relative manufacturing wages in the southern European nations. The point of this paper is to argue that this is not necessarily true. While complete elimination of obstacles to trade always raises the competitiveness of the peripheral regions, partial elimination may in principle have a perverse effect.

The reason for this ambiguity may be conveyed by a highly oversimplified example. Imagine that there is some product that could be produced either in Belgium (a central nation) or in Spain, or in both. We assume for simplicity that the demand for the good is completely inelastic, so that total shipments can be taken as given. We also suppose that, if only direct production costs were considered, it would be more expensive to make the good in Belgium than in Spain; but because there are economies of scale, it is still more expensive to produce in both. In addition to production costs, however, there are shipping costs; if the good is produced only in the centre, some units must be shipped to the periphery; if the good is produced only in the periphery, a larger number of units must be shipped to the centre. Finally, we assume that somehow a cost-minimizing location of production is chosen.

Under these assumptions, the situation might look like that in Table 3.2. As described, it is cheapest to *produce* the good in Spain alone, and most expensive to produce in both locations. However, the shipping costs may change this decision. In the 'high' shipping cost case, the cheapest locational structure overall is to produce in both locations: the savings in transportation outweigh the extra production cost.

What we can now note is that reducing shipping costs does not necessarily cause production to move to the low-cost location. A *complete* elimination of these costs, shown as the 'low' cost case in Table 3.2, will indeed give Spain the advantage. However, a shift from the 'high' to the 'medium' cost case – in which all shipping costs are reduced to half their level in the 'high' case – actually causes production to shift to Belgium.

The point is that while high barriers to trade encourage local production, moderate barriers interacting with economies of scale may encourage concentration of production in high-cost locations with good market access rather than in low-cost locations. While this is a contrived and oversimplified example, it conveys a general point. In the remainder of this paper we will consider a more sophisticated (although still highly abstract) model to demonstrate the nature of the ambiguity in a less *ad hoc* way.

	Production costs	Shipping costs		
		High	Medium	Low
Produce in Belgium	10	3	1.5	0
Produce in Spain	8	8	4	0
Produce in both	12	0	0	0

Table 3.2. Hypothetical effects of lowering trade barriers

2   A model of trade liberalization

In order to focus on the effects of market access in trade liberalization, we make some severe simplifications in terms of the representation of economic geography, market structure, and the sources of international differences in per capita income.

First, despite some reservations, we maintain the long tradition of international economics by representing countries as if they were dimensionless points. Increasingly it makes sense in practical terms to think of economic Europe as consisting not of a collection of internally homogeneous countries, but of a collection of regions, of varying degrees of peripherality from a centre located somewhere around Brussels; although Belgium and the Netherlands are small countries, they have close and (especially after 1992) easy access to very large markets. For the purposes of this exercise, however, we will represent the centre-periphery issue by considering trade liberalization between a single relatively small economy and its larger partner. The smallness of the 'small' country should be taken to represent, not actual small size, but a peripheral position that gives it less good access to markets, while the 'large' country's size really represents a central location. In other words, you should think of Spain as part of the small country and Belgium as part of the large. Trade liberalization is modelled as reduction in the costs of getting access to the 'foreign' market. These trade costs should be interpreted as a synthetic measure of a wide range of barriers to trade including trade taxes, transport costs, and costs of frontier formalities and differing product standards.

Second, the model presented here is one of the simplest possible models of intra-industry trade, capturing two motives for such trade. One is the efforts of oligopolistic firms to raid each other's markets, in the tradition of Brander and Krugman (1983), Dixit (1984) and Venables (1986). The other is that each firm produces a product type differentiated from that of other firms, and demanded by consumers in both countries.

Third, since the aim of the paper is to make a point rather than to be realistic, a number of extreme simplifying assumptions are made. For example, firms compete in quantities sold in segmented markets, and also firms are assumed to have linear demand and cost functions (as in Dixit, 1984). These assumptions produce quite sharp and clearcut results, but exaggerate some effects while minimizing others. For example, quite small price changes generate large quantity changes. This produces huge changes in the location of production in response to modest changes in trade barriers; it also implies implausibly small effects of trade barriers on relative factor prices. We choose to present most of our results by developing a numerical example. This is an efficient way of illustrating the insights generated by the model, but is intended to illustrate qualitative not quantitative effects. The numerical results reported below should not be taken as even stylized estimates. To model the quantitative effects of policy change requires a significantly richer model, and one fitted to data.

Finally, the model is developed in a series of stages, moving from the simplest to the more complex. In order to focus on the effects of peripherality vs/centrality, we initially assume away comparative advantage. Until Section 6, the countries are permitted to differ *only* in relative size; differences in both technology and relative factor endowments are assumed away.

The two countries described in the model are labelled 1 and 2. The size of the market in each country is measured by a parameter s_1, s_2, and we shall call the country with the smaller market country 1, so $s_1 < s_2$. Each economy has two sectors. One is a perfectly competitive sector producing a tradeable output which will be taken as the numeraire. The other is imperfectly competitive, and it is this sector on which attention will be focussed. We shall call this sector 'manufacturing'. The number of firms in the manufacturing sector of countries 1 and 2 are denoted n_1 and n_2. Each of these firms produces its own variety of differentiated product, but we shall assume that all products produced in a particular country are symmetric. We may then use p_{ij} and x_{ij} to denote the price and quantity of a single one of these products produced in country i and consumed in county j, where the indices i and j take values 1 and 2. We shall assume that demand curves for these products are linear. The inverse demand curve for a single variety produced in country i and sold in country j, $(i, j = 1, 2)$ then takes the form,

$$p_{ij} = a - \frac{1}{s_j} \left\{ \frac{(1 + \theta)}{2} x_{ij} + \theta[(n_i - 1)x_{ij} + n_j x_{jj}] \right\}$$

$$p_{ii} = a - \frac{1}{s_i} \left\{ \frac{(1 + \theta)}{2} x_{ii} + \theta[(n_i - 1)x_{ii} + n_j x_{ji}] \right\} \tag{1}$$

$$a > 0, \quad \theta \in [0, 1], \quad i, j = 1, 2, \quad i \neq j.$$

That is, the price of the single variety depends on the quantity of this product sold, (with coefficient $(1 + \theta)/2$) and on the quantities of the $n_i - 1$ other varieties from country i and n_j from country j (with coefficient θ). The demand parameter θ measures the extent of product differentiation, with products being homogeneous if $\theta = 1$ and differentiated when $\theta < 1$; since $\theta > 0$ products are substitutes.

Firms have increasing returns to scale, represented by linear cost functions. Each firm in country i has a fixed cost of f_i, and marginal cost c_i; t is the cost of shipping one unit of output between countries. The profits of a country i firm, π_i, may be expressed as,

$$\pi_i = (p_{ii} - c_i)x_{ii} + (p_{ij} - c_i - t)x_{ij} - f_i \qquad i, j = 1, 2, \quad i \neq j. \tag{2}$$

We assume that firms compete as Cournot competitors in each market separately. Choosing sales in each market to maximize profits implies,

$$x_{ii} = (p_{ii} - c_i)s_i(2/(1 + \theta))$$

$$x_{ij} = (p_{ij} - c_i - t)s_j(2/(1 + \theta)) \qquad i, j = 1, 2, \quad i \neq j. \tag{3}$$

Because of the linear structure of the model it is possible to derive explicit expressions for equilibrium prices and quantities, given the number of firms operating in each country. Using equations (1) and (3) we obtain,

$$p_{ii} = \frac{c_i(1 - \theta)}{2} + \frac{(1 + \theta)}{2} \left\{ \frac{a + \theta n_i c_i + \theta n_j(c_j + t)}{1 + \theta(n_1 + n_2)} \right\}$$

$$p_{ij} = \frac{(c_i + t)(1 - \theta)}{2} + \frac{(1 + \theta)}{2} \left\{ \frac{a + \theta n_j c_j + \theta n_i(c_i + t)}{1 + \theta(n_1 + n_2)} \right\}$$

$$i, j = 1, 2, \quad i \neq j. \tag{4}$$

$$x_{ii} = s_i \left\{ \frac{a - c_i + \theta n_j t + \theta n_j(c_j - c_i)}{1 + \theta(n_1 + n_2)} \right\}$$

$$x_{ij} = s_j \left\{ \frac{a - c_i - (1 + \theta n_j)t + \theta n_j(c_j - c_i)}{1 + \theta(n_1 + n_2)} \right\}$$

$$i, j = 1, 2, \quad i \neq j. \tag{5}$$

In order to highlight the economic forces at work, this model will be developed as follows. In Sections 3 and 4 we shall assume that costs, c_1, c_2, f_1, f_2 are constant, and are the same in both countries, so that no comparative cost considerations enter the analysis. In Section 3 we also assume that the numbers of firms in each country, n_1 and n_2, are constant and unchanged by integration. This assumption is relaxed in Section 4, and entry and exit of firms may occur; Section 4 therefore develops the model from one of oligopoly to monopolistic competition. In Sections 5 and 6, we remove the assumption that costs are constant, by making factor prices depend on the level of manufacturing employment. Until Section 6 it is assumed that the two countries differ only in size, having no other sources of comparative advantage. In Section 6 we adopt a Heckscher–Ohlin framework, in which countries may differ both in size and in relative factor abundance.

3   Oligopoly

Suppose that the initial situation is one in which market access is restricted by high trade barriers, although these are not so high as to choke off intra-industry trade. What is the effect on the industry of a reduction in these barriers, as represented by a fall in the trade cost, t? Given the numbers of firms and cost levels in each country, the effects are immediate from equations (5). As would be expected the reduction in t reduces home sales, x_{ii}, but raises trade volumes, x_{ij}. The effect of a small reduction in trade costs, $-dt$, on total production in country 1 is,

$$\frac{dx_{11}}{-dt} + \frac{dx_{12}}{-dt} = \frac{s_2 + \theta n_2(s_2 - s_1)}{1 + \theta(n_1 + n_2)} \tag{6}$$

Country 1, the small country ($s_2 > s_1$), therefore experiences increased production as barriers are reduced, although it is possible that production in the large country contracts. The reason for this is simply that firms in the small country are getting improved access to the larger market, while firms in the larger country only gain access to a smaller market.

This effect is mirrored in the balance of trade. If costs are the same in both countries, ($c_i = c$, $i = 1, 2$), then country 1's net manufacturing imports are (in physical units),

$$n_2 x_{21} - n_1 x_{12} = \left\{ \frac{(a - c - t)(n_2 s_1 - n_1 s_2) + n_1 n_2 t \theta(s_2 - s_1)}{1 + \theta(n_1 + n_2)} \right\} \tag{7}$$

Providing country 1's share of firms is not more than its relative size, i.e. $s_1/s_2 \geq n_1/n_2$, then, from equation (7), country 1 is a net importer of manufactures and as t is reduced net imports fall. These effects are

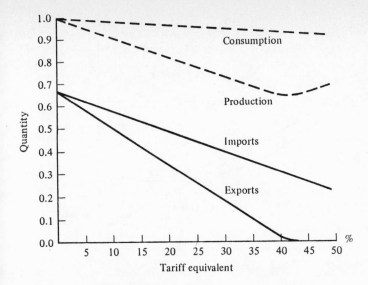

Figure 3.1   Oligopoly: output and trade

illustrated in Figure 3.1, which, for an example described in the Appendix, traces out quantities produced, traded, and consumed in the small country as a function of t. (In this and all following figures quantities are expressed as a proportion of consumption at $t = 0$, and, t, the tariff equivalent, is expressed as a proportion of marginal costs). Figure 3.1 extends to values of t high enough to drive country 1 exports to zero; reductions in t at levels greater than this reduce country 1 output, as they increase imports while leaving exports at zero.

The price effects of a reduction in trade barriers can also be obtained from equations (4). As is apparent, reductions in t reduce price, and therefore raise consumer surplus. Notice that if there are more firms in the large economy than the small ($n_2 > n_1$), then positive t implies a relatively high goods price in the small economy, i.e., consumers in the small economy are disadvantaged by the lower level of competition. Corresponding to this, reductions in t bring relatively larger gains to consumers in the small economy than in the large.

The behaviour of profits is more complex, as it involves the interaction of price and quantity effects. We know that, in the symmetric case, going from autarky to free trade reduced profits (Donsimoni & Gabsziewicz, 1989), but this need not be a monotonic process. This is illustrated by the profits curve in Figure 3.2, which gives country 1 profits per firm as a function of t. Profits fall in the early stages of liberalization (as increased

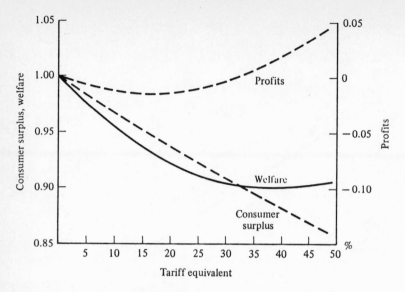

Figure 3.2   Oligopoly: profits and welfare

competition from imports erodes market power), but rise in the later stages as exports become very large, so the direct cost saving effects of reductions in t come to dominate. The fact that profits move in this way has two implications. First, possible reductions in profits mean that the welfare effects of trade liberalization are ambiguous. This is illustrated in Figure 3.2 which reports, in addition to profits, consumer surplus, and, as a welfare indicator, the sum of country 1's total profits and consumer surplus (expressed as a proportion of their value when $t = 0$). With a given number of firms we see welfare falling in the early stages of liberalization. Second, changing profit levels suggest that we should expect to see the number of firms in each country changing as trade barriers are removed. It is to this that we now turn.

4   Monopolistic competition

The preceding story was incomplete, as it took as exogenous the number of firms in each country. We now endogenise these, but, in order to bring out the importance of the effect of relative market size, we maintain the assumption that the two countries have identical and unchanged costs whatever the size of the trade barriers. What we can show in this case is that the smaller country is always a net importer of manufactured goods, because its firms are placed at a disadvantage by their inferior market access. Perhaps more surprisingly, this trade deficit in manufactured goods will actually be greater, the lower the barriers to trade. The reason is that already suggested by the example in Table 3.2: a reduction in barriers to trade reduces the incentives for self-sufficiency faster than it reduces the incentives to concentrate production near the larger market, so causing relocations of firms towards the larger market.

In terms of the formal model, the equilibrium number of firms, n_1 and n_2 are obtained by adding the condition that firms in each country should earn zero profits. Using equations (3) in the definitions of profits, equations (2), the industry equilibrium conditions can be written as[1]

$$\pi_1 = 2(p_{11} - c_1)^2(s_1/(1 + \theta)) + 2(p_{12} - c_1 - t)^2(s_2(1 + \theta)) - f_1 = 0$$

$$(8)$$

$$\pi_2 = 2(p_{22} - c_2)^2(s_2/(1 + \theta)) + 2(p_{21} - c_2 - t)^2(s_1(1 + \theta)) - f_2 = 0$$

Providing there is a positive number of firms in each country equilibrium prices and numbers of firms can be solved from this pair of equations, together with equations (4).

The first point to note is that if $c_1 = c_2$, then the number of firms, comparative prices and the pattern of trade depend on relative country size. Specifically, it is straightforward but tedious to show that if $s_1 < s_2$, country 1 will have a higher price of manufactured goods and also be a net importer of manufactured goods (and a net exporter of the other good). A formal demonstration is given in Venables (1986) for the case when $\theta = 1$; the point, of course, is that firms in the smaller country are at a disadvantage, and they can only cover their fixed costs if the home market is less competitive than the foreign.

How does this result change if the barriers to trade are reduced? The effects of reductions in t can be derived directly from differentiation of equations (8) and (4). Doing this gives,

$$\frac{dp_{11}}{-dt} = \frac{(1 + \theta)x_{12}(x_{21} - x_{22})}{2(x_{11}x_{22} - x_{12}x_{21})} \quad \frac{dp_{21}}{-dt} = \frac{dp_{11}}{-dt} - \frac{(1 - \theta)}{2} \quad (9)$$

The denominator of the right hand side of the first of these equations is certainly positive if $t > 0$. The numerator term $x_{21} - x_{22}$ is the difference between export and home sales for firms in country 2 and is certainly negative (see equations (5)). This means that reductions in t reduce p_{11}; p_{21}, the price of imports to country 1, falls by more, because of the direct effect of the reduction in t (see second equation (9)). So the small country will find that prices of manufactured products necessarily fall.[2] If we can ignore any possible costs of adjustment, this represents a clear gain. This is especially true if the trade barriers captured by t are taken to represent the kinds of nuisance costs that 1992 is supposed to reduce, rather than revenue-generating tariffs; if government revenue is unchanged by the reductions in t, then reductions in p_{11} and p_{21} necessarily mean an increase in social welfare, since it raises consumer surplus and, in the free entry case, producer surplus is always zero. Ignoring problems of adjustment, reductions in t raise welfare in the small economy.

Unfortunately, adjustment problems are all too likely to arise, because reductions in trade barriers are associated with dramatic effects on the number of firms operating in country 1. We know that if trade barriers are large enough, then both n_1 and n_2 are positive – as must be the case under autarky.[3] However, for a sufficiently small but positive level of trade barriers the number of firms in the small economy is zero. To see this subtract π_2 from π_1 (equations (8)), use equations (4), and rearrange to obtain,

$$(\pi_1 - \pi_2)\left\{\frac{1 + \theta(n_1 + n_2)}{1 + \theta}\right\}$$

$$= 2t(a - c)(s_1 - s_2) + t^2\{\theta(s_1 + s_2)(n_2 - n_1) + s_2 - s_1\}/2 \qquad (10)$$

For small enough values of t, t^2 is approximately equal to zero. Since $(a - c) > 0$ and n_1 and n_2 are bounded, $s_1 < s_2$ implies $\pi_1 < \pi_2$. Neither π_2 nor π_1 can be positive at equilibrium, so this tells us that $\pi_1 < 0$, i.e., for small enough t there can be no surviving firms in the small economy's industry.

For intermediate levels of trade barriers it turns out that reductions in barriers lead to a progressive reduction in the number of firms in the small country. The implications of this relocation of firms for production and trade are illustrated in rather stark terms in Figure 3.3 (details of the example underlying this are given in the Appendix). Production declines steadily (despite rising output per firm, as in Section 3), and imports rise to meet domestic consumption (which rises somewhat as p_{11} and p_{21} are falling). Country 1 exports per firm increase as t falls, but as the number of firms falls total exports reach a peak and decline thereafter. The small economy's *net* manufactured imports increase steadily as t falls.

5   Variable costs

The example given in the last section points up rather clearly the idea that a reduction in barriers to trade may actually cause production of manufactured goods to shift toward rather than away from regions with better market access. In one way, however, this model conveys a misleading

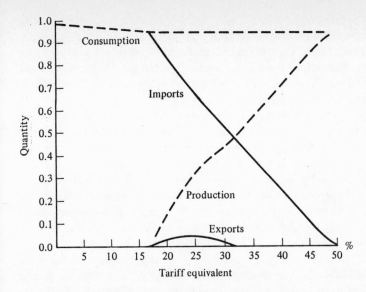

Figure 3.3   Monopolistic competition: output and trade

impression: that barriers to trade actually seem to become more important the lower they are. The reason for this impression is that when costs
are both fixed and equal, the only countervailing force against concentration of production is self-sufficiency. As the barriers to trade go down, the
incentive for self-sufficiency is reduced while the advantages of concentrating in the larger market remain, (except in the limit, when there are no
trade costs of any sort). Realistically, however, there may also be general
equilibrium effects causing changes in factor prices and costs, and these
effects may work against the concentration of production.

One source of general equilibrium effects could be changes in the price
of the perfectly competitive sector's output in each country. So far we
have assumed that the price of this good is the same in both economies at
all levels of trade costs. This assumption is correct if trade costs on this
good are negligible, or if the price of the good is set on an integrated world
market. But what if trade costs between the two countries cause the price
of this good to differ between countries? Suppose that trade costs apply to
trade in the perfectly competitive good, as well as to manufactures, and
that these costs are reduced by trade liberalization. As noted above, the
small economy is the exporter of this good, and the large economy the
importer. When trade costs are positive the internal price of the perfectly
competitive good is therefore higher in the large economy than in the
small. This is translated into higher wages in the large economy, so

putting manufacturing in the large economy at a cost disadvantage relative to the small economy. How does this modify the argument of the preceding section, as illustrated in Figure 3.3? It can be shown that the qualitative shape of the diagram is unchanged, but the decline in the small economy's manufacturing output is now less steep. At high levels of t the small economy has a cost advantage so giving higher output (but remaining a net importer). As trade costs go to zero (for both sectors of the economy) the wage and cost differences between countries disappear and country 1's output goes to zero, as in Figure 3.3.

A second source of general equilibrium effects will arise if there are upward sloping supply curves of resources to manufacturing. In this case changes in the size of manufacturing will induce factor price changes, and these will tend to offset the forces for concentration of production. In order to capture this the remainder of this section reworks our analysis for the case where the imperfectly competitive sector faces an upward sloping input supply curve. For simplicity we suppose that labour is the only input in the imperfectly competitive industry, f denoting the labour employed in fixed costs, and c the labour per unit of output. If w_i is the wage rate in country i, then country i marginal and fixed costs take the form

$$c_i = cw_i \quad f_i = fw_i \qquad i = 1, 2. \tag{11}$$

We assume that the perfectly competitive sector produces output y_i, using labour and a sector-specific factor of production k_i which has price r_i. The unit cost function for the perfectly competitive industry is denoted $b(w_i, r_i)$ and the equality of price to unit cost gives equilibrium condition

$$b(w_i, r_i) = 1 \qquad i = 1, 2, \tag{12}$$

where the price of the perfectly competitive sector's output is unity.

Each economy has labour endowment l_i, and we assume that factor endowment ratios in the two economies are the same, i.e., $l_1/k_1 = l_2/k_2$. Factor market clearing is given by

$$l_i = y_i b_w(w_i, r_i) + n_i[(x_{ii} + x_{ij})c + f]$$
$$k_i = y_i b_r(w_i, r_i) \qquad i = 1, 2. \tag{13}$$

Equilibrium is now characterized by equations (4), (5), (8), (11), (12) and (13).

If the cost function b is independent of r then this model is identical to that of the preceding section; there are constant returns to the use of labour in the perfectly competitive sector, and the marginal product of labour and wage rate are constant. If $b_r > 0$ then there are diminishing returns to labour, and the wage rate is lower the greater is employment in

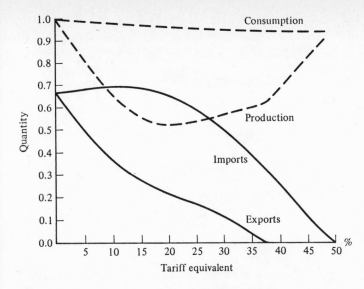

Figure 3.4 Output and trade when wages are flexible

this sector. Since the algebra of this case is fairly complex, we restrict ourselves to a pair of numerical examples. We let b take the form $w_i^\alpha r_i^{1-\alpha}$, where α is the share of labour in the industry and investigate the cases when $\alpha = 0.9$ and $\alpha = 0.5$.

Figure 3.4 shows the consequences of varying trade barriers for the case $\alpha = 0.9$, for the consumption, output, and trade of the manufacturing sector of the smaller country. When a high trade barrier is reduced, the results appear similar to those in Figure 3.3: the small country's output falls. At sufficiently low trade barriers, however, further reduction actually leads to a rise in production. The same U-shaped production locus emerges for other values of α, with the minimum point occurring at higher output levels the lower is α.

The reason for this shape is that once labour supply to the manufacturing sector is less than perfectly elastic, the smaller country will have a lower wage rate (providing intra-industry trade is occurring). Precisely because it is a net importer of manufactured goods, the smaller country will have smaller manufacturing employment relative to its total labour force, and hence a lower marginal product of labour in the constant returns sector. Now when barriers to trade are lowered, there are two opposing effects. On one side, the incentive to produce in the smaller country for its own market, as opposed to concentrating production in the large country, is reduced; this was the only effect in the

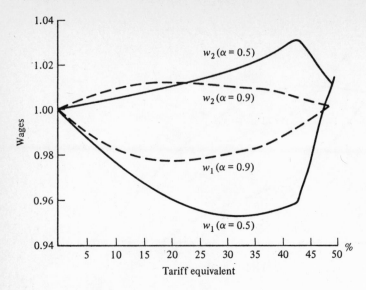

Figure 3.5   Relative wages

zero-wage-differential case considered above. On the other side, however, there is a greater incentive to export from the low-wage to the high-wage country.

In the limit, with no barriers to trade, the latter effect would predominate: it would always be desirable to produce wherever production was cheaper. So not surprisingly, as one approaches that limit, production moves toward the smaller rather than the larger country. Conversely, when the tariff equivalent is large, this effect is small, and the concentration of production in the larger country dominates.

For peripheral countries attempting to get their initial exchange rates right, a key question is the effect of reduced trade barriers on equilibrium wage rates. Given what we have already seen about output, it is not surprising to see the results shown in Figure 3.5. When the tariff equivalent is reduced from a high level, the wage rate (in terms of the competitive good) rises in the large country, falls in the small; so the relative small-country wage falls. At sufficiently low tariff rates, however, relative wage rates move the other way, with the relative wage of the smaller country rising. In the limit, with no barriers to trade, the equilibrium wage rates are equal.

We therefore see that in this extended model it is not true that trade barriers matter more for location, the smaller they are. What emerges instead is that the tendency to concentrate production in the centre, and the resulting wage differential of centre against periphery, is largest when there are moderate barriers to trade – not too high to prevent concentration of production, but not so low as to promote factor price equalization. This example captures perfectly both the positive and the negative positions we described in the introduction. Starting from high trade barriers the smaller economy experiences falling manufacturing production and downward pressure on wages as barriers fall. As the process continues manufacturing production increases and there is a convergence of peripheral wages to those of the centre.

6   Factor abundance and comparative advantage

The previous section developed the simplest possible model to illustrate the way in which factor market interaction countervailed the centripetal forces due to market access. In this section we go one stage further, by embedding our model of imperfect competition in a 2-factor Heckscher–Ohlin trade model. This means that countries may now differ in two respects – market size, and relative factor abundance. We do this in order to address the following question. Suppose that the small economy has a comparative advantage in manufacturing; how does this interact with the market access effects studied in preceding sections? Specifically, suppose that the small economy is relatively labour-abundant, and the manufacturing sector is relatively labour-intensive. What then happens to the small economy's wages and manufacturing output during the process of trade liberalization?

In order to model this the model of the previous section needs only slight modification. We suppose that both industries use labour and sectorally mobile capital. The perfectly competitive sector's cost function is as in the previous section, and the manufacturing sector now has marginal and fixed costs given by

$$c_i = c(w_i, r_i), \quad f_i = f \cdot c(w_i, r_i) \qquad i = 1, 2. \tag{14}$$

In this formulation we assume that both fixed and marginal costs have the same capital–labour ratio. Factor market clearing conditions are

$$l_i = y_i b_w(w_i, r_i) + n_i[(x_{ii} + x_{ij}) + f]c_w(w_i, r_i)$$

$$k_i = y_i b_r(w_i, r_i) + n_i[(x_{ii} + x_{ij}) + f]c_r(w_i, r_i) \tag{15}$$

$$i = 1, 2.$$

Equilibrium is now characterized by equations (4), (5), (8), (12), (14) and (15).

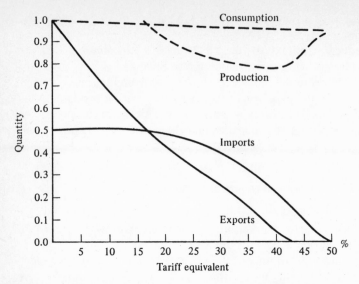

Figure 3.6   Output and trade when manufacturing is labour-intensive

Once again we use numerical techniques to illustrate levels of production, trade and wages associated with different values of t. The example underlying Figure 3.6 is constructed to give the small economy a comparative advantage in manufacturing, and parameters are chosen such that at free trade the small economy produces 50% more manufacturing output than it consumes, so its net exports of manufacturing are one-third of production. (Details of this example are given in the Appendix). The main result apparent from Figure 3.6 is that, even with this comparative advantage in manufacturing, early stages of trade liberalization are associated with a decline in manufacturing output. This means that the direction of net trade is in the opposite direction to that predicted on the basis of factor endowment; at relatively high levels of t the small economy is a net importer of manufactures, this switching round only at lower levels of t. The result that there is some interval of t on which the small country is a net importer seems quite robust. Increasing the difference in relative factor endowments reduces the range of t on which this result holds, but does not eliminate it.

Figure 3.7 gives the wage paths associated with this case, and these are as would be expected. Under autarky the labour-abundant economy has a lower wage, and with free trade there is factor price equalization. However, because of the decline in the small economy's manufacturing output at high levels of t, wage convergence is not monotonic. There is an interval of t on which trade liberalization brings relative wage divergence.

So far we have assumed that factors of production are internationally

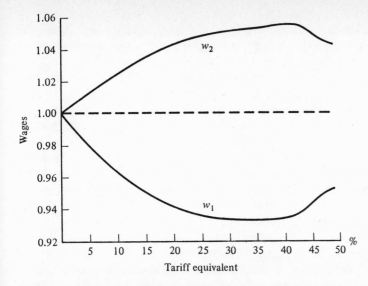

Figure 3.7   Relative wages when manufacturing is labour-intensive

immobile. Several remarks can be made on the consequences of relaxing this assumption. First, consider international capital mobility. Suppose that, in the model of this section, we allow capital to be perfectly mobile. This will equate the rate of return in the two economies, $r_1 = r_2$, and, if there is free trade in the perfectly competitive good, (equation (12)), must also equate wages, $w_1 = w_2$. Essentially one mobile factor and one freely traded good are sufficient to bring about factor price equalization even in the presence of trade barriers on other traded goods. The model of this section then collapses back to that of Section 3, with the manufacturing production path illustrated in Figure 3.3. The general point here is that forces which tend to equalize factor prices across countries will increase the importance of market access considerations in determining the location of manufacturing.

The same remarks apply if labour is internationally mobile. But in this case we must also add that as labour migrates so does demand. Labour mobility therefore reinforces the centripetal tendencies associated with integration both by reducing the magnitude of wage differentials, and by accentuating market size differences between the centre and the periphery.

7   Concluding remarks

The analysis of this paper is suggestive of what may occur to a small country engaged in mutual and equal reductions in barriers to trade with a larger economy. Smallness seems to have the following consequences.

First, it is important to stress that there are large potential gains in welfare. The traditional gains from exploitation of economies of scale are reinforced in a world of imperfect competition. In a position of restricted trade the small country does relatively badly as it is unable to achieve both economies of scale and a high level of competition. This cost of smallness is removed by trade.

On the other hand, it is quite possible that there will be a reduction in the number of firms in the small country, and relocation of the industry towards the larger country. When trade barriers are high large national markets require national firms to serve them. As the barriers come down, there is a tendency for production to relocate to be close to the larger market even if this goes against the direction of trade predicted on the basis of relative factor endowments. The resulting decline in manufacturing production in the peripheral regions may be accompanied by a decline in wages. However, this tendency toward concentration in the centre may be offset by the fact that peripheral regions have lower wages. While the U-shaped curves shown in our Figures are the result of particular numerical examples, they are suggestive of a general tendency for the process of concentration to reverse itself when barriers to trade fall sufficiently.

These results suggest a fundamental ambiguity in the effects of Europe 1992 on the relative competitiveness of manufacturing in the peripheral nations. Lower barriers to trade could make it more attractive to move production out toward the lower-wage periphery, and thereby allow a rise in peripheral wages; or they could make it more attractive to concentrate production in the centre, requiring a fall in peripheral wages at least relative to those in the centre. Anything that impedes the necessary changes in relative wages will reinforce the tendency to concentrate production in the centre.

One might naively suppose that since 1992 is supposed to produce a Europe without borders, it is equivalent to setting $t = 0$ in our simulations. The parameter t, however, is meant to include such 'natural' trade barriers as transport cost, difficulty of communication, and cultural differences as well as governmentally imposed costs. The strong income gradient in the Community shown in Table 3.1 is much larger than could be explained by official barriers alone, suggesting that the natural barriers are substantial. The point is that we do not know which side of the U-shaped curve we are on – whether 1992 will improve or worsen the competitiveness of peripheral industry.

Appendix: numerical simulations

All the numerical simulations have demand parameters:

$$a = 5; \quad \theta = 0.333; \quad s_1 = 2.5; \quad s_2 = 5.0.$$

In Sections 3, 4 and 5 cost parameters are:

$$c_1 = c_2 = 1; \quad f_1 = f_2 = 0.4.$$

In Section 3 the number of firms is set at $n_1 = 13$, $n_2 = 26$. These values of n_1 and n_2 give zero profits in both countries when $t = 0$, i.e., the oligopoly values of n_i (Section 3) are an equilibrium of the monopolistic competition model (Section 4) when $t = 0$. At this equilibrium price is 19% above marginal cost.

In Section 5 $b(w_i, r_i) = w_i^\alpha r_i^{1-\alpha}$. When $\alpha = 0.9$, $k_1 = 6.55$, $l_1 = 91.7$, $k_2 = 13.1$, $l_2 = 183.4$. When $\alpha = 0.5$, $k_1 = 32.7$, $l_1 = 65.5$, $k_2 = 65.5$, $l_2 = 131.0$. When $t = 0$ the equilibrium is $w_i = r_i = 1$, and prices and quantities in the manufacturing sector are exactly as in Sections 3 and 4. These values imply that at $t = 0$ one-third of consumers' expenditure is on manufacturing, the remainder on the perfectly competitive good.

In Section 6 $b(w_i, r_i) = w_i^\alpha r_i^{1-\alpha}$, $c(w_i, r_i) = w_i^\beta r_i^{1-\beta}$ and $f_i = 0.4$. Figures 3.6 and 3.7 were constructed with $\alpha = 0.6$ and $\beta = 0.8$, $k_1 = 36$, $l_1 = 78.6$, $k_2 = 62.2$, $l_2 = 117.9$. When $t = 0$ the equilibrium has the same manufacturing sector prices and quantities as in Sections 3–5.

NOTES

1 For the remainder of the paper we assume that the equilibrium number of firms, $n_1 + n_2$ is large enough to be treated as a continuous variable, so we ignore integer problems.
2 This is not necessarily true for the larger country. It is possible that reductions in t raise p_{22} as the export sales of small country firms (x_{12}) may exceed home market sales (x_{11}).
3 We assume that the economies are large enough, relative to the degree of returns to scale, to support at least one firm each under autarky.

REFERENCES

Brander, J.A. & P. Krugman (1983). 'Intra-industry trade in identical commodities', *Journal of International Economics* **15**, 313–21.
Dixit, A.K. (1984). 'International trade policy for oligopolistic industries', *Economic Journal*, Supplement, **94**, 1–16.
Donsimoni, M. & J. Gabszewicz (1989). 'Le commerce international profite-t-il aux industries oligopolistiques?', in D. Laussel & C. Montet (eds.), *Commerce International en Concurrence Imparfaite*, Paris, Economica.
Krugman, P.R. (1990). 'Macroeconomic adjustment and entry into the EC: a note', this volume.
Venables, A.J. (1986). 'Trade and trade policy with imperfect competition; the case of identical products and free entry', *Journal of International Economics* **19**, 1–19.

Discussion

ANDRE SAPIR

This is a paper with an unusual message for most economists: location matters. The motivation arises from the fear that trade liberalization within Europe might result in a reallocation of manufacturing activity from the peripheral South to the centrally-located North.

The paper presents four models that share a number of common features. There are two countries: a relatively small economy, 'the periphery', and a relatively large one, 'the centre'. Each economy has two sectors: one, which is perfectly competitive, where constant returns to scale prevail and the other, which is imperfectly competitive, characterized by increasing returns to scale – 'manufacturing'.

Krugman and Venables conduct the following experiment with their different models. Starting from an initial situation of high trade barriers, they progressively lower the barriers between the two countries and observe the impact on manufacturing output in the periphery.

In the last two models (Sections 5 and 6), which combine features of the first two, trade liberalization has an interesting U-shaped impact on the size of the manufacturing sector in the South. Initially, the lowering of trade barriers leads to the progressive dismantling of the manufacturing sector in the periphery. Production moves to the large country whose size, combined with trade barriers, confers cost advantages in the production of the increasing-returns-to-scale good. Later on, however, as trade barriers become negligible, size becomes less important and manufacturing production moves back to the periphery which enjoys lower wages.

There are two ways of interpreting the paper from the viewpoint of the periphery. Optimists will argue that initial barriers are only modest. Their removal will, therefore, take place entirely in the left part of the U-curve, implying that manufacturing output in the periphery will continuously rise. Pessimists, on the other hand, will insist that initial barriers are high, so that trade liberalization will result, for a while, in the reallocation of manufacturing output from the periphery to the centre.

Is there any reason to side with the pessimists? Is there a danger that the manufacturing sector in the periphery will shrink? I think not. In the models of Krugman and Venables, the centre and the periphery are defined in terms of location. To my mind, infrastructure and human capital are more important factors in determining whether a country will expand or shrink its manufacturing sector. In other words, being peripheral is *not* irreversible. Although Korea was and remains badly located, it has shifted from the periphery to the centre by accumulating human and physical capital. Similarly, neither Greece nor Portugal will remain in the periphery if they succeed, like Spain, in building a sufficient infrastructure.

4 The market for cars in the enlarged European Community

ALASDAIR SMITH

1 Introduction

The objective of this paper is to provide some estimates of how the European car market may be affected by the integration and enlargement of the European Community and by possible changes in taxation and external trade policy associated with the 1992 programme. The motivation for looking at the car market is that it is of considerable quantitative significance to the European economy, and is likely to be strongly affected by the changes analysed here. Further it is an industry with a significant presence both in the 'South' and the 'North' in the Community.

One particularly interesting question which might be asked in the context of the project to which this paper contributes is whether competition between the North and the South in the car market is likely to result in a notable 'victory' for one side or the other. Unfortunately the model presented in this paper cannot provide an answer to this question. The most significant part of the 'Southern' motor car industry is the Spanish industry, which however consists entirely of the Spanish operations of multinational producers. Predictions of the future of that industry requires predictions both of the future of the multinational producers involved, which the model will provide, and of the future location of multinationals' production, on which the model is silent.

Trade policy in the European car market is studied here in a formal model incorporating economies of scale and imperfect competition. The model is calibrated to data relating to 1988, and also uses empirical estimates of some key parameters. This work derives from earlier partial equilibrium modelling of trade policy in imperfectly competitive industries (Venables and Smith, 1986; Smith and Venables, 1988). However, the present paper differs from these in the detail of the empirical information which it is possible to incorporate in the model. The earlier work

78

was applied to industries for which the available data was rather aggregated, in which there were difficulties in reconciling trade data and industrial production data, on which much of the information about scale economies and industrial structure was somewhat sketchy, and in which trade and industrial policy was modelled in fairly general terms. By contrast, in the car market, there are very detailed (and presumably reliable) data on sales (and some on prices) at quite disaggregated levels, the market shares of individual firms are known, some detailed estimates of economies of scale are available, and it is also possible to give fairly precise descriptions of the tools of trade policy.

The modelling of the industry as imperfectly competitive allows us to focus on the possible anti-competitive effects of voluntary export restrictions (VERs); and the detailed country and producer structure of the model permits the running of a wide range of policy simulations (tax harmonization, the reduction of non-tariff barriers, the abolition of VERs, the replacement of national VERs with an EC-wide VER) relevant to the European Community's 1992 programme. The implications of the model for the ranking of policy instruments in imperfectly competitive industries is discussed in a related paper (Smith and Venables, 1989) and more general issues concerning the model, such as its sensitivity to changes in the level of aggregation and in the values of key parameters, are addressed in Smith (1989). The present paper focusses on the results of the policy simulations.

2   The model

The formal model is presented and discussed in Smith and Venables (1989) and Smith (1989) and outlined in the Appendix to this paper. It follows Smith and Venables (1988) in treating the industry under study as an imperfectly competitive industry producing differentiated products.

Firms, which each produce several different 'models' of car, see the demand for their products as depending on the price of the individual model, and also on the overall price of cars. Firms maximize profits, taking account of the impact of scale economies on marginal costs, of the effect of taxes, tariffs and transport costs on the wedge between producer and consumer prices, and of the elasticity of demand in different markets on their marginal revenues. I make the Cournot assumption that in equilibrium firms maximize profits, taking their rivals' outputs as given (modified in the presence of sales restrictions in a way described below). National markets are assumed to be segmented, so that firms can set different prices in different markets. A producer with a large market share in a particular national market sees its own behaviour as having a strong influence on the overall price of cars in that market and thus perceives a relatively inelastic demand for its product; and this leads such firms to have higher price–cost margins.

The model also has to take account of sales restrictions, of which I consider two types; both of them taking the form of a 'voluntary' export restraint (VER) which limits the *share* that a Japanese firm may have in a market. In the first, I suppose that each Japanese firm is restricted to fixed shares of each of a subset of European national markets. However, I alternatively want to allow there to be a restriction on the firm's overall market share in the EC market as a whole. When a Japanese firm is subject to either type of sales restriction, it is assumed to maximize profits subject to the restriction, and this modifies the relation between its marginal cost and marginal revenues, in a way spelled out in the Appendix.

Firms in markets in which the Japanese are not subject to sales restrictions, and the Japanese firms themselves in markets where they are not restricted, are assumed to behave as Cournot competitors. This assumption would, however, be an unreasonable assumption to make of unrestricted firms in markets where Japanese firms are subject to restrictions on their market shares. In this case, an unrestricted firm is assumed to take account of the effect that a change in its sales will have on the sales of Japanese firms. To give a concrete example, in the UK market, Japanese firms are restricted to an 11% market share. A non-Japanese firm planning to sell 1,000 more cars in the UK market should therefore take into account not only the impact on prices of these sales, but also the fact that Japanese firms would thereby be enabled to sell 124 more cars as a result (as $124/1124 = 0.11$). The implication is that firms will behave less competitively in the presence of a VER than they would in the presence of, say, a tariff 'equivalent' to the VER. In the Appendix, this argument is formalized, and it is shown that the non-Japanese firms behave as if their market shares were larger than they actually are, and therefore have higher price–cost margins than they would in the absence of the VER.

3   Data and model calibration

The model is calibrated to data for the world car market in 1988. The world is divided into eight markets: France, West Germany, Italy, the United Kingdom, Iberia (Spain and Portugal), the rest of the European Community (RoEC) (an aggregation of Benelux, Ireland, Greece and Denmark), EFTA, and the rest of the world (RoW). This level of country disaggregation is needed in order to model the differences in trade policy in 1988 between different members of the European Community; and to deal with the fact that the Iberian countries are still in the process of harmonizing their trade policy with the common external tariff of the Community.

The producers are divided into eight groups: French (two producers, Peugeot and Renault), Volkswagen (VAG), Fiat, Rover, the US multinationals in Europe (Ford and GM in Europe), the 'specialist' producers (Mercedes, BMW, Volvo, Saab, Jaguar and Porsche), the Japanese, and the rest of the world (who are mainly the North American producers). Ford and GM in Europe are treated as independent of their American parents. This level of producer disaggregation is necessary in order to capture in the model the strong differences in national sales patterns. Within each group, firms are assumed to be identical. In the case of the French and the Americans in Europe, this is very close to reality: in each pair the firms are of roughly equal size and have similar sales patterns. The specialists and the Japanese are more heterogenous; and calculation of Herfindahl indices suggests it is appropriate to assume the existence of three equal-sized specialist manufacturers and five equal-sized Japanese firms.

It is also worth noting for future reference that the American firms in Europe, which have production facilities in several European countries, are not the only multinational producers: both French firms have production in Spain (and one of them in the UK also), and the Volkswagen group includes SEAT of Spain. Thus when we come to look at the national distribution of the welfare effects of policy changes, we have to be cautious about attributing to particular countries changes in the profits of these firms.

Table 4.1 summarizes the shape of the European car market in 1988. The top panel of the table shows sales in the eight markets, and the distribution of those sales by producer group, based on registration data in the Automotive Industry Data 1989 Car Yearbook. Both the rest of the world market and the sales by 'other' producers in Europe are included only to close the model and no attention has been given to accurate modelling of the non-European markets, so in reporting the effects of policy changes both the effects on 'other' producers and in the rest of the world market are ignored.

The shares of Japanese producers in the different markets display the effects of trade restrictions. In the base year of 1988 VERs were in operation on imports from Japan to France, Italy, the UK, and Spain. The French negotiated an agreement with the Japanese in 1977 limiting the imports of Japanese cars to a 3% volume share of the French market. Since 1977, Japanese car imports have been restricted to an 11% volume share of the UK market. (The 11.4% Japanese share of the UK market

	France	Germany	Italy	UK	RoEC	Iberia	EFTA	RoW
Market sales total (million cars)								
	2.2	2.8	2.2	2.2	1.1	1.3	1.2	17.2
Market shares (percent)								
French	63.2	6.7	14.8	12.6	18.3	38.0	9.3	2.6
VAG	8.6	29.4	11.7	5.9	13.0	17.5	14.2	1.6
Fiat Group	7.2	4.7	59.9	3.7	5.3	9.7	5.2	0.0
Rover	1.9	0.3	1.1	15.0	1.2	1.9	0.2	0.2
Ford/GM	11.3	25.4	6.9	40.1	22.5	26.9	19.2	0.6
Specialists	3.6	17.7	3.4	7.9	8.4	3.3	17.5	2.6
Japanese	3.0	15.2	0.9	11.4	26.6	2.1	31.9	39.0
Others	1.3	0.8	1.2	3.4	4.6	0.6	2.5	53.4
	100.0	100.0	100.0	100.0	100.0	100.0	100.0	100.0
Estimated sales value (billion ecu)								EC total
	26.2	28.9	25.2	25.3	17.1	16.1		138.9
Sales tax rates (percent)								
	28	14	20	25	55	39	20	20

	Sales (million)	Model numbers	Firm numbers	Sales/model (000)
French	3.443	7	2	246
VAG	2.205	7	1	315
Fiat Group	1.929	6	1	322
Rover	0.475	6	1	79
Ford/GM	2.935	5	2	293
Specialists	1.622	3	3	180
Japanese	8.190	6	5	273
Others	9.422	12	2	393

Table 4.1. The European car market in 1988

shown in Table 4.1 includes a small number of UK-produced Nissan cars, but in the model all Japanese cars are treated as being imports.) Italy has a long-standing agreement with Japan restricting the number of Japanese cars sold in Italy to 2,300 units per year – virtually a complete inhibition – though a further 14,000 units are imported indirectly each year through other European countries. Spain and Portugal also have virtual prohibitions of Japanese imports. Both the Italian and Iberian restrictions are modelled, like the French and UK restrictions, as limiting Japanese market shares. This is not strictly accurate, but the levels to which Japanese imports are restricted in these markets are so low that the distinction between levels and shares is of little significance. In the

German market there is no explicit restraint on Japanese sales, though there is some evidence of pressure being applied for sales growth in Germany to be moderated. (There is some degree of 'monitoring' by the European Commission of Japanese sales in the Community as a whole; and given the existence of restrictions in all the other large markets, this may have the effect of limiting the growth of Japanese sales in Germany.) The Japanese share of the West German market is, however, not inconsistent with the absence of a VER in that market, given the strength of the German producers and the presence of the US multinationals, and I have therefore assumed that the German market has no VER.

It is assumed that cars imported across national borders in Europe incur a transport cost of 10% (or 5% in the case of sales in the Southern EC by multinationals which have Spanish production); while Japanese cars imported into Europe are assumed to face transport costs of 20%. Multinationals are assumed not to incur transport costs in selling in markets where they have production facilities (except that the presence of Jaguar in the UK is assumed to reduce the transport costs of specialist producers only to 5%.) These costs should not be interpreted literally as transport costs but are intended to account partially for the extraordinary asymmetry of sales patterns shown in Table 4.1. While some of this asymmetry may be the result of genuine demand differences, it seems reasonable to account for some of it by differences in producers' distribution networks and other non-tariff barriers to imports, and it is such effects that the transport cost term attempts to capture.

Cars produced in the EC and EFTA have tariff-free access to all EC and EFTA markets; but Japanese cars face a common external tariff (CET) of 10.3% in the EC. (In 1988 the level of production of Nissan cars in the UK was sufficiently small to be ignored for this purpose also.) In the absence of a satisfactory description of Portuguese trade policy, I have assumed that the Spanish 1988 tariff levels of 35% on Japanese cars and 23% on EC cars apply to the whole Iberian market. Producers in Spain are assumed to have tariff-free access to the Iberian market, ignoring the possible costs that they may have incurred in investment in Spain in order to obtain market access, and the fact that they do not in fact have tariff-free access to Portugal. The inclusion of Greece in the rest of the EC implies an assumption that Greek trade policy was fully aligned with the Community by 1988.

The second panel of Table 4.1 reports the estimated value of car sales in each of the EC markets and in the EC market as a whole. These estimates are based on the prices calibrated in the model, as described below. They are useful in translating into proportions of consumption the welfare changes reported in later tables. Based on information from Motor

Industry Research Unit (1988) on VAT rates and other special sales taxes on cars, the sales tax rates shown in Table 4.1 are incorporated in the calibration.

In earlier work (Venables and Smith, 1986, Smith and Venables, 1988), variation in number of models per firm was used as a device to account for the difference in the scale of different firms. In the case of the car industry, however, it is possible to give the device a concrete interpretation. The Ludvigsen study for the European Commission (Ludvigsen Associates Limited, 1988) centred its description of scale economies on the concept of a 'platform', essentially a floorplan on which a family of cars can be based. The Ludvigsen information on the numbers of platforms per producer is used to give the model numbers shown in Table 4.1 (where, however, the model numbers for Japanese and 'other' producers are simply assumed).

Ludvigsen provides a great deal of information about the relation between variable costs and scale of output per platform; and rather sketchier information about fixed costs. On the basis of that information, I chose a cost function to satisfy the properties: (i) average variable cost declines by 5% for every doubling of output per platform; (ii) fixed costs are 20% of total costs for a firm producing 5 platforms, and 200,000 cars of each platform; (ii) a proportion of fixed costs is independent of the number of platforms, while the rest of fixed costs rise linearly with the number of platforms, and for a producer of 5 platforms, the proportion of fixed costs independent of the number of platforms is half. The Appendix provides details of the function which satisfies this property and which is used in the model.

Ludvigsen also provides some information on the prices of cars of different types in different markets. I chose the German market prices as a base, on the grounds that this is the market least distorted by taxes and protection of the markets on which Ludvigsen provides data. Assuming that the distribution of cars of different types (utility, small, lower medium, etc.) in each firm's output is the same as in the firm's German sales gives a price for each producer group's 'typical' car in Germany.

On the demand side, there have been many econometric estimates of the aggregate industry elasticity of demand, for different countries in different time periods. OECD (1983) reports a range from 1 to 3. Hess (1977) surveys many previous studies and re-estimates demand equations to obtain a value of 1.63. More or less arbitrarily, I use the value 1.5. For the elasticity of demand for an individual model of car, estimates in Cowling and Cubbin (1971) (see also Maxcy and Silberston, 1959) suggest a value of around 7; and it is a value in this area which is consistent with the calibration of our data to a long-run equilibrium in which the average of profits across firms is zero. However, the work of Bresnahan (1981) suggests a value of 2.3. Feenstra and Levinsohn (1989), obtain a much smaller elasticity of 0.467 from estimated demand functions, but a very much larger value from the pricing equation in their model. Levinsohn (1988) and Feenstra and Levinsohn (1989) argue that it is not very sensible to apply a single elasticity value at a rather aggregate level. It would be desirable to disaggregate the present model, which at present treats the car market as a single market, and to treat separately five or six sub-markets. In the absence of such disaggregation, I have chosen to use the value of 4 for the elasticity of demand for individual car models.

The calibration of the model then consists of the choice of firm-specific cost levels to reproduce the German prices, and, in the absence of VERs, choice of parameters to scale the demand functions to observed sales; that is to say, to explain the pattern of sales displayed in Table 4.1. However, this procedure cannot be adopted where sales by Japanese firms are affected by a VER. In such cases, we would simply 'observe' a very low demand for Japanese cars. In markets where VERs are in operation we have no observations on Japanese market shares in the absence of constraints, and are therefore unable to use these to infer the demand parameters. These parameters are therefore obtained by assuming first that consumers in France and Italy have the same preference for Japanese cars relative to German cars as do consumers in 'rest of the Northern EC'. This particular assumption was chosen as being the comparison least contaminated by the relatively large market shares of domestically produced cars in all markets. However, it produces unrealistic numbers for the UK and Iberia; for the UK it was the ratio of French to Japanese sales in the 'rest of the EC' and for Iberia the ratio of Ford/GM to Japanese sales in the 'rest of the EC' that were used as the benchmarks.

4 Simulation of policy changes

Tables 4.2–4.9 look at a range of policy changes; from which some lessons may be learned both about the model and about the effects of policy changes in the European car market. The numbers presented should be interpreted as plausible illustrative calculations rather than detailed predictions. The evidence presented in the present paper would not justify the latter interpretation, as there is no discussion of the robustness of the results to changes in the parameters or the structure of the model. Only a limited amount of sensitivity analysis has been undertaken. The results are not reported here. They suggest that the model is fairly insensitive to changes in the assumed value of the industry-level demand elasticity. There is a higher degree of sensitivity to changes in the elasticity of demand for individual cars, but the qualitative conclusions of the analysis remain unchanged. It should also be noted that one disadvantage of the level of aggregation of the model is that it does not allow for the possibility of quality upgrading by the constrained producers in response to VERs. Jones (1987) suggests that there is little evidence of upgrading in the UK market, though Messerlin and Becuwe (1987) argue that upgrading has occurred in France.

The structure of each of the tables is the same. The top panel reports the predicted sales changes by each producer (row) in each market (column), and on the right the total sales change of each producer. The second panel reports the associated price changes. The Japanese shares of each of the EC markets and of the EC market as a whole before and after the change are reported in the third panel. Finally the fourth panel reports (in million ecu) the impact of the policy change on producers' profits, consumer welfare and government revenue. As I have already noted, the multi-nationality of much of the European industry means that it is impossible to attribute profit changes to individual countries. It would also be inappropriate to attribute changes in common external tariff revenue to individual countries, as it goes to the Community budget. Therefore, a welfare total is calculated only for the EC as a whole. The EC total includes half of the profit changes of Ford and GM, on the assumption that part of their economic profits will be reflected in workers' and managers' incomes. It is questionable whether changes in tax revenue should be counted as a welfare gain: insofar as taxes on cars are the same rate as on other goods or reflect the social costs of pollution and congestion, tax revenue changes should not be counted as welfare gains. Therefore, the EC welfare total is reported both with and without tax revenue included. In contemplating the EC total welfare change reported in their tables, one can use as a standard of comparison the 135.22 billion ecu shown in Table 4.1 as the estimated value at consumer prices of sales of cars in the EC market.

Table 4.2 presents the effects of removing the tariffs in Iberia on European cars (which effectively, though not quite appropriately, means removing the tariffs on European producers without Spanish manufacturing facilities) and reducing the Iberian tariff on Japanese cars to the level of the CET (although this latter change is irrelevant in the presence of the quantitative restriction). The most noteworthy feature of the results shown in this Table is the size of the aggregate welfare effect in the Iberian market: the gain to consumers of almost 900 million ecu is a large fraction of the base value of consumption of 16 billion ecu in that market.

Table 4.3 shows the effects of halving the levels of the assumed non-tariff barriers between EC markets, as a crude representation of the 1992

	France	Germany	Italy	UK	RoEC	Iberia	EFTA	Total (incl RoW)
Quantity changes (percent)								
French	−0.2	−0.5	−0.7	−0.5	−0.4	−8.1	−0.5	−1.5
VAG	−0.3	−0.3	−0.6	−0.4	−0.3	−8.8	−0.4	−1.2
Fiat	1.6	1.6	0.7	1.5	1.7	80.8	1.6	6.0
Rover	1.8	1.8	1.4	1.3	1.8	97.9	1.8	6.3
Ford/GM	−0.4	−0.4	−0.8	−0.4	−0.4	−9.5	−0.5	−1.5
Specialist	1.0	0.8	0.6	0.8	0.9	96.9	0.8	3.4
Japanese	−0.0	−0.1	0.2	0.1	−0.0	6.4	−0.1	0.0
Consumer price changes (percent)								
French	0.1	0.1	0.1	0.1	0.1	−1.3	0.1	
VAG	0.1	0.1	0.1	0.1	0.1	−1.1	0.1	
Fiat	−0.4	−0.4	−0.3	−0.4	−0.4	−16.6	−0.4	
Rover	−0.4	−0.5	−0.5	−0.4	−0.5	−18.5	−0.5	
Ford/GM	0.1	0.1	0.1	0.1	0.1	−0.9	0.1	
Specialist	−0.2	−0.2	−0.2	−0.2	−0.2	−18.4	−0.2	
Japanese	0.0	0.0	−0.2	−0.1	0.0	−4.8	0.0	

Market shares of Japanese (percent)								EC total
initial	3.0	15.2	0.9	11.4	26.6	2.1		9.3
final	3.0	15.2	0.9	11.4	26.6	2.1		9.2

Welfare change in m ecu per year

	Profits		Con surp	Tax rev	CET rev
French	−164.5	France	−6.1	−0.7	0.1
VAG	−70.2	Germany	8.1	0.5	−0.2
Fiat	249.7	Italy	40.9	3.4	−0.1
Rover	46.5	UK	14.0	1.4	−0.1
Ford/GM	−111.6	RoEC	0.6	0.1	0.0
Specialist	121.4	Iberia	891.4	125.0	−86.6
Japanese	66.2	EFTA	5.1	0.4	0.0

EC	Profits	Con surp	Tax rev	CET rev	Total	(less tax)
	127.1	948.9	129.7	−86.9	1,118.8	989.1

Table 4.2. Iberian integration

reduction in border costs. The changes shown in Table 4.3 are calculated from a base that includes the effects shown in Table 4.2. The effects are in line with the kind of effects generated in Smith and Venables (1988): significant increases in intra-EC trade, a modest reduction in imports, and an overall gain to the EC of some 2.5% of base consumption.

Table 4.4 presents the results of another '1992'-related policy change:

	France	Germany	Italy	UK	RoEC	Iberia	EFTA	Total (incl RoW)
	Quantity changes (percent)							
French	−1.2	18.6	12.4	14.8	11.7	3.2	0.8	4.2
VAG	13.9	0.1	12.2	15.2	11.6	3.3	0.9	4.9
Fiat	14.2	18.5	0.4	15.8	12.4	10.8	1.0	4.9
Rover	14.1	18.7	12.5	−2.4	11.8	11.2	0.0	1.9
Ford/GM	13.6	−0.9	12.4	−1.9	11.0	2.6	0.3	2.3
Specialist	14.6	−0.7	12.9	6.0	12.0	11.7	0.5	3.3
Japanese	3.8	−1.8	4.9	2.9	−6.6	5.1	−0.4	−0.3
	Consumer price changes (percent)							
French	−1.1	−4.6	−4.6	−4.5	−4.6	−2.8	−0.3	
VAG	−4.6	−0.5	−4.6	−4.6	−4.6	−2.8	−0.3	
Fiat	−4.6	−4.6	−1.9	−4.7	−4.8	−4.5	−0.3	
Rover	−4.6	−4.7	−4.6	−0.5	−4.6	−4.6	−0.1	
Ford/GM	−4.5	−0.3	−4.6	−0.7	−4.5	−2.7	−0.2	
Specialist	−4.7	−0.3	−4.7	−2.6	−4.7	−4.7	−0.2	
Japanese	−2.3	−0.0	−3.0	−1.8	−0.3	−3.2	0.0	

								EC total
Market shares of Japanese (percent)								
initial	3.0	15.2	0.9	11.4	26.6	2.1		9.2
final	3.0	14.6	0.9	11.4	23.5	2.1		8.8

Welfare change in m ecu per year

	Profits		Con surp	Tax rev	CET rev
French	118.0	France	593.1	64.9	−0.5
VAG	169.5	Germany	225.3	13.8	−6.9
Fiat	−47.6	Italy	738.2	61.5	−1.3
Rover	−1.8	UK	463.4	46.4	−0.9
Ford/GM	59.5	RoEC	540.4	95.9	−21.5
Specialist	114.8	Iberia	552.0	77.5	−0.4
Japanese	−100.0	EFTA	21.3	1.8	0.0

EC	Profits	Con surp	Tax rev	CET rev	Total	(less tax)
	382.6	3,112.4	360.0	−31.5	3,823.6	3,643.6

Table 4.3. NTB reduction (Iberian integration base)

replacing the different national sales tax levels in EC markets with a single rate of 26.5%, chosen to be virtually revenue-neutral for the EC as a whole. The distribution of the effects is as one would expect, and the overall effect on EC welfare is positive. A more satisfactory treatment of fiscal harmonization demands a model disaggregated in two directions from the present model. At present, both the Iberian and the 'rest of the EC' market aggregates include countries with quite different sales tax

	France	Germany	Italy	UK	RoEC	Iberia	EFTA	Total (incl RoW)
Quantity changes (percent)								
French	2.4	− 13.4	− 6.5	− 0.8	37.0	16.2	1.2	4.1
VAG	0.8	− 14.9	− 8.1	− 2.6	34.6	14.3	− 0.7	− 2.8
Fiat	0.6	− 15.2	− 8.0	− 2.8	34.2	14.2	− 0.9	− 3.4
Rover	1.9	− 14.1	− 7.1	− 1.6	36.1	15.5	0.4	1.2
Ford/GM	1.8	− 14.1	− 7.2	− 1.6	35.9	15.4	0.3	1.1
Specialist	0.8	− 14.9	− 8.0	− 2.5	34.7	14.4	− 0.5	− 2.2
Japanese	1.9	− 14.2	− 7.7	− 1.7	35.8	15.2	0.2	0.6
Consumer price changes (percent)								
French	− 1.4	10.7	5.1	0.9	− 18.6	− 9.2	− 0.3	
VAG	− 1.0	11.1	5.6	1.4	− 18.2	− 8.8	0.2	
Fiat	− 1.0	11.2	5.6	1.4	− 18.2	− 8.8	0.2	
Rover	− 1.3	10.9	5.3	1.1	− 18.5	− 9.1	− 0.1	
Ford/GM	− 1.3	10.9	5.3	1.1	− 18.4	− 9.1	− 0.1	
Specialist	− 1.0	11.1	5.6	1.4	− 18.3	− 8.9	0.2	
Japanese	− 1.3	10.9	5.5	1.2	− 18.4	− 9.0	− 0.0	

Market shares of Japanese (percent)							EC total
initial	3.0	14.6	0.9	11.4	23.5	2.1	8.8
final	3.0	14.7	0.9	11.4	23.5	2.1	9.0

Welfare change in m ecu per year

	Profits		Con surp	Tax rev	CET rev
French	327.9	France	346.0	− 209.3	2.0
VAG	− 187.6	Germany	− 2,995.2	2,206.9	− 52.3
Fiat	− 414.5	Italy	− 1,351.1	954.4	− 4.8
Rover	5.8	UK	− 293.0	211.9	− 5.5
Ford/GM	54.1	RoEC	3,709.5	− 2,129.0	103.3
Specialist	− 99.2	Iberia	1,633.3	− 1,028.1	8.7
Japanese	104.1	EFTA	− 2.3	− 0.2	0.0

	EC	Profits	Con surp	Tax rev	CET rev	Total	(less tax)
		− 340.6	1,089.5	6.8	51.4	807.1	800.3

Table 4.4. Tax harmonization (on rate of 26.5%)

rates, and a full accounting of the effects of fiscal harmonization would treat each national market separately. Secondly, just as the aggregation level of the model precludes quality upgrading effects of VERs, it also precludes analysis of the effects on firms' product mix of fiscal distortions. Both considerations suggest that the present treatment of fiscal harmonization understates the likely benefits.

The rest of the tables show the effects of changes in trade policy which

	France	Germany	Italy	UK	RoEC	Iberia	EFTA	Total (incl RoW)
Quantity changes (percent)								
French	−4.4	−1.7	−21.0	−5.4	−1.8	−12.2	−2.1	−6.6
VAG	−11.6	−1.1	−19.3	−5.6	−1.6	−13.1	−1.7	−6.0
Fiat	−11.4	−0.6	−0.4	−5.9	−0.9	−11.6	−1.0	−2.9
Rover	−14.1	−1.6	−23.8	−1.9	−1.8	−17.5	−1.7	−5.8
Ford/GM	−12.2	−0.9	−22.3	0.6	−1.2	−13.8	−1.3	−4.3
Specialist	−14.0	−1.1	−23.3	−6.9	−1.5	−17.5	−1.4	−4.8
Japanese	378.6	4.3	1,816.6	47.3	3.9	758.0	3.7	15.2
Consumer price changes (percent)								
French	−2.4	0.5	−0.6	−0.4	0.4	−1.6	0.5	
VAG	−0.5	0.3	−1.1	−0.4	0.4	−1.3	0.4	
Fiat	−0.5	0.2	−6.2	−0.3	0.2	−1.8	0.2	
Rover	0.2	0.4	0.3	−1.4	0.4	−0.0	0.4	
Ford/GM	−0.3	0.3	−0.2	−2.0	0.3	−1.1	0.3	
Specialist	0.2	0.3	0.1	−0.1	0.3	−0.0	0.3	
Japanese	−34.8	−1.0	−55.2	−10.9	−1.0	−44.3	−1.0	

Market shares of Japanese (percent)							EC total
initial	3.0	14.6	0.9	11.4	23.5	2.1	8.8
final	13.7	15.3	16.2	16.3	24.5	17.6	16.5

Welfare change in m ecu per year

	Profits		Con surp	Tax rev	CET rev
French	−940.3	France	1,543.4	168.8	177.6
VAG	−305.6	Germany	−27.2	−1.6	11.3
Fiat	−966.0	Italy	2,736.4	228.0	283.1
Rover	−90.7	UK	756.9	75.7	69.7
Ford/GM	−416.7	RoEC	7.1	1.2	6.7
Specialist	−190.8	Iberia	1,332.5	186.9	164.9
Japanese	1,050.0	EFTA	10.7	0.9	0.0

EC	Profits	Con surp	Tax rev	CET rev	Total	(less tax)
	−2,701.8	6,349.1	659.0	713.3	5,019.6	4,360.6

Table 4.5. Removal of national VERs (Iberian integration and EC NTB reductions in base)

might be associated with the '1992' programme. National trade restrictions are incompatible with the single European market. The key question is whether the national restrictions on imports from Japan will simply be removed or will be replaced by a Community-wide restriction. There is a third possibility: that some means will be found to maintain national

	France	Germany	Italy	UK	RoEC	Iberia	EFTA	Total (incl RoW)
Quantity changes (percent)								
French	−14.1	−21.2	−36.3	−20.4	−22.9	−26.1	−18.8	−20.9
VAG	−25.8	−13.6	−34.4	−21.0	−21.7	−27.7	−16.2	−21.1
Fiat	−25.8	−20.1	−5.4	−21.6	−23.9	−25.7	−17.9	−12.3
Rover	−71.0	−68.6	−75.6	−61.2	−69.8	−72.4	−67.7	−64.9
Ford/GM	−16.9	−8.3	−29.6	−3.2	−12.1	−20.1	−6.5	−10.5
Specialist	−19.6	−9.8	−31.2	−12.4	−14.8	−24.9	−7.4	−13.3
Japanese	798.4	88.4	3,346.6	174.7	75.6	1,445.8	27.6	53.1
Consumer price changes (percent)								
French	−4.6	0.2	−1.1	−0.9	−0.7	−2.9	0.1	
VAG	−1.0	−2.1	−1.9	−0.7	−1.0	−2.4	−0.7	
Fiat	−1.7	−0.9	−11.1	−1.2	−1.0	−3.7	−0.8	
Rover	−1.2	−0.5	−0.8	−6.4	−0.8	−1.8	−0.4	
Ford/GM	0.0	0.2	0.2	−1.9	−0.1	−1.0	0.5	
Specialist	0.8	0.6	0.8	0.5	0.7	0.5	0.7	
Japanese	−40.7	−10.1	−59.3	−18.8	−9.7	−49.3	−0.1	

Market shares of Japanese (percent)	France	Germany	Italy	UK	RoEC	Iberia	EC total
initial	3.0	14.6	0.9	11.4	23.5	2.1	8.8
final	25.2	27.0	27.8	30.0	39.9	31.2	29.1

Welfare change in m ecu per year

	Profits		Con surp	Tax rev	CET rev
French	−1,956.0	France	1,996.0	218.3	205.1
VAG	−1,005.9	Germany	915.3	56.2	32.6
Fiat	−1,877.3	Italy	3,638.2	303.2	301.5
Rover	−111.6	UK	1,147.7	114.7	99.0
Ford/GM	−830.3	RoEC	927.3	164.5	0.7
Specialist	−549.8	Iberia	1,840.4	258.1	178.0
Japanese	5,538.8	EFTA	252.5	21.0	0.0

EC	Profits	Con surp	Tax rev	CET rev	Total	(less tax)
	−5,915.8	10,464.9	1,115.0	816.9	6,481.0	5,366.0

Table 4.6. Removal of national VERs and Japanese expansion into EC

restrictions, but this would imply a considerable retreat from the principles of 1992.

In all of the subsequent tables, the effects shown in Tables 4.2 and 4.3, but not those in Table 4.4, are built in to the base of the calculation. Table 4.5 looks at the effects of one version of 1992 policy: simple removal of the national import restrictions. Japanese sales in the free markets rise substantially. Increases in Japanese sales are associated with reductions in

Japanese prices, and smaller reductions in the prices of non-Japanese cars. The details of the price reductions display the anti-competitive effect of the VER discussed in Section 2: in the freed markets it is the market leaders which cut their prices most in response to Japanese competition. The effects, as one should expect, are generally good for consumers in freed markets and bad for European producers. The overall welfare benefit is of the order of 3% of base consumption. Any surprise at the fact that this simulation shows the Japanese share of the EC market rising only to 16.5% from the base of 8.8% should be tempered by the observation that this is a short-run change, in which the number of models per firm is held constant.

Table 4.6 modifies the policy change shown in Table 4.5 by adding an exogenous assumption that the model range of each Japanese producer expands by 2, the model ranges of the French producers, VAG and Fiat contract by 1, and the Rover model range contracts to 2. In addition the CET on Japaneses cars is reduced to 6% to allow for the possibility that many of these cars would be supplied by European plants, and the non-tariff barrier faced by the Japanese is reduced to 60% of its former level, to reflect the assumption that the Japanese distribution network would become more extensive. Now there is a more substantial expansion of Japanese market share in response to the removal of the VERs; and the welfare effects are generally larger than in the short-run case shown in Table 4.5, in spite of the potentially adverse effect on consumer welfare of a loss of some product varieties. The effects on profits in this simulation are very large, and would surely result either in the exit of some producers from the market or in mergers and collaborations. The present model is not very suitable for dealing with such changes in the market structure, and in the remaining simulations I revert to studying only the short-run effect of policy changes on a market with fixed numbers of firms producing fixed product ranges.

Table 4.7 shows the effects in the model of simulation of the principal alternative trade policy on the EC's 1992 agenda: relacement of the national VERs with a European VER holding the Japanese producers to their existing market share. (So that the Table shows the effects only of the VER shift, it is assumed that the European VER holds the Japanese to the share that they hold after the two experiments shown in Tables 4.2 and 4.3). In France, Italy and Iberia the effects on sales follow the same pattern as in Table 4.5, though with all effects reduced; but there is a significant difference in the effects on prices, with only the market leaders now cutting their prices in response to Japanese entry and other firms actually raising prices. In the UK, the model finds that the EC-wide VER would be more restrictive than the existing national VER, and Japanese

	France	Germany	Italy	UK	RoEC	Iberia	EFTA	Total (incl RoW)
Quantity changes (percent)								
French	−2.0	4.5	−13.5	0.2	6.5	−7.2	−0.7	−2.5
VAG	−7.7	0.6	−13.3	−1.0	4.8	−8.7	−0.7	−2.8
Fiat	−9.5	1.6	−1.9	−3.4	4.9	−9.4	−0.9	−3.0
Rover	−4.8	9.3	−12.1	6.0	13.1	−7.4	0.9	2.6
Ford/GM	−6.3	4.3	−13.8	4.9	7.1	−7.7	0.3	1.0
Specialist	−4.6	7.8	−11.7	2.8	12.2	−7.4	0.6	2.3
Japanese	139.0	−47.8	895.8	−26.0	−45.2	338.8	−0.0	−0.2
Consumer price changes (percent)								
French	−0.7	1.3	0.4	0.5	1.7	−0.2	0.2	
VAG	0.8	2.3	0.3	0.8	2.1	0.2	0.2	
Fiat	1.3	2.0	−2.7	1.4	2.1	0.4	0.2	
Rover	0.0	0.1	0.0	−0.9	0.2	−0.1	−0.2	
Ford/GM	0.4	1.3	0.5	−0.7	1.6	−0.1	−0.1	
Specialist	0.0	0.5	−0.1	−0.1	0.4	−0.2	−0.2	
Japanese	−20.6	20.5	−45.5	8.4	20.1	−32.3	0.0	

Market shares of Japanese (percent)   EC total

	France	Germany	Italy	UK	RoEC	Iberia	EC total
initial	3.0	14.6	0.9	11.4	23.5	2.1	8.8
final	7.1	8.0	8.9	8.5	13.6	9.3	8.8

Welfare change in m ecu per year

	Profits		Con surp	Tax rev	CET rev
French	−251.3	France	520.2	56.9	75.5
VAG	77.6	Germany	−1,098.4	−67.4	−125.6
Fiat	−481.4	Italy	1,327.9	110.7	165.7
Rover	10.7	UK	−220.0	−22.0	−45.5
Ford/GM	176.0	RoEC	−897.4	−159.2	−74.8
Specialist	150.8	Iberia	565.5	79.3	86.1
Japanese	814.1	EFTA	−0.1	0.0	0.0

EC	Profits	Con surp	Tax rev	CET rev	Total	(less tax)
	−405.6	197.8	−1.7	81.4	−128.1	−126.4

Table 4.7. Replacement of national VERs by an EC VER

sales fall and prices rise. The EC-wide VER also, of course, has effects in the two markets which formerly had no VER; with reductions in Japanese sales, and rises in prices, of non-Japanese as well as Japanese cars. Thus there are substantial consumer surplus losses in these markets, and increases in the profits of those producers for whom the European VER provides more protection than the national VERs. There is also a substantial increase in Japanese producers' profits, as the removal of national

	France	Germany	Italy	UK	RoEC	Iberia	EFTA	Total (incl RoW)
Quantity changes (percent)								
French	−2.4	−5.9	−8.7	−5.6	−7.8	−5.3	−1.4	−4.2
VAG	−4.3	−1.7	−7.0	−4.6	−6.2	−4.8	−1.0	−3.3
Fiat	−2.2	−2.2	1.6	−2.5	−5.5	−2.4	−0.2	0.1
Rover	−9.8	−10.0	−13.3	−7.5	−13.2	−10.9	−2.6	−8.2
Ford/GM	−6.3	−5.0	−9.9	−4.1	−7.7	−6.7	−1.5	−5.2
Specialist	−9.8	−8.3	−13.1	−9.4	−12.2	−10.9	−2.0	−6.9
Japanese	100.3	99.9	92.5	99.1	89.7	95.5	3.8	15.5
Consumer price changes (percent)								
French	−1.7	−0.8	−1.0	−0.9	−1.3	−1.4	0.3	
VAG	−1.3	−1.9	−1.5	−1.2	−1.7	−1.5	0.2	
Fiat	−1.8	−1.8	−3.6	−1.7	−1.9	−2.1	−0.0	
Rover	0.2	0.3	0.3	−0.4	0.2	0.1	0.6	
Ford/GM	−0.8	−1.0	−0.7	−1.3	−1.3	−1.0	0.3	
Specialist	0.2	−0.2	0.2	0.1	−0.1	0.1	0.5	
Japanese	−17.9	−17.8	−17.9	−17.8	−17.6	−17.7	−1.0	

Market shares of Japanese (percent)   EC total

	France	Germany	Italy	UK	RoEC	Iberia		EC total
initial	7.1	8.0	8.9	8.5	13.6	9.3		8.8
final	13.7	15.3	16.2	16.3	24.5	17.6		16.5

Welfare change in m ecu per year

	Profits		Con surp	Tax rev	CET rev
French	−689.0	France	1,023.2	111.9	102.1
VAG	−383.2	Germany	1,071.2	65.8	136.9
Fiat	−484.6	Italy	1,408.5	117.3	117.4
Rover	−101.4	UK	976.9	97.7	115.2
Ford/GM	−592.7	RoEC	904.5	160.4	81.5
Specialist	−341.6	Iberia	767.0	107.6	78.8
Japanese	235.9	EFTA	10.8	0.9	0.0

EC	Profits	Con surp	Tax rev	CET rev		Total	(less tax)
	−2,296.2	6,151.3	660.7	631.9		5.147.8	4.487.0

Table 4.8. Removal of European VER

constraints allows them to redistribute their sales between markets. To emphasize the point that the major effect of this policy change is on the distribution of welfare within Europe, the change in overall EC welfare is tiny.

Table 4.8 presents the same information in a different way, by showing the effects of removing the European VER (so Tables 4.7 and 4.8 taken together show the same policy experiment as Table 4.5). Removal of the

	France	Germany	Italy	UK	RoEC	Iberia	EFTA	Total (incl RoW)
Quantity changes (percent)								
French	−1.6	−2.0	−3.4	−2.0	−5.2	−3.8	−0.8	−2.2
VAG	−0.7	−1.0	−2.5	−1.1	−4.2	−2.8	−0.5	−1.4
Fiat	3.4	3.1	1.6	3.0	−0.3	1.2	0.3	1.7
Rover	−6.0	−6.3	−7.7	−6.4	−9.4	−8.1	−1.7	−6.4
Ford/GM	−2.6	−3.0	−4.4	−3.0	−6.1	−4.8	−1.0	−3.3
Specialist	−6.0	−6.3	−7.7	−6.3	−9.4	−8.0	−1.4	−4.9
Japanese	57.8	57.3	55.0	57.2	52.1	54.4	2.4	9.8
Consumer price changes (percent)								
French	−1.1	−1.1	−1.1	−1.1	−1.1	−1.1	0.2	
VAG	−1.3	−1.3	−1.3	−1.3	−1.3	−1.3	0.1	
Fiat	−2.3	−2.3	−2.3	−2.3	−2.3	−2.3	−0.1	
Rover	0.0	0.0	0.0	0.0	0.0	0.0	0.5	
Ford/GM	−0.8	−0.8	−0.8	−0.9	−0.8	−0.8	0.2	
Specialist	0.0	0.0	0.0	0.0	0.0	0.0	0.3	
Japanese	−12.1	−12.1	−12.1	−12.1	−12.1	−12.1	−0.6	

Market shares of Japanese (percent)							EC total
initial	6.9	8.8	5.2	9.7	17.3	11.6	8.8
final	10.6	13.4	7.8	14.8	25.2	17.3	13.2

Welfare change in m ecu per year

	Profits		Con surp	Tax rev	CET rev
French	−452.4	France	677.8	74.1	62.2
VAG	−254.1	Germany	749.9	46.0	89.5
Fiat	−397.5	Italy	917.7	76.5	55.3
Rover	−67.7	UK	674.4	67.4	77.6
Ford/GM	−389.9	RoEC	668.0	118.5	57.8
Specialist	−213.5	Iberia	576.9	81.0	54.3
Japanese	25.8	EFTA	8.6	0.7	0.0

EC	Profits	Con surp	Tax rev	CET rev	Total	(less tax)
	−1,580.1	4,264.7	463.5	396.7	3,544.8	3,081.3

Table 4.9. Removal of European VER with integrated markets

European VER leads to a more or less uniform Japanese expansion in European markets which is bad for all European producers and good for all European consumers. The gain to Japanese producers is modest, but the overall gain to EC welfare of not having a VER is substantial.

Smith and Venables (1988) find the biggest effects of completing the Community's internal market arise if firms are induced to treat the European market as a single integrated market rather than a set of separate national markets. The same conclusion is obtained in the present model: shifting from segmented markets to an integrated European market in which each firm sets one price for the whole market leads to price reductions, especially by national market leaders, and the consequent welfare gains are much larger than the gains shown in Table 4.3. Table 4.9 displays not the results of this shift, but rather the effect of the removal of a common European VER in the case of market integration. The results have the same shape as the results of Table 4.8, but are consistently smaller, reflecting the fact that the VER has less strongly anti-competitive effects in the more competitive market structure.

If one takes a simple welfarist view of economic policy-making, the conclusion is clear: restrictions on imports of Japanese cars into European markets are costly, whether the restrictions are operated at the national or the Community level. However, public policy decisions do not invariably seem to be motivated solely by welfarist considerations. In the case of the Community's external trade policy towards Japanese cars, there is concern for the adjustment costs which will be imposed on producers, especially the French and Italian producers who enjoy strongly protected home markets. Comparison of Tables 4.5 and 4.7 makes the point that even though an EC-wide VER cushions the 1992 blow somewhat, it does not protect the French and Italian producers from painful adjustment. Furthermore, this imperfect cushioning is provided at considerable expense to those consumers who previously had unrestricted access to Japanese cars. Finally, it should be noted that among the largest beneficiaries of the replacement of national restrictions with an EC-wide restriction are the Japanese producers. All in all, an EC-wide import restriction seems no more attractive from a political than a welfarist standpoint.

5   Conclusions

The analysis of economic policy changes using calibrated models is not uncontroversial. It is a procedure that gives rather more weight to the structure of the underlying theoretical model than to the modest amount of data used to calibrate the model numerically, and the results have to be interpreted in this light. Both the theoretical structure and the data impose discipline on the calculation of the likely welfare effects of policy changes, so the results are surely more reliable than back-of-the-envelope calculations based on informal modelling, though less reliable than the results one might obtain from an econometric model estimated on a run of reliable and consistent data, if the production of such a model were feasible.

I noted at the outset that the model could not answer questions about the distribution of gains and losses between countries, because of the multinational production structure. For a contribution to a project on 'North–South' relations in the Community, this may seem a serious drawback, but the point being made is a point about the real world rather than the present model: when multinationality is a strong feature of an industry, it is difficult to make predictions about the location of production effects.

In a more general sense too, the message of the examples presented here is that it may be a mistake to see economic policy choices in terms of 'national' interests: whether 'North' versus 'South' or 'France' versus 'Germany'. In none of the trade policy examples is there a single example where the interests of one country's consumers and its national champion producer strongly coincide.

Appendix: The model

1   The basic model

The formal model follows Smith and Venables (1988) in treating the industry as an imperfectly competitive industry producing differentiated products. The world is divided into J countries, indexed j, and production is undertaken by I firms, indexed i. (In the empirical implementation of the model, some firms are grouped together and all of the firms in the same group are assumed to be identical, but for the purposes of theoretical exposition it is clearer to treat all firms as distinct.) Each firm produces m_i different varieties of the product. The quantity of a single product variety produced by a firm in producer group i and sold in country j is denoted x_{ij}. In addition to the industry under study, each economy contains a perfectly competitive sector producing a single tradeable output under constant returns to scale, and this output is taken as the numeraire.

Demand for the differentiated product is represented by a two-stage budgeting process, following Dixit and Stiglitz (1977). Welfare is separable between the differentiated product and the numeraire good, with the sub-utility function representing welfare in country j obtained from consumption of the differentiated product represented by the constant elasticity of substitution function

$$y_j = \left[\sum_{i=1}^{I} m_i a_{ij}^{1/\epsilon} x_{ij}^{(\epsilon-1)/\epsilon} \right]^{\epsilon/(\epsilon-1)} \tag{A1}$$

where $\epsilon > 1$ and $j = 1, \ldots, J$. The function y_j can be regarded as a quantity index of aggregate consumption of the good, with the parameters a_{ij}

describing consumer preferences between products of different origin. Dual to the quantity index is a price index q_j which takes the form

$$q_j = \left[\sum_{i=1}^{I} m_i a_{ij} p_{ij}^{1-\epsilon} \right]^{1/(1-\epsilon)} \tag{A2}$$

and represents the price of the aggregate product, where the p_{ij} are the prices of the individual varieties.

I ignore income effects, so that demand for the aggregate product is a function only of the price index q_j. I assume that this function is iso-elastic, so

$$y_j = b_j q_j^{-\mu} \tag{A3}$$

for $j = 1, \ldots, J$, where the b_j reflect the size of the respective country markets. Utility maximization implies that demand for individual product varieties depends both on the price of the individual variety and on the aggregate price index:

$$x_j = a_{ij} b_j (p_{ij}/q_j)^{-\epsilon} y_j = a_{ij} b_j p_{ij}^{-\epsilon} q_j^{\epsilon-\mu} \tag{A4}$$

where $i = 1, \ldots, I, j = 1, \ldots, J$; and the corresponding inverse demand functions are

$$p_{ij} = a_{ij}^{1/\epsilon} (x_{ij}/y_j)^{-(1/\epsilon)} q_j = a_{ij}^{1/\epsilon} b_j^{1/\mu} x_{ij}^{-(1/\epsilon)} y_j^{[(1/\epsilon)-(1/\mu)]} \tag{A4'}$$

The market share, in value terms, in country j of a firm from producer group i is

$$s_{ij} = \frac{m_i p_{ij} x_{ij}}{q_j y_j} = \frac{m_i a_{ij} p_{ij}^{1-\epsilon}}{\sum_k m_k a_{kj} p_{kj}^{1-\epsilon}} = \frac{m_i a_{ij}^{1/\epsilon} x_{ij}^{(\epsilon-1)/\epsilon}}{\sum_k m_k a_{kj}^{1/\epsilon} x_{kj}^{(\epsilon-1)/\epsilon}} \tag{A5}$$

The profit of a typical firm in producer group i is

$$\pi_i = \sum_{j=1}^{J} m_i x_{ij} p_{ij} \tau_{ij} - C_i(x_i, m_i) \tag{A6}$$

where the factor τ_{ij} represents the *ad valorem* costs of selling in market j, including transport costs, non-tariff barriers, import taxes and sales taxes. (For notational convenience the factor τ measures the inverse wedge so $\tau_{ij} < 1$ where such costs are positive). The function C_i is the firm's cost function assumed to depend positively on the output per variety, $x_i = \Sigma x_{ij}$, and on the number of varieties m_i.

Firms choose sales x_{ij} to each of their markets independently. Where sales are not restricted, the first-order condition for profit maximizing choice of x_{ij} is the equality of marginal revenue to marginal cost:

$$p_{ij}\tau_{ij}\left[1 - \frac{1}{e_{ij}}\right] = \frac{1}{m_i}\frac{\partial C_i}{\partial x_i} \tag{A7}$$

this equality holding for all j if $i \notin R$, and for $j \notin E$ if $i \in R$, where E is the set of markets in which there are sales restrictions, R is the group of firms subject to sales restrictions in the markets E, and where e_{ij} is the perceived elasticity of demand.

2   Trade restrictions

I model two types of sales restrictions; both of them taking the form of a 'voluntary' export restraint (VER) which limits the *share* that a firm from the set R (assumed to be foreign firms) may have in a market. In the first, I suppose that each firm in the set R is restricted to fixed shares of each of a subset E of world markets, so that if $j \in E$ the market share σ_{rj} is constrained not to exceed some fixed level. However, I alternatively want to allow there to be a restriction on the firm's *overall* market share in a set of markets E, σ_r. Note that these shares are volume shares as opposed to the value shares s_{ij} defined earlier.

When a firm r is subject to a restriction on its share of each of a set of markets E, the Lagrangean for its profit maximization problem is

$$L_r = \sum_{j=1}^{J} m_r x_{rj} p_{rj}\tau_{rj} - C_r(x_r, m_r) - \sum_{k \in E} \lambda_k\left(m_r x_{rk} - \sigma_{rk}\sum_{i-1}^{I} m_i x_{ik}\right)$$

with first-order conditions in each restricted market j

$$p_{rj}\tau_{rj}\left(1 - \frac{1}{e_{rj}}\right) = \frac{1}{m_r}\frac{\partial C_r}{\partial x_r} + \lambda_j(1 - \sigma_{rj}) \tag{A7$'$}$$

while for a restriction on the overall share of a set of markets E, the Lagrangean is

$$L_r = \sum_{j=1}^{J} m_r x_{rj} p_{rj}\tau_{rj} - C_r(x_r, m_r) - \lambda \sum_{k \in E} \left(m_r x_{rk} - \sigma_r\sum_{i=1}^{I} m_i x_{ik}\right)$$

giving first-order conditions for each market j in the set E

$$p_{rj}\tau_{rj}\left(1 - \frac{1}{e_{rj}}\right) = \frac{1}{m_r}\frac{\partial C_r}{\partial x_r} + \lambda(1 - \sigma_r) \tag{A7$''$}$$

The perceived elasticity of demand e_{ij} is derived by assuming that firms are Cournot competitors, except in the case where firms which are not themselves subject to restrictions perceive that the behaviour of rivals from producer group R is constrained. Cournot behaviour therefore applies to all firms in markets without restrictions and to all firms from the constrained group of producers. The perceived elasticity of demand is then derived from equations (A4′) and (A1), holding sales of competitors constant, as

$$\frac{1}{e_{ij}} = \frac{1}{\epsilon} + \left(\frac{1}{\mu} - \frac{1}{\epsilon}\right)s_{ij} \tag{A8}$$

for all j if $i \in R$, and for all i if $j \notin E$.

Consider now the behaviour of unconstrained firms in the presence of a VER limiting the *overall* market share of a group R of firms in the set E of national markets. An unconstrained firm i maximizes (A6), taking account of effects of changes in x_{ij} on x_{rk} in *all* $k \in E$, so

$$x_{ij}\frac{\partial C}{\partial x_i} = m_i p_{ij} x_{ij} \tau_{ij} + \sum_{k \in E} m_i p_{ij} x_{ik} \tau_{ik} \frac{x_{ik}}{p_{ik}} \frac{dp_{ik}}{dx_{ij}}$$

From (A4′) it follows that

$$\frac{x_{ij}}{p_{ij}}\frac{dp_{ij}}{dx_{ij}} = -\frac{1}{\epsilon} - \left(\frac{1}{\mu} - \frac{1}{\epsilon}\right)\frac{x_{ij}}{y_j}\frac{dy_j}{dx_{ij}}$$

and for $k \neq j$

$$\frac{x_{ik}}{p_{ik}}\frac{dp_{ik}}{dx_{ik}} = -\left(\frac{1}{\mu} - \frac{1}{\epsilon}\right)\frac{x_{ik}}{y_k}\frac{dy_k}{dx_{ij}}$$

so the first-order condition for an unconstrained firm is

$$x_{ij}\frac{\partial C_i}{\partial x_i} = m_i p_{ij} x_{ij} \tau_{ij}\left(1 - \frac{1}{\epsilon}\right) - \left(\frac{1}{\mu} - \frac{1}{\epsilon}\right) + \sum_{k \in E} m_i p_{ij} x_{ik} \tau_{ik} \frac{x_{ik}}{y_k}\frac{dy_k}{dx_{ik}}$$

However, from the fact that

$$y_k = \left[\sum_{i \in F} m_i a_{ik}^{1/\epsilon} x_{ik}^{(\epsilon-1)/\epsilon}\right]^{\epsilon/(\epsilon-1)} \tag{A2}$$

where F is the set of all firms, it follows that

$$\frac{x_{ij}}{y_k}\frac{dy_k}{dx_{ik}} = \frac{m_i a_{ik}^{1/\epsilon} x_{ik}^{(\epsilon-1)/\epsilon}}{\displaystyle\sum_{i \in F} m_i a_k^{1/\epsilon} x_{ik}^{(\epsilon-1)/\epsilon}} = s_{ik}$$

so

$$\frac{x_{ij}}{y_k}\frac{dy_k}{dx_{ij}} = s_{ij}\sigma_{jk} + n_r s_{rk}\frac{z_{ij}}{x_{rk}}\frac{dx_{rk}}{dx_{ij}}$$

where n_r is the number of (identical) restricted firms, and the first-order condition becomes

$$x_{ij} \frac{\partial C}{\partial x_i} = m_i p_{ij} x_{ij} \tau_{ij} \left[1 - \frac{1}{\epsilon} - \left(\frac{1}{\mu} - \frac{1}{\epsilon} \right) s_{ij} \right]$$

$$- \left(\frac{1}{\mu} - \frac{1}{\epsilon} \right) \sum_{k \in E} m_i p_{ik} x_{ik} \tau_{ik} n_r s_{rk} \frac{x_{ik}}{x_{rk}} \frac{dx_{rk}}{dx_{ik}} \tag{A9}$$

The constrained firms' behaviour enters the unconstrained firms' first-order condition. The constraint which must be met is that

$$\sum_{k \in E} m_r x_{rk} = \sigma_r \sum_{k \in E} \sum_{i \in F} m_i x_{ik}$$

where σ_r is the fixed share of the aggregate market in E to which each of the firms r is constrained. Differentiating with respect to x_{ij} gives

$$\sum_{k \in E} m_r \frac{dx_{rk}}{dx_{ij}} = \sigma_r \left(m_i + \sum_{k \in E} n_r m_r \frac{dx_{rk}}{dx_{ij}} \right)$$

so

$$(1 - \sigma_r n_r) \sum_{k \in E} m_r x_{rk} \frac{x_{ij}}{x_{rk}} \frac{dx_{rk}}{dx_{ij}} = \sigma_r m_i x_{ij} \tag{A10}$$

We assume that firm i conjectures that restrained firms will, in equilibrium, change their sales in each of their markets equiproportionately in response to the change in their constrained output resulting from a change in x_{ij}, and let

$$\xi = \frac{x_{ij}}{x_{rk}} \frac{dx_{rk}}{dx_{ij}} \qquad \text{for all } k$$

which implies that (A10) can be written as

$$\xi = \frac{\sigma_r m_i x_{ij}}{(1 - \sigma_r n_r) \sum_{k \in E} m_r x_{rk}}$$

and the first-order condition (A9) now becomes

$$p_{ij} \tau_{ij} \left[1 - \frac{1}{\epsilon} - \left(\frac{1}{\mu} - \frac{1}{\epsilon} \right) s_{ij} \right] - \frac{\displaystyle\sum_{k \in E} m_i x_{ik} p_{ik} \tau_{ik} n_r s_{rk}}{\displaystyle\sum_{k \in E} \sum_{i \notin R} m_i x_{ik}} \left(\frac{1}{\mu} - \frac{1}{\epsilon} \right)$$

$$= \frac{1}{m_i} \frac{\partial C_i}{\partial x_i} \tag{A8$'$}$$

In the case of there being a share quota in *each* of a group of markets j, the argument above can be applied to the market j individually and (A8$'$)

then implies that the unrestricted firm's optimum choice in market j is given by (A7) but with inverse elasticity

$$\frac{1}{e_{ij}} = \frac{1}{\epsilon} + \left(\frac{1}{\mu} - \frac{1}{\epsilon}\right)\left\{s_{ij} + n_r s_{rj}\frac{m_i x_{ij}}{\displaystyle\sum_{i \notin R} m_i x_{ij}}\right\} \qquad (A8'')$$

The case of a market with no share quotas, which we have already seen in (A7) and (A8), can be derived from (A8') by letting $n_r = 0$, in which case (A8') does indeed reduce to (A7) and (A8).

3   Integrated markets

The analysis above is based on the assumption of nationally-segmented markets in which firms set different prices in each market. In the Cournot model, the modelling of the integration of a set of national markets is a little complicated, but if we make the simplifying if incorrect assumption that the sum of the national market constant elasticity demand functions will give rise to an integrated demand function which also has constant elasticity, then equations (A8) and (A8') can be applied to the set of integrated markets.

4   Long-run adjustment

The firms' choice of the number of models is not modelled here, so that the m_i are formally exogenous. However, in the paper some policy simulations are presented in which the values of the m_i are changed. Long-run adjustment is therefore not ignored, but it is treated in a much more *ad hoc* fashion than the short-run sales decisions modelled above.

5   The cost function

Finally, the cost function used in the paper is chosen to satisfy the properties: (i) average variable cost declines by 5% for every doubling of x; (ii) fixed costs are 20% of total costs when $x = 200{,}000$ and $m = 5$; (iii) half of fixed costs are independent of m, when $m = 5$. These properties are satisfied by the function:

$$C(x, m) = c(5 + m + 0.0001x^{0.925}m)$$

where the parameter c is chosen in the calibration of the model.

NOTE

I am grateful for funding from the Economic and Social Research Council (grant no. R000231763), research assistance from Michael Gasiorek, help with data sources from Deborah Stroud of McKinsey and Company, London, and comments on an earlier version of the paper from John Black and David Newbery.

REFERENCES

Bresnahan, T. (1981). 'Departures from marginal-cost pricing in the American automobile industry'. *Journal of Econometrics* **17**, 201–27.

Cowling, K. and J. Cubbin (1971). 'Price, quality and advertising competition: an econometric investigation of the United Kingdom car market'. *Economica* **38**, 378–94.

Dixit, A. and J. Stiglitz (1977). 'Monopolistic competition and optimum product diversity'. *American Economic Review* **67**, 297–308.

Feenstra, R. and J. Levinsohn (1989). 'Estimating demand and oligopoly pricing for differentiated products with multiple characteristics'. Typescript.

Hess, A.C. (1977). 'A comparison of automobile demand equations'. *Econometrica* **45**, 683–701.

Jones, D. (1987). 'Prudent marketing and price differentials in the UK car market: a case study'. In OECD (1987).

Levinsohn, J. (1988). 'Empirics of taxes on differentiated products: the case of tariffs in the U.S. automobile industry'. In R.E. Baldwin (ed.), *Trade Policy Issues and Empirical Analysis*, Chicago, Ill.: University of Chicago Press.

Ludvigsen Associates Limited (1988). 'The EC92 Automobile Sector'. In Commission of the European Communities, *Research on the 'Cost of Non-Europe'*, *Basic Findings*, Vol. II. Luxembourg: European Communities Publications Office.

Maxcy, G. and Z.A. Silberston (1959). *The Motor Industry*. London: George Allen and Unwin.

Messerlin, P. and S. Becuwe (1987). 'French trade and competition policies in the car industry'. In OECD (1987).

Motor Industry Research Unit (1988). *A Single European Market? An Automotive Perspective*. Norwich: University of East Anglia.

OECD (1983). *Long Term Outlook for the World Automobile Industry*. Paris: Organisation for Economic Cooperation and Development.

(1987). *The Costs of Restricting Imports: the Automobile Industry*. Paris: Organisation for Economic Cooperation and Development.

Smith, A. (1989). 'Alternative models of trade policy in the European car market'. Paper presented to the NBER/CEPR conference on Empirical Studies of Strategic Trade Policy, Cambridge, Mass., October 1989.

Smith, A. and A.J. Venables (1988). 'Completing the internal market in the European Community: some industry simulations'. *European Economic Review* **32**, 1501–25.

(1989). 'Counting the cost of voluntary export restrictions in the European car market'. Paper presented to the Pinhas Sapir conference, Tel Aviv, May 1989.

Venables, A.J. and A. Smith (1986). 'Trade and industrial policy under imperfect competition'. *Economic Policy* **1**, 622–72.

5 Financial market integration, macroeconomic policy and the EMS

WILLIAM H. BRANSON

1 Introduction and summary

The new and prospective entrants to the EC join an economic environment that itself is undergoing rapid change. The combination of the European Monetary System (EMS) and the integration of European financial markets in 1992 will substantially alter the environment of monetary and fiscal policy in Europe. This paper reviews the constraints placed on macroeconomic policy, and the remaining options, in a system that appears to be integrating with regard to monetary, but not fiscal, policy. We begin by noting that integration is taking place at a time when the countries in Europe have large and persistent current account imbalances, and discuss the conditions under which these will be automatically financed within Europe. We go on to discuss the constraint that the combination of 1992 and the EMS will place on monetary policy, and the role of local financial intermediation in this environment. We end by discussing issues of structural reform of the financial system of the new entrants, and the possible need for an EC fiscal authority.

Section 2 of the paper reviews projections and recent outturns of world and European current accounts. In the world context, OECD Europe and the EC have roughly balanced current accounts. Within Europe, however, we see growing imbalances. A 'core' group of Germany, Belgium–Luxembourg, the Netherlands, and Switzerland, have a growing aggregate surplus, while the other 'peripheral' countries have deficits, mostly growing. How these developments are viewed depends on the viewer's perception of the degree of financial integration of these two groups. With an integrated financial system, Europe would be approximately self-financing, with the excess saving in the surplus countries flowing to investment in the deficit countries.

In Section 3 we turn to the problem of financing current account deficits in the integrated financial system. We analyze current account

104

deficits as the sum of excess private investment and the government budget deficit. This is done in the context of increasing financial integration and external balance in Europe. The conditions for sustainable financing of private or public imbalances are reviewed; these are the conditions under which the current account imbalances will be financed without growing risk premia or, ultimately, balance-of-payments crises. The conclusion of Section 3 is that in the integrated financial system of 1992, European governments will have to finance their deficits on the open market, at risk premia that reflect the market's assessment of the difficulty the country will experience in servicing its debt, much like states in the US. In Section 4 we briefly note the problem that lack of fiscal unification in the EC poses for a European System of Central Banks (ESCB): in whose debt are open-market operations to be conducted?

The 1992 legislation in financial markets will remove almost all obstacles to capital movement in the area. This will place a substantial, if not completely binding, constraint on the freedom of domestic monetary policy for any member that chooses to manage its exchange rate relative to the EMS grid. This is most obvious for members that join the exchange rate arrangements of the EMS, but it is equally true for members that peg their real exchange rate to the EMS grid, as suggested for some of the new entrants by Rudiger Dornbusch (1988). In these cases monetary policy will be fully occupied with the task of keeping the nominal rate moving in such a way that the real rate remains constant. This effectively eliminates any role for aggregate domestic monetary policy in stabilizing the domestic economies against relative real disturbances across member countries. Section 5 lays out a model that illustrates the constraint on aggregate domestic monetary policy in both the fixed nominal and real rate cases, based on William Branson (1981).

The constraint on aggregate monetary policy discussed in Section 5 does not mean that domestic monetary policy, broadly considered, can play no role in stabilization. Recent work on financial intermediation, both theoretical and empirical, has focussed on the costs of monitoring local borrowers as a reason for the existence of local intermediaries. John Montgomery (1988) analyzes a situation in which a local intermediary incurs the fixed costs of local monitoring and acquires a monopoly (or, in general, market power) position relative to the local borrower. This gives the local intermediary an advantage over international intermediaries and creates a two-tiered system of international intermediaries that deal with each other and with international firms and local intermediaries that lend locally. Steven Fazzari et al. (1988) present evidence that implies that this structure is relevant within the US, and Charles Goodhart (1987) argues that it would be relevant in the EC of 1992. The existence of this structure of intermediation within Europe would make selective monetary or credit policy that operates on the local intermediation system potentially effective as a stabilization instrument, as analyzed in William Branson (1976). It also raises the issues of whether, how, and under what conditions the member governments would wish to take steps to preserve their local intermediation systems. The role of local intermediation, and the extent that it provides some freedom for local or domestic credit policy with the expanded EC, is discussed in detail in Section 6.

A related problem is the competitive pressure on local banking systems in the entrants as the 1992 legislation is implemented. The banking systems of Greece, Portugal, and Turkey are burdened with backlogs of non-performing loans that grow as their service is capitalized into new loans. The extent of the problem is not known precisely, but it is considered to be serious. See, for instance, William Branson (1985) for the case of Portugal. As new international banks enter local markets, there is the likelihood that they will skim off the most credit-worthy borrowers, worsening the position of the already fragile local banks. Thus for the new entrants, substantially more than the minimal harmonization of banking regulation will have to be achieved to preserve the desired degree of local intermediation. Mergers of domestic banks, in some cases with foreign EC banks, and consolidation of non-performing loans, at least those of state enterprises, using a one-time issue of government debt, may be among the needed measures. Issues of the health of the domestic banking systems in the new or potential entrants are taken up in Section 7.

With the role of monetary policy in stabilization severely constrained, fiscal policy and labour migration will have to play greater roles in stabilizing the EC of 1992 against relative real disturbances. Integration of financial markets and the spread of the EMS exchange-rate arrangements will effectively create a unified currency area. Whether, or perhaps when, a single monetary authority will emerge is not clear, but the independence of domestic monetary policy will be severely constrained. Peter Kenen (1969) has argued that the domain of fiscal policy should coincide with the currency area. Since the existence of the currency area effectively eliminates relative monetary policy within it, an area-wide tax and transfer system that automatically cushions incomes against relative real disturbances becomes an esssential adjustment mechanism. In its absence, a temporary disturbance due to a technology shock or a fluctuation in the price of oil, for example, could trigger an unstable cumulative local decline. As an example, consider a shock that causes a temporary rise in local unemployment. As income falls, so does tax revenue. If this leads to a reduction in the provision of local public goods, the result may be outward migration of individuals or business, exacerbating the

Area or Country	OECD Projections		IMF
	$ billion	% GNP	% GNP
OECD	− 57	− 0.4	− 0.3[a]
North America	− 128	− 2.1	
US	− 116	− 2.1	− 2.8
Canada	− 12	− 2.0	− 2.3
Japan	83	2.7	2.8
OECD Europe	− 1	0	
Australia–New Zealand	− 11	− 3.0	
Asian NICs	18	—	5.4[b]
Korea	8	—	
Taiwan	7	—	
Hong Kong	2	—	
Singapore	1	—	
Rest of World (ROW)	− 25		
(OPEC)	− 5	—	
World Total	− 64	—	

Table 5.1. World current accounts, 1990

[a] IMF datum for total industrial countries, which excludes OECD countries Greece, Portugal, and Turkey.
[b] IMF estimated range for Asian NICs.

Sources: OECD (1989), IMF (1989).

fall in tax revenue. This might be the right response to a permanent shock, but not to a temporary one. It could be prevented by an inward transfer from a fiscal system that is integrated across the currency area. The problems of adjustment without an integrated fiscal system, and some possible steps to alleviate them, are discussed in Section 8.

2   Current account balances: the world and Europe

The projected world current account balances for 1990 are shown in Table 5.1. The first column gives the OECD projections in $ billion, and the second in percent of GNP, where available. The third column compares the IMF projections as percent of GNP. The table is based on the OECD projections because they include the dollar amounts and more countries. The OECD current account deficit in 1990 is projected to be

Area or Country	OECD Projections		IMF
	$ billion	% GNP	% GNP
OECD Europe	−1	0	
Surplus Countries	69.25	—	
Belgium–Luxembourg[ab]	2.75	1.8	
Germany[ab]	53.0	4.2	3.9
Ireland[ab]	0.5	1.7	
Netherlands[ab]	4.75	2.0	2.4
Norway	3.5	3.6	
Switzerland	4.75	2.6	3.0
Deficit Countries	−69.0	—	
Austria	−1.0	−0.8	
Denmark[ab]	−1.25	−1.2	
Finland	−5.25	−4.2	
France[ab]	−4.0	−0.4	−0.3
Greece[a]	−2.25	−3.9	
Iceland	—	−3.2	
Italy[ab]	−10.0	−1.1	−0.2
Portugal[a]	−2.25	−4.8	
Spain[ab]	−11.0	−2.7	
Sweden	−3.5	−1.8	
Turkey	−0.5	−0.8	
UK[a]	−28.0	−3.1	−1.1
EC	1.0	0	
EMS ERM[b]	34.75	—	

Table 5.2. OECD Europe current accounts, 1990

[a] EC Member.
[b] Member of EMS Exchange Rate Mechanism.
Sources: OECD (1989), IMF (1989). Differences in degree of rounding are in the source tables.

$57 billion, about the same as in 1989. The OECD projects deficits of $128 billion in North America and $11 billion in the Antipodes, a surplus of $83 billion in Japan, and balance in Europe. The Asian NICs show a surplus of $18 billion and the ROW a $25 billion deficit.

The world deficit, or current account discrepancy, in the OECD projections of Table 5.1 is $64 billion. The world deficit in the IMF projections for 1989 is $100 billion. The IMF breaks this down into a world trade *surplus* of $17 billion, with deficits of $109 billion on services and $8 billion on transfers. (See IMF, 1989, p. 156).

Aside from the world deficit, the main impression we get from Table 5.1 is that North America (mainly, of course, the US) and Japan have large imbalances, both in levels and as fractions of GNP, and that Australia–New Zealand, the NICs, and the ROW also have marked imbalances. These are smaller in levels, but larger in terms of GNP, and about the same size. Among the industrial countries, the impression is one of large imbalances in the US, Japan, and the NICs, with much smaller ones in Europe and the Antipodes. OECD Europe, especially, has a current account balance near zero. The data of Table 5.1 show Europe in balance, at the world level.

The distribution of imbalances within Europe in the 1990 projections is shown in Table 5.2, which follows the same format as Table 5.1. In Table 5.2 we see the large amplitude of imbalances across Europe. The biggest imbalance in levels is Germany's, while Portugal's is the biggest in terms of GNP.

There are several ways to look at the data of Table 5.2. Clearly there is a large offset to the $53 billion German surplus within Europe. The surplus of the EMS ERM countries is $35 billion, so the rest of the ERM countries show an $18 billion deficit, on aggregate. The rest of the offset is a deficit in the non-ERM countries. The EC has surplus of $2 billion, so the EC non-ERM members have a collective deficit of $32.5 billion, with $28 billion in the UK. A non-institutional way to look at the data is suggested by the separation of surplus and deficit countries in Table 5.2. The surplus countries are a core group around Germany. Viewed from this perspective, all of the periphery except Ireland and Norway is in deficit.

The pattern of imbalances in the 1990 projections of Table 5.2 has persisted for several years. The data since 1987 are shown in Table 5.3, grouped as in Table 5.2, with the exception of Norway, which moves from deficit to surplus in 1990. In Table 5.3 we see the OECD Europe and EC surpluses actually diminishing since 1987. The imbalances within Europe seem to be growing, including those within the EC. The surpluses seem fairly stable as fractions of GDP. Among the deficit EC countries, only Denmark's deficit has decreased as a percent of GDP, while those of Italy, Portugal, Spain, and the UK have increased. Thus the trend shows increasing imbalances within Europe and the EC, within a stable total.

The extent to which we should consider the German, or the core, surplus as an independent imbalance, rather than submerge it into a European aggregate, depends on how integrated we think the aggregate is. We do not break out states or regions in the US for purposes of this analysis because we consider the US to be financially integrated. Suppose we considered the EMS ERM group to be integrated from the point of

Area or Country	% of GDP/GNP 1987	1988	1989	1990
OECD Europe	−0.9	0.3	0.0	0.0
Surplus Countries				
Belgium–Luxembourg[ab]	2.0	2.0	1.8	1.8
Germany[abc]	4.0	4.0	4.0	4.2
Ireland[abc]	1.5	2.3	1.8	1.7
Netherlands[ab]	1.4	2.3	1.4	2.0
Switzerland	4.2	3.5	3.1	2.6
Deficit Countries				
Austria	−0.2	−0.4	−0.7	−0.8
Denmark[ab]	−3.0	−1.7	−1.5	−1.2
Finland	−2.2	−2.9	−3.8	−4.2
France[ab]	−0.5	−0.4	−0.5	−0.4
Greece[a]	−2.6	−1.9	−3.3	−3.9
Iceland	−3.2	−4.3	−3.3	−3.2
Italy[ab]	−0.1	−0.5	−1.0	−1.1
Norway	−4.9	−4.0	−0.9	3.6
Portugal[a]	1.3	−1.4	−3.4	−4.8
Spain[a]	0.0	−1.1	−2.1	−2.7
Sweden	−0.6	−1.4	−1.6	−1.8
Turkey[c]	−1.4	−1.1	−1.0	−0.8
UK[a]	−0.7	−3.2	−3.3	−3.1
EC	0.9	0.3	0.0	0.0

Table 5.3. OECD Europe current accounts, 1987–90

[a] EC Member.
[b] Member of EMS Exchange Rate Mechanism.
[c] Calculated as a percentage of GNP.

Sources: OECD (1989).

view of financing external imbalances. Then we would see the core ERM surplus as automatically financing any ERM deficits, with an external ERM surplus of $35 billion. If we accept the Single European Act as expressing a definitive decision on integrating the EC from this point of view, then the ERM surplus is automatically available to finance the rest of the EC imbalances, and the external EC imbalance disappears. If we think that the non-EC members will take the necessary steps to be within the single European market, they would share in the financing of imbalances within Europe. Thus how we view the core ERM surplus in a world analysis depends on the degree of integration of the core with concentric groups of increasing economic distance, and this degree of integration itself is changing rapidly.

3   Capital markets and risk premia

As the EC, and effectively Europe, moves towards the unified financial markets of 1992, the governments and private sectors will be borrowing in increasingly integrated bond markets. This will mean that to continue to finance current account deficits within Europe, both government and private borrowers will be required to pay risk premia that are related to their underlying economic condition, that is, the probability that they will have difficulty servicing their debt. The situation can be analyzed using the classic framework from Robert Mundell (1963).

The national income identity can be written in a flow-of-funds form as

$$CAB = (S - I) - D,\qquad\qquad (1)$$

where CAB is the current account balance ($+$ is surplus), S and I are private saving and investment, and D is the consolidated government deficit. The form of equation (1) emphasizes the fact that the current account deficit ($CAB < 0$) is composed of the sum of an excess of private investment over saving ($S < I$) and a government deficit ($D > 0$). Thus the current account deficit is the sum of net private sector and government borrowing internationally. In a case where the government runs a deficit but does not borrow directly abroad, that is, borrows from its private sector or Central Bank, the private sector must borrow abroad enough to finance both its deficit, $(I - S)$, and the government's. Then the private capital inflow would equal the CAB deficit, and finance both $(I - S)$ and D.

The data of Table 5.2 show that Europe is essentially self-financed. The sum of the OECD Europe current account balances is approximately zero. If exchange rates were fixed in Europe, then borrowing and lending within Europe would not entail the exchange risk that would come with external financing such as borrowing from Japan or lending to the US. Thus intra-European financing of current account imbalances is likely to be more efficient than gross external financing with surplus countries lending in dollars and deficit countries borrowing in yen. So we can think of Europe of 1992 as an integrated and largely self-financed capital market, with relatively small flows outside the area, to finance net external imbalances.

Borrowers within Europe, both private and public, will borrow at rates i_i that are marked up over the perceived risk-free rate i^* by the risk premium rp_i:

$$i_i = i^* + rp_i \tag{2}$$

Here the risk-free rate might be the lowest national government borrowing rate, or it could be the rate on a debt issue connected with the new ECSB. Equation (2) assumes that exchange rates are immutably fixed between the relevant countries. If not, an additional term must be added to equation (2) for the expected rate of change of the exchange rate, and the risk premium will include currency risk. This would weaken the argument that self-finance within Europe is more efficient than external finance.

The risk premium in equation (2) reflects the market's perception of the probability that the borrower will run into trouble in servicing the debt. The market's expression of the risk premium is in points over Libor, or on premia that depend on credit rating, as in the US market. In this way, governments borrowing on the unified European Market will resemble states borrowing in the US. The market will provide fiscal discipline for both private and public borrowers. That discipline will provide an incentive not to overextend on $(I - S)$ in the private case or D in the public case in equation (1), and thereby provide discipline for the national CAB.

It may be worth noting that the role of a change in the exchange rate in this view of the current account balance would be to change the relative profitability of the private sectors of the relevant countries, as well as to change relative goods prices. Thus in an extreme case in which two countries were producing essentially the same goods, a devaluation would increase the profitability of the devaluing country's private sector, and vice-versa for the upvaluing country. This would improve financing conditions for the devaluing country, and worsen them for the upvaluing country. This adjustment mechanism for financing deficits is assumed away here.

In this market-oriented system, individual borrowers, corporations or governments, can find the needed discipline in the arithmetic of debt dynamics set out by Daniel Cohen (1985). The growth rate of the ratio of debt to income b is given by

$$db = (r - n)b + d - s \tag{3}$$

where r is the real borrowing rate, n is the growth rate of real income, d is the ratio of the non-interest deficit to real income, and s is the ratio of seigniorage (including the inflation tax) to nominal income. If n exceeds r, with a non-interest deficit that exceeds seigniorage, the equilibrium debt–income ratio b^* is given by

$$b^* = (d - s)/(n - r), \quad \text{if } r - n < 0 \tag{4}$$

In this case the market will be trying to determine whether the debt service on this level of debt is feasible. If r is greater than n, then a non-interest surplus ($-d$) plus seigniorage is required to keep the debt–income ratio from rising indefinitely. In this case the ratio of the non-interest surplus to income should be at least equal to the difference $(r - n)$ times the debt–income ratio b less seigniorage:

$$-d^* = (r - n)b - s, \quad \text{if } r - n > 0 \tag{5}$$

In this case the market will be trying to evaluate the ability of the borrower to sustain the required surplus $-d^*$. If the government deficit is seen to be unsustainable, its risk premium will rise. Concern for future taxation to service the government's debt would also increase the private sector's risk premium. If both the private sector and the government respect the debt arithmetic, the resulting current account deficit can be financed at the existing risk premium.

This system of European financial markets will not, of course, be perfect or self-regulating. Some borrowers will overextend, as New York City did in the middle of the 1970s. They will face a drying up of the capital market and the need for a drastic retrenchment. But the knowledge that this is the consequence of overextension will itself be stabilizing. The markets will require regulatory attention at the European level, either by the ESCB or by the Commission. This regulation would in general prevent private borrowers from overextending, as well as governments. If all private borrowers and governments respect the debt arithmetic, under system-wide regulation, then the entire system will be stable. This indicates the direction for regulation.

4   Interaction with the monetary system

Within the exchange-rate arrangements of the EMS, and I assume eventually within the entire expanded EC, monetary policy at the national level will be tied to the exchange-rate commitment. Thus the national central banks, even in 1989, are not free to finance the budget deficits of their governments. They can finance them to the extent allowed by exchange-rate stability, but that extent is determined by the financial markets, not by the bank or the government. Over time, as freedom of capital and monetary movements within the EC increases, this constraint will become tighter. So increasingly, governments will have to finance their deficits in the markets, under the constraints discussed in Section 3. This will pose a difficult problem for the ESCB: in whose debt will it conduct monetary policy?

In order to conduct joint intervention and sterilization operations, and to provide for monetary growth (non-inflationary, of course) in the entire area, the ESCB will have to accumulate a portfolio of debt. To the extent that it buys the debt of one country, it provides that government with the seigniorage from the attendant money creation. This will require some rules for the composition of open-market operations by the ESCB. These rules will have to be formulated with the resulting fiscal incentives in mind. For example, a rule that says the ESCB should buy debt in proportion to the outstanding stocks, or one that maintains a constant distribution within the ESCB's portfolio, would provide an incentive for any one government to increase its deficit, in order to capture more of the seigniorage. It seems that the rule for the composition of additions to the ESCB's portfolio should be insensitive to the fiscal behaviour of all member countries, as suggested by Alessandra Casella and Jonathan Feinstein (1989). This would eliminate any incentive for a fiscal authority to manipulate the central monetary authority.

This problem does not exist in an area with a central fiscal authority, such as the US. The Federal Reserve does open-market operations in US government debt, not state debt. This is one aspect of Kenen's (1969) observation that in an optimal currency area the single monetary authority would face a unified fiscal authority. The political problems of designing the rules for the composition of the ESCB's open-market operations are evident. The Europe of monetary but not fiscal integration will not yet be an optimal currency area.

5   The constraint on monetary policy

The constraint on monetary policy that is imposed by the combination of free capital movements and fixed nominal exchange rates is well known and understood. For example, the 'Note from the President of the Commission to the President of the Council' for the Knokke meeting puts it:

> 'The EMS is going to have to face a challenge when capital movements are liberalized . . .: how to manage the triangle of incompatibilities which results from the coexistence of exchange rate stability and the free movement of capital, with the relative autonomy of monetary policies of certain member countries'. [*European Economy*, May 1988, p. 37.]

In this case the free movement of capital and exchange-rate stability preclude relative autonomy of monetary policy. This is the case even if it is the real exchange rate that is stabilized. This section of the paper lays out a basic model of exchange rate determination that can be used to illustrate this constraint.

Let us consider the basic textbook model of equilibrium in the market for domestic money in an EC member in 1992. The equilibrium condition is given by

$$m - p = ay - bi + x \tag{6}$$

Here m, p, and y are the logarithms of the stock of domestic money, the domestic price level, and the level of real GDP, respectively, i is the domestic interest rate, and changes in x represent any shifts in portfolio preferences between domestic money and bonds that earn interest i. The parameter a is the income elasticity of the demand for money, and b is the semi-elasticity of the demand for money with respect to the interest rate.

With the free capital and monetary movements, the domestic interest rate is tied to the centre's by

$$i = i^* + de + rp \tag{7}$$

Here e is the logarithm of the exchange rate so that de is its expected rate of change, added to equation (2), and the index i has been removed from equation (2). The centre under current arrangements is Germany. In a completely unified system, it would be whatever dominant financial centre emerges. Any change in rp would represent a shift in portfolio-holders' preferences between domestic and foreign (centre) bonds. Within the EMS, de would be zero except around times of expected realignments. In the 'soft-currency' option of Dornbusch (1988), de would be given by the inflation differential. The risk premium will be assumed to be exogenous here, although in principle it depends on relative asset supplies, as shown in William Branson and Dale Henderson (1985). Equation (7) is a financial markets arbitrage condition; with open financial markets, the domestic interest rate will be fixed by the centre rate plus any expected rate of depreciation plus the risk premium.

With open goods markets and similar consumption baskets across countries, the domestic price level is tied to the centre's by

$$p = e + p^* \tag{8}$$

Here p, p^*, and e are the logarithms of the domestic and centre price levels and the exchange rate, respectively. In arithmetic terms, equation (8) would just be $P = EP^*$. Equation (8) is essentially a goods market arbitrage condition; the price of the same goods in two member countries must be (approximately) the same, measured in a common currency. It holds strictly if all goods are traded. With some non-traded goods still remaining in a unified Europe, equation (8) would only hold approximately, consistent with the existence of local intermediation, discussed in Section 6 below. Equation (8) implies the relation of inflation rates, at least between traded goods, and the rate of change of the exchange rate:

$$de = dp - dp^* \tag{9}$$

This is the rate of depreciation in the soft-currency option.

Equations (7) and (8) can be put into equation (6), and m isolated on the left-hand side, to see the constraint on domestic monetary policy:

$$m = e + p^* - b(i^* + de + rp) + ay + x \tag{10}$$

The term $e + p^*$ reflects goods market arbitrage, the term in $b(\ )$ reflects financial market arbitrage across bonds denominated in the home and centre currencies, the term ay gives disturbance to the demand for money coming from shocks to domestic output, and x represents shifts in portfolio demands between domestic money and bonds.

For members of the EMS that adhere to the exchange-rate arrangements, e in equation (10) would be constant, and de would be zero. To hold the nominal exchange rate e constant, monetary policy would have to accommodate disturbances to the demand for domestic money coming from the price level or interest rates in the centre, portfolio shifts between domestic and centre bonds and between domestic bonds and money, and shocks to real output. For example, an increase in portfolio-holders' estimate of the riskiness of holding domestic bonds would be represented by an increase in rp in equations (7) and (10). From equation (10), the domestic money supply must be reduced to achieve this increase in the interest rate. If monetary policy does not respond by raising the domestic rate, portfolio holders will continue to move into foreign bonds by selling domestic bonds. To keep the interest rate from rising, the Central Bank would have to buy domestic bonds in exchange for domestic money. Then, to hold the exchange rate as portfolio-holders exchange money for foreign exchange in order to buy foreign bonds, the Central Bank will have to sell foreign exchange reserves. This disequilibrium will continue until the Central Bank permits the domestic interest rate to rise to restore the arbitrage condition, equation (7). Thus for the members that join the exchange-rate arrangements, equation (10) gives the path for monetary policy that will fix e, given the various sources of financial disturbances.

Some of the entrants may come into the EMS with initially high rates of inflation. For example, the rate in Greece was about 20% in 1988. If the rate of inflation itself is not fully flexible, the output cost of reducing inflation to the EC average quickly may be unacceptable. Or, as noted by Dornbusch (1988), Francesco Giavazzi (1989), and others, the high rate of inflation may play an important, if temporary, role in the country's public finance. This would be the case if the marginal cost of rapidly increasing tax effort is high. A rapid decrease in inflation would reduce the inflation tax portion of seigniorage as rapidly. This would require the expansion of normal tax revenue to replace the loss in inflation tax, which might be too costly in the short run. Thus, if a revenue-raising tax reform is planned, but not to take effect immediately, retaining the inflation tax may be desirable in the short run. Thus, some new members may want to bring their inflation rates down gradually, and not join the exchange-rate arrangements immediately.

In these cases, the rate at which inflation can be reduced is controlled by public finance issues, as shown by Ritu Anand and Sweder van Wijnbergen (1989). As the budget deficit is reduced, the rate of inflation needed to close the budget gap is reduced. In terms of the balance between aggregate demand and supply, reduction of the budget deficit reduces demand. By presumption, in these cases the process of inflation reduction takes time. During this adjustment period, the domestic rate of inflation dp in equation (9) can be taken as exogenous, driven by the process of fiscal adjustment. Then the rate of depreciation that maintains goods arbitrage is given by equation (9), with presumably dp and de declining over time. In this case the monetary constraint is given by equation (10) with equation (9) substituted for de:

$$m = e + p^* - b(i^* + dp - dp^* + rp) + ay + x \qquad (11)$$

With de from equation (9) positive, e on the right-hand side of equation (11) is rising relative to p^*, so m is increasing. If the domestic rate of inflation is itself decreasing, dp is falling, so m is growing on that account, too. A successful and anticipated disinflation adds to the demand for domestic money, adding to the required growth rate from equation (11). Thus the constraint expressed in equation (11) for a member that opts for gradual inflation reduction includes both the direct effect of a rising price level and the effect of a falling inflation rate on the demand for domestic money.

With the constraint on monetary policy set by equation (11) for the non-members of the exchange rate arrangements, it is clear that they do not achieve independence for monetary policy by not joining. At each point in time, the nominal rate of the non-member is pegged to the centre. The rate at which it is pegged is moving according to the relative inflation rate, but the rate is not floating. Monetary policy is committed to moving the nominal exchange rate along its prescribed path. Non-members do achieve some independence for the rate at which they reduce their inflation rates, however. If the output cost of a rapid reduction in inflation or the cost of immediate explicit tax reform is high, not joining the exchange-rate arrangements until after the rate of inflation has been reduced to the range of existing members may be preferable to joining the exchange rate arrangements immediately upon entry into the EMS.

6   The role of local financial intermediaries

The constraint on aggregate monetary policy described in Section 5 does not mean that Central Bank policy can have no effect on economic activity in individual members of the EMS, even with completely open capital markets. Recent empirical work on the importance of local intermediaries as sources of finance for small firms in the US has shown that only the largest firms have access to non-bank sources of debt financing, that is, the bond market. Recent theoretical work on asymmetric information and costs of monitoring borrowers' activity provides a basis for the view that a concentration of local intermediation on smaller firms is not an 'imperfection' of the financial markets, but rather an equilibrium result once the assumption of complete and costless information is abandoned.

Consideration of these factors leads to a structure in which large entities trade on open international financial markets, constraining aggregate monetary policy, but local intermediaries stand between local depositors and borrowers and the international market, with a form of market power locally. In this case, the domestic financial system contains a spectrum of instruments and agents, ranging from large agents trading internationally known instruments on integrated international markets to local agents trading instruments with costly local knowledge. The latter can be considered to be non-traded internationally, and the Central Bank can affect their relative returns or availability, and therefore local activity. This section of the paper outlines a typical theoretical structure, summarizes the empirical evidence, and draws some preliminary conclusions for the potential effectiveness of locally-targeted monetary or credit policy. Fazzari *et al.* (1988) provide a brief survey of the theoretical literature and empirical evidence of the relevance of local intermediation and the resulting financing constraint on investment in the US.

One example of a theoretical structure that provides a role for local intermediaries and non-traded assets is presented in Montgomery (1988). In his model, local lenders have an advantage over foreign intermediaries in monitoring local borrowers. The cost of monitoring is lower for local lenders. Montgomery makes monitoring by foreign lenders prohibitively expensive, but this is not necessary for the essence of the model. The local intermediary incurs a significant fixed cost in establishing its business, including the capacity to monitor locally. The fixed cost gives it market power, because once it is incurred, it deters entry by other potential local lenders. In Montgomery's model, the local intermediary is a monopolist, but that too is inessential.

The local intermediary, and local savers, can transact on an international capital market at given interest rates. This can be thought of as an international market in the debt of governments, banks, and large corporations. On it, local intermediaries can borrow or lend, savers lend, and governments borrow. However, because of the cost of monitoring local firms, they do not enjoy access to the international market. The international interest rate is the i^* of Section 5, and the rate on domestic government and large-scale business debt is the i of Section 5. They are linked by the arbitrage condition of equation (7). The local intermediary may also be able to borrow freely at this rate plus a fixed premium, or it may face an upward-sloping supply curve of funds on the international market.

Domestic savers can hold deposits earning i_d at the local intermediary or government debt at the rate i that is fixed by the international arbitrage condition. Local deposits are assumed to have a liquidity value relative to international debt, so the rate the intermediary pays for them, i_d, is less than the international rate i. Montgomery assumes that the differential $i - i_d$ is fixed, but again this is inessential. In the model below, we will assume that the monetary authority sets i_d by regulation.

The local intermediary lends to local borrowers at a rate i_l that is above the international arbitrage rate i. This reflects the market power of the local intermediary. Local investors' demand for loans increases with the marginal product of their investment projects, and decreases as the lending rate i_l increases. The spread between the loan and deposit rates must be large enough to justify the intermediary's investment in monitoring ability plus the cost of any international borrowing it does to service the local market, and yield the profit that keeps it in the business.

In this situation, the local intermediary stands between the international market and the local investor due to the high cost of monitoring the activities of the local investor from afar. The local intermediary must enjoy some degree of market power to exist, that is, to justify sinking the costs needed to do the monitoring, and it acquires market power by sinking those costs, deterring entry by potential competitors. The monopoly or oligopoly position of the local intermediary *vis-à-vis* local investors will generate political pressure on the monetary authority or the government to regulate the intermediary's activities. This pressure will be justified by the natural existence of the intermediary's market power. The monetary authority, through its regulation, can influence the amount of local lending done by the intermediary, and therefore local economic activity. Regulation can be through reserve requirements, credit ceilings or more direct credit surveillance, or by setting deposit rates. All of the new entrants into the EC use some such form of regulation of local intermediaries.

The macroeconomic representation of the model of local intermediation can be adapted from the model with non-traded assets in Branson (1976). Local savers allocate their total relevant financial wealth between holdings of the internationally-traded asset and deposits, which they hold for transactions purposes. This gives us a deposit function of the form

$$D = D(i, i_d, Y) \tag{12}$$

where the rate on international assets i is determined by the arbitrage condition (7), deposits decrease as i rises and increase as i_d or income Y rises. We assume here that regulation takes the form of the authority setting the deposit rate i_d.

The intermediary has a demand for international loans that depends positively on the domestic loan rate i_l and negatively on the rate at which it borrows i_b, and it faces a supply that is increasing in i_b and a variable z which represents all other influences on supply:

$$f(i_l, i_b) = g(i_b, z) \tag{13a}$$

A natural simplification would be to assume that the borrowing rate is fixed at a premium v over i, which would replace (13a) by

$$i_b = i + v \tag{13b}$$

The intermediary then lends deposits plus the proceeds of international borrowing to local borrowers:

$$D + f(i_l, i_b) = L(i_l, q) \tag{14}$$

Here L is the local demand for loans and q represents the marginal product of investment projects.

The structure of the solution of the model should be clear. Given the deposit rate, deposits are determined by equation (12). Then equations (13a) and (14) together determine the loan rate and the rate at which the local intermediaries borrow on the international market. Or, if that rate is fixed by equation (13b), equation (14) determines the loan rate. The latter can be put into the loan demand function to determine local borrowing. In this model, an increase in the deposit rate, the supply of international lending represented by an increase in z, or an increase in q will increase local borrowing and investment. Thus by controlling the deposit rate, the monetary authority can influence the level of investment by that segment of local economic activity that does not have direct access to the international capital market, that is, must borrow through the local intermediary.

Fazzari *et al.* (1988) show that this 'financial hierarchy' model is relevant within the US, and that its implied financing constraint influences investment. Their focus is on the role of retained earnings as a source of investment finance for firms that are too small to have access to the corporate bond market within the US. In the model described above, retained earnings would also be an important source, since firms must borrow from the local intermediary at a rate above their own internal rate of return, and cannot borrow on the international market at all. The firms' managers presumably have better knowledge of their prospective returns than the intermediary does, so part of the premium charged by the intermediary is due to this information asymmetry. Thus, in our model, firms prefer to finance with retained earnings, and will increase investment with an increase in retained earnings, as well as with an increase in the availability of funds from the intermediary.

Sources of funds, by size of manufacturing firm, in the US are summarized in Table 5.4, taken from Fazzari *et al.* There, size is measured by total assets. The next-to-last column of the table shows that firms with assets under $100 million did 75 percent of their borrowing from banks. As size increases to over $1 billion in assets, the share of banks in total borrowing falls to 13 percent. As Fazzari *et al.* point out, in the US banks are lending institutions that specialize in monitoring borrowers through ongoing customer relationships. Banks are the local intermediaries in the model presented here. The last column of the table shows the fraction of total earnings that are retained, that is not paid out as dividends. This 'retention ratio' falls from 79 percent for the smallest firms to 52 percent for the largest, suggesting the importance of retained earnings for the small firms.

Fazzari *et al.* go on to test the importance of the financing constraint in several models of investment spending. Cash flow is a highly significant variable for all sizes of firms, and its effect on investment spending is significantly greater for smaller firms. The points for Fazzari *et al.* were that in the US the financing hierarchy model holds, and that investment spending is finance-constrained. The point for the EC and, especially for the new entrants, is that this constraint in the US does not come from 'market imperfections' that take the form of barriers against lending to small firms, or legal barriers to their financing on the capital markets. The constraint arises naturally from the asymmetry of information between borrowers and lenders. These asymmetries must be greater across the EC than in the US, and even greater in the new entrants, with their relatively less-developed capital markets.

Two major points emerge from the discussion of finance-constrained investment in a financing hierarchy generated by intrinsic information asymmetries. First, the local monetary authorities will retain some degree of influence over local investment activity via their control over the local

Firm size	Source of funds (percent of total)[a]				Percentage of long-term debt from banks	Percentage of total debt from banks	Average retention ratio
	Short-term bank debt	Long-term bank debt	Other long-term debt	Retained earnings			
All firms	0.6	8.4	19.9	71.1	29.6	31.1	0.60
Asset class							
Under $10 million	5.1	12.8	6.2	75.9	67.3	74.3	0.79
$10–50 million	5.9	17.4	6.9	69.8	71.6	77.2	0.76
$50–100 million	3.1	12.9	5.3	78.7	71.0	75.1	0.68
$100–250 million	−0.2	13.3	12.0	74.9	52.4	52.2	0.63
$250 million–$1 billion	−2.3	10.6	15.4	76.3	40.8	35.0	0.56
Over $1 billion	−0.6	4.8	27.9	67.9	14.7	13.1	0.52

Table 5.4. Sources of funds for US manufacturing firms, by asset class, 1970–84

[a] Funds raised from new equity issues are excluded from the calculations.

Source: Authors' calculations based on data taken from U.S. Department of Commerce, Bureau of the Census, Quarterly Financial Reports of Manufacturing, Mining, and Trade Corporations, various issues. The data underlying the calculations are expressed in 1982 dollars.

intermediaries, essentially the local banking system. The quantitative importance of this point is not clear, however. Fazzari *et al.* show that the financing constraint is quantitatively important in the US, but it is not clear whether this means that local Federal Reserve Banks can systematically and differentially influence investment spending in their districts. Presumably for some time information asymmetries and the resulting market segmentations will be stronger in the EC than in the US, so EC central banks will retain more local power than the local Federal Reserve Banks have. Second, the governments and monetary authorities in the member countries, especially the ones with less developed financial systems, cannot be indifferent to the existence and health of local intermediaries. A main point of the literature on information asymmetries and financing constraints is that investment spending is likely to exhibit sharp reactions to swings in income that disturb cash flow and local lending. In these cases, as Fazzari *et al.* put it, 'A "financial collapse" may occur, in which some or all classes of asymmetric-information borrowers are denied loans' (p. 153). If local intermediaries are taken over by international banks, there is the risk that small local borrowers will be screened out of the market, at least in the short run, until a new equilibrium market structure is established. This may appropriately be a policy concern for the local government.

7   Structural reform in the financial sector

In addition to the intrinsic problems caused by asymmetric information, the banking systems in the new entrants into the EC generally had administered interest rates and credit rationing to favoured sectors of the economy at the time of entry. This was true at least for Greece and Portugal, and is now the case in Turkey. Thus entry into the EC required reform of the banking system even prior to the 1992 legislation. This reform is more urgent in the light of the role of the local intermediary discussed in Section 6. In this section, the consequences of the prior existence of financial repression are discussed, and some guidelines for a reform policy are suggested.

The current structure of financial markets in the new entrants generally reflects a history of government intervention. The forms of government intervention have included credit preference for large-scale enterprise and agriculture, and episodes of financial repression and credit rationing. These result in a type of dualism in the industrial sector, with an over-capitalized large-scale sector, partly in public hands, and a small-scale, labour-intensive private sector. This dual structure poses difficulties as financial markets are liberalized. Rising real interest rates will increase the cost of capital to previously-subsidized, large-scale industries. This will threaten possible failures in the private sector, or an explicit drain on the government budget to the extent they are in the public sector. This, in turn, could cause difficulties for macroeconomic stabilization. Liberalization can also provide an increase in lower-cost credit to the small-scale sectors that were earlier not favoured by government intervention. These may then increase their capital-intensity by shedding labour. The result could be a combination of business failures or budget deficits and rising unemployment that threatens the liberalization policy itself. Thus, a sudden lurch toward liberalization could so destabilize the economy of the new entrant in the short run that long-run benefits are never obtained. This suggests that the liberalization policy should be carefully designed to prevent such destabilization. This is likely to be difficult if the liberalization is thrust on the financial system by external events such as entry into the EC. Therefore, the governments of new entrants may want to have their well-considered liberalization programs well in train *before* the refreshing winds of EC financial competition begin to blow too hard!

The risk to the financial system of the new entrant to the EC of 1992 are exacerbated by the tendency for a high fraction of 'non-performing' loans in the portfolio of the local commercial banking system. In several of the new entrants, arrears in the service of 'non-performing' loans seem to be a significant and increasing problem. Portugal, at the time of entry, was an example. In the Portuguese reporting system, non-performing debts were reported in three categories of 'bad and doubtful debts'. The total of such debts was 10.2 percent of all domestic credit at the end of 1983 for the commercial banks, and 7.3 percent for the savings and investment banks. (See Branson, 1985, pp. 15–16 for details, and World Bank, 1988, chapter 4, for the case of Turkey.) Equity was significantly smaller than bad and doubtful debts, 3.7 and 6.2 percent of domestic credit, respectively. So one could have said that the banking system in Portugal was formally, if only implicitly, bankrupt. A similar situation existed in Greece in 1981, and exists in Turkey in 1989.

The data, however, presents the most minimal view of the problem. Data on bad and doubtful debt generally include only debtors that are in arrears for varying durations on principal payments. Thus they do not include two major categories of non-performing loans: (a) those formally in arrears on interest payments but not amortization, (b) those large (but bad) borrowers for whom the banks are capitalizing the arrears into new loans. Inclusion of these non-performing loans would increase the total of 'bad and doubtful' debt significantly. The exact amount is of course unknown. Boissieu (1984, p. 26) put the proportion at 32–40% of the total portfolio for the commercial banks in Portugal. A conservative estimate from a commercial banker who cited this as the most serious problem facing the banking system was 20%. Thus estimates of the aggregate of non-performing loans were a multiple of equity, anywhere from 3 to 5 times the level of equity. In this new entrant, the banking system was a potential source of serious instability.

As the banks capitalize debt service, their portfolios of bad loans grow. With positive real interest rates, deposits grow at roughly the same rate as interest earnings are written into deposits. Thus the entire system could appear to be growing stably in real terms, with the central bank providing the necessary growth in real reserves, but the growth might be on a base of bad debt. A major explicit failure of an industrial firm could expose its major creditor bank and begin a run of depositors out of that bank into others. This provides one incentive for banks to keep a bubble growing by not declaring bankruptcy against any major borrower. This practice is well known in Portugal, Greece, and Turkey.

The non-performing loan problem also contributes to the interest spread. As bad debts rise, banks will increase their interest charges on successful borrowers. This will partially compensate for losses on bad debts. The spread will tend to rise, depressing investment and increasing the problem of potential financial instability. The dynamic forces generally point to the development of an unstable growth path.

A gradual expansion of demand in the economies of the new entrants is necessary to create the conditions for stabilizing the situation of the banking system. If firms that would be solvent under normal demand conditions could meet their debt service, the banks could institute a gradual program of declaring bankruptcy against the minority of nonviable firms. This would have to be part of a policy package that would progressively clean the balance sheets of the banks while the government maintains its implicit guarantee of deposits. Mergers of smaller banks and sales of existing banks to newly entering foreign banks as conditions of entry could also be part of the package. It seems essential that a program to stabilize the banking sector in the new entrants be instituted, especially before competition from EC Banks becomes too severe.

The potential instability in the financial system in the new entrants could be exacerbated by the entry of major foreign banks into competition with the local intermediaries. Entry requires the banking system to be opened to competition from the EC countries, with free entry after 7 years. The 1992 legislation will further reduce barriers to entry. In most countries, the process of entry and expansion of potential competition has already begun.

Normally, competition from abroad would provide a welcome stimulus to a sheltered domestic industry, and in the end be expected to increase efficiency. However, the foreign entrants do not have the burden of non-performing loans that the banks in the new entrants have. Even though foreign banks lack broad networks for attracting deposits, they can be expected to grow, and new entrants will appear. With better profit situations, the new banks can attract large depositors with favourable terms. With modern banking technology and a perception by borrowers of greater stability than the domestic banks, the new entrants may draw the better loan customers away from the local intermediaries. This would further weaken the position of the domestic banking system, which in some cases is already effectively bankrupt. The probability of a major financial failure simply increases.

It thus appears urgent that the financial sector in the new entrants be reformed and the existing stock of bad debt be consolidated and cleared off the balance sheets of the local banks *before* widespread competition from EC banks begins to undermine their position further. Once their balance sheets are cleared up, the monetary authorities might consider consolidation or merger of some units with entering foreign banks as part of a broader package of reform in the financial sector.

Reform of bankruptcy law and proceedings may also be an essential part of the reform package, at least in Greece, Portugal, and Turkey. The existing system of arrears grew up because major units are not allowed to become bankrupt. Banks may proceed quickly against small debtors, but they capitalize the arrears of large debtors into new loans. This weakens the financial structure. It also engenders the belief that major firms will not be allowed to enter bankruptcy, weakening financial incentives. Thus the bankruptcy law seems to require revision such that non-viable firms are taken into proceedings by their creditors, and that the proceedings be reasonably swift. Effective reform of the law along these lines may require action on the macroeconomic level, as mentioned earlier. Expanding demand is needed to distinguish viable from non-viable firms; in a depression they all make losses. Again, a macro-level framework may be necessary for the success of micro-level reform, and the urgency of the latter is increased by impending competition from EC banks under 1992.

8   An integrated EC fiscal system?

The limited scope for monetary policy to stabilize income in the member countries, especially under the combination of the EMS and 1992, throws the weight of stabilization against relative real disturbances onto fiscal policy and factor mobility. The EC lacks a unified fiscal system that could automatically cushion incomes against such disturbances and prevent them from setting off unstable spirals as described in Section 1. This places an even larger burden on factor mobility. The need for a unified fiscal system was described by Kenen (1969). This will be discussed below. More recently, Giuseppe Bertola (1989) has strengthened Kenen's case by showing the positive interaction between a stabilizing fiscal policy and factor mobility.

Bertola presents an interesting exploration of the connections between recent work on factor flexibility under uncertainty and the older literature on optimum currency areas. The research on factor flexibility models the worker facing the choice between remaining in his current occupation or location or moving to another, with income in both uncertain and with fixed moving costs. In this case, the expected income differential that induces movement must exceed the fixed moving cost by an amount that is related to the probability that the agent may want to reverse the movement in the future. In this framework, the pattern of movement exhibits hysteresis. Within a range of expected income differentials, there is no movement, and the width of this range depends positively on the degree of uncertainty. Thus an increase in income uncertainty reduces factor mobility, and feeds back on itself, further increasing uncertainty. Since one criterion for an optimum currency area is factor mobility within, but not between, areas, it seems reasonable that the new results on factor flexibility could put the literature on optimum currency areas on a better footing. Bertola explores this possibility, and implicitly shows how a stabilizing fiscal policy within the EC could increase factor mobility, and reduce the cost of relative real disturbances. His general point is that anything that stabilizes income increases factor mobility, thereby making it easier to stabilize income.

In the basic Mundell–Fleming model of stabilization in an open economy, if monetary policy is targeted toward stabilizing the exchange rate, relative fiscal policy will be effective in stabilizing output. Since any policies that stabilize income make factors more mobile, thus making it easier to stabilize income, the EC–EMS decision to use monetary policy to stabilize the exchange rate will increase the payoff from using fiscal policy to stabilize income. Here increasing returns to stabilization using fiscal policy come from exchange-rate stability obtained by monetary policy. This is most relevant for the EMS and the EC of 1992. With monetary policy tied down by the EMS, adjustment is left to factor mobility and fiscal policy. From Bertola's analysis, we see that stabilizing fiscal policy will generate increasing returns as it increases factor mobility within the area.

In the analysis of the stabilizing role of relative fiscal policy, the important distinction between permanent (or, more precisely, indefinite) and transitory (or temporary) relative real disturbances must be made.

Existing EC policy deals partially with permanent shocks; the transfer mechanisms we are discussing here are more relevant for transitory shocks. An example of a permanent shock would be a technological innovation that makes some line of industry obsolete. This may be happening now in basic steel. In this case, the need is for structural adjustment, closing the obsolete lines of production and redeploying the non-fixed resources, writing off the fixed ones. This calls for a policy of structural adjustment assistance, such as that written into Objective 2 of the 'Objectives and Tasks of the Structual Funds' of the EC (see The Council of the EC, 1988, pp. 9–20).

An example of a temporary shock would be a shift in tastes of consumers among auto models. This will generate a temporary boom in the area producing the favoured model, and a temporary slump in the area producing the disfavoured model. In this case, the auto producers can re-tool and change their product mix, but this takes time, perhaps an entire model year. Here, the need is not for structural adjustment, but for income support for the temporarily redundant workers and their communities. This is the example given in Section 1. Support for incomes is needed in order to prevent an unstable adjustment that becomes a costly structural problem. Here is where the need for relative fiscal policy that stabilizes incomes against transitory disturbances arises.

The importance of the availability of fiscal policy as an instrument to stabilize income was emphasized in a slightly different context by Kenen. He pointed out that in the face of relative real disturbances in the US, the federal fiscal system makes fiscal transfers automatically between the affected areas. When New England is booming and Texas is in a recession, tax payments rise and unemployment benefits and welfare claims fall in New England and the opposite in Texas. The fiscal transfer is made automatically, without a negotiation between the governments of New England and Texas. In fact, the federal fiscal system communicates directly with the affected individuals in the two areas, without going through the intermediation of the state governments. This automaticity of the federal fiscal transfer mechanism led Kenen to add an integrated fiscal system at the area level to the set of criteria for an optimal currency area.

As Europe approaches 1992 with the EMS expanding and capital mobility rapidly increasing, the limited mobility of labour between states, compared to the US, and the virtual non-existence of a fiscal system at the Community level make it seem likely that given relative real disturbances will generate more instability in real incomes than otherwise, and more than within the US. And following Bertola's analysis, this will reduce labour mobility, further destabilizing real incomes. This could lead to political resistance to the further integration of the EC and perhaps to some disintegration. Thus problems of labour immobility and fiscal inflexibility, and their Bertola interactions, deserve prominence on the Community's research and policy agendas.

REFERENCES

Anand, S. and S. van Wijnbergen (1989). 'Inflation and the financing of government expenditure: an introductory analysis with an application to Turkey'. *The World Bank Economic Review* 3, 17–38.

Bertola, G. (1989). 'Factor flexibility, uncertainty, and exchange rate regimes', in M. de Cecco and A. Giovannini (eds.), *A European Central Bank?* Cambridge University Press.

Boissieu, C. de (1984). 'Some reflections on the Portuguese financial system'. Mimeo, World Bank.

Branson, W.H. (1976). 'Portfolio equilibrium and monetary policy with foreign and non-traded assets', in E. Claassen and P. Salin (eds). *Recent Issues in International Monetary Economics*. North-Holland. 241–50.

(1981). 'Monetary stability and exchange rate objectives in Singapore', in Monetary Authority of Singapore (ed.), *Papers on Monetary Economics*. Singapore University Press. 112–29.

(1985). 'Portugal's Entry into the European Communities: Challenges and Opportunities'. Unpublished World Bank report in mimeo.

Branson, W.H. and D.W. Henderson (1985). 'The specification and influence of asset markets', in R.W. Jones and P.B. Kenen (eds.), *Handbook of International Economics*, vol. II. North-Holland. 749–805.

Casella, A. and J. Feinstein (1989). 'Management of a common currency', in M. de Cecco and A. Giovannini (eds.), *A European Central Bank?* Cambridge University Press.

Cohen, D. (1985). 'How to evaluate the solvency of an indebted nation'. *Economic Policy* 1, 139–56.

Dornbusch, R. (1988). 'The European Monetary System, the dollar, and the yen', in F. Giavazzi, S. Micossi and M. Miller (eds.), *The European Monetary System*. Cambridge University Press. 23–41.

Fazzari, S.M., G. Hubbard and B.C. Peterson (1988). 'Financing constraints and corporate investment', *Brookings Papers on Economic Activity* 1, 141–95.

Giavazzi, F. (1989). 'The exchange rate question in Europe', in R.C. Bryant, D.A. Currie, J.A. Frenkel, P.R. Masson and R. Portes (eds.), *Macroeconomic Policies in an Interdependent World*. IMF, Washington. 283–304.

Goodhart, C. (1987). 'Structural changes in the British capital markets', in *The Operation and Regulation of Financial Markets*. Macmillan.

International Monetary Fund (1989). *World Economic Outlook*. Washington, D.C. April.

Kenen , P.B. (1969). 'The theory of optimal currency areas: an eclectic view', in R.A. Mundell and A.K. Swoboda (eds.), *Monetary Problems of the International Economy*. University of Chicago Press. 41–60.

Montgomery, J. (1988). 'Financial intermediation, contracts and international capital mobility'. Mimeo, Princeton University, November.

Mundell, R.A. (1963). 'Capital mobility and stabilization policy under fixed and

flexible exchange rates', *Canadian Journal of Economics and Political Science*
29, 475–85.
Organization for Economic Cooperation and Development (1989). *OECD
Economic Outlook*. Paris. June.
World Bank (1988). 'Evaluation of Structural Adjustment Lending in Turkey'.
Report No. 7205. April 13. Washington.

6 Macroeconomic adjustment and entry into the EC: a note

PAUL R. KRUGMAN

The enlargement of the European Community is in a direct sense concerned with real trade and investment flows, not with macroeconomic policy. In practice, however, the 'EC cum 1992' shock poses macroeconomic challenges as well. The most dramatic consequence of these challenges has been the dilemma of monetary policy in Spain, which has oscillated between restriction intended to curb a growing inflation problem and loose policy designed to keep the peseta from appreciating against other European currencies. Since both objectives cannot be served, neither has been served fully, the result being both an acceleration of inflation and a current account that has moved from modest surplus to substantial deficit.

The purpose of this note is to present a general framework for thinking about the macroeconomic policy dilemmas posed by enlargement for the entering countries. This framework is largely inspired by the case of Spain, as covered in the papers by Viñals (1989) and Viñals et al. (1990). It does not attempt, however, to provide an empirical case study. Instead, its objective is to suggest some underlying structure to the problem.

The note is in four parts. Section 1 reviews some general considerations that set the background for the macroeconomic dilemma. Section 2 discusses what I will argue is the source of the dilemma of macroeconomic policy for new entrants to the EC: uncertainty about the ultimate effect of integration on equilibrium exchange rates. Section 3 discusses the implications of anticipated integration on medium-term capital flows and exchange rates. Finally, Section 4 discusses the short-run monetary policy dilemma.

1   General considerations

The European Economic Community began as a pure trade agreement, without any implied subtext of European monetary coordination or

131

integration. Almost as soon as the Bretton Woods fixed rate system broke down, however, European nations began attempting to establish regional regimes of exchange-rate stability. The surprising success of the Exchange Rate Mechanism of the EMS has persuaded even many doubters that Europe is an optimum currency area, within which exchange rates should change at most rarely or within limited ranges.

Spain joined the ERM on June 19th, 1989; it will probably be reluctant to realign its rate too soon or too often, and the other Southern European countries will probably feel compelled at minimum to shadow the ecu, and eventually to join the ERM as well. There are a variety of reasons militating for close currency ties between the Southern entrants and the EC core:

– The large volume of trade between the Southern countries and the EMS countries means that the costs in terms of risk and uncertainty associated with unstable exchange rates are fairly large;

– The administration of EC programs, notably the Common Agricultural Policy, is considerably complicated by large exchange rate fluctuations;

– Given the freeing up of capital movements that is part of 1992, small countries will have difficulty avoiding eroding use of their currencies (we might call this 'ecuization') unless these currencies have a strongly credible stability in terms of the major currencies[1];

– Finally, all the Southern European countries have recent histories of fairly serious inflation. As in the case of such large countries as Italy and France, they will require a Teutonic anchor to make their future price stability credible.

For all these reasons, it seems clear that the Southern European nations will want to keep their currencies relatively stable in terms of the core EC nations after their entry.

Given this future prospect of stable exchange rates, it becomes important that the entering countries get the initial exchange rates right. In particular, an overvalued initial exchange rate will ensure the necessity of either an embarassing and credibility-threatening early realignment, or a prolonged period of depressed economic activity as monetary policy is obliged to gradually deflate the country relative to the rest of the EC.

The problem, of course, is that nobody is certain about what exchange rates are appropriate, since entry into the EC not only involves large changes in the specific trading relationship between the relevant country and the EC, it involves the entering countries in the massive changes now taking place in the economic relationships among the major European economies. Thus entrants are obliged to fix an exchange rate that they will be reluctant to change, without any accurate way of choosing the right rate.

One might suppose that the best policy in this case would be to take one's best shot: to make the best possible estimate of the post-entry equilibrium real exchange rate, and to set the nominal rate at a level that allows establishment of this real rate without inflation or deflation. This policy recommendation would be appropriate if the costs of getting the price of the ecu too high and those of getting it too low were symmetrical. This is, however, very unlikely. Experience and common sense suggest that the cost of the few years' inflation that would be needed to eliminate a 10 percent undervaluation fall far short of the cost of the prolonged recession that would be needed to correct a 10 percent overvaluation. Thus a commonsensical view is that the entering countries should try to err on the side of undervaluation – to first enter the ERM at exchange rates that will probably turn out to have been undervalued.[2]

In effect, this is the policy that Spain has attempted to follow: to keep the peseta low against the ecu (and the DM in particular) so that Spanish industry will be in a favourable competitive position in the early post-entry years. The problem is that the capital markets try to set the rate at a level that makes sense to them, not at the level that is optimal from a policy point of view. It is this conflict that poses the macroeconomic policy dilemma.

Before turning to this conflict, however, it is useful to take a look at the reasons for uncertainty about the effect of enlargement on equilibrium real exchange rates.

2   Long-run exchange-rate effects of integration

The basic idea of enlargement is that the Southern European countries will remove trade barriers against the EC core products, and the EC core countries will reciprocate. The key macroeconomic question is what this will do to the equilibrium exchange rates of the entrants.

In most models, and for most definitions of the real exchange rate, protection will lead to an appreciation of the equilibrium real exchange rate. The partial equilibrium logic seems obvious: protection reduces imports, other things equal, and will therefore lead to an incipient trade surplus. Unless net capital outflows for some reason increase to offset this, the incipient trade surplus must be offset by a real appreciation that leads to lower exports and/or higher imports in unprotected sectors. The general equilibrium case is a little harder to make, but basically comes out the same (see Dornbusch, 1974).

Since imposing protection ordinarily leads to a real appreciation, removing this protection should normally lead to a real depreciation.

Conversely, a removal of foreign protective barriers against a country's exports should lead to a real appreciation: in partial terms, exports will rise, so unless there is some reason to expect capital outflows to offset this, there will have to be a real appreciation. Essentially, a removal of foreign protection acts in macroeconomic terms just like a rise in demand for an export good; the real exchange rate effects of such an export boom are familiar from the 'Dutch disease' literature (see Corden, 1985, for a survey).

The entry of the Southern European nations into the EC combines a liberalization of imports by the entrants and an opening for their exports by the core nations. The first pushes toward real appreciation; the second toward real depreciation.

Efforts to decide which of these effects predominates are complicated by several cross-cutting considerations:

– First, the visible protective barriers that need to be brought down by the entrants are much higher than those that need to be brought down by the EC core. The reason is partly that the Southern European countries have historically followed much more protectionist and interventionist policies than the North, partly that the special trading arrangements already in force have an element of *noblesse oblige* in which the wealthy core granted concessions to the poorer periphery without demanding comparable concessions in return. Partly because of this asymmetry, the assessment of the initial trade effects of Spanish entry by Viñals *et al.* (1990) stresses the increase in Spanish imports, finding little sign of favourable effects on exports.

– On the other side, however, the huge difference in size between the EC core and the entrants pushes the other way. As stressed in Venables and Krugman (1990), the elasticity of a large country or trading bloc's demand for imports from a small country is likely to be larger than the small country's elasticity, because the large bloc is more likely to produce close substitutes. Thus an equal reciprocal tariff will tend to worsen the small country's trade balance and improve the large bloc's, and will normally require a real depreciation on the part of the small country. Conversely, when a small country joins a trading bloc, it will find its real exchange rate appreciating even if tariff rates were initially the same. Essentially, Spain has more to gain from its union with the EC than the EC has to gain from union with Spain, and this asymmetry should be reflected in the exchange rate.

– Finally, the Southern European countries are entering a changing entity. 1992 may be viewed in part as a general lowering of remaining trade barriers; as such it will tend to lead to real appreciation on the part of the more peripheral regions. (Again see Krugman and Venables, 1990).

Putting all of these together, it is possible to make virtually any case: that with access to the European market, the entrants will be able to appreciate substantially in real terms; that their industry will be unable to compete in an integrated market without a substantial real depreciation; or that not much real adjustment is necessary. What seems clear in the Spanish case is that the *capital markets* have concluded that a substantial real appreciation is likely. The Spanish government, however, is not so sure, and reasonably (as discussed above) would like to err on the side of undervaluation. The result is a policy dilemma.

3 Expectations and the real exchange rate in the medium term

It is useful at this point to introduce a simple formal model of the real exchange rate, capital flows and the balance of payments. This model is a slight variant of that developed by Branson (1985). It takes output as given, and is a wholly real model in which monetary policy has no role to play; however, its conclusions can be readily modified to think about monetary implications, as we will see in the next part of the paper. The model provides a useful peg on which to hang our discussion of the effects of anticipated trade opening.

The Branson model builds on the familiar identity,

Net Exports = Saving − Investment

with the assumption that net exports depend on the real exchange rate, savings and investment on the real interest rate:

$$NX(e) = S(r) - I(r) \tag{1}$$

Assuming the usual signs, equation (1) defines the upward-sloping line *GG* in Figure 6.1.[3]

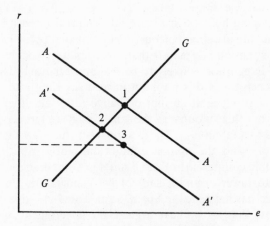

Figure 6.1 Open-economy equilibrium

	1980–85	1986	1987	1988
	%	%	%	%
GDP growth	1.4	3.3	5.5	5.0
Investment growth	−0.9	10.0	14.6	14.0
Consumer prices, increase	12.8	8.8	5.3	4.8
Current account (% of GDP)	−1.0	1.8	0.0	−1.1

Table 6.1. Spanish macroeconomic developments, 1980–88

For a country that is open to capital mobility, NX need to equal zero at any particular moment. Instead, capital will flow until expected yields in different countries are equal up to some risk premium. To a first approximation, we can ignore the risk premia and require that the expected rate of return in this country equal the expected rate of return abroad. Expected rates of return abroad include capital gains resulting from appreciation or depreciation, however, so the equality of expected returns must be written

$$(1 + r) = (1 + r^*)(\hat{e}_{t-1}/e_t) \tag{2}$$

where r^* is the foreign real rate of interest, e_t the current real exchange rate, and $\hat{e}_{t+1}$ the expected real exchange rate next period. This may be rearranged to give the exchange rate equation

$$e_t = \hat{e}_{t+1}(1 + r^*)/(1 + r) \tag{3}$$

Suppose that we simply take $\hat{e}_{t+1}$ as given. Then (3) defines the downward-sloping line AA in Figure 6.1. The real interest rate and the real exchange rate are simultaneously determined at point 1.

The basic situation of Spain is that investors have concluded that the net effect of integration is likely to be real appreciation. (They may not frame their decision in this way, but instead say simply that Spain is a good place to produce at current exchange rates, and therefore worth investing in; but this amounts to the same thing). In terms of the model, this amounts to a fall in $\hat{e}_{t+1}$. The asset-market curve AA therefore shifts down to $A'A'$, and the market equilibrium shifts from 1 to 2. The macroeconomic counterpart of these shifts is a simultaneous investment boom (due to lower r) and a shift of net exports into deficit. This is precisely what has happened in Spain, as indicated in Table 6.1.

But suppose that, as we have argued, the government of the entrant nation does not agree with the market about the appropriate level of the exchange rate. This might occur because the government has a different assessment, but equally it may occur, as already stressed, because the market is interested in the mean, while the government prefers with good reason to err on the side of undervaluation in the face of considerable uncertainty. Then the appreciation associated with the move from 1 to 2 will not be welcome. The government will then be tempted to try to use monetary policy to hold down the currency. In terms of Figure 6.1, it looks as though it could do this by keeping the real interest rate low, so as to get the economy to point 3. However, this implies an excess of investment over savings plus net exports, which cannot happen; something must give.

What gives in the first instance is output. Since output is not truly fixed in the short run, an incipient excess of investment over planned savings at the initial interest rate will be reflected in an expansion of the domestic economy. In the slightly longer run, this expansion gets reflected in inflation.

To look at the role of monetary policy more easily, however, it is useful to switch models slightly and look at the problem in terms of a model in which money is explicitly introduced.

4   Money and exchange-rate policy

We can now turn to the role of monetary policy. For this purpose we can think in terms of a slight variant of the Mundell–Fleming model.[4] Prices are taken as predetermined at any point in time, so that output may vary in response to changes in demand. There is an *IS* curve, relating demand for domestic output to the nominal interest rate and the nominal exchange rate:

$$y = A(i, E) \tag{4}$$

There is also an *LM* curve, relating real money demand to output and interest rates:

$$M/P = L(y, i) \tag{5}$$

Finally, capital mobility ensures that the domestic interest rate must equal the foreign rate plus expected depreciation:

$$(1 + i) = (1 + i^*)(\hat{E}_{t+1}/E_t)$$

or

$$i = \bar{\imath} = (1 + i^*)(\hat{E}_{t+1}/E_t) - 1 \tag{6}$$

As emphasized by Branson (1990), in this kind of model – which Europe is increasingly approaching – there is no room for separate

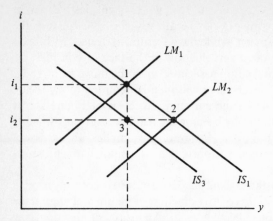

Figure 6.2   The monetary consequences of expected appreciation

monetary and exchange-rate policies. Either one sets a target for the money supply, or an exchange-rate, never both.

In Figure 6.2, we draw the *IS* curve IS_1 conditional on some initial exchange rate E_1. Given E_1, i_1 is the initial interest rate consistent with (6). In order to fix the exchange rate at E_1, the monetary authority must choose a money supply that produces the *LM* curve LM_1. If it does, the economy is in equilibrium at point 1.

Now suppose that prospects of European integration lead investors to expect a future appreciation of the currency. Then the interest rate consistent with the exchange rate falls to i_2. Clearly the monetary authority must make a decision. If it wants to keep the exchange rate unchanged, it must expand the money supply, so as to produce the *LM* curve LM_2. The new equilibrium at point 2, however, will have higher output than at point 1. If the economy was already operating at its non-accelerating-inflation level of output, then this will be inflationary; this inflation will over time undercut the effort to maintain competitiveness. On the other hand, if the monetary authority attempts to avoid an inflationary increase in demand it must accept an appreciation of the currency.[5]

Assuming that the monetary authority dislikes both inflation and appreciation, it is caught in a dilemma.

The only way out of this dilemma without imposing capital controls is through tight fiscal policy. Suppose that the central government can raise taxes and/or cut spending, shifting the *IS* curve to the left at any given exchange rate. Then it can reduce the size of the expansion in money and output required to stabilize the exchange rate. Ideally, a fiscal contraction that pushed the *IS* curve all the way back to IS_3 would allow the stabilization of both output and the exchange rate at point 3.

It is worth turning briefly to the Spanish case to get some idea of the orders of magnitude involved. As pointed out in Table 5.1, Spain's current account balance went from a surplus of 1.8 percent of GDP in 1986 to a deficit of 1.1 percent in 1988; given the continuing deterioration of the trade figures, Goldman, Sachs (1989) predicts a deficit of 3.3 percent of GDP in 1989. It should be recalled that this took place in spite of a fairly determined effort to prevent the exchange rate from appreciating, an effort that led to an acceleration of inflation from 4.4 percent in mid-1988 to 7.1 percent in mid-1989. It follows that in order to avoid any real deterioration of the current account, Spain would have to have had a huge fiscal contraction – in excess of 5 percentage points of GDP.

5   Conclusions

This note has offered a framework for thinking about the macroeconomic dilemmas faced by Spain, in particular, in its effort to enter smoothly into the ERM; difficulties that will probably also arise for other entrants. In essence, it argues that the dilemmas arise from the conflict between the reasonable exchange rate goals of the entrant's government and the expectations of the market. The government, faced with great uncertainty about the appropriate exchange rate, reasonably prefers to err on the side of undervaluation. Investors, however, have no such incentive and try to drive the currency up toward its expected future level.

Monetary policy alone cannot resolve this conflict. A monetary policy that attempts to preserve a competitive exchange rate leads to inflation; a policy that attempts to control inflation leads to a riskily strong currency. A policy that oscillates between these goals gets a little of both problems.

Aside from capital controls, the only available recourse is fiscal tightening. A rough calculation for Spain suggests, however, that only a very severe fiscal contraction could resolve the dilemma.

NOTES

1 One might make a counter-argument: that fluctuating exchange rates make diversification attractive, and thus increase the demand for small-country currencies. This is so, however, only if the additional hedging demand for the small-country currencies by large-country residents exceeds the flight from these currencies by risk-averse small-country residents – which seems unlikely.

2 Much of the macroeconomic welfare analysis of the 1970s and 1980s, which tended to view positive and negative deviations from the natural rate of unemployment as equally harmful, would seem to contradict this view. The new

revival of Keynesian economics, however, with its stress on imperfect competition and coordination failures, restores the traditional view that more output is usually good. The reason is that the same externalities among price setters that lead to the possibility of economic slumps also imply that the economy *normally* produces too little and has too many workers unemployed. See Blanchard and Fischer (1988) for a survey.

3 It would of course be possible to introduce other factors, notably fiscal policy, explicitly into the *S* and *I* functions. Their role is however clear, and we will be able to consider the role of fiscal policy in a straightforward fashion in the next section.

4 Alogoskoufis (1989) has pointed out that there are some differences in behaviour between macroeconomic models that simplify a trading economy by imagining that it produces only one good, as in the Mundell–Fleming approach, in which real exchange rates and terms of trade are the same thing; and those that take a 'dependent economy' approach in which the economy's terms of trade are taken as given, but the relative price of nontraded goods can vary. He also presents evidence that for Greece, at least, the dependent economy model is a much better approximation. The points made here are easier to see in the one-good model, however; a restatement in terms of a dependent economy model would be straightforward but time-consuming.

5 It is straightforward to show in this case that a policy of keeping the money supply completely unchanged would actually lead to a *contraction* of output. So even to keep output the same would mean some expansion of the money supply, but not as much as is required to avoid appreciation.

REFERENCES

Alogoskoufis, G. (1989). 'Macroeconomic policy and the external constraint in the dependent economy: the case of Greece', CEPR Discussion Paper No. 330.

Blanchard, O. and S. Fischer (1988). *Lectures on Monetary Theory*, Cambridge: MIT Press.

Branson, W. (1985). 'Causes of appreciation and volatility of the dollar', in Federal Reserve Bank of Kansas City, *The US Dollar: Prospects and Policy Options*.
    (1990). 'Financial market integration, macroeconomic policy, and the EMS', this volume.

Corden, W.M. (1985). 'Booming Sector and Dutch Disease Economics: Survey and Consolidation', in *Protection, Growth and Trade*. Oxford: Basil Blackwell.

Dornbusch, R. (1974). 'Tariffs and nontraded goods', *Journal of International Economics* **4**, 177–85.

Goldman, Sachs (1989). *The International Economics Analyst*, July/August.

Krugman, P. and A. Venables (1989). 'Integration and the competitiveness of peripheral industry', this volume.

Viñals, J. (1989). 'Europe's capital account shock', prepared for CEPR project on North–South integration in the enlarged European Community.

Viñals, J. *et al.* (1990). 'Spain and the "EC cum 1992" shock', this volume.

Discussion of chapters 5 and 6

VITOR GASPAR

Branson's and Krugman's papers share a concern with the macro-economic consequences of the increased integration of new entrants' economies into the EC. Both stress the importance and nature of macroeconomic policy constraints and identify remaining options for the national policy makers. Furthermore both point to the central role of public sector budget balances.

In different ways both papers contribute substantially to the understanding of the macroeconomic environment in which the new entrants' economies will have to perform.

The purpose of this comment is only to pursue some of the points raised in the two papers. The note will present an alternative to the mechanism of macroeconomic adjustment put forward by Krugman. Then, it provides some remarks on Branson's assessment of the sustainability of fiscal deficits based on the intertemporal nature of government budget constraints.

1 Macroeconomic adjustment to economic integration

Krugman's paper proposes a very interesting story. Uncertainty about the long-run equilibrium exchange rate and asymmetric costs for nominal and real adjustments make it preferable for new entrants to have an undervalued currency. One way to make specific this general remark is simply to assume that the adjustment of the real sectors of the economy determines a target for the real exchange rate. Then, different beliefs about the evolution of capital markets – modelled as an exogenous shift in future exchange rate expectations – induce an appreciation of the national currency.

Given that the national policy maker would like to keep the exchange rate stable the tendency towards appreciation leads to increased money supply and inflationary pressures. If one assumes that monetary policy is the only available instrument then the policy maker is confronted with a dilemma: nominal exchange-rate appreciation or inflation. But, given the nominal exchange-rate path, which is determined with reference to the exchange-rate mechanism of the European Monetary System, inflation means real appreciation. Therefore, there is no choice but real appreciation.

141

This story is certainly persuasive and it seems to agree with recent experience of the Spanish economy. Nevertheless, the expectations of the future exchange rate should be an endogenous variable and exogenous reasons should be found to motivate the outcome of the model. Such is the purpose of this comment.

One may start by writing the balance between income and expenditure on domestic goods (*IS* equation) as:

$$y = (e - p + p^*)h - i(r - \dot{p}) + (g - s) \tag{1}$$

where y is the log of income, e the log of the nominal exchange rate, p the log of the domestic price level, p^* the log of the foreign price level. Therefore, $(e - p + p^*)$ is the real exchange rate representing the relative price of foreign to domestic goods. Also, r is the domestic nominal interest rate on bonds, a dot denotes a time derivative so that $\dot{p}$ is the domestic inflation rate, and $i(.)$, g and s are shift factors associated with investment, public deficits and private savings respectively. In the initial equilibrium $i(.) = g = s = 0$. Finally, h represents the real exchange rate elasticity of domestic goods expenditure ($h > 0$).

Following Krugman, the (uncovered) interest rate parity will be used which may be written as:

$$r = r^* + \dot{e} + \delta \tag{2}$$

where r^* is the interest rate on foreign bonds, $\dot{e}$ the rate of depreciation of the national currency, and δ reflects risk premium and transaction costs.

Monetary equilibrium is represented in a conventional *LM* equation as:

$$m - p = \gamma y - \omega r \tag{3}$$

where m is the log of the nominal money supply and γ and ω are parameters. One simple way to close the model is to assume super-neutrality, that is a perfectly inelastic aggregate supply:

$$y = \bar{y} \tag{4}$$

In a steady state all real variables will be constant. In particular, the real money supply will be constant assuring that:

$$\dot{m} = \dot{p} = \pi \tag{5}$$

On the other hand, the constancy of the real exchange rate implies that:

$$\dot{e} = \pi - \pi^* \tag{6}$$

where π^* is the foreign inflation rate. Substituting (6) into (2) one gets:

$$r = r^* + (\pi - \pi^*) + \delta \tag{7}$$

Equation (6) means that the purchasing power parity and equation (7) that the open-economy Fisher relation both hold in a steady state.

One may therefore use (5), (6), and (7) in (1) to solve for the steady state equilibrium real exchange rate:

$$e - p + p^* = \frac{\bar{y} + i(r^* - \pi^* + \delta) - g + s}{h} \tag{8}$$

One interesting feature of equation (8) is that it allows one to discuss some likely consequences for a new entrant of increasing monetary and financial integration. First, the integration process is likely to decrease the risk premium and transaction costs – a decrease in δ. And from (8) it is apparent that a decrease in δ causes a decrease in the real exchange rate, $(e - p + p^*)$.

Another possible rationalization for the same phenomenon (mentioned by Krugman) would be simply to assume that investors believe that the growing integration of a new country into the EC makes such a country a good place to invest – an autonomous shift in the $i(.)$ function. This shift would also bring a real appreciation of the national currency. The similarity of results is not at all surprising because both stories may be interpreted as reflecting an increased substitutability between domestic and foreign assets and a general fall in transaction costs (given that capital is relatively scarce in the new entrant's economy).

Furthermore, if appreciation of the national currency is regarded as undesirable, equation (8) suggests two possible ways to counteract this outcome, by causing the domestic currency to depreciate: a program of fiscal restraint (as suggested in Krugman's paper); and stimulation of private savings.

2   Sustainability of public sector budget deficits

The remarks in Branson's paper concerning public debt dynamics and the sustainability of fiscal deficits are based on:

$$\dot{b}_t = (r_t - n_t)b_t - s_t - \frac{1}{v}\rho_t \tag{9}$$

where b is the debt to GDP ratio, r is the interest rate, n is the real growth rate of national GDP, s is the primary surplus (disregarding interest payments) to GDP ratio, v is the income velocity of money and ρ the growth rate of the money supply. The ultimate criterion for sustainability of a given deficit is its compatibility with the intertemporal budget constraint for the public sector. To see this, one has to integrate (9) to obtain:

$$b_t = b_0 \exp \int_0^t (r_v - n_v) dv - \int_0^t S_\tau \left[\exp \int_0^{t-\tau} (r_v - n_v) dv \right] d\tau \quad (10)$$

where $S_t = s_t + \dfrac{1}{v} \rho_t$.

Assuming asymptotic boundedness on public debt, which prevents it from growing faster than the discount factor $(r - n)$, one may write:

$$\lim_{t \to \infty} b_t \left[\exp \left(- \int_0^t (r_v - n_v) dv \right) \right] = 0 \quad (11)$$

then rearranging (10) and using (11) one obtains:

$$b_0 = \int_0^\infty S_\tau \left[\exp \left(- \int_0^\tau (r_v - n_v) dv \right) \right] d\tau \quad (12)$$

Equation (12) is the public sector intertemporal budget constraint, meaning simply that the initial public debt to GDP ratio has to equal the discounted present value of primary surpluses (including seigniorage revenues) to GDP ratios, the discount factor being the difference between the interest rate and the growth rate of the economy.

It should be noticed that in using (9) one has implicitly assumed away liquidity constraints. The existence of liquidity constraints would make the sustainability criterion for the path of the public sector budget more stringent than what is implied by (12) alone.

There is something to be gained in using (12) instead of (10). First, (12) is fully compatible with Ramsey type models in which the interest rate exceeds the growth rate of the economy. Notice that the transversality condition (12) is not appealing at all if $(r < n)$. Secondly (12) gives full meaning to the remark made by Branson that unsustainability simply means that adjustments in the intertemporal pattern of public sector budgetary policies (perhaps drastic) is required. Since the intertemporal public sector budget constraint has to be met somehow that is exactly what should be expected. Thirdly, (12) shows that, although anticipating revenues by correspondingly increasing future liabilities has potentially large effects on reported deficits, this should be of no concern when analyzing the public sector balance component of fiscal adjustment programs.

7 Spain and the 'EC cum 1992' shock

JOSÉ VIÑALS *et al.*

1 Introduction

The major recent change in the Spanish economy has been its opening up to the rest of the world and specifically to the European Community. Although the internationalization of the economy first started when autarky ended in 1959, it is only now that Spain is really becoming an open economy – at least relative to Community countries. In this regard, the integration of Spain into the EC in 1986 and the forthcoming vast economic reforms associated with the 1992 European Internal Market are major anticipated permanent shocks with both real and financial elements which constitute both a challenge and an opportunity. Consequently, it is of critical importance to identify which main economic issues are raised by the 'EC cum 1992' integration shock so that potential problems may be identified and suitable policies may be implemented at the appropriate times.

Spain's full integration into the EC has short, medium and long-term[1] effects. The long term is the appropriate horizon to assess the potential gains to be made from the integration process. This paper, however, concentrates on the transitional period associated with the short and medium term, when most of the costs of adjustment to the new structure will have to be borne. Specifically, this paper analyzes the likely effects on the Spanish economy resulting from the opening up of the current account, the opening up of the capital account and the establishment of free banking and a free supply of financial services. In this regard, the main conceptual questions to be answered are the following:

First, what are the major opportunities and problems for Spain associated with EC integration? Are they more likely to come from the opening up of the current account, from the opening up of the capital account or, rather, from the free establishment of banking and the free supply of financial services envisaged to take place in 1993? That is, do the major opportunities and problems have mainly a real origin, in trade flows and industrial structure, or a financial origin, in capital flows and financial structure?

Second, what specific structural characteristics of goods, factors and financial markets seem to contribute most to the problems mentioned above?

And third, how far can automatic market mechanisms (e.g. autonomous labour and capital flows, exchange-rate flexibility) be trusted to take adequate care of the problems envisaged? What should be the appropriate policy responses to reduce the short-run costs of integration without simultaneously preventing the economy from making desirable long-run adjustments?

In order to answer these questions adequately, the paper is organized as follows: Section 2 gives a compact view of the Spanish economy at the time of EC membership and describes the major structural characteristics and initial conditions of the markets most directly affected by the liberalization of the current account (goods and labour markets), by the liberalization of the capital account, and by the freedom of banking and the free supply of financial services (financial markets). Section 3 analyzes the pattern of structural adjustment in the Spanish economy that results from Spain's EC membership when account is taken of the changes envisaged for 1992. Section 4 looks at the relative roles of automatic market adjustment mechanisms and of economic policy in helping the economy adjust in the optimal way to the new situation. Finally, Section 5 summarizes the conclusions.

The review of the structural characteristics of the Spanish economy prior to the 'EC cum 1992' shock carried out in Section 2 indicates that Spain's relatively less open current account and rigid labour markets, its relatively more open capital account, and its solvent, although not too efficient, financial systems, are likely to lead to larger adjustment costs in goods and labour markets than in financial markets as a result of the 'EC cum 1992' shock. Nevertheless, given the close links existing between banks and industry, bad industrial performance could cause financial distress.

The analysis of Section 3 shows that Spain may enjoy substantial long-term economic benefits from its full integration into the EC. On the one hand, since approximately half of Spain-EC trade is inter-industry trade, overall gains can be made by exploiting Spain's comparative advantage in the production of relatively labour-intensive products. On the other hand, since intra-industry trade is also important and since Spain's industrial firms have an insufficient size and low technology, the country can further increase the long-run gains by benefiting from increasing competition and from the exploitation of scale and scope economies. Consequently, while Spain should exploit its comparative advantage by moving towards being a net exporter of broad categories of labour-intensive goods, scale and scope economies should also be exploited by specializing within each of these broad categories of goods in certain specific products.

But the adjustment from the old to the new economic structure is not without costs. In this regard, the paper also assesses the size of the efficiency costs involved in the reallocation of production from contracting to expanding sectors. The analysis in Section 3 shows that the rationalization of production due to both inter and intra-industry trade changes is likely to be across sectors rather than within sectors, involving a fair amount of inter-sectoral capital and labour flows. Moreover, adjustment costs will be larger the lower is the degree of inter-sectoral labour and capital mobility and the lower is the degree of aggregate and sectoral wage flexibility. Unfortunately, the rigid and excessively centralized wage-setting process, the low degree of labour mobility, the relatively high labour firing costs, the lack of sufficiently deep and developed long-term capital markets, and the not very efficient provision of bank credit indicate that such costs may be far from negligible in the case of Spain.

Another important implication from Spain's liberalization experience since 1986 is about the order in which the current and capital accounts of the balance of payments should be opened up. While the literature suggests that opening up the current account first is the correct policy to follow, in the case of Spain the current account started being opened after many segments of the capital account had already been opened. Perhaps, the lesson to be drawn is that the order in which the current and capital accounts are opened is not so critical as long as the domestic financial system is solvent prior to the external opening up of the economy.

The analysis of the role of automatic market forces *vis à vis* policy in Section 4 concludes that while it is true that 1992 by itself will bring about a number of efficiency-enhancing changes in goods and financial markets, only with a well designed economic policy strategy will the country succeed in making effective the long-run potential benefits associated with the process of economic integration while keeping the short and medium-run adjustment costs within tolerable limits. The appropriate economic policy strategy should combine labour market, tax, budgetary and financial policies, and have as its top priorities the improvement of the allocational efficiency of labour and financial markets within a sustained growth scenario, the preservation and exploitation of Spain's comparative labour cost advantage, and the of scale and scope economies in production and distribution.

panish economy on the eve of EC membership

tly, Spain's economy has remained very regulated and pro-
ιϲϲιϲυ .... external competition. This situation has led over the years to
the introduction of significant tariff and non-tariff trade barriers, controls
on international capital flows, very strict rules on wage-setting and union-
ization, restrictive banking laws, administrative price and interest rate
setting, etc. . . . which have influenced the structure of the economy
deeply and unfavourably. Since the advent of democracy in 1977,
however, there has been a less interventionist attitude. Unfortunately,
between 1974 and 1984, and specially since 1977, the country suffered a
deep, long and severe economic crisis when initially unfavourable
external developments (i.e. the oil shock and world recession) were
combined with an unstable domestic political situation after the death of
General Franco. Moreover, the negative economic effects of the crisis
were amplified by the many structural rigidities and inefficiencies present
in Spain's goods, labour and financial markets, leading over time to
massive job destruction and disinvestment accompanied by a sharp
increase in inflation.

Given the significant role of Spanish private banks as lenders and
shareholders of industrial firms, the industrial crisis also provoked a deep
and long banking crisis. As a result, several banks failed, although a bank
panic was avoided thanks to the timely and firm attitude of the authorities. During the period, a stabilization package was adopted to curb
inflation and to prevent a balance of payments crisis, with wage moderation and a gradual monetary tightening being its most visible elements.
Moreover, several liberalization measures were taken in financial
markets, labour markets, public industry, etc. . . . at various points during
the 1977–84 period.

In sum, on the eve of Spain's entrance into the EC on January 1, 1986
the economy had just started recovering from a major economic crisis
whose most visible, and socially painful, consequence was a dramatic
jump in the unemployment rate from 2.9% in 1974 to 21.4% in 1985. On
the other hand, some of the most worrying internal and external economic
disequilibria during the crisis period had been corrected. In particular,
inflation had come down from a maximum of 24.5% in 1977 to 8.3% in
1986, the current account had improved from a maximum deficit of 3.4%
of GDP in 1976 to a surplus of 1.7% in 1986, and annual real growth had
gone above 2% for the first time since 1977.

These were the initial macroeconomic conditions of Spain's economy

Period	Trade Account	Services Account	Transfers	Current Account
1964–69	− 6.2	3.4	1.5	− 1.2
1970–73	− 4.5	3.7	1.8	1.1
1974–77	− 6.7	2.4	1.2	− 3.0
1978–79	− 2.8	2.6	1.0	0.6
1980–85	− 4.5	2.6	0.7	− 1.1
1964–85	− 5.2	3.0	1.2	− 0.9

Table 7.1. The components of Spain's current account balance, 1964–85 (percent of GDP)

Source: Secretaría de Comercio.
Note: Numbers may not add up due to rounding.

on the eve of its entry to the EC. The rest of this section discusses in detail structural conditions in goods, labour and financial markets with the aim of identifying which specific features may be most significant in shaping the effects of the 'EC cum 1992' shock.

2.1 Goods markets

At the time Spain joined the EC in 1986 its total GDP was about 8.6% of the total EC12 GDP, and its per capita GDP was 72.1% of the EC12 average.[2] The sectoral composition of Spanish GDP shows that only 7% of Spain's total GDP came from agriculture, while 37% came from industry and construction, and about 56% from services. By a rough measure, tradeable goods represented a bit more than one-third of GDP, and nontradeable goods a bit less than two-thirds. In this section we look both at the tradeable and nontradeable goods markets.

Tradeables and trade flows[3]

Overview The 'EC cum 1992' shock means – among other things – the full opening up of the current account. To better assess its impact it is essential to identify the most important characteristics of Spain's trade pattern on the eve of EC entry.

A first characteristic is the tendency towards deficit in the current account balance shown in Table 7.1, which presents the long-term evolution of the Spanish current account balance in the 1964–85 period in terms of its components: the trade balance, the services account, and

Table 7.2. Evolution of Spanish manufacturing trade prior to EC membership (percent)

	Average growth 1978–85		Structure				Net Exports Revealed Comparative Advantage (1)	
	Imports	Exports	Imports		Exports		1978	1985
			1978	1985	1978	1985		
Strong-demand	19.4	27.2	31.4	34.2	11.4	16.2	−45.9	−27.1
Moderate-demand	16.9	19.7	38.1	36.0	46.9	43.5	19.1	18.7
Weak-demand	17.6	20.5	30.4	29.8	41.7	40.3	16.1	24.0
Total manufacturing	17.9	21.0	100	100	100	100	3.6	9.4
Energy	24.1	47.6	—	—	—	—	−88.3	−65.4
Total industry	20.1	22.5	—	—	—	—	−15.2	−10.7

Sources: Dirección de Aduanas.

Notes: (1) Numbers correspond to revealed comparative advantage indices (*RCA*), calculated as follows: $RCA_i = (X_i - M_i)/(X_i + M_i) \times 100$, where X_i and M_i correspond respectively to exports and imports of sector i, $i = 1, \ldots 13$ *NACE–CLIO* R–25 manufacturing branches. The index RCA_i varies between −100 (maximum disadvantage) and 100 (maximum advantage).

transfers. On average, this tendency to deficit is due to the strong and continuous deficit shown by the trade balance. Nevertheless, the continuous surpluses in the services account, due to the booming tourist industry, and in transfers due, until recently, to emigrants' remittances, are responsible for improving the performance of the current account relative to the trade balance in every subperiod. A second characteristic is that, contrary to popular misperceptions, Spain's trade balance has relied only to a small extent on agricultural products, since on the eve of EC membership foodstuffs were just about 11% of total exports of goods and 3% of total imports of goods. The above is, nonetheless, not surprising given that only 7% of total GDP came from the agricultural sector at that time.

A third characteristic is the relatively low degree of openness of the Spanish economy. On the eve of EC membership Spain still had a low degree of openness when compared with other European economies, and even with new or recent entrants like Portugal or Greece. While imports plus exports of goods and services were only 44.3% of GDP in Spain, they were 61% in the EC-12, 55% in Greece and 69% in Portugal. This fact was most probably related to Spain's large degree of nominal and effective protection, which has been estimated to be 11% in nominal terms, and 13% in effective terms.[4] A fourth characteristic is the heavy concentration of manufacturing trade in moderate and weak-demand products,[5] which jointly account for about 84% of total manufacturing exports and 66% of imports, as shown in Table 7.2. The table also indicates the heavy dependence of the Spanish economy on energy imports, which is reflected in a sizeable deficit.

A fifth characteristic is that prior to EC entrance most of Spanish manufacturing trade was with the OECD, and still is. Specifically, according to Table 7.3, in 1985 85.7% of total imports and 78.6% of total exports consisted of trade with OECD countries. Among these countries, the largest share was taken by the EC, which received about 49.3% of Spanish exports and contributed 58.1% of Spanish imports in 1985. It can be said that even prior to formal EC membership, Spain already had major and increasing trade linkages with Community countries. On the other hand, regarding the geographical composition of net exports, Spain had a deficit with the OECD – due to trade with the US and Japan – and a surplus with non-OECD countries which, on balance, led to an overall surplus.

Inter and intra-industry trade Having given a general overview of Spanish foreign trade, it is now time to perform a more systematic analysis of its inter and intra-industry nature.[6] This is an important issue

	Imports (1)		Exports (1)		Net Exports (2)	
	1978	1985	1978	1985	1978	1985
OECD	80.8	85.7	65.7	68.3	−126	−85
EC	54.3	58.1	48.0	49.3	−51	39
US	12.6	12.6	10.1	10.1	−21	−10
Japan	4.5	6.1	1.7	1.5	−24	−116
Rest of OECD	9.4	8.9	5.8	7.4	−30	1
Non-OECD 1964–69	19.2	14.3	34.3	31.7	134	660
Total World	100	100	100	100	7	575

Table 7.3. Geographical structure of Spanish manufacturing trade, 1978–85

Notes:
(1) percent.
(2) billion pesetas.

for two reasons. On the one hand, adjustment costs from Spanish integration into the EC are likely to be more important if most of the changes in the trade pattern take the form of inter-industry trade than if they take the form of intra-industry trade.[7] And, on the other hand, there are generally extra benefits to be gained in the long run from trade liberalization when intra-industry trade is also present.

To get a rough idea of the extent to which industrial trade has an *inter-industry* component, the last two columns of Table 7.2 present the revealed comparative advantage of Spain in strong, moderate and weak-demand sectors in both 1978 and 1985. As can be seen, Spain's merchandise trade is characterized by exhibiting a continuous, though shrinking revealed comparative disadvantage in strong-demand products, a stable comparative advantage in moderate-demand products, and an increasing comparative advantage in weak-demand products. It may be of interest also to analyze how these revealed comparative advantages are distributed across geographical areas, as is done in Table 7.4. This shows that Spain has a revealed comparative disadvantage with the OECD in strong-demand products, and a comparative advantage in moderate and weak-demand products. With respect to non-OECD countries, it has a revealed comparative advantage in strong, weak, and – especially – moderate-demand products, and a comparative disadvantage in energy.

	EC	OECD	Non-OECD
Strong-demand	− 31.3	− 39.9	37.9
Moderate-demand	13.4	7.9	59.0
Weak-demand	10.7	17.4	38.1
Total manufacturing	1.2	− 1.8	45.5
Energy	32.0	11.1	− 87.7
Total industry	4.1	− 0.6	− 27.2

Table 7.4. Revealed comparative advantage in Spanish industrial trade by geographical areas, 1985 (index, in percent)

Sources: Dirección General de Aduanas.
Notes: Same as in Table 7.2.

The impression that results from looking at this data is that Spain's foreign trade has an important inter-industry component, since it seems reasonable to expect that Spain exports relatively more sophisticated products to non-OECD countries and relatively less sophisticated products to OECD countries. However, in order to see how much of Spain's trade can be explained according to traditional comparative advantage more formal tests are needed.

In a recent paper, Fariñas and Martín (1990) perform a test of the Heckscher-Ohlin model for Spain's manufacturing trade using the Leontief-Leamer approach for 75 industrial sectors, excluding energy and mining, and data from 1981. They calculate the capital-labour ratios obtained from the total (direct plus indirect) input requirements which are incorporated into an output of 1 million pesetas worth of exports and import substitutes. Their results show that Spain's imports from the OECD are slightly more capital-intensive than exports to the OECD, which is reflected in the relative capital-labour ratio of 1.064. At the same time, Spain's imports from non-OECD countries are less capital intensive than exports to non-OECD countries, as indicated by the ratio of 0.839. Consequently, it seems to be confirmed that Spain's exports to the OECD are relatively labour-intensive compared with her imports from the OECD, while her exports to non-OECD countries are relatively capital-intensive compared with her imports from them.[8]

It should be pointed out, however, that the calculated differences in relative capital-labour intensities are larger for trade with non-OECD countries than for trade with OECD countries, as shown by the respective ratios of 0.839 and 1.064. To get a further insight into this, Fariñas and

Martin (1990) follow the approach of Baldwin (1971) and Branson and Junz (1971), and run pooled cross section-time series regressions to determine the explanatory factors of Spain's net exports for 74 manufacturing industries during the 1981–84 period. Since the explanatory variables used are physical and human capital, labour, natural resources and trade barriers, it is possible to determine how important are 'comparative advantage' variables in explaining trade flows both with OECD and non-OECD countries. Their results tend to confirm that while net exports from Spain to non-OECD countries tend to be mostly influenced by 'comparative advantage' elements, net exports from Spain to OECD countries cannot be so well explained in terms of these elements alone, and need the presence of variables like economies of scale.

After having described and analyzed Spain's inter-industry trade pattern, we now turn to studying Spain's *intra-industry trade* pattern. The justification for this is threefold. First, the results of the last section suggest that intra-industry trade may be important in explaining trade between Spain and OECD countries. Second, intra-industry trade appears to be a significant and rising proportion of total trade in other industrialized countries, as shown by Tharakan (1983). Thirdly, the adjustment costs and welfare implications from trade liberalization may differ significantly depending on whether the changes in trade patterns take the form of inter-industry or intra-industry trade.

To get a first idea of the relevance of intra-industry trade in Spain, we calculate the Grubel-Lloyd index.[9] This index indicates that intra-industry trade was a significant element in Spain's trade pattern before EC integration, although it exhibits high variance among specific industries. Moreover, when the index is computed for the different geographical areas, it shows, as it is reasonable to expect, a smaller proportion of intra-industry trade between Spain and non-EC countries (27%), and a larger proportion of intra-industry trade between Spain and EC countries (43.6%). Still, casual evidence, such as that presented in Culem and Lundberg (1986) indicates that the role of intra-industry trade, although by no means insignificant, is not as important in Spain as in other industrialized countries.[10]

After having identified the practical importance of intra-industry trade it still remains to isolate and analyze its main determinants. For this purpose, Fariñas and Martín (1988) perform an econometric analysis of the main determinants of intra-industry trade by taking a sample of 70 manufacturing branches in 1981. After trying alternative specifications and estimation methods, the study concludes that product differentiation in conjunction with scale economies and, to a lesser extent, foreign investment have a significant and positive effect on Spain's intra-industry trade.

	1978			1985		
	Spain	EC	S.I.	Spain	EC	S.I.
Strong-demand	16.9	19.6	0.86	19.3	22.6	0.85
Moderate-demand	39.6	46.1	0.86	41.7	46.5	0.90
Weak-demand	43.5	34.3	1.27	39.0	30.9	1.26
Total manufacturing	100	100		100	100	

Table 7.5. The structure of Spanish industrial value added, 1978–85 (percent)

Sources: Encuesta industrial of Instituto Nacional de Estadística (INE) and Eurostat.
Notes: All percentages calculated from data at 1980 prices. S.I. is the specialization index which is obtained by dividing Spain's share by EC share in each product category.

Scale economies and sources of comparative advantage   So far we have examined the structure and determining factors of Spain's industrial trade flows, which represent approximately 90% of total trade flows. As indicated, both inter and intra-industry trade considerations need to be taken into account when explaining Spain's trade flows. In what follows, it is analyzed what sort of comparative advantages/disadvantages of Spanish industry underlie this trade pattern, focussing on dimensions such as industry specialization, firm size and scale economies, technology, financial structure and labour costs.

The *lack of flexibility* of Spanish industry to move quickly enough towards manufacturing products with more dynamic markets is illustrated in Table 7.5. This Table shows the changes in the pattern of industrial specialization in Spain and in the EC between 1978 and 1985. During that time, Spain's industrial crisis prompted a severe drop in real industrial value added – at a rate of 1.1% per year – which was more marked in weak and moderate-demand sectors. However, on the eve of Spain's entry to the EC, Spanish industry remained relatively less specialized than the EC in strong and moderate-demand products and relatively more specialized in weak-demand products. Moreover, Spain was by then as over-specialized in weak-demand products and under-specialized in strong-demand products relative to the EC as in 1978. But, why didn't Spain's industry move quickly enough into the most dynamic markets? Since manufacturing the most dynamic goods involves production with large-scale firms using high-technology capital-intensive techniques, one

	Number of workers per plant					
	1–9	10–19	20–49	50–99	100–499	500 or more	Average size (2)
Strong-demand (3)	58.0	13.4	13.3	5.8	8.0	1.4	45
Moderate-demand (3)	81.5	8.7	5.9	2.0	1.7	0.2	14
Weak-demand (3)	80.5	9.9	6.5	1.7	1.3	0.1	11
Total manufacturing (3)	80.1	9.5	6.5	2.0	1.7	0.2	13

Table 7.6. Size distribution of the number of plants in Spanish manufacturing, 1985

Notes:
(1) Size is measured in terms of workers, 1985 data.
(2) Numbers of workers.
(3) In percent.

must look at the size and technology of Spain's industrial firms to find some of the answers.

Regarding *size*, it is well known that there exists a relationship between size, at the product, plant and firm level, and cost of production. If we define the minimum efficient size (MES) as the size where unit costs are minimized for a given activity, then it is the case that units of production with lower than efficient size may have more problems when facing external competitive pressures, and also more to gain from exploiting economies of scale. Therefore, a sense of optimal firm size may be useful.

Table 7.6 gives the size-distribution (in terms of employment) of Spanish plants in the manufacturing sector in 1985. As can be observed, the average size of Spanish plants is extremely small, and tends to go up as one moves from weak, to moderate, to strong-demand sectors. Indeed, 80.1% of plants employ less than 10 workers and only 0.2% of plants employ more than 500 workers. Moreover, as might be expected, there are remarkable differences between branches. For instance, within the weak-demand sector, plants in the subsector of 'ferrous and nonferrous ores and metals' have an average size of 196 workers, with 30.9% of plants employing less than 10 workers. On the other hand, plants in the 'miscellaneous manufacturing products' sector employ on average 5 workers, with 88.7% of the plants employing less than 10 workers.

In order to get a better idea of the technical efficiency of each manufacturing sector, minimum efficient technical scale (METS) indices have been calculated according to the procedure of Weiss (1963); that is, taking the median plant size on the basis of output in each sector.[11] We have also looked at the sectoral METS-output ratio, which indicates the number of METS plants that could be in each sector according to total market size. Our results confirm the very small size of Spanish plants, although the lack of plant size data for other EC countries prevents us from making international comparisons.

Where international comparisons are possible is with firm-level data. Using the data collected by Dun & Bradstreet-ELC on the basis of the International Standard Industrial Classification, we have looked at the relative size of Spanish firms in comparison with those of other EC countries, when size is measured by sales. Again, our findings show a much smaller firm size in Spain relative to other EC countries and especially to France, Germany, and the United Kingdom.[12]

Having a suboptimal size is a problem when facing international market competition. Having a relatively outdated *technology* is another serious problem which may explain why a country does not adapt its production structure flexibly enough to produce strong-demand products, most of which are relatively intensive in high technology.

As is known, there are two main ways of gaining access to new technologies: generation through R&D activities, and imports from other countries. Although it is not always clear how to measure 'technological effort', it may be of interest to notice that in spite of the remarkable increase in firms' R&D expenditures in Spain during the previous decade, by 1985 these expenditures were just 0.9% of industry's value added, whereas in the EC they were 3.9%.

The former impression is confirmed for all branches of industry in Spain by the data shown in Table 7.7. In particular, Spain's technological effort is smaller than in the EC in strong, moderate, and weak-demand products, the differences being largest for strong-demand products. Moreover, at a more disaggregated level it is found that these differences are most important in the 'transport equipment' and 'machinery' subsectors, which is particularly worrying since these concentrate most of the embodied technical change.

Turning now to the output, rather than the input, side of technological innovation as an alternative measure, it is the case that Spanish residents are less active in registering patents than other EC residents. First, while in the EC almost 30% of the total patents registered correspond to residents, this number is just 15% in Spain; and second, while EC residents register abroad more than twice the number of patents that they register at home, in the case of Spanish residents this figure is just two-thirds. Moreover, Spanish firms are less able to register patents abroad than their foreign counterparts. This, in turn, is reflected in

	Spain (1)		EEC (2)	
	R&D/ Value Added	%	R&D/ Value Added	%
Strong-demand	2.5	43.8	12.1	53.6
Moderate-demand	1.2	37.8	3.8	36.9
Weak-demand	0.3	12.4	1.0	6.7
Total manufacturing	1.1	94	4.6	97.2
Energy	0.3	6	0.6	2.8
Total industry	0.9	100	3.9	100

Table 7.7. Relative effort in R&D and sectoral structure of Spanish R&D expenditures, 1983–85 (percent)

Sources: INE, Eurostat and OECD (STIC).
Notes:
(1) 1985 data.
(2) 1983 data.

Spain's absorption of technology through international transfers. Specifically, while the percentage of payments for technology services imports covered by revenues from technology services exports was 13% in 1985 in Spain, it averaged 72.3% in the most developed EC countries. On the other hand, while the proportion of all resources devoted to technological activities (R&D plus technology imports) which is absorbed by domestic R&D was 45.2% in Spain, it averaged 87.4% in the most developed EC countries.

In sum, Spain's industry seemed to have an important relative disadvantage *vis-à-vis* the EC regarding the production of technology.

Turning now to financial issues, although they are treated in considerably more depth later in the paper, it may nevertheless be useful to take brief note of the *financial structure* of industrial firms at this point. Since the conditions for the validity of the Modigliani-Miller theorem are rarely fulfilled in reality, it is reasonable to think that financial structure and investment decisions are connected. In fact, the relative scarcity of certain types of financing may decisively influence the investment and production decisions of firms and, consequently, their competitiveness.[13]

To get a first idea about the financial structure of Spanish industrial firms, Table 7.8 gives the debt-equity and bank debt-total debt ratios at the time Spain joined the EC. While the debt-equity ratio is 122.9% for the whole of industry, this is due to the much higher ratio in the energy

	Debt/ Equity	Bank debt/ Total debt
Strong-demand	63.3	88.2
Moderate-demand	85.9	91.0
Weak-demand	101.1	82.9
Total manufacturing	84.2	87.7
Energy	146.1	60.1
Total industry	122.9	67.2

Table 7.8. The financial structure of private Spanish industrial firms, 1985–86 (percent)

Sources: Central de Balances, Banco de España.
Notes: Average of 1985–86 values.

sector than in the manufacturing sector. Another interesting fact is that firms' debt-equity ratios seem to be, on average, higher in the weak-demand sector than in moderate-demand sector, and higher here than in the strong-demand sector. This, in turn, can perhaps be explained by the faster growth of retained profits in the stronger-demand sectors which makes less necessary recourse to debt financing. Overall, firms' leverage in the industrial sector is very similar to that of other EC countries, like Italy and the United Kingdom.

Table 7.8 also shows the very high weight of bank debt in total debt, especially in the manufacturing sector. This feature, however, seems to correspond quite well with other EC countries, pointing towards the very important role played by bank credit conditions in the financing of industry. Since, as we will see in detail later on, the Spanish banking system seems to be one of the least efficient in the EC, the observed heavy dependence on expensive bank credit may indeed be a burden for Spanish industrial firms. This is even more so at a time when changing international market conditions require making new investments so as to move into new and more dynamic markets.

So far, we have just pointed out the major kinds of comparative disadvantage of Spain's economy. There is, however, a general presumption that Spain has a non-negligible comparative advantage in terms of *labour costs*. In relation to this, Figure 7.1 illustrates the recent evolution of relative industrial unit labour costs between Spain and industrialized countries when expressed in a common currency. As can be seen, from 1970 till 1979 Spain lost labour competitiveness both relative to the EC and to the larger group of industrialized countries. However, after that

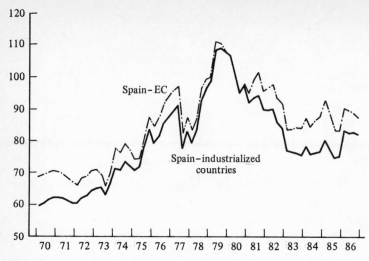

Note: A higher number means an increase in Spain's relative unit labour costs.
EC excludes Ireland, Greece, Portugal and Spain.

Figure 7.1   Spain: relative real unit labour costs measured in a common currency, 1970–86

year and until the eve of Spanish entry to the EC in 1985 there was an impressive improvement in competitiveness which recovered part of the lost ground.

It can be argued, convincingly, that the above calculations are capable, at best, of indicating the evolution over time of the labour cost advantage (or disadvantage) of Spain *vis-à-vis* other industrialized countries but that they do not give information about the relative levels of unit labour costs at a given point in time. To make these comparisons, it is necessary to adjust the competitiveness index in the form proposed by Hooper and Larin (1988), by using base-year Purchasing-Power-Parity exchange rates.

In a recent paper, Laborda *et al.* (1986) perform such a calculation and make a comparison between the relative levels of unit labour costs in Spain and a selected group of industrialized countries, which is shown in Figure 7.2. The vertical axis measures the ratio between the level of Spanish industry's unit costs and a weighted average of those of a representative group of industrialized countries. When the number is above (below) 100 it means that Spanish labour costs are lower (higher) than those of the other countries and, therefore, that Spain has a labour cost advantage (disadvantage). It is clear from the Figure that in 1970 Spain had a considerable labour cost advantage, between 1970 and 1979

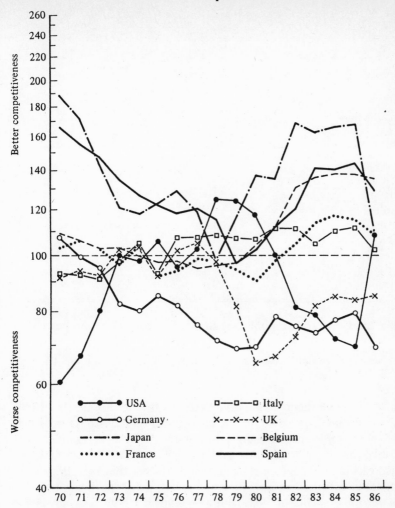

Source: Laborda, Lorente, and Prades (1986).

Figure 7.2   Labour costs – competitiveness, 1970–86

Spain gradually lost this advantage over other industrialized countries, and from 1979 to 1985 Spain regained much of the lost competitiveness, with unit labour costs in 1985 about 43% lower than in other industrialized countries when measured in a common currency.

Summarizing, Spain's industrial structure shows a considerable lack of flexibility to move quickly enough towards products with more dynamic

	1973	1985	1988
Total expenditures			
EC	37.2	49.0	47.4
Spain	22.7	42.1	40.5
Total revenues			
EC	36.1	43.8	43.6
Spain	23.8	35.1	37.5
Budget balance			
EC	−1.1	−5.2	−3.8
Spain	1.1	−7.0	−3.0
Gross public debt			
EC	36.9	56.6	60.0
Spain	12.8	46.5	48.5
Debt interest			
EC	1.9	5.0	4.8
Spain	0.6	3.2	3.3

Table 7.9. Comparative public sector structures, 1973–88 (in percent of GDP)

Sources: European Commission, OECD, Ministry of the Economy, and Banco de España.

markets. Among the most important reasons behind this are the insufficient, and probably also inefficient, size of Spanish industrial firms, their relatively less efficient technology, their more expensive access to financial resources and, as will be discussed later, the substantial functional mismatch existing in Spain's labour market. However, thanks to the important labour cost moderation of the first half of the 1980s, Spain was able to enter into the EC in 1986 with a significant labour cost advantage relative to its major trading partners. Whether Spain is able to maintain this sort of comparative advantage in the future or not will critically affect the economy's performance following the 'EC cum 1992' shock.

Nontradeables: the public sector[14]
While there has traditionally been a substantial degree of public sector intervention in Spain in most spheres of economic life, it has been mostly during the last fifteen years, with the introduction of democracy, that there has been a very rapid growth of the role of the public sector through the budget. Consequently, as shown in Table 7.9, while general government spending represented a bit less than 23% of GDP in 1973, it rose to

	Actual figures in 1985 (percent of GDP)		Adequacy ratios Spain/EC4 (a) (percent)	
	EC4	Spain	1976	1985
1 General Public Services	4.3	4.1	130.7	111.9
2 Defence	3.5	2.0	50.4	58.3
3 Education	5.5	3.6	34.8	59.5
4 Health	5.9	4.5	77.6	78.3
5 Social Security	18.2	14.9	62.6	85.7
6 Housing	2.2	1.8	33.2	71.4
7 Other Social Services	0.6	0.9	88.9	174.8
8 Economic Services (b)	4.8	6.6	78.6	102.5
9 Other (c)	4.0	4.0	101.4	111.8
Total expenditure	48.9	42.5	63.0	86.0

Table 7.10. Government spending comparisons, Spain and EC4, 1985

Sources: Lagares *et al.* (1988).
Notes: (a) The ratio of actual expenditure in a given functional component to the 'EC Standard' expenditure. The 'EC Standard' is the value of the per-capita expenditure that would have been obtained in an EC country with the socio-economic and demographic characteristics of Spain. The EC model of public expenditure is constructed upon panel data econometric estimates of functional expenditure equations using data of the Federal Republic of Germany, France, Italy and the United Kingdom.
(b) Includes: energy, gas, agriculture, mining, industry, transport, communications, and other services.
(c) Public debt interest and other minor expenditures.

42% by 1985, with an average annual increase of 1.8 points of GDP. This almost doubled the increase registered in the EC average, which was of 1 percentage point of GDP per annum.

The very rapid growth of government spending was mainly due to three factors. First, the deep economic crisis that started in 1977 led to a sharp increase in transfers, subsidies and income-maintenance expenditures. Second, the advent of democracy led to the fulfilment of many unsatisfied social demands which had been neglected under the previous regime, as illustrated by the figures in Table 7.10. And third, political demands for regional autonomy led to a considerable transfer or spending power to the new regional governments which often caused a duplication of spending.

At the same time, on the eve of Spain's entry to the EC, the country had a progressive modern tax system which, however, still compared

	EC	Spain
1 Income taxes	33.8	24.6
Personal	26.5	19.3
Corporate	7.3	5.3
2 Social Security contributions	29.7	39.4
3 Property taxes	4.0	4.3
4 Consumption taxes	29.8	28.6
5 Other taxes	2.7	3.1

Table 7.11. The structure of Spanish taxation in 1985 (per cent of total tax revenues)

Sources: OECD, INE and Banco de España.

unfavourably with those of EC countries in terms of the degree of tax fraud, as exemplified by the official estimate that non-declared incomes constituted about 45% of the potential tax base. Other features of our tax system, shown in Table 7.11, were the relatively low share of income tax revenues, and particularly of personal taxes, in total tax revenues, and the relatively high share of social security contributions in total tax revenues compared with the average EC country.

The unprecedented increase in government spending experienced since the mid-1970s, mostly reflected in transfers, could not be entirely financed by raising taxes. On the one hand, this would have depressed even more the already feeble rhythm of economic activity at that time. And, on the other hand, even after the substantial and progressive major tax reform of 1977–78, the ease with which tax on non-labour incomes could be evaded meant that a general tax increase would have been effectively borne mostly by labour-income recipients, which would have been socially and politically costly. All in all, however, tax revenues rose, as a percent of GDP, from 24% in 1973 to 35% in 1985.

All this meant that the budget deficit had to rise. In fact, it went from a surplus of slightly above 1% of GDP in 1973 to a deficit of 7% in 1985, with approximately half of this deterioration corresponding to an increase in the cyclical deficit and half to an increase in the structural deficit. At the same time, the explosion of the deficit was accompanied by an almost four-fold increase in the debt-GDP ratio, which went from 13% in 1973 to more than 46% in 1985, and by an increasing weight of debt interest payments in the total deficit, as shown by Table 7.9.

It is very curious to observe that while in the first half of the 1980s there were major liberalization measures taken in financial markets, public industry, etc., nevertheless there was a large increase in the role of the public sector through the budget. The risks posed by the continuously expanding public spending and budget deficit were, no doubt, a major threat to the real and financial stability of the country. Indeed, as shown by Viñals (1985), if the primary structural deficit then existing had been maintained it could have led either to a debt explosion with major unfavourable effects or to a substantial increase in the average inflation rate of the economy which, at the minimum, would have almost doubled the 8.3% rate experienced at that time.

However, reducing the deficit was not just a necessary condition for financial stability. Causality tests performed by Raymond-Bara and González-Páramo (1988) show that there is also causality running from deficits to public expenditure. This can be rationalized as saying that the less visible 'inflation tax' contributed to overcome taxpayers' resistance to financing public expenditures and this, in turn, led to higher public expenditure on average in the 1975–86 period. Consequently, reducing the deficit was also helpful for controlling public expenditure. The growth in public spending was also stimulated by several budgetary practices like laxity in the concession of supplementary credits by Parliament, and the possibility of carrying forward unused appropriations under certain conditions.

The need to preserve and even improve the international competitiveness of the Spanish economy in the light of the imminent integration of the country into the EC made it necessary to continue the path of inflation reduction started since 1978. That, however, was clearly inconsistent with the presence of high budget deficits which were caused by public spending mostly oriented to current transfers and consumption. It was therefore of critical importance to engineer a deficit-reduction strategy consistent with price stability together with a substantial reorientation of public spending towards public capital formation to reduce the infrastructural gap of the country, shown in Table 7.12.

2.2 The labour market

There are two striking characterstics of the Spanish labour market which are keys to analyzing the impact of the 'EC cum 1992' shock. The first is the existence of a significant labour cost advantage relative to most of the other EC countries which has already been explored in Section 2.1. The second is the extraordinarily high unemployment rate, which on the eve of EC membership was 21.4%, and remains to this day the highest in the EC.

It could be objected that the presence of an informal sector in the Spanish economy may in fact be exaggerating the measured Spanish

	Germany	France	Italy	UK	Spain
1 Length of road networks (000 km)	492.8	801.4	297.0	370.9	167.2
2 Road km per 000 vehicles	18.4	33.8	13.1	19.3	16.3
3 Length of motorways (000 km)	7.8	5.7	5.7	2.9	2.0
4 Motorway density (km per 000 km^2 of land)	30.0	9.7	19.7	10.8	3.8
5 Private vehicles per 000 capita	412.0	340.0	366.0	304.0	229.0
6 Passenger-km by train (billion)	38.4	60.3	37.1	30.1	15.6
7 Passenger-km by aircraft (billion)	24.4	32.8	13.6	43.6	16.5
8 Telephone sets per hundred capita	60.0	60.0	43.0	52.0	36.0
9 Total factor productivity change in postal services (per cent)	2.6	−0.2	−1.0	5.0	−6.0
10 Public expenditure on transport and communications per km^2 of land (1985 PPP Ecu)	6,956	1,820	7,103	4,875	1,189

Table 7.12. Selected infrastructure indicators in the EC and Spain, circa 1985

Sources: Eurostat, *Basic Statistics of the Community*, Luxemburg, 1987; United Nations Organization, *Statistical Yearbook 1984*, New York, 1986; S. Perelman and P. Pestieau (1988); own calculations.

unemployment rate. However, even discounting for this factor, 'real' unemployment in Spain seems still to be the highest in Europe. It is clear that starting the economic integration process with such a high rate of unemployment constitutes a fundamental reason for trying to soften as much as possible the short and medium-term adjustment costs due to the 'EC cum 1992' shock. On the other hand, such a high unemployment rate may also be indicative of a severe malfunctioning of the labour market which, by itself, may exacerbate the adverse short and medium-term costs coming from the adjustment process.

In this section we analyze several key features of the Spanish labour market in order to understand why unemployment is so persistently high, how some of those features, wage-setting and labour mobility, can shape the adjustment process of the economy to the 'EC cum 1992' shock, and whether the existing relative labour cost advantage is likely to be kept in the future.[15]

Employment and unemployment
In recent years Spain has experienced unemployment rates which are not only historically high but also internationally high among the group of industrialized nations. The roots of the current unemployment problem date, however, at least from 1974, when Spain's industrial crisis erupted through the combined negative effects of the first oil price shock and the wage explosion, passed onto prices by firms and accommodated by the monetary authorities, which took place following the death of General Franco at the end of 1975.

Since then, the economy's unemployment rate jumped from 2.9% in 1974 to 21.5% in 1985, with 2.5 million additional people becoming unemployed during the period. That the unemployment problem was mainly due to a contraction in labour demand rather than to an unprecedented expansion of labour supply is suggested by the fact that of the total 2.5 millions of people who became unemployed, 2.1 millions came from reduction of employment, and only 0.4 millions from increase in the labour force.[16] In turn, the very unfavourable labour market outlook led to a drop in participation rates from above 52% in 1976 to less than 49% in 1985, fully due to the reduction in the male participation rate, while the female participation rate remained constant.

The tremendous job-destruction process in the Spanish economy was by no means symmetric in terms of its effects. On the one hand, while agriculture continued after 1974 its secular trend of employment reduction, the previously favourable job-creation process in industry and construction turned into a severe job-destruction process after 1974. Only the services sector continued creating jobs after that year, although at a lower rate than before. On the other hand, the evolution of employment was very different by occupations, and hit the youngest groups of employees hardest, with particular severity in the cases of females, and workers with less education. Finally, although public employment played a counter-cyclical role it could not prevent the net loss of 2.1 millions jobs between 1974 and 1985.

Since the initial conditions of the Spanish economy in 1986 are so critical to understanding the effects of the country's integration into the EC, it is of great interest to ask why employment fell so much. Unfortunately, there is no single cause of the massive job losses in the economy. The story that best seems to fit the facts goes as follows: the oil-price shock and the wage explosion that followed General Franco's death caused a severe decline in the demand for labour plus inflationary

	1968–74	1974–81	1981–85	1985–87
π_d	0.21	0.59	0.74	0.46
π_p	0.41	0.31	0.26	0.54
π_s	0.37	0.10	0.00	0.00

Table 7.13. The percentage of Spanish firms with local constraints, 1968–87

pressure which, at the end of the 1970s, led the monetary authorities to sharply decrease monetary growth, deepening the recession. Faced with low demand prospects and a very high cost of capital, firms severely reduced their investment plans, curtailing productive capacity and, consequently, reducing the amount of employment that the economy could support.

A more precise interpretation of what happened can be obtained with the help of disequilibrium econometric techniques. In this regard, Andrés *et al.* (1988) have recently applied Sneessens and Drèze's (1986) disequilibrium model to the Spanish economy. This model postulates that observed employment at any point in time cannot exceed labour demand or labour supply, whichever is lower. At the same time, if firms have near-zero *ex-post* substitution elasticities, actual labour demand depends on installed capacity, provided demand is high enough to absorb total output, or on actual output demand, if demand is not high enough. Specifically, the model differentiates between the percentage of firms whose marginal or local constraint is either lack of demand (π_d) (i.e. demand is not high enough to employ as many people as are needed to produce the output that can be supplied with the current installed capacity and labour productivity), existing installed capacity (π_p) (i.e. firms can at the maximum employ the number of workers that are required to operate the installed capacity at normal utilization rates for given factor proportions), or labour supply (π_s).

Table 7.13 looks at the evolution of the percentage of firms in the Spanish economy which are locally constrained by demand (π_d), capacity (π_p) or labour supply (π_s). It turns out that, on average, in the years 1981–85 about 74% of the firms had demand as the local binding constraint, 26% had installed capacity as the locally binding constraint, and none of them were locally constrained on the labour-supply side.

These numbers, however, should be interpreted carefully since they mean that both capacity and demand constraints were constraining the

	1965–73	1974–81	1982–85	1986–88
Real labour costs	5.5	3.6	0.9	−0.9
Real take-home pay	5.6	0.8	−1.3	1.0
Unit labour costs	0.3	0.7	−2.3	−2.4
Wage-rental ratio	6.7	2.9	1.6	1.9
Productivity	5.3	4	3.1	1.5

Table 7.14. Spanish factor prices and productivity, 1965–88 (annual % growth rates)

employment creation process on the eve of Spain's entry to the EC, although the second was stronger than the first in 74% of the firms, while the first was stronger than the second in 26% of the firms. Also, while no firm was locally constrained in terms of workers available to be employed, this does not mean either, as we will see later, that sectoral bottlenecks due to skills mismatch, etc. . . . did not exist.[17] Finally, while the Table tells us that demand was the dominant constraint in the Spanish economy by 1985, this does not mean that 'demand causes' were solely responsible for the low activity levels, since the large increase in real wages and in the wage-rental ratio experienced since 1974 (Table 7.14) decreased the labour-intensity of production, and therefore the amount of employment needed to produce a given quantity of output. Simultaneously, capacity constraints which put a supply-side limit to how much the economy could produce and how many workers it could employ, were probably exacerbated by the low investment of the period due to the poor demand prospects of firms, and also by the rise in the wage-rental ratio that increased the capital-intensity of production and, therefore, lowered the amount of employment needed per unit of capacity.[18] Consequently, both unfavourable supply and demand developments were constraining employment creation in Spain in 1985. A combination of demand expansion, real wage moderation, and other supply-side policies was therefore needed to get out of the unemployment trap.

Wage-setting
The high rates of unemployment in Spain and their persistence over time indicate the existence of non-competitive forces in the labour market. This persistence effect is found not only in aggregate but also in sectoral terms, a feature shared by other European countries. Most probably, the persistence of unemployment has a lot to do with wage-setting practices in the Spanish labour market. In what follows, we review some of the main determinants of wage-setting.

A first striking stylized fact about the Spanish labour market is the relatively high and increasing degree of indexation of wages in the presence of unexpected supply and demand shocks leading to price changes. The econometric evidence on aggregate wage equations indicates that *de facto* wage indexation is at least as high in Spain as in other EC countries, although it is not complete. A high degree of wage indexation means that nominal and real unexpected demand shocks have few real consequences for unemployment since nominal wage growth offsets price changes. On the other hand, wage indexation exacerbates the unemployment consequences of real supply-side shocks, which is an undesirable feature. However, the differences in the degree of wage indexation between Spain and other Western countries are not large enough to lead us to conclude that this is a key distinguishing feature of the Spanish labour market's discomforting past performance.

A second and most important question to be asked is what are the reasons that prevent a big enough adjustment in wages from taking place so as to accommodate more employment in Spain. Here there are two possible, and not totally mutually exclusive, explanations. On the one hand, it may be the case that the existence of relatively very high firing costs, as documented in Emerson (1988), and the predominance of permanent employment contracts exacerbate the size of the real wage cut needed for the labour market to start reducing unemployment.[19] On the other hand, it may be that wages do not come down in the presence of excess labour supply either because firms are forced to pay more or because they are willing to do so.

In the Spanish case, probably both explanations are responsible for the observed persistence of unemployment, although the available econometric evidence is more abundant for the second explanation. One such piece of evidence is provided by sectoral wage equations which try to identify how much sectoral wages move with sector-specific unemployment and productivity, and how much they move with economy-wide unemployment and productivity. The paradigm of a well-functioning competitive and integrated labour market has sectoral wages depending only on sectoral productivity (workers therefore getting full reward for their efforts without damaging the firm's position) and overall unemployment (since all unemployed are fully eligible for existing jobs). However, our econometric evidence from sectoral industry wage equations shows few, if any, of the desirable features of a competitive labour market. In fact, what is found is that sectoral real wages in Spain are heavily indexed with the aggregate industry consumption real wage but respond very little to own sector-specific productivity or general industrial excess labour conditions.[20] Indeed, a possible interpretation of these results not rejected by the data is that current sectoral nominal wages evolve so as to catch up past deviations in the desired relative wage position *vis-à-vis* the industry-wide wage.

The previously described evidence suggests that the unemployed ('outsiders') do not exert sizeable downward pressures on wages, and this results in increasing unemployment persistence.[21] It also suggests that the observed lack of flexibility of wages in Spain may have to do not just with legal or institutional constraints but also with how firms select their labour force. In such circumstances, if firms try to recruit and keep the better workers through relative wage differentials, then these will not vanish even if there is very high unemployment, and only those unemployed with similar skills and experience as those now employed will exert downward wage pressures. If mismatch is large or if there are barriers to sectoral/regional labour mobility, then the labour market may be tight and wages may not come down even if unemployment is high and rising.

Wage differentials and labour mobility

A further question to be asked is to what extent the sectoral wage-setting process mentioned above leads in practice to systematic wage differentials. When regional wage differentials are computed, it is found that there is a very low degree of dispersion, the lowest regional wages being paid in Valencia (90% of the national average wage) and the highest wages being paid in the Basque Country (120% of the national average wage). However, there seem to be very sizeable wage differentials across occupations, and also by sex, education, marital status and type and contract tenure. And what is most significant, wage differentials across sectors show a high degree of dispersion, with some sectors paying as little as half the national wage (domestic services) and others getting up to almost a half more than the national wage (insurance and finance). Therefore, while sectoral wage differentials do exist they may fail to show up at the regional level because regions contain different portions of different sectors, and, most important, because national wage agreements set wages by sectors on a nation-wide scale.

But, are these observed sectoral wage differentials consistent with a competitive labour market, in the sense of reflecting different labour characteristics of individuals, or do firms pay wages in excess of what is warranted by such characteristics? To answer this question precisely an econometric analysis was carried out to see how much of the reported sectoral differentials could be explained by both the personal characteristics of the employed (sex, marital status, education, etc. . . .) and by job characteristics (tenure, full-time or part-time, permanent or temporary, etc. . . .). The results indicate that although a very significant proportion of differentials is explained, there still exist important unexplained sectoral wage differentials.[22]

The next question to be asked is to what extent these differentials are indicating the existence of significant barriers to the free mobility of labour in Spain. Surely, low labour mobility is very much linked to the observed differentials. However, while legal and institutional constraints to labour mobility may cause these wage differentials, it is also very likely that both wage differentials and the low degree of labour mobility are jointly determined variables.

Among the legal and institutional constraints existing on the eve of Spain's entry to the EC, the most important were costly and complicated firing procedures, very high levels of severance pay, and difficulties in writing part-time and temporary labour contracts as well as the existence of legal provisions – like Empleo Comunitario which makes it profitable to remain unemployed while working seasonally – as pointed out by Emerson (1988), and Bentolila and Blanchard (1990). Nevertheless, it is our impression that low labour mobility was not just the result of legal and institutional constraints. Here, in turn, there are two alternative and possibly complementary explanations.

A first explanation, due to Bentolila and Blanchard (1990), relies on the very high rate of unemployment to explain the observed lack of labour mobility. The reason is that when a worker becomes unemployed in Spain she/he can rely on family support to survive, therefore making unemployment more bearable. Simultaneously, if the unemployment rate is high in the economy, this means a lower probability of finding a job and, if the unemployed have to move outside their region in order to seek a job, this means losing the economic support derived from staying at the family home. Moreover, there is a presumption that housing problems impair the ability of workers to move to the expanding sectors, often located in areas where housing costs are high. Consequently, the higher the unemployment rate, the lower is labour mobility, and therefore the smaller is the downward pressure on wages and the more persistent is unemployment.

In support of this explanation, Bentolila and Blanchard (1990) provide high observed correlations between reductions in employment and increases in unemployment by region (0.59 in 1976–79 and 0.91 in 1980–85) which is taken to indicate that workers do not move from the region where they lose their employment. However, the small explanatory power of regional wage differentials in our econometric equations explaining the sectoral differentials gives only partial support to this explanation. At the same time, it is true that a worker does not have to leave her/his region while looking for a job across different sectors in that same region.

An alternative explanation relies on the argument that firms may pay the observed wage premia because of efficiency considerations so as to attract and keep the better employees. This, in turn, may lower training and turnover costs, as econometric tests confirm, and, consequently, increase firms' profits. In such circumstances, observing high wages and low unemployment in a particular sector does not mean excess labour demand or a 'higher chance of getting a better job' for anyone else, and therefore should not lead to labour inflows. Accordingly, if workers are not homogeneous, and their probability of leaving unemployment varies widely across different groups of workers, low sectoral mobility is not the cause of wage differentials but something jointly determined with them.

To provide empirical support for this explanation based on the existence of mismatch between labour supply and demand, it must be the case that if firms choose to pay higher wages for more productive workers – above what would be justified by their relative generic and specific human capital – rather than employ others at a lower cost, this is because there are non-negligible differences among them. Consequently, to give the mismatch explanation some credibility, it must be the case that the probability of leaving unemployment is different across social groups formed according to different personal or labour market characteristics of the individual.

In this regard, an initial piece of evidence is provided by the very different incidence of Spanish unemployment among different groupings (age, sex, duration, sectors, occupations). As shown in Table 7.15, unemployment seems to be more heavily concentrated on the younger, females and the longer-term unemployed, and to vary widely both across sectors and occupations. In sum, the incidence of unemployment on the population seems to be very asymmetric in Spain.

However, a more precise test is needed in order to estimate which are the effects of the personal characteristics of the individual (age, education, marital status, etc.) and of the labour market conditions (sector, occupation, region, etc. . . .) on the probability of becoming unemployed, and also to estimate how this probability is decomposed into the probabilities of receiving and accepting a job offer. With those goals in mind, the following econometric evidence was constructed: first, a probit model to analyze the significance of the total impact of the relevant variables; second, a duration model to evaluate the expected duration and the probability of entering unemployment across different characteristics; and, third, a test of how duration affects the probability of leaving unemployment. Among the empirical findings,[23] several stand out as most relevant.

A. By *age and sex* (unemployment rates)

Age	Total			Males			Females		
	1976	1985	1988	1976	1985	1988	1976	1985	1988
16–19	14	55	43	12	51	36	15	60	50
20–24	8	42	35	8	38	29	8	48	44
25–54	3	16	14	3	14	11	3	19	21
55+	2	8	8	2	9	9	0.5	5	6
Total	5	21	18	4	19	14	5	28	27

B. By *duration* (percentages of the total)

Months	1976	1985	1988
1 or less	9	3	1
1–3	27	11	14
3–6	25	12	11
6–12	20	17	13
12–24	13	22	17
24+	4	35	42
Unclassified	2	1	1

C. By *sectors* (unemployment rates)

	1976	1985	1988
Agric. and Fish.	2	11	12
Energy	1	5	4
Mining, Chem.	2	13	7
Prepar. Metals	2	14	6
Other Manufactures	3	17	12
Building	10	31	15
Retail, Hotel	3	13	10
Transport and Commun.	1	7	6
Finance	1	8	5
Other services	1	9	9
Total	3	14	10

D. By *occupation* (unemployment rates)

	1976	1985	1988
Prof. and Tech.	1	6	3
Managers and Admin.	0.4	4	2
Clerical	2	10	7
Retail sales	2	9	7
Other services	3	15	13
Farmer	2	11	12
Other occup.	4	19	11
Army	0	0	1
Total	3	14	13

Table 7.15. The distribution of unemployment in Spain, 1976–88

Note: Numbers have been rounded.

	Probability of entering unemployment	Expected duration
A. *By region* (b, c)		
High	Valencia, Andalucía, Madrid, La Rioja	Cantabria, Basque Country, Asturias, Extremadura
Low	Murcia, Castilla–La Mancha, Basque Country, Asturias, Cantabria, Aragón	Aragón, Madrid, La Rioja, Baleares
B. *By occupation* (d)		
High	Non-specialized workers, services supervisors, qualified workers, highly qualified technical workers, miscellaneous services	Miscellaneous services, clerical, non-specialized
Low	Clerical, professionals, administrators and managers	Foreman, services supervisors, administrators and managers, highly qualified technical workers
C. *By sector* (e)		
High	Building and civil engineering, hotels and catering, footwear, retail distribution, leather	Textiles, clothing, timber and furniture, paper, printing and publishing, other manufacturing
Low	Extraction and preparation of metals, education and research, paper, printing and publishing, public administration, army, textiles, insurance and finance, clothing	Building and civil engineering, foods, drink and tobacco, public administration, army, education and research, agriculture, forestry and fisheries

Table 7.16. Spain: the probability of entering unemployment and its expected duration, 1976–88[a]

Notes:
(a) The reference individual is a male aged 32, with an intermediate or higher qualification, married, working as supervisor of services in a firm of services to the firms, and living in Castilla–León.
(b) The different regions, occupations and sectors are listed in order of significance.
(c) Same reference individual as in (a) except for the region.
(d) Same reference individual as in (a) except for the occupation.
(e) Same reference individual as in (a) except for the sector he works in.

On the one hand, it is found that the probability of being employed varies a lot according to sex, marital status, the number of wage earners in the family, and education. Consequently, the probability of having a job is higher when the worker is a married male, a single female, when other family members also have jobs, and when the educational level is high.

On the other hand, we find that by comparison with the reference individual, whose personal characteristics are such that her/his expected unemployment duration is similar to the sample mean, the probability of becoming unemployed and the expected duration of unemployment vary widely across different regions, sectors and occupations, as shown in Table 7.16. This is indicative of the existence of sizeable mismatch in the Spanish labour market in both a geographical and functional sense which, undoubtedly, is a factor behind the size and persistence of unemployment.

Finally, when we test econometrically for the impact of unemployment duration on the probability of leaving unemployment, we find that duration significantly lowers this probability. Indeed, for the reference individual the probability of leaving unemployment within a month of first becoming unemployed is as low as 7.4%, and this probability decreases to 5.9% after six months, to 5.4% after a year, to 5.0% after two years, and to 4.7% after three years. Consequently, people who fall into the 'unemployment trap' find it hard getting out of it, and this becomes harder as duration increases and as the educational level is lower (if our reference individual had no intermediate or higher education his probability of leaving unemployment within a month would be 4.9%, and after three years only 3.1%).

With such low probabilities of leaving unemployment due to the severe mismatch problems before mentioned, it is not surprising that workers have little incentive to move around looking for new jobs. In turn, this lowers the downward wage pressure from unemployment, and increases the human capital depreciation of the unemployed the longer they stay unemployed, thereby increasing the size of the mismatch and helping continue – or even augment – current unemployment. Downward wage resistance and low labour mobility are therefore two sides of the same coin in Spain. This can explain why unemployment was so high on the eve of entry to the EC, and give us some clues as to what sort of short-run adjustment costs may be forthcoming following the 'EC cum 1992' shock. Fortunately, it also tells us how these costs can be reduced.

2.3   Financial markets

Capital flows[24]
After having analyzed the structure of Spain's goods and labour markets and trade flows prior to the country's entrance into the EC, it is now

time to turn to the analysis of financial markets and capital flows. It is important, however, to emphasize an important difference between both analyses: In the case of trade flows, 'goods mobility' experiences a major, albeit gradual, shock starting in 1986 as a result of the clauses included in the Accession Treaty signed by Spain and the EC. On the other hand, the worrying aspect of 'capital mobility' – and especially short-term capital mobility – is not so much the changes resulting from the Treaty of Accession of 1986 but those resulting from the establishment of completely free capital mobility by the end of 1992 as envisaged in recently approved Community legislation.

With this important distinction in mind, in what follows we describe the logic and structure of the system of capital controls in Spain prior to her 1986 entry to the EC, and also analyze its effective economic impact on the most sensitive component of capital flows: short-term capital flows.

The logic and structure of Spanish capital controls   The origin of the Spanish system of capital controls dates back to the autarkic policy imposed by the authorities in 1939 after the Civil War. Although the country started to open up to foreign competition with the adoption of a package of reforms in 1959, it has not been until the late part of the 1970s and, most importantly, until the entry of Spain into the EC in 1986 and the passing of recent EC legislation that the structure of capital controls has started to be dismantled.

Since the use of capital controls in Spain has been, and still is, significant, it is important to consider what may be its economic justification. In this regard, it is convenient to start by pointing out the desirability of free capital flows in a world without distortions. As the literature on the intertemporal open economy models teaches us,[25] free capital mobility allows domestic residents to reallocate resources optimally over time so as to achieve the desired time path of consumption. Consequently, in a first-best world with perfectly functioning markets and fully flexible prices and wages, capital controls have no place. In reality, however, things may be quite different from the above idealized paradigm. In fact, both the short-run stickiness of wages and prices and other distortions may well explain why exchange controls have been and are still used by so many countries.

In the specific case of Spain, the use of capital controls can be attributed to the following reasons:

First, the almost chronic trade and current account deficits of the balance of payments during many years after the end of the Civil War led to a system of capital controls which tended to discourage capital outflows, so that scarce foreign reserves were not depleted. Although in recent years Spain's trade and current account balances have improved quite significantly, the system of capital controls has continued to discourage 'net outflows' by being legally more severe on outflows than on inflows.

Second, capital controls were established during a period when Spain was pursuing a fixed exchange-rate policy, which lasted until 1974. This allowed the authorities to achieve simultaneously exchange-rate targets and interest-rate targets (money-targets have not been pursued until very recently) which made it easier to reconcile their domestic (growth, inflation) and external (exchange-rate) goals. Although the authorites formally abandoned the fixed exchange rate policy in 1974 following the example of most industrialized nations, they have continued to pursue a 'managed' exchange-rate policy in the past few years which has now been made explicit with the integration of the peseta in the European Monetary System since mid-June, 1989.

Finally, the authorities understood that capital controls had to be in effect as long as the domestic financial system was subject to significant restrictions and regulations, to avoid severe 'spillover' effects towards external financial markets that might undermine the stability and growth prospects of the domestic financial market. At the same time, the authorities found it natural that the capital account be subject to restrictions since the current account was also subject to restrictions, perhaps – unconsciously – following the recommendations of the existing literature on the order of economic liberalization. This literature suggests that it may be convenient not to get rid of capital controls before the current account is substantially open. Otherwise, the relative faster speed of adjustment in assets markets relative to goods markets may produce significant short-term capital flows and exchange rate pressures that might compromise the whole liberalization process.[26]

Broadly speaking, at the time of entry to the EC the Spanish network of capital controls had two main features. First, although controls were imposed both on long-term and short-term capital flows, they were much stricter on short-term capital flows. Second, although there were controls both on inflows and outflows the second were more numerous and stricter than the first, giving an asymmetric bias which favoured inflows.[27]

The effective degree of capital mobility   It is clear from our previous discussion that legal capital controls were relatively more restrictive on short-term flows, while longer-term capital flows already enjoyed a substantially greater degree of freedom – especially regarding inflows – on the eve of Spain's entry to the EC. Because of this and also because of the critical macroeconomic role of short-term capital mobility, we now turn

	1982	1983	1984	1985	1982–85
Average (1)	−0.41	0.20	0.19	0.10	0.02
Standard deviation (1)	0.99	0.44	0.58	0.39	0.60
Percentage of observations in excess of ± 0.5% from covered interest parity	40.0	26.9	30.8	13.5	27.8
Total weeks	52	52	52	52	208

Table 7.17. Covered interest-rate differential between the peseta and the Eurodollar, 1982–85 (3-month deposit, January 1982–December 1985)

Note:
(1) Percentage points, annualized.

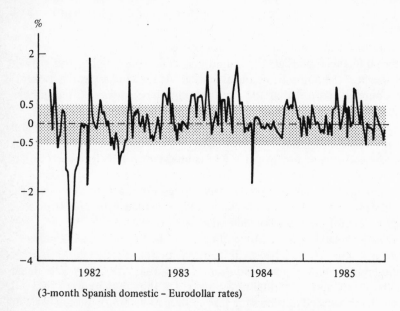

(3-month Spanish domestic – Eurodollar rates)

Figure 7.3   Spain: deviations from covered interest parity, 1982–85

to analyze how effectively open was the short-term capital account of the Spanish economy prior to 1986.

From the above description of the very strict system of Spanish capital controls (more than 150 legal norms, each with many clauses), one would suspect that domestic and foreign financial markets must not have been very integrated. However, what really matters is whether or not these controls were really effective. Once this is known, it will be possible to speculate whether the opening up process of the capital account dictated by EC entry and '1992-related' EC Directives should be considered a 'large' or a 'small' shock.

The easiest and most appropriate way to measure the degree of short-term capital mobility is to check the extent to which the data violate the benchmark of covered interest-rate parity. If covered interest-rate parity holds continuously, there are no unexploited profit opportunities for investors, and therefore they are indifferent between placing their funds in domestic or foreign short-term assets. If, on the other hand, deviations from covered interest-rate parity are found, there exist profit opportunities whose exploitation is prevented by the existence of binding capital controls.

Figure 7.3 represents the observed deviations from interest-rate parity during the 1982–85 period.[28] It shows, quite surprisingly, that the deviations from covered interest-rate parity were quite small during the period, especially given the extensive network of legal controls on international capital flows between Spain and the rest of the world previously described. In fact, if one allows for a ± 0.5% band around covered interest-rate parity to take account of transaction costs, it can be concluded that there is no hard evidence of very large unexploited profit opportunities in the 1982–85 period.[29]

More precisely, Table 7.17 contains several useful statistics that show the sign, average size and standard deviation of measured covered differentials as well as the frequency with which these differentials were in excess of ± 0.5%. As can be seen in the Table, the annual average covered differential was well below 0.5% in every year, and after 1983 it was always positive. At the same time, with the exception of 1982, the percentage of observed deviations in excess of ± 0.5% was relatively small. Therefore, it can be concluded that except in the first half of 1982 the data do not show the existence of substantial arbitrage opportunities. In other words, capital controls do not seem to have been binding for the most part of the 1982–85 period in Spain, i.e. 72% of the time. It is, nevertheless, necessary to investigate a bit further the reasons why Spain has had such an apparently large effective degree of openness on capital account transactions even prior to EC entry.

In this regard, it should be noted that Spanish monetary authorities had regularly intervened in the forward exchange market until February 6, 1984. The reason why this is relevant is because the intervention forward rate was set so as to minimize deviations from covered interest-rate parity and therefore avoid tensions in the peseta foreign-exchange market.

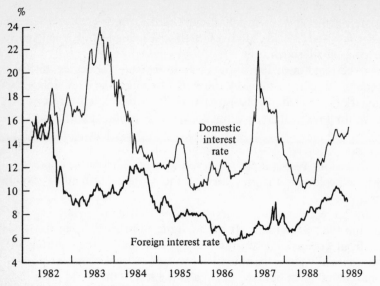

Figure 7.4   Peseta and Eurodollar 3-month deposit interest rates, 1982–89

Consequently, the very small covered interest-rate differentials observed between the peseta and the Eurodollar until 1984 are due, not so much to the existence of unimpeded private capital flows as to official forward market interventions.

What still remains to be explained is why covered interest-rate parity is so precisely satisfied from February 1984 till the end of 1985. Figure 7.4 gives us the clue: between these two dates the differential between the peseta and the dollar interest rate was rather stable and small when compared with the preceding periods. In such a context, exchange market tensions were relatively small, and the desired arbitrage operations took place through the loopholes in the law (over-invoicing and under-invoicing in foreign trade), and also through the lengthening and shortening of the maturity of commercial credits. As is often said, 'capital controls work only when they bite'.

A few conclusions emerge from the above analysis: first, long-term capital flows were already substantially liberalized by the time of Spain's entry into the EC in 1986. Short-term capital flows were, on the other hand, legally quite restricted especially regarding capital outflows. And second, in spite of the very complex and extensive network of capital controls, measured deviations from covered interest-rate parity have been relatively small – and certainly smaller than generally believed – in the 1982–85 period. In fact, 72% of the observations satisfy the criterion of covered interest-rate parity once account is taken of transaction costs.

From our analysis of the structural characteristics of Spain's current and capital account on the eve of EC integration, it would be reasonable to conclude that while the change in 'goods mobility' derived from Spain's EC membership is likely to constitute a very significant shock in goods markets, the change in the degree of 'capital mobility' is not likely to be as important for financial markets.

Banks and asset markets[30]

Although the Accession Treaty between Spain and the EC did not have a major economic impact on the structure of the financial system, important changes are envisaged in recently passed EC Directives leading to the establishment of unrestricted banking activities by member countries Community-wide and to the free supply of financial services. In this section we analyze the most salient characteristics of Spain's present financial system and identify what are likely to be the main issues raised by 1992. In what follows, we examine the main segments of the Spanish financial system: the banking system, money markets and capital markets.

Banks   Until very recently the Spanish banking system has remained a rather static, sheltered, over-regulated, and relatively inefficient sector. This has been the case both for commercial banks and for savings banks. Unlike in other European countries, banks have had close ties to industry. Banks have often been important shareholders as well as lenders to industrial firms. While this feature may have economic advantages like the reduction of informational asymmetries between lenders and borrowers, it also has a major disadvantage in terms of excessive concentration of debt and equity risk in banks' assets. Those risks materialized in the deep and severe banking crisis that occurred after 1978 – and which affected almost half of the banks existing in 1977 – as a result of the strong industrial crisis suffered by the Spanish economy. Although the crisis ended with a recomposition of banking groups and with the creation of public institutions in charge of closely monitoring the performance of banks in trouble, the continuing close links between some of the major banks and industry still prevail. In September 1988 Spanish banks held almost 1 billion pesetas in shares, which is equivalent to 10% of the total stock market capitalization at the end of 1988, and to almost 50% of total bank equity (capital plus reserves). Accordingly, the future of important segments of the banking system cannot be detached from the future of industry.

The performance of the Spanish banking system relative to its European

		Spain	France	Germany	Italy	Year
1	Share of GDP (%)	6.1	4.5	5.6	5.6	1985
2	Share of employment (%)	3.9	3.4	3.7	2.5	1985
3	Bank loans/GDP (%)	99	93	139	96	1984
4	Labour costs/Assets (%)	2.1	1.3	1.5	2.1	1986
5	General Costs (Banks)/Assets (%)	3.0	2.1	2.2	3.0	1986
6	General costs (savings)/Assets (%)	3.8	—	2.2	2.2	1986
7	Inhabitants per branch	1,191	2,636	1,530	4,192	1986
8	Interest spread (%)	6.1	5.1	5.3	4.5	1988
9	Intermediation margin/GDP (%)	7.2	4.3	4.7	—	1986
10	Average fall in prices (%)	34	25	33	18	1986

Table 7.18. Comparative measures of output and costs in banking, 1984–88

Sources and brief explanation

1 *European Economy* (1988): Value added by the credit and insurance industries ('branches') GDP.
2 Id.: Employment in the credit and insurance branches over total employment. Information for Italy refers to 1985.
3 Id.: Ratio of outstanding bank loans to GDP.
4 *Boletín Económico* (1988), primary source OECD, 'Bank Profitability': Labour costs (including contribution to pension schemes) over average assets.
5 Id.: Non-financial transformation costs of banking sector, including contributions to deposit insurance funds, over average assets.
6 Id.: Idem for savings banks.
7 Steinherr and Gillibert (1988): Total population divided by the number of branches.
8 Id.: Prime or base rates minus average interest rate on saving deposits having maturity of one year.
9 Torrero (1988): Margin of intermediation obtained by the credit system over GDP.
10 *European Economy* (1988): 'Implied potential price fall' of banking services.

counterparts is usually characterized as exhibiting both high transformation costs and high profitability. Spanish banks have substantial intermediation margins that allow them to incur high operating costs and still maintain a good level of profitability. The popular interpretation of these two facts – accepted as conventional wisdom in the literature – is that Spanish banks are highly inefficient, but are able to remain profitable thanks to their exercise of market power. These issues are analyzed in what follows.

Looking first at *transformation costs*, Table 7.18 presents some comparative ratios for Spain and other EC countries which seem to support the idea that the Spanish banking sector has relatively high costs per unit of output. The higher share of the financial sector in Spanish GDP (row 1) can be interpreted either as indicating that Spain is 'overbanked' or that financial services are 'overpriced' – either because of inefficiencies or non-competitive pricing. This is consistent with the finding that the share of employment in the financial industry over total employment (row 2) is also relatively high in Spain.

If we compare the value of outstanding bank loans over GDP (an output measure) shown in row 3 with the share of banking value added in GDP, a rough measure of unit costs is obtained. This indicator reveals that these costs are higher in Spain than in other European countries, which is consistent with the inefficiency-hypothesis of the Spanish banking sector. Rows 4 to 7 provide alternative indicators which seem also to support this hypothesis.

The margin of intermediation is measured in rows 8 to 10 in the Table. As can be seen, Spain's banking sector has the highest interest spread between deposit and lending rates, and it is estimated that the degree of 'overpricing' in banking services[31] is 34%, a number higher than in the other countries shown in the Table. Although part of the interest spread is due to the relatively high legal reserve requirements imposed on commercial banks and savings banks, it nevertheless points to an inefficient financial intermediation process. In turn, there are several reasons that may account for this behaviour: non-competitive pricing, x-inefficiency, and other factors like tastes, technological and geographical constraints, and regulation. In this respect, our hunch is that the fast process of deregulation that has been affecting Spanish financial markets over the last few years (freeing of interest rates and commissions) can make banks look temporarily inefficient while they adjust their human and physical capital to the new *status-quo*.

Turning now to *profitability*, there is a popular belief that Spanish banks are highly profitable, which is usually interpreted as meaning that they exercise some degree of monopoly power. But first let us see if this belief is supported by facts. Table 7.19 gives two alternative measures of profitability in the banking sector (return on assets, and return on equity) for Spain and several other EC countries. As can be observed, the performance of Spanish commercial and savings banks is better than that of the other countries when we measure profitability as accounting profits over total assets (shown in rows 1 and 4). However, Spanish banking sector profitability is relatively lower than in the other countries when measured relative to equity (rows 2 and 5). The third and sixth rows of

	Spain	France	Germany	Italy
Commercial banks				
1 Return on assets	0.81	0.38	0.79	0.50
2 Return on equity	14.4	14.9	16.9	17.1
3 Equity/Assets	5.7	2.6	4.7	5.1
Savings banks				
4 Return on assets	0.9	—	0.94	0.92
5 Return on equity	16.9	—	25.1	26.1
6 Equity/Assets	5.4	—	3.8	3.5

Table 7.19. The comparative profitability of EC banking industries, 1985–86[1] (percent)

Sources: Boletín Económico (1988), Torrero (1988), Drazen (1988), Ballarin *et al.* (1988).

Note:
(1) Data refer to 1986, and for Italy to 1985. French data refer to both commercial and saving banks. Profits are before-tax profits.

Table 7.19 point to the cause of these differences in measured profitability: the lower leverage of Spanish banks due to the tough solvency requirements imposed by the authorities following the banking crisis.

In sum, although there is no clear-cut evidence either supporting or rejecting the popular belief that Spanish banks have a relatively high profitability *vis-à-vis* other national banking systems, it is clear, nevertheless, that there are no profitability or solvency problems in Spanish banking. In fact, it can be claimed that Spanish banking constitutes the most profitable sector of the economy at present, judged by the 14.7% average annual return on equity obtained in the 1985–87 period, which substantially exceeds the 6.2% obtained by private non-financial firms.[32]

Given the coexistence of high intermediation costs and significant profitability, can we safely conclude that Spanish banks exercise some degree of monopoly power? Under the traditional I.O. paradigm of 'market structure-conduct-performance', the most relevant structural dimension for the study of the possession of monopoly power is the degree of *market concentration*. Table 7.20 contains two alternative indices of concentration. In part A is shown the total market share in total deposits by the biggest 5, 10, 20 and 50 banks in different years, and according to varying institutional criteria. As can be seen, during the 1980s there was a process which tended to reduce the market share of the largest 5 commercial banks. This process – which continued the trend

	Individual banks			Banks Groups			Private and savings banks			
	1980	1988	1988 (1)	1980	1988	1988 (1)	1980	1988	1988 (1)	1988 (2)
A. *Number of Banks*										
5	50	46	52	58	58	66	33	28	31	39
10	68	66	68	84	83	86	49	45	47	57
20	80	80	81				62	59	60	71
50	93	95	96				80	79	80	89
B. *Herfindahl index*	0.062	0.056	0.066		0.090	0.109	0.031	0.026	0.030	0.045

Table 7.20. Indices of concentration in the Spanish banking sector, 1980–88

Sources: Consejo Superior Bancario, Confederación Española de Cajas de Ahorro, and own computations.

Notes:
(1) Consolidated data for BBV used.
(2) Data corresponds to commercial bank groups (after mergers) and savings banks.

observed between 1952 and 1980 – was reversed in 1988, with the merger of two of the six big banks into Banco Bilbao-Vizcaya (formerly Banco de Bilbao and Banco de Vizcaya).

The existence of a trend towards lower concentration is not so clear, however, when we look at bank groups. This implies that the relative size of the group with respect to the parent company increased, which may be either a consequence of the process of absorption of smaller banks after the banking crisis or, rather, a deliberate strategic choice. Again, the merger breaks the stability of the market share of the five big banks, which suddenly jumps to 66% in 1988.

When one looks at commercial and savings banks together a process towards lower concentration between 1980 and 1988 is also detected. This may be due to the faster rate of expansion of savings banks during the period – as some of the regulatory constraints imposed on them were partially relaxed – together with their smaller size relative to the major commercial banks. Indeed, the market share of savings banks in total deposits has gone from 24.1% in 1975, to 39.7% in 1982, and to 47% as of September 1988. However, the merger previously discussed breaks the trend towards lower concentration, as also happened in the other cases examined.

Part B of Table 7.20 looks at the Herfindahl index, which is defined as the sum of squares of market shares of firms in a particular market or industry. This index ranges from near zero (pure competition) to 1 (pure monopoly), and its inverse gives the equivalent number of firms of identical size that generate the same market concentration. This index is attractive because its properties can be interpreted in terms of Cournot competition, and because it does not have the drawbacks of the absolute concentration index just discussed: dependence on the number of firms, and not accounting for differences in size. The computed values of the Herfindahl index in the Table seem to corroborate quite precisely the trend towards lower concentration observed in the 1980s until it was sharply reversed by the recent mergers.

Several conclusions can be drawn from the previous analysis of concentration. First, from 1980 to 1988 there was a continuation of the trend towards lower concentration that persisted during the 1952–80 period. Second, the 1980–88 period has witnessed an increase in the market share of savings banks, which has dynamized competition. Competition has also increased due to the active role played by foreign banks, which have contributed to enlarge quite considerably the menu of financial products in the market. Competition has also been possible thanks to the recent de-regulation of the Spanish banking system[33] (freeing of borrowing and lending interest rates, relaxed constraints on operations allowed to savings banks, etc. . . .). Third, the merger of two major banks into the new biggest bank of the country represents a reversal of the previous long-term trend towards lower concentration. The merger was justified in terms of unexploited scale economies and improved competitiveness to face the 1992 challenge. However, the fact is that it may also have increased the industry-specific risk of the banking sector and led to future negative effects on competition, particularly in some banking products in which the new banks may have a disproportionate share of the market. And, fourth, this pessimistic view of competition in the Spanish banking industry may be tempered by the beneficial effects of the financial integration process due to take place after 1992.

Money, bond and stock markets The previous sections have been devoted to the analysis of some of the most relevant features of the Spanish banking sector. In this section, we provide a brief description of the present features of Spain's money, bond, and stock markets.

The stage of development of Spanish financial markets is very asymmetrical: highly developed markets with a degree of sophistication comparable to the most advanced European markets have been living alongside sleepy markets with some regulations and practices dating back to the nineteenth century. In the mid-1970s, the strict regulation and control of every financial activity by the Bank of Spain and/or the Ministry of the Economy, together with the cosy *status-quo* of the banking sector, led the financial sector to a level of underdevelopment that contrasted with other parts of the Spanish economy. Regulations started to be loosened up and reform was very different across markets. The chief explanation for this asymmetry in the evolution is probably that reforms were implemented only when they contributed to solve some urgent needs of the public sector. These urgent needs were mainly the necessity of creating flexible ways of deficit financing (in a scenario of runaway public sector deficits until 1985) and, also, the necessity of flexible monetary policy instruments that could provide the Bank of Spain with the necessary tools for bringing two-digit inflation under control.

The previous explanation is corroborated by an examination of the situation of the Spanish financial sector at the time of the accession to the EC, and its evolution to the present. The most developed markets are the interbank market and the market for short and medium-term government debt. Their degree of sophistication contrasted (especially in 1986) with the situation of the other segments of the money and capital markets, such as the stock market and the markets for private debt instruments (long-term private bonds, mortgages and derivative instruments, etc.). As we shall see, the demands of a booming economy together with the spectre

	1982	1985	1987	1988
A. Interbank market (1)				
Total daily flows	138	412	790	
Deposits outstanding	300	962	2,695	
B. Short-term bond market (2)				
T. bills (Pagarés)				
Gross issue	131	4,708	3,314	2,965
Outstanding stock	115	5,100	5,332	5,051
T. notes (Letras)				
Gross issue	—	—	2,538	3,658
Outstanding stock	—	—	—	—
C. Long-term bond market (2)				
T. bonds (Bonos)				
Gross issue	151	387	1,038	1,163
Outstanding stock	606	1,100	3,287	4,276
Private fixed interest rate bonds				
Gross issue	574	1,086	640	759 (3)
Outstanding stock	2,120	3,655	4,220	4,350
D. Stock exchange (4)				
Volume	172	621	4,766	3,021
Net issue	141	207	456	495
Capitalization	1,403	3,007	7,240	9,640
Market Index	69	122	358	397
(1970 = 100)				

Table 7.21. Spanish money, bond and stock markets, 1982–88 (billion pesetas)

Sources and notes:
(1) Daily averages. Taken from Trujillo *et al.* (1988).
(2) From Banco de España Data Bank.
(3) Flows from January to November, and stocks outstanding in November.
(4) From Banco de España Data Bank and Bolsa de Madrid.

of the 1992 liberalization have led to rapid movement in the right direction for many of these markets.

Table 7.21 presents the main stylized facts of Spain's money, bond, and stock markets. Part A shows the growing importance of the *interbank market*, which is closely linked to the process of liquidity creation of the Bank of Spain. Nowadays, the market is sizeable, deep, and works very efficiently with a simple and direct clearing system. Part B shows that the development of the *short-term bond market* has been less gradual than in the interbank market. This, in turn, has been due to the changing needs of the Treasury regarding the financing of sizeable budget deficits, to the relative after-tax real unattractiveness of deposit interest rates in the late 1970s and early 1980s, and also to the increasing sophistication of monetary control. As may be observed, total market volume has grown quite spectacularly between 1982 and 1988, representing in this last year about 22% of Spanish GDP.

Other short-term bond markets are the mortgage market and the commercial paper market. The first has not taken off yet, and the second enjoyed a large success before the appearance of Treasury notes. Nowadays, the commercial paper market is particularly ripe for development, given the recent strong growth of private investment and the relatively high transformation costs of the banking sector. Nevertheless, the market will not be consolidated until the unfavourable fiscal treatment – relative to T-bills – is eliminated, and until the archaic operating mechanics of the market are changed.

Part C of Table 7.21 summarizes the recent evolution of the Spanish *long-term bond market*. The main instruments traded are private fixed interest rate bonds ('obligaciones privadas'), and Treasury bonds ('obligaciones' for maturities above 5 years, and 'bonos' for maturities below). The T-bond market started from a very low level and grew slowly until 1986, when the outstanding stock almost tripled as a result of the aggressive issuing policy of the Treasury in that year in an environment where the private sector held expectations of future lower interest rates and of the development of a sophisticated T-bond market. Since then, the delay in the introduction of the expected market reform and the restrictive monetary policy stance since 1987 have led to a T-bond supply and demand contraction which has slowed down market growth. Nevertheless, the future of the Treasury bond market looks bright if and when the current demand management problems leading to very high short-term interest rates are solved. Once this is accomplished, the recent technical improvements in the market will make it deep, liquid, efficient, and transparent, and it will become a centrepiece of the Spanish financial system.

Where things look rather less encouraging is in the private long-term bond market. As shown in Table 7.21, while the relative size of this market was rather large in 1982, its growth since then has been much slower than in the public long-term bond market, even suffering a decline in gross issues since 1987. This recent setback was linked to the near-bankruptcy of one of the major utility companies in the country which prompted a very negative reaction in the market. This episode – which surprised most market participants – points out the problems caused by the absence of a reliable debt rating service that could orientate investors.

Other negative factors in the market are the recent increase in interest-rate volatility, the low degree of development of pension funds and other natural buyers of long-term bonds, and the lack of long-term public bond issues which leaves the private market without a reference point. In any case, the lack of development of the long-term private bond market has fairly negative implications for the access of firms to badly-needed long term capital, as is the case with utilities and other capital-intensive industries. This makes firms resort to the Euromarket, to higher than desirable short-term financing, or to tapping the less reliable equity market. Still, for many small firms bank credit is the only option to finance long-term capital needs.

Turning now to the *stock market*, there is a presumption – both in public and private circles – that this is the segment of the financial market that could be most negatively affected by the 1992 Single European Market.[34] However, it should be pointed out that this vulnerability is also shared by most of the continental stock markets of the Community, including the French, Italian, and German markets.

Figures 7.5 and 7.6 show that the Spanish stock market is not very different either in terms of capitalization or liquidity from those of other major continental European nations. However, to complete the picture of the Spanish stock market it is necessary to make some additional remarks. First, the exceptional performance of the market from 1985 till October 1987 (shown in Table 7.21) in relation to other national markets may have artificially increased Spanish capitalization above normal values. Second, the market is very narrow, with fewer than 400 quoted companies, out of which only about 60 have enough liquidity to be acceptable in the port-folios of large investors. Moreover, banks and public utilities account for about 75% of total assets traded, prices are still subject to the manipu-lations of large shareholders, and insider trading has not until now been regulated. Finally, until mid-1989 the compensation and liquidation process was very archaic, the official intermediary agents charged a fixed fee (independent of volume) that discriminated against small investors, and there was a lack of self-regulatory power of the Exchanges. All these features have hindered the efficiency of the Spanish stock market until now.

The fear that the Spanish stock market would be badly hurt by 1992 has led the authorities to issue legislation to overhaul the market and to get rid of most of the above mentioned problems, starting in mid-1989. Given the important role that the stock market can play in helping Spanish firms adjust to increasing international competition derived from the 'EC cum 1992' shock, it is criticial that additional legal reforms take place soon and that incentives are provided to simultaneously expand market supply and demand.

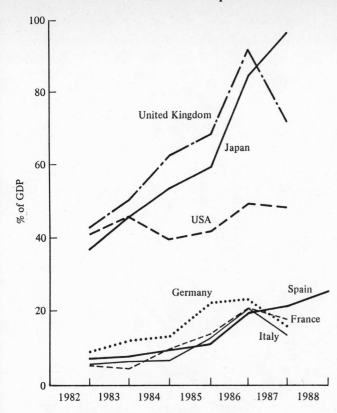

Source: Gutiérrez and Segura (1989).

Figure 7.5   Stock market capitalization, 1983–88

Overall assessment of the Spanish economy

From our review of the structural characteristics of Spain's economy prior to the 'EC cum 1992' shock, it can be concluded that the darkest spot is the very high and persistent unemployment rate which, in turn, reveals major mismatch problems in the Spanish labour market. Spain's relatively less open current account, its relatively more open capital account and its relatively healthy financial system suggest that, if anything, the adjustment costs from EC integration may be larger in goods and labour markets than in financial markets, although given the close links between banks and industry bad industrial performance could cause financial distress. Moreover, since Spain's industrial trade shows a high and increasing degree of concentration in the OECD, and most significantly in the EC, it is to be expected that the free trade adjustment

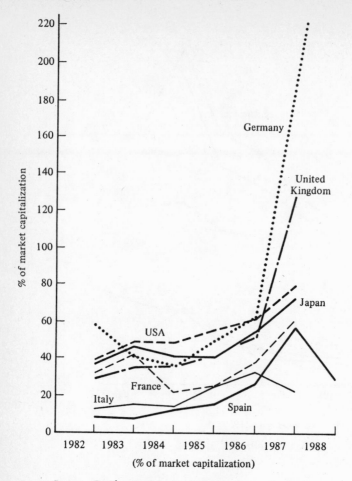

Source: Gutiérrez and Segura (1989)

Figure 7.6   Annual stock rotation, 1983–88

started in 1986 and to be completed in 1992 will significantly affect Spain's industrial structure. Finally, since Spain's trade pattern shows both important inter-industry and intra-industry components, this seems to depart also from the typical case of a 'Southern' economy entering into a 'Northern' Common Market.

The review of Spain's industrial structure reveals important short-comings and comparative disadvantages in terms of insufficient size and low technology. A large part of the gains from trade that Spain can achieve within the EC have to be based on exploiting the country's comparative labour-cost advantage. For this to be so, relative wage and non-wage labour costs have to be kept down in the future. Simultaneously, improving labour market functional and geographical mobility will help reduce short-run employment costs. And last, moving to a more efficient financial system will facilitate the required capital reallocations between sectors, and finance the investment process in more favourable conditions.

3   Adjustment to the 'EC cum 1992' shock

3.1   Goods market integration and trade flows

In this section we analyze the economic adjustment process of the Spanish economy to the 'EC cum 1992' shock. We start by examining the recent experience of Spain inside the EC in the 1986–88 period with the hope of finding some clues as to the likely evolution of trade flows, output and employment following the completion of the Single Internal Market in 1992. Then we go on to discuss what kind of long-run potential gains and medium-run adjustment costs are likely to come from the full integration of Spain's goods markets with those of the rest of the EC.

What can be learned from the 1986–88 experience?

Output, employment and investment   From our discussion of the major structural characteristics of the Spanish economy on the eve of EC integration, it seemed as if the country could suffer a major real shock from the trade liberalization process, given the weaknesses there detected. However – and fortunately for Spain – the trade liberalization process that started in 1986 occurred simultaneously with a drop in world energy prices, as well as with an ongoing expansion in the major economies. These events, coupled with the pursuit of an economic policy strategy directed at removing some of the fundamental rigidities of the economy has led to excellent overall macroeconomic performance since 1986.

In fact, as Table 7.22 shows, in the 1986–88 period Spain's macroeconomic performance inside the EC has been quite satisfactory. Real growth has accelerated, unemployment and inflation have declined, there has been an impressive investment boom, and public finances have improved. Moreover, behind this performance there has been an interaction of market forces with domestic policy actions which has had important effects on goods and labour markets.

Regarding *tradeable goods markets*, it is nowadays still true that the typical Spanish industrial firm continues to suffer from a relatively

	1985	1986	1987	1988
Quantities				
Real Growth (GDP) (1)	2.3	3.3	5.5	5.2
Unemployment (2)	21.4	21.0	20.6	19.5
Fixed Investment (1)	4.1	10.0	14.6	14.2
Current Account (3)	1.7	1.8	−0.0	−1.1
Budget Balance (3)	−7.0	−6.1	−3.6	−3.0
Public Debt (3)	46.4	47.4	48.1	48.0
Prices				
Inflation (CPI) (1)	8.3	8.8	5.2	4.8
Real long-term interest rate (4)	5.1	2.6	7.6	7.2
Real exchange rate, CPI-based (1)	1.2	5.5	3.0	5.1
Real wages (1, 5)	1.3	−0.4	2.4	1.8

Table 7.22. Spain's macroeconomic performance, 1985–88

Sources: EC and Banco de España.

Notes:
(1) Percent annual growth rate.
(2) In percent.
(3) In percent of GDP.
(4) In levels. Deflated by CPI.
(5) Hourly wage deflated by GDP deflator.

insufficient size and a low technological level. However, during the past years there has been an impressive investment boom in the country which has improved the quantity and quality of the industrial capital stock, as documented by González-Romero and Myro (1989). In fact, while gross manufacturing investment has been growing in the EC at an average annual rate of 5.7% in 1986–88, in Spain it has grown at an average annual rate of 26.8% during the same period.

No doubt, the investment boom experienced in the Spanish economy in these past years has favoured the process of capital allocation towards the expanding sectors, which explains the dynamism of the economy in that period. On the other hand, this impressive investment performance has been due to the sustained increase of aggregate demand – at an average annual rate of 7.4% – to the substantial recovery of profit margins in the private sector – from 4.1% of equity in 1984 to 9.1% in 1987 – and also to the prospects of continuing economic and political stability.

Mention should also be made of the important contribution made by foreign direct investment[35] to the overall investment process. This contribution is illustrated by the fact that while in the 1981–85 period foreign

	% of total FDI (a)	Imports as a % of demand (b)	Exports as a % of output (b)	% change in real imports (c)	% change in real exports (c)	% change in revealed comparative advantage (c)	% change in output (c)	% change in employment (c)	% change in labour productivity (c)
Sectors with high FDI	86	24	17	123	28	−27	27	7	22
Sectors with low FDI	14	18	15	87	−9	−36	16	11	7
Total manufacturing	100	22	16	109	10	−32	22	9	15

Table 7.23. Foreign direct investment in Spanish manufacturing and sectoral performance, 1985–88

Sources: Own elaboration.

Notes:
(a) Average 1986–88.
(b) In 1988.
(c) Change over the 1985–88 period.

direct investment inflows amounted to 0.7% of GDP and 9% of total investment, in 1986–88 they amounted to 1.33% and 15.6% respectively, half of them going to industry. The very important role played by foreign investment in the reorganization of the Spanish manufacturing sector is also revealed by the fact that about 35% of the total investment made in the 1986–88 period has been due to foreign direct investment. At the same time, the foreign direct investment coming into strong, moderate, and weak-demand sectors has been respectively 88%, 52%, and 11% of the total investment in each of these sectors during the period.

Since most of the direct foreign investment flows have gone into the more dynamic manufacturing sectors, this may have contributed to the exploitation of scale economies, to the use of more advanced technology, new management, better and larger distribution networks, etc. Indeed, as shown in Table 7.23, the group of sectors which received most of the foreign direct investment in these past years are also those sectors which had a higher rate of output growth, larger productivity increases, a larger propensity to export and import, and a lower deterioration of their net external trade positions. Given the current technological gap of Spain's industry, the role of foreign direct investment as a vehicle for the transfer of technology is most critical. That this has indeed been the case is exemplified by the remarkable increase of Spain's payments for technology imports since 1986, 60% of these payments coming from manufacturing activities where the presence of foreign direct investment was high.

Finally, the far-reaching reorganization of the public industrial sector in the past few years also deserves mention. In fact, although by 1985 Spanish public firms only represented 4.5% of the total employment of the economy – as compared with 12.3% in the EC4 – and 15.9% of total gross fixed investment – as compared with 27.7% in the EC4 – there was a widespread perception that their very large consolidated losses reflected major inefficiencies in the organization of production. Consequently, during these past years there has been a significant overhaul of Spanish public industry. As a result, the absorption of private firms has halted, employment has been reduced, public-sector wages have moderated and several major privatization operations have been undertaken.

In sum, although some of the most salient relative disadvantages in Spain's tradeables goods sector are still present, nevertheless there have been significant improvements in the past few years relative to the situation prior to entering the EC.

With respect to the *nontradeable goods market*, there have also been important changes. Most significantly, during the 1986–88 period there has been a very substantial reduction of the budget deficit basically due to the faster increase in tax revenues – coming from direct taxation and VAT

– but also helped by the moderation of current transfers and public consumption. This has made it possible to go from a total general government deficit of 7% of GDP in 1985 to a deficit of 3% in 1988, while the primary deficit has gone respectively from 4.8% to a surplus of 0.3% in the same years. This, in turn, has made it easier to preserve a low inflation rate in the future. The above notwithstanding, it is still the case that the proportion of public expenditure devoted to capital formation continues to be small relative to the size of the infrastructural gap of the country, a problem to be dealt with as a matter of urgency in future years.

Another development that deserves attention is that the nontradeables goods market has remarkably increased its importance as a recipient of direct foreign investment. While the nontradeables sector received about 23.4% of total direct foreign investment flows in 1986, it received 62.1% in 1988 – most of it going into finance, insurance and real estate. It is likely that the real appreciation of the peseta during the period and the booming financial services industry are the main causes of the increasing attractiveness of the nontradeables sector. For these reasons, it is important to avoid a real overvaluation of the currency that damages the tradeables sector in the future, given that the share of the tradeables sector in total GDP has dropped from 36.1% in 1985 to 35.7% in 1988.

All of the above developments in goods markets have also been reflected in the *labour market*. Thus, the 1986–88 period has witnessed an increase in employment for the first time since 1974, and a reduction in unemployment for the first time since 1969, although the current unemployment rate – slightly below 18% – still remains too high. Nevertheless, the creation of jobs has been rather unevenly divided between the tradeables and nontradeables sectors, with the most important increases taking place in the second sector.

At the aggregate level, it is very important to ask what fundamental developments in the labour market brought the significant increase in employment. Table 7.13 gives us some clues. As can be seen, while a few years ago aggregate demand was the most important locally binding constraint on the labour demand of firms (in 74% of the cases), the very high increase in aggregate demand in the past years has, undoubtedly, favoured an increase in labour demand. This seems to be consistent with the fact that in 1985–87 a smaller percentage of firms (46%) had aggregate demand as the locally binding constraint on labour demand.

On the other hand, the analysis synthesized in Table 7.13 also shows that 54% of firms are still locally constrained in their labour demand by the lack of sufficient productive capacity. In this instance, it has also probably been the case that the substantial increase in capital formation that has taken place in these past years has relieved some of these capacity constraints, leading to the increase in labour demand of many firms. However, it seems to also be the case that the relaxation of the capacity constraint has been slower than the relaxation of the aggregate output demand constraint, as indicated by the larger percentage of firms – 54% – now experiencing local capacity constraints on labour demand. A final reason why labour demand has increased in the past years is the moderation of real-wage costs, which have gone from increasing at an annual average rate of 0.9% in 1981–85 to decreasing at a rate of 0.9% in 1986–88.

On the labour-supply side, however, developments have been rather mixed. True enough, Table 7.13 does not indicate any constraints on employment creation coming from lack of workers being available for work. However, what the aggregate figures in the Table cannot capture is the extent to which there has or has not been labour mismatch, although our labour-market analysis suggests that this has been indeed a serious problem. This notwithstanding, it must be said that the new legislation issued in 1984 allowing for temporary and training contracts probably helped to create new jobs and, particularly, reduced the unemployment rate of young people as shown in Table 7.15, part A. However, a very unpleasant characteristic of the recent recovery has been that the structure of unemployment has worsened in terms of duration. Specifically, the long-term unemployed have gone from representing about 57% of the total unemployed in 1985 to 59% in 1988, a historical peak. This, in turn, has two undesirable implications: first, it leads to a gradual reduction of the human capital of the unemployed which lowers their probability of finding a job; and second, this gradual deterioration of the skills of the unemployed contributes to further increasing the degree of mismatch, lowering the capacity of the economy to transform demand growth into output growth without inflationary pressures.

Trade flows   Table 7.24 summarizes the main characteristics of the changes in Spanish external protection derived from the clauses of the Treaty of Accession signed with the EC. As can be seen, the liberalization of trade in agricultural products postpones that of fruits, vegetables, and vegetable fats until 1996. As a result, looking at the 1986–88 experience may underestimate the extent of the trade changes and potential welfare gains that Spain can reap from exploiting its natural comparative advantage in agricultural products within the EC. In what follows we analyze the most visible implications of the trade liberalization process on trade flows both at the aggregate and sectoral levels.

At the *aggregate* level, the most visible impact of Spain's integration into the EC has been the very significant increase in the degree of

A. *Industrial* products:
  1. Gradual tariff rate reduction process from the base rate (approximately 14%) to zero in the case of other EC countries, and from the base rate to the (lower) Common External Tariff rate (CET approximately 4–5%).
  2. The time-table for the above tariff reduction is as follows:

		% reduction	
March 1st	1986	....	10
January 1st	1987	....	12.5
,,	1988	....	15
,,	1989	....	15
,,	1990	....	12.5
,,	1991	....	12.5
,,	1992	....	12.5
,,	1993	....	10
Total		....	100

  3. Most quantitative restrictions between Spain and the EC can be maintained only until 1-1-1990. In fact, Spain got rid of many quantitative restrictions in 1986.

B. *Agricultural* products
  1. Products originating in any EC country have preference (relative to products originating in non-EC countries) in other EC countries.
  2. Common Agricultural Policy accepted as of 1986.
  3. Gradual tariff rate reduction for agricultural products to be completed by 1–1–1993. The time-table for fruits, vegetables, and vegetable fats extends to 1–1–1996.

Table 7.24. Changes in Spain's commercial protection derived from EC membership, 1986–93

openness of the economy which – measured by the ratio of exports plus imports over GDP – has risen from 39% in 1985 to 47% in 1988. However, since the elimination of tariffs and quantitative restrictions has had a negative effect on the competitiveness of Spanish products, it is not surprising that the increasing volume of trade has been reflected to a larger extent in the expansion of imports – rather than exports – leading to the gradual worsening of the trade and current account balances shown in Table 7.25.

What is perhaps most striking is that while real imports of goods and services have gone from representing 17.6% of GDP in 1985 to 25.6% in 1988, real exports have stagnated around 21%. Moreover, this process has taken place simultaneously with an important geographic reorientation of trade flows in the direction of increasing the share of Spain-EC

	1985	1986	1987	1988
1 Trade balance	−2.5	−2.7	−4.5	−5.2
2 Services balance	3.5	4.0	3.5	2.9
3 Transfers	0.7	0.5	0.9	1.3
4 Current balance (1 + 2 + 3)	1.7	1.8	−0.0	−1.1
5 Long-term capital balance	−0.9	−0.7	3.2	2.9
(direct investment)	(0.4)	(0.7)	(0.6)	(0.9)
6 Short-term capital balance	−2.1	−0.1	1.1	0.6
7 Current plus long-term capital balances	0.8	1.1	3.2	1.8
8 Current plus direct investment balances	2.1	2.5	0.6	−0.2

Table 7.25. Spain's external accounts adjustment, 1985–88 (percent of GDP)

Source: Secretaría de Comercio.

Note: Numbers may not add up due to rounding.

trade at the expense of the non-EC area. Specifically, the proportion of Spain's imports coming from the EC has gone from 36.6% in 1985 to 56.8% in 1988, while the proportion of Spain's exports going to the EC has gone up from 52.1% in 1985 to 65.6% in 1988.

Of course, as already mentioned, not all of the trade balance changes during the period can be attributed exclusively to the trade liberalization process caused by EC membership. In this regard, in a recent paper, Fernández and Sebastián (1989) perform an econometric analysis of import and export functions which tries explicitly to detect the importance of the EC shock. Their results indicate that the overall effect of EC integration on the goods and services balance is quite asymmetrically divided between imports and exports. Specifically, they detect a very substantial positive long-run impact on total non-energy imports (although the authors caution about the disappearance of this effect when investment is also included as a scale variable), and a short-run negative impact on total exports, after 1986.

How can this last negative effect on exports be explained? Perhaps, the already very advantageous treatment of Spanish exports by EC countries in accordance with our Preferential Treaty prior to integration, and the unchanged legal status of our exports to non-EC countries after integration, can explain why there was not a surge in exports. On the other hand, the disappearance of hidden export subsidies caused by the introduction of VAT may be behind the negative impact on exports already discussed since this led exporters to advance exports in 1985, therefore reducing export growth in 1986.

The authors also look at how much of the geographical reorientation of Spain's goods trade flows towards the EC is due to the trade liberalization process linked to EC membership. They estimate bilateral export and import functions, and try to distinguish between the contribution of scale, competitiveness, and 'EC-shock' variables in explaining the long-run evolution of Spain's trade flows with the EC in the 1986–88 period relative to the 1980–85 period. According to their results, the total explained change in exports (45.0 points) is decomposed between the contribution of the scale (45.6 points), competitiveness (− 53.2 points) and 'EC-shock' (53.5 points) variables. With respect to imports, the total effect (89 points) is also decomposed between the scale (14 points), competitiveness (16 points), and 'EC-shock' (59 points) variables. Consequently, it does seem that EC integration has been very important in promoting imports and exports of goods with the EC.

Another independent piece of evidence to assess the impact of EC entrance on trade flows can be obtained by looking directly at the effects of the elimination of quantitative trade restrictions, many of which were suppressed in 1986–87. To calibrate the importance of this effect, a set of manufactured products (6-digit level Brussels Trade Nomenclature) accounting for about 25% of total manufacturing imports from the EC in 1985 were identified as subject to the elimination or relaxation of quantitative restrictions. Their import performance during the 1986–87 period was compared with that of similar products which had not experienced any change in their trade regime. The cumulative percentage change of the imports of the first group of goods was 157%, as compared with 70.3% for the second group. If it is assumed that in the absence of trade liberalization both groups of goods would have grown at the same rate, then we can infer that elimination of trade restrictions accounts for about 20% of actual real import growth in non-energy products from the EC.[37]

In the light of the above evidence it seems that Spain's entry to the EC has had a significant impact on the external accounts. Moreover, the gradual and significant worsening of the trade and current account balances in the 1986–88 period relative to the situation before EC integration has led – in spite of Spain's satisfactory overall economic performance – to some worries about the ability of the Spanish economy to withstand external competition. In particular, those worries have been triggered not so much by the take-off of imports but by the stagnation of exports.

If it turns out to be the case that the lack of attractiveness of Spanish products in world markets is the reason behind the progressive trade

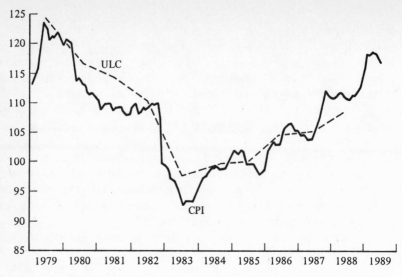

Source: Banco de España.
Note: 1985 = 100. Position relative to industrialized countries according to CPI
and unit labour costs (ULC). An upward movement is a real appreciation
of the peseta.

Figure 7.7   The peseta real exchange rate, 1979–89

balance deterioration, then it should be a cause for concern. Indeed, as
shown in Figure 7.7, the real appreciation of the peseta during the trade
liberalization process has been quite significant, and econometric estimates confirm that it has contributed negatively to the expansion of
exports, thus offsetting the positive effects of world demand growth
during the period. On the other hand, the impressive surge in imports has
been caused – more than anything – by the rapid growth of domestic
demand and, in part, has reflected the investment boom of the economy in
these past years.

To analyze further the nature of the current account deterioration, it is
convenient to look at the evolution of the external accounts from a
saving-investment perspective. Table 7.26 presents a decomposition of
total net saving into private and public saving and investment. As can be
observed, the overall worsening of the economy's current account has
been due to an increase in private investment which could not be financed
by the combined savings of the private and public sectors. Therefore,
from the welfare point of view, there seems to be little objection to a
current account deficit financing a domestic investment expansion.
However, it should be noticed that, as the drop in the private saving rate

	Private sector			Public sector			Total		
	S_p	I_p	$S_p - I_p$	S_g	I_g	$S_g - I_g$	S	I	$S - I$
1985	23.9	15.2	8.6	−3.4	3.6	−7.0	20.4	18.8	1.6
1986	24.1	16.3	7.8	−2.5	3.5	−6.1	21.6	19.8	1.8
1987	22.2	18.3	3.9	−0.1	3.5	−3.6	22.1	21.8	0.2
1988	22.0	19.9	2.1	0.7	3.7	−3.0	22.7	23.6	−0.9
Change 1985–88	−1.9	4.7	−6.5	4.1	0.1	4.0	2.3	4.8	−2.5

Table 7.26. Spanish savings and investment, 1985–88 (percent of GDP)

Sources: Banco de España; own elaboration.

Notes: 'S' is saving, 'I' is investment; 'p' refers to the private sector, and 'g' to the public sector. Numbers may not add up due to rounding.

indicates, part of the current account deficit went also to finance an increase in current consumption which may not be sustainable.

Moreover, as rows 5 and 7 of Table 7.25 show, so far the current account deficit has been financed fully by long-term capital flows. However, there are reasons to be skeptical about the permanency of these capital flows, especially regarding portfolio and real estate investment – which seem to have been heavily influenced by speculative reasons. Consequently, if we take direct investment flows as the rough measure of structural long-term capital flows, we can see from row 8 of the Table that nowadays they are barely financing the current account deficit, while in 1985 and 1986 they financed it well in excess. It is the downward trend in this 'basic' balance which – we believe – may be behind some of the currently existing worries about not letting the trade and current account balances worsen much more in the future, especially if their worsening results from the expansion of consumption rather than investment.[37]

After having analyzed the overall effects of the EC-1986 shock on trade flows, we now turn to *sectoral issues*.[38] The main questions here are the following: how much of the observed changes in the trade pattern take the form of inter-industry as opposed to intra-industry trade? Can the observed changes be explained according to traditional comparative advantage and/or according to imperfect competition and scale economies?

As already mentioned, while Spain's total and manufacturing imports grew at a relatively higher rate after Spain's integration into the EC, the opposite was the case for exports. Moreover, while the surge of imports

	Imports			Exports		
	EC	Non-EC	World	EC	Non-EC	World
Strong-demand sectors	28.8	25.4	27.4	20.5	5.5	13.9
Office and data-processing machinery	15.9	22.2	18.9	5.0	−5.4	2.1
Electrical and electronics goods	33.5	31.3	32.5	23.0	4.0	16.2
Chemical and pharmaceutical products	34.1	22.9	30.4	27.7	8.0	17.1
Moderate-demand sectors	38.4	20.9	32.5	16.3	−5.1	8.1
Rubber and plastic products	−10.2	−10.7	−10.3	−0.5	−16.1	−8.3
Transport equipment	47.9	47.6	47.8	18.1	2.6	14.6
Food, beverages, tobacco	17.0	−11.8	1.2	3.2	−11.5	−4.7
Paper and printing products	30.2	19.6	25.2	20.0	−4.5	8.7
Industrial and agricultural machinery	50.05	41.8	48.1	36.8	1.6	18.4
Weak-demand sectors	20.7	8.1	15.1	9.0	−16.5	−4.7
Metal products	28.7	22.0	27.3	15.7	−8.2	2.8
Miscellaneous manufactured products	13.9	4.7	8.5	13.0	−4.1	5.6
Ferrous and non-ferrous ores and metals	10.3	5.9	8.5	−0.2	−30.9	−19.2
Textiles, leather, clothing	45.3	12.8	27.8	7.3	−9.0	−0.2
Non-metallic minerals (construction materials)	26.3	7.1	17.7	22.6	−7.2	5.8
Total manufacturing sectors	30.8	18.6	25.9	14.8	−8.2	4.4
Energy	−10.2	−25.8	−24.7	−24.3	−8.8	−16.9
Total industry	28.8	−3.1	10.9	11.5	−8.3	2.6

Table 7.27. Spanish manufacturing trade after accession, by branches, 1985–88 (cumulative annual nominal rate of growth)

Sources: Dirección General de Aduanas.

	1985	1988	% Change
Strong-demand sectors	−259	−665	−156
Office and data-processing machinery	−87	−168	−93
Electrical and electronics goods	−54	−170	−215
Chemical and pharmaceutical products	119	−327	−375
Moderate-demand sectors	195	−367	−288
Rubber and plastic products	−5	14	380
Transport equipment	240	48	−80
Food, beverages, tobacco	61	18	−70
Paper and printing products	10	−6	−160
Industrial and agricultural machinery	−111	−442	−298
Weak-demand sectors	104	−66	−163
Metal products	5	−28	−660
Miscellaneous manufactured products	5	5	0
Ferrous and non-ferrous ores and metals	−59	−131	−122
Textiles, leather, clothing	138	69	−50
Non-metallic minerals (construction materials)	14	19	36
Total manufacturing sectors	39.2	−1,097	−2,898
Energy	107.0	13	−88
Total industry	146.2	1,084	−841

Table 7.28. Post-accession changes in Spain's net exports to the EC
Sources: Dirección General de Aduanas.
Notes: In billion pesetas. Numbers have been rounded.

was mainly due to Spain's trade with the EC, the slowdown of exports was mainly related to the actual decrease of Spain's exports to non-EC countries, Table 7.27 indicates that the increase of imports of manufacturing products in the 1986–88 period was concentrated mainly in moderate-demand products, while imports of strong and weak-demand products grew at lower rates. In turn, the reduction of Spanish exports was concentrated in weak-demand products.

Table 7.28 shows the combined net export changes of Spain *vis-à-vis* the EC. Not surprisingly, Spain's revealed comparative advantage positions have experienced a rapid and generalized deterioration in strong, weak and – above all – moderate-demand manufacturing products.

Some authors have suggested that the structure of revealed comparative advantage on the eve of a trade liberalization episode might be revealing of the underlying competitive positions, and, consequently, could be used as a leading indicator of potential sectoral vulnerability when trade restrictions are removed. Leaving aside the significant conceptual weaknesses of this view, the data in Table 7.28 corresponding to 1985 would have suggested that following integration strong-demand sectors would have deteriorated by relatively more than weak and moderate-demand sectors, in this order. The column corresponding to 1988, however, indicates that precisely the opposite has happened. In fact, the comparative advantage of the strong-demand sector has worsened the least, and that of the moderate-demand sector the most.

When one goes beyond the general heading of the strong, moderate, and weak-demand sectors to examine what happens to the specific industries within each of these sectors, the former result is confirmed. We find, however, that this behaviour seems to be influenced by the structure of protection. But this should be no surprise since it is precisely what the traditional theory of comparative advantage would predict following a tariff reduction process of different intensity in different sectors. Indeed, the deterioration of revealed comparative advantage has been higher in the sectors and industries that beforehand were more heavily protected, and which therefore have experienced a larger reduction in protection. For instance, nominal and effective protection was highest in the moderate-demand sector and lowest in the strong-demand sector, the weak-demand sector being in an intermediate position. From Table 7.28, it is clear that the worsening has been biggest in relative terms in the moderate-demand sector, and smallest in the strong-demand sector.

In sum, while the major changes in trade flows which have followed Spain's entry to the EC are of an inter-industry nature this is certainly not the whole story. In fact, the preliminary evidence available suggests that there has also been a non-negligible degree of specialization within sectors

Table 7.29. Simulated sectoral effects on Spain of the 'EC cum 1992' shock (percentage changes)

Sources: Dirección General de Aduanas.

Notes:
(1) Tariff reduction from Jan 1, 1986 to Jan 1, 1988 (37.5% of total). A fixed number of firms is assumed.
(2) Tariff reduction from Jan 1, 1986 to Jan 1, 1993 (100% of total). A variable number of firms is assumed.
(3) Non-Tariff Barriers reduction equivalent to a direct cost saving of 2.5% of base year intra-EC trade. Case where firms can discriminate among national EC markets. A variable number of firms is assumed.
(4) Same as in (3), except that the markets are perfectly integrated and firms have to set a single producer price in all national markets in the EC.
(5) Increase in overall welfare as a percentage of consumption.

	Effects of tariff reductions started 1986		Effects of 1992 internal market	
	1988 (1)	1993 (2)	Segmentation (3)	Integration (4)
A. *Output*				
Cement	−0.5	−0.8	−0.9	1.8
Pharmaceuticals	−5.2	−13.4	−15.3	−11.1
Machine Tools	−36.1	−100	−100	−100
Electrical H-hold appliances	−22.2	n.a.	n.a.	n.a.
B. *Welfare* (5)				
Cement	−0.0	−0.0	−0.01	1.14
Pharmaceuticals	−0.3	0.6	1.07	1.99
Machine Tools	5.9	12.4	13.2	13.2
Electrical H-hold appliances	5.3	n.a.	n.a.	n.a.
C. *Exports to*: EC (non-EC)				
Cement	−0.7 (−0.6)	−0.9 (−0.8)	122.7 (−0.8)	−75.4 (5)
Pharmaceuticals	0 (0)	−13.9 (−13.4)	0.2 (−15.5)	−14.4 (−18.9)
Machine Tools	−10.3 (−10.3)	−100 (−100)	−100 (−100)	−100 (−100)
Electrical H-hold appliances	−21 (−21.6)	n.a.	n.a.	n.a.
D. *Imports from*: EC (non-EC)				
Cement	56.3 (145.8)	226.9 (147.6)	576.7 (146)	51.1 (95.7)
Pharmaceuticals	32.2 (69.1)	150.5 (82.4)	204 (81)	149.8 (75.6)
Machine Tools	77.1 (197.2)	253.6 (90.4)	262.2 (74.1)	262 (74)
Electrical H-hold appliances	134.0 (1,196.7)	n.a.	n.a.	n.a.

in the production of several goods, leading to significant amounts of additional intra-industry trade between Spain and the EC so far. Specifically, the share of intra-industry trade in manufacturing has increased from 43.5% in 1985 to 52.1% in 1987, when measured by the Grubel-Lloyd index.

To provide additional evidence on this issue, we have constructed a model à la Smith and Venables (1988) for Spain to assess empirically the extent to which there can be changes resulting from the rationalization of production in several representative key sectors experiencing different degrees of increasing returns to scale and scope, as well as product differentiation. The results of the model simulations – described in detail in Gual *et al.* (1989) – are summarized in the first column of Table 7.29 which shows the overall effects of the tariff reduction process completed between January 1, 1986 and January 1, 1988 under the assumption of a fixed number of firms. As can be observed in part A of the Table, the model predicts a considerable contraction of production in two sectors, and a zero or small contraction of production in the other two. Notice also that the two sectors whose output is severely curtailed are those whose exports decline by more, and that the two sectors whose output is cut by little are those whose exports decline by less. This can be interpreted as saying that not only inter-industry but also intra-industry adjustments in production and trade flows must have taken place in Spain in the 1986–88 period as a result of the trade liberalization that has occurred so far. This may also help explain – together with the favourable external conditions of the period – why the output and employment costs of the 1986–88 period have not been as large or evident as first envisaged.

Moreover, it is likely to be the case that the simulations shown in Table 7.29 overestimate to a certain extent the sectoral changes that result from the trade liberalization process implemented in the 1986–88 period. Specifically, the substantial increase in foreign direct investment inflows in the 1986–88 period – half of which went into the manufacturing sector – has certainly improved the efficiency of significant segments of Spain's industrial sectors, therefore avoiding some of the most dramatic negative output and employment consequences of the trade liberalization process in these past years. However, the exclusion from the simulations of the elimination of quantitative restrictions to trade tends to offset the size of the overestimation.

Potential gains and adjustment costs
The integration of Spain's tradeable goods markets with the rest of the EC – started in 1986 and to be completed in 1992 – may lead to important *long-run gains*. On the one hand, since approximately half of Spain-EC

trade is inter-industry trade, overall gains can be made by exploiting Spain's comparative advantage in the production of relatively labour-intensive products. In this regard, it is to be expected that the new set of relative prices resulting from trade liberalization will make production shift away from import-competing goods and move towards labour-intensive exportables. On the other hand, since the other half of Spain-EC trade prior to integration was intra-industry trade, the country can further increase the long-run gains by benefiting from increased competition and the exploitation of scale and scope economies.[39] Consequently, while Spain should exploit its comparative advantage in moving towards being a net exporter in broad categories of labour-intensive goods, scale and scope economies should be exploited by specializing within each of these broad categories of goods in certain specific products. This will help Spain compete successfully in servicing the EC market with other non-EC countries with even larger labour cost advantages.[40]

These are not, however, the only long-run benefits to be gained by Spain. This is because the imposition of the Common External Tariff (CET) on trade with non-EC countries *de facto* implies a tariff reduction on the part of Spain, since the pre-existing tariff with those countries exceeded the CET. These gains will be of two types: inter-industry and intra-industry gains in trade with other OECD countries, and mostly inter-industry gains in trade with non-OECD countries. Consequently, Spain's long-term gains are likely to come both from the exploitation of differences in endowments and technology and through the exploitation of scale and scope economies.

Regarding the likely size of the long-term potential gains to be obtained in the process of integration there are several pieces of rough evidence.

First, the significant differences in labour costs observed between Spain and its EC competitors indicate that the traditional gains from exploiting the country's comparative advantage may be far from negligible. However, while wages are taken to be lower the more abundant is labour in the competitive factor markets Heckscher-Ohlin paradigm, our previous description of the Spanish labour market indicates that in Spain the future evolution of wages may be not so much influenced by labour abundance as by non-competitive wage-setting practices: i.e., there may be very high unemployment, and wages still not come down. Consequently, whether Spain can or cannot fully exploit the gains from specializing in relatively labour-intensive products will depend on how easy it is to maintain relative wage and unit labour cost moderation.

Second, the long-term potential gains to be obtained from exploiting scale and scope economies within a larger and more competitive market are also likely to be very significant, given our previous description of the insufficient and inefficient size of Spanish industrial firms. In this regard, Table 7.29 contains a sequence of simulations that assess the long-run consequences resulting from the integration of goods markets. As part B of the Table shows, the 'EC cum 1992' shock has very significant effects on welfare in several sectors, especially when allowing for complete market integration and free entry and exit of firms (column 4).

But the adjustment from the old to the new structure is not without costs. These *adjustment costs* can be of two types: distributional and efficiency costs.[41] The first come from the reallocation of resources from contracting to expanding sectors. While it would be a mistake to stop this process from taking place so as to reduce these costs, it is nevertheless necessary that they be taken care of through appropriate distributional policies. Efficiency costs, on the other hand, imply an important waste of resources, like unemployment and spare capacity. These social costs are to be avoided for Spain's integration into the EC to be a success.

The question is how much is Spain likely to suffer from these costs. The answer depends on two things: how much of the change in trade patterns involves inter and intra-industry trade, and how well factor markets work.

While inter-industry trade changes involve the movement of capital and labour from some industries to others, intra-industry trade changes may – in certain circumstances – be achieved with smaller intersectoral factor movements. Given that Spain's new trade flows are likely to contain both inter and intra-industry trade components, these adjustment costs are potentially significant.

The adjustment costs coming from trade liberalization in the presence of intra-industry trade will be – as recently stressed by Richardson (1989) – relatively small when the rationalization of production takes place within sectors, with firms specializing in some variety of the products that they produce. However, when the rationalization of production takes place across sectors, it may lead to the closing down of plants or firms in a par-ticular sector, with major drops in the output produced by that sector. In this second case, and contrary to the first, there will be large notional labour and capital flows going from the shrinking to the expanding sectors.

In this regard, the long-run simulations of the Smith and Venables model carried out by Gual *et al.* (1989) for Spain can be of some help in distinguishing how much of the rationalization of production caused by trade liberalization is within or across sectors, precisely in those sectors which are subject to increasing returns to scale and scope, and product differentiation. As indicated by part A of Table 7.29, there are sectors – like cement and pharmaceuticals – which experience relatively minor

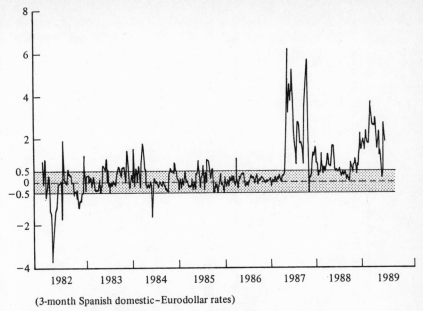

(3-month Spanish domestic–Eurodollar rates)

Figure 7.8   Spain: deviations from covered interest parity, 1982–89

changes in overall output even in the most extreme cases of complete
market integration and free exit and entry of firms (column 4), while
others – like machine tools – are potential candidates for severe output
changes. Consequently, even for the part of the trade pattern that is of an
intra-industry trade nature, it is conceivable that trade liberalization will
lead over time to significant labour and capital flows between sectors.

On the other hand, adjustment costs will be larger or smaller depending
on the degree of inter-sectoral mobility of labour and capital, and depending also on the degree of real wage flexibility. Unfortunately, as already
documented, the specifics of the wage-setting process, low functional and
geographical labour mobility, relatively high labour firing costs, lack of
sufficiently deep and developed long-term bond and stock markets, and
the not very efficient provision of bank credit, indicate that such costs
may be far from negligible in the case of Spain.

3.2   Financial market integration and capital flows

The opening up of the capital account: the 1986–89 experience[42]
So far we have looked at the effects of the closer integration of goods
markets brought about by the opening up of Spain's current account since

	1982	1983	1984	1985	1986	1987	1988	1989	1982–83	1984–85	1986–89	1982–89
Average	−0.41	0.20	0.19	0.10	0.10	1.74	0.75	2.04	−0.1	0.14	1.03	0.49
Standard deviation	0.99	0.44	0.58	0.39	0.22	1.79	0.49	0.82	0.83	0.50	1.28	1.13
Percentage of observations in excess of ±0.5% from covered interest rate parity	40.0	26.9	30.8	13.5	1.9	53.8	63.5	92.6	38.4	22.1	47.53	37.03
Total weeks	52	52	52	52	52	52	52	27	104	104	183	391

Table 7.30. Covered interest-rate differentials between the peseta and the Eurodollar, 1982–89 (3-month deposits, January 1982–June 1989)

1986. However, and most surprisingly, things have been rather different regarding the capital account. In fact, while it is true that the long-term capital account has become more open since 1986 thanks to the freer regulatory framework on inflows and – most specifically – on outflows, things have run in just the opposite direction for the *short-term capital account*, at least regarding inflows. Consequently, it turns out that nowadays the economic effects associated with the suppression of short-term capital controls from January 1, 1993, seem more worrying than they would have a few years ago.

More precisely, Figure 7.8 shows the new computed deviations from interest-rate parity which result from extending the empirical analysis of Section 2 of the paper[43] to the 1986–89 (June) period. As can be seen, the years when capital controls have been most effective in the 1982–89 period are precisely 1987, 1988 and 1989. Indeed, as Table 7.30 shows, the annual average interest parity deviation during the 1986–89 period is 1.03%, which goes beyond the ± 0.5% transaction costs band. Moreover, the percentage of observations beyond the ± 0.5% band in the 1986–89 period is 47.5%, the most frequent and important occurring in 1989.

The reduced effective degree of short-term capital mobility has, in turn, been the result of the imposition of new exchange controls on inflows at various times since 1987. But why were controls imposed or reintroduced? The explanation is relatively simple: the economic recovery that has been taking place in Spain since 1985 – and specially since 1986 – has been associated with a major wave of financial innovation. In 1987, the substantial portfolio shifts of agents motivated by the new financial innovations, and the changes in the tax-treatment of short-term public debt instruments, prompted a large increase in money demand. Nevertheless, at the time it was not as clear as it is perhaps nowadays how much of the increase was due to purely financial reasons and how much of it was reflecting an excessive output demand growth, given the substantial supply-side limits existing at the time.[44] Under this uncertainty, there was a strategy of partial accommodation of the increase in money demand which, however, did not prevent interest rates from rising substantially above international rates, as can be seen in Figure 7.9.

It was then feared that the higher domestic rates might attract large amounts of speculative capital which would either push the peseta even beyond what at the time was taken to be an already substantial nominal and real appreciation or, alternatively, force the Banco de España to intervene in the foreign exchange market, leading to money supply increases and to a revival of inflation. To make both exchange-rate and money-supply targets compatible, capital controls were introduced on short-term inflows in the second quarter of 1987. And, although

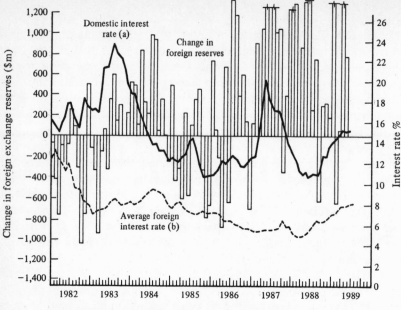

Source: Banco de España.

Notes: (a) Madrid interbank 3-month rate.
           (b) Euromarket 3-month rates, weighted according to the foreign
               currency composition of Spain's external debt.

Figure 7.9   Spanish interest rates and foreign-exchange reserves, 1982–89

foreign-exchange reserves accumulated in 1987 and 1988 as shown in Figure 7.9, they were to a substantial extent sterilized so as to permit achieving disinflation and moderating the appreciation of the peseta.

The second round of capital controls on short-term inflows came in mid-1989 because the economic authorities feared that inflation might take off as a result of the overheating of the economy which, for the last three years, had been growing above 5% in real terms. Since fiscal policy did not move quickly and strongly enough to moderate the nominal demand growth of the economy, the authorities decided to tighten monetary policy gradually. This made short-term interest rates rise again quite significantly, leading to capital inflows which both put upward pressures on the already very appreciated peseta and provoked the overshooting of money-targets. Concerned – as the authorities seemed to be – with the prospects of a widening external deficit and higher inflation, they decided to impose capital controls on short-term inflows so as to achieve simultaneously money and exchange-rate targets.[45]

From this perspective, and given Spain's recent entry to the discipline mechanism of the EMS, the future elimination of controls on short-term inflows due to take place by December 31, 1992 will make it impossible for the Spanish authorities to continue with the current fiscal-monetary policy mix, and still achieve price and exchange rate stability simultaneously. A more flexible use of fiscal and monetary policy – and not just of the latter – will be needed for this purpose. As is well known, it is necessary to have two instruments, at least, to achieve two targets.

Banking and financial markets after 1992[46]
Contrary to the cases of the current and capital accounts just described, there is no 'small-scale' experience in the 1986–88 period that can help us assess what is going to happen to Spain's financial system following the sweeping financial reforms due to take place in the European Community in 1992. As a result, this section will be highly speculative.

It may be useful to recall that our analysis of Spain's *banking sector* in Section 2 of the paper concluded that there seem to be no serious issues of financial fragility that might threaten the health of the real side of the economy. It was pointed out, however, that the Spanish banking sector was relatively inefficient when compared with other European banking sectors. This fact, supported by the presence of relatively high intermediation costs and other indicators, has been interpreted by some authors as indicating that Spain's banking sector may not be able to survive in its present state with open competition. While we also offered some reasons that could account for these higher costs – temporary inefficiency, tastes, reserve requirements – there is no doubt that some important parts of Spain's banking sector do have an inefficient performance. There is therefore room for banks to further lower costs, modernize processes, and become more aggressive.

One of the main reasons for the persistence of this misallocation of resources is that banks have been overprotected. Indeed, they have been shielded from both domestic and external competition and, until very recently, there were no ways to shake up bad management through the usual capitalistic measures of takeover threats or proxy fights. Given that there is a presumption that banks have exercised some degree of market power, the relative inefficiency just described has not necessarily translated into low profitability. As a matter of fact, the measurement of relative profitability of Spanish banking is far from being settled, as we saw. Nevertheless, our impression is that – once all measurement problems involved in international profitability comparisons are taken into account – Spanish banks are nowadays relatively more profitable than their EC counterparts, but that this was not the case in the late 1970s and early 1980s, at the height of the banking crisis. On the other hand, even if banks have been able to keep non-competitive margins, we should not forget that an important part of these profits has been taxed away through the existing reserve and investment ratios.

Given that the recent merger process has reversed the long-run trend towards lower market concentration in the sector and, other things equal, lowered competition, the key question is whether Spanish banks will be able to stand the external competitive pressures associated with the 1992 financial reforms.

A tentative and highly speculative answer to that question is that while market forces will undoubtedly lead to much more competition than before in the wholesale market, it is not at all clear that EC financial liberalization will greatly affect the dominant position of major banks in the retail market.[47] While it may be true that other more sophisticated and longer-established foreign financial institutions may take away some share of the wholesale banking market, the reduced size of this market relative to the overall Spanish banking market (wholesale plus retail) suggests that this is not likely to be a major problem. With regard to retail banking, the lower competitiveness of Spanish banking may not pose a serious threat in the short run, given that the extensive existing branch networks constitute important entry barriers. Nevertheless, while this makes the adjustment towards more efficient performance of the Spanish banking sector less urgent, it does not make it less necessary. In fact, recent banking attitudes indicate that the 'right' moves are already being made so as to exploit the natural comparative advantage represented by those branch networks. It is therefore to be expected that banks will be able to intermediate between ultimate suppliers and users of funds more efficiently.

All in all, while some significant financial changes may take place in the Spanish banking scene, it is not foreseeable that they will by themselves lead in the short to medium run to important problems; in fact, a gain in efficiency is to be expected. However, the close links between banks and industry – both in equity and loans – suggest that, other things equal, future banking performance may be closely influenced by industry performance since the trade liberalization process may have a negative impact on certain industrial sectors in which banks participate importantly. Conversely, the new solvency requirements of the 'Second Banking Directive' may entail a severe limitation of bank industrial holdings relative to bank equity (estimated to be around 50% in September, 1988). If, as a result, Spanish banks had to sell a substantial proportion of their industrial participations, there would be a major impact on Spanish industry, since many big firms would experience a change in their controlling shareholders.

Turning now to *money and capital markets*, there seems to be a need to improve the workings of the private long-term bond market and the stock market. However, things have started moving already in the right direction with the promotion of pension funds – which are typically major institutional investors in the bond market – and plans to make the long-term public bond market deeper and more active. Both of these developments will undoubtedly help the market enlarge its demand and get a better reference point for the issuing of public bonds. Another important modernization step has been the development of a fairly active over-the-counter market in public debt futures and options since the beginning of 1989. It should also be mentioned that the process of creating a futures exchange has already started. Finally, the recently implemented Stock Market Reform Law will make it easier and more attractive for smaller firms and for investors to enter the market.

In fact, since July 29, 1989, Spanish stock exchanges have experienced their 'little-bang' as the law started being effective. As a result, it is no longer required that stocks be physically exchanged; the old oligopolistic intermediaries have been replaced by a new and more efficient system of brokers and dealers; Stock Exchange Organizations have been set up to manage the four existing Stock Exchanges; an equivalent of the US SEC has been created (Comisión Nacional del Mercado de Valores) with regulatory, supervisory and control powers; very liberal rules have been set to regulate market price-setting behaviour; insider trading has been regulated; and finally, the four stock exchanges have been connected so as to create a National Stock Exchange with a single price for any share at a particular time.

An important issue arises, however, regarding the future role of the Spanish bond and stock markets after 1992.[48] Specifically, will bond and stock markets in Europe concentrate in just a few financial centres? To answer this question it seems reasonable to be guided by considerations of comparative advantage and scale economies. Accordingly, it would not be cost-effective for Spain to try to compete with more developed financial centres like London, Frankfurt, or Paris in servicing the financing needs of large international firms. Instead, Spanish bond and stock markets have to specialize in servicing the needs of medium-to-small national firms. If the markets make these adjustments successfully, they may even grow faster than at present, and play a crucial role in helping Spanish firms adapt to the new market conditions. Once again, the recent legal changes that have been introduced seem to go in the right direction.

4   Policy responses

There is little doubt that Spain's entry to the EC has started having very significant effects on the Spanish economy, especially on the real side. Moreover, it is the case that the gradual trade liberalization process has still to be completed, and that there is the further liberalization of goods, labour and financial markets coming from the 1992 European Internal Market. Consequently, since only a portion of the 'EC cum 1992' shock has been borne so far by the Spanish economy, it is of critical importance to examine how future economic policy should be shaped so as to maximize the long-term potential gains from integration while keeping the adjustment costs within economically and socially tolerable limits.

In order to maximize the long-term potential gains resulting from integration, it is necessary that the Spanish economy proceeds to reap the long-run inter-industry gains by specializing in labour-intensive sectors so as to exploit its present labour-cost advantage. Moreover, it must also seek specialization in specific products within each of those sectors to adequately exploit long-run intra-industry gains. At the same time, for the adjustment costs associated with the process of structural change to be kept low it is of critical importance that the inter-sectoral reallocation of labour and capital flows from contracting to expanding sectors takes place as smoothly as possible. This, in turn, is more easily accomplished within a context of sustained growth.

4.1   The adjustment process

To keep adjustment costs within economically and socially acceptable bounds there should be major policy initiatives directed towards improving the resource allocation process through the labour and capital market, especially since nominal exchange-rate flexibility is no longer available as an adjustment mechanism following Spain's entry to the EMS in mid-1989. The goal would be to avoid unemployment and idle productive capacity resulting from the changes in the sectoral composition of production caused by the international integration of goods markets.

In the *labour* market, the specifics of the sectoral wage-setting process and the substantial lack of functional and geographical mobility indicate a far from smooth functioning on the labour supply side. Moreover, labour demand is constrained by relatively high firing costs, by the existing productive capacity, and by output demand. It is therefore critical that future economic policies relax the constraints that nowadays still bind the employment-creation process.

On the labour demand side, the real product wage cost moderation experienced in the recent past should be maintained in the future since the available econometric evidence indicates that wage cost moderation influences positively and proportionally labour demand in the medium run. Moreover, since tariffs, exchange controls, and devaluations will not be available in the future to compensate for excessive wage increases, and since the likely reduction of price mark-ups brought about by increased goods-market competition means that wage increases will be reflected even more in profit reductions, it is increasingly necessary that wage moderation continues in the future. This will not only directly enhance Spain's international competitiveness but will also attract foreign investment which will further improve Spain's competitiveness by raising labour productivity.[49]

In this respect, the relatively higher weight of social security contributions and the relatively lower weight of VAT taxes in Spain *vis-à-vis* other EC countries would suggest engineering a reduction in social security contributions financed by higher VAT. However, the economic policy scenarios presented by Spain's economic authorities for the 1989–92 period do not contemplate such policy change and VAT revenues are forecast to modestly increase by 0.6% of GDP. In addition, it is very important that employers and unions reach an agreement so that real wage increases do not exceed – on average – the growth in labour productivity, allowing real unit labour costs to be kept stable. Finally, lowering the economic and bureaucratic firing costs of labour will also have a beneficial effect on labour demand.

Important as it is to maintain moderation in wage and non-wage labour costs this must be supplemented by an adequate sustained growth of output demand, and a sufficiently large productive capacity to lead to significant increases in labour demand in the near future. From this viewpoint, it is of critical importance that the Spanish economy prolong as much as possible the current investment process.

The former policies oriented towards expanding labour demand have to be complemented, necessarily, by supply-side policies geared to increasing the geographical and functional mobility of labour. Otherwise, the expansion of labour demand in some sectors may just lead to an overall increase in wages – as firms try to compete in getting the scarce available workers with the appropriate skills – without significant increases in employment.

In this regard, it is critical to lower severance-pay compensation, and to simplify the bureaucratic procedures for the termination of labour contracts and, at the same time, provide less restrictive regulations on part-time and temporary labour contracts. However, the lack of functional and labour mobility in the Spanish labour market is not just a matter of legal restrictions. As emphasized earlier in the paper, both the existence of a very high rate of unemployment coupled with the security of family support, and a substantial degree of mismatch, may be behind low labour mobility.

It is therefore necessary that policy be directed towards making the currently unemployed more competitive in the job-search process. One possibility would be to establish training policies oriented to giving workers the new specific skills which are in high demand. While it is true that the private sector is already offering training opportunities to certain types of workers – youngsters, women – these are however not fully reaching the long-term unemployed. Consequently, public initiatives should be targetted to restoring the human capital of the long-term unemployed through specific training programmes, temporary public employment contracts, temporary subsidizing of labour contracts, etc. . . . . Other supplementary measures to enhance the job-search process would be to make the size and/or duration of unemployment benefits conditional on the recipient participating in professional recycling programmes, and to improve the housing market to facilitate the geographical mobility of workers.

Unfortunately, the modest increase in the funds allocated to employment promotion policies in the government budget for the 1989–92 period only represents an average increase of 0.2% of GDP over the low figure of 0.5% of GDP in 1988. Moreover, the officially proposed policies seem to be targetted towards youngsters and entrants to the labour market rather than to the long-term unemployed.

A final and very important issue is how the wage-setting process should be modified to respond best to the adjustment needs of 1992. The reasons why this is of paramount importance are several. First, unless the wage-setting process is perceived to be fair by social partners there will be disagreements over income shares which may fuel inflation and unemployment again. Second, because the remaining part of the 'EC cum 1992' shock is going to affect sectors very asymmetrically it is necessary that the relative real wage structure be flexible enough to reflect changes in the structure of relative productivities.[50] Third, if wage-setting does not lead to the appropriate degree of real wage variability across sectors, unemployment will result and – given the structure of the Spanish labour market – persist over time.

Unfortunately, the empirical evidence available from sectoral industrial wage equations in Spain suggests that sectoral real wages do not move to reflect changes in sectoral labour productivity or in aggregate unemployment. Quite the contrary, sectoral real wages are heavily indexed with respect to the industry real wage. It is therefore necessary to modify the current nation-wide relatively centralized wage-setting process so as to facilitate – and not prevent as seems to be the case at present – an efficient allocation of labour. One option could be to decentralize the wage-setting process so that real wages become responsive to sectoral productivity fluctuations. Simultaneously, the policies – formerly described – aimed at reducing the degree of mismatch in the Spanish labour market can contribute to increasing the sensitivity of wages to overall unemployment conditions. As a result of the proposed reforms, sectoral real wages would be more responsive to sectoral productivity developments and to overall unemployment, reducing the persistence of unemployment and allowing a more efficient channelling of labour flows from contracting to expanding sectors.[51]

So far, we have just looked at what must be done to improve the national inter-sectoral allocation of labour under the new economic conditions brought about by the European Internal Market. Regarding international labour flows between Spain and the rest of the EC, and their potential role in helping lower Spain's unemployment rate and improving the efficiency of the labour market, it seems sensible to envisage a future scenario where massive, inter-industry international labour migration to and from Spain will be minimal given existing cultural and language barriers. Moreover, if such migrations do take place it must be because wage differentials are high enough to overcome these barriers, which itself would signal that domestic policies have failed to do their job.

As important as ensuring an adequate growth of employment and its efficient sectoral allocation is to ensure an adequate rate of *capital formation* and its efficient sectoral allocation towards expanding sectors. In the case of Spain, the available empirical evidence indicates that for investment to keep up policy should provide sustained demand growth, support appropriate profitability, and remove the constraints present in credit markets.

Clearly, while wage moderation is necessary for maintaining adequate profit margins, it would also help if the currently internationally high domestic real interest rates were to be brought down in the future towards more reasonable levels. Moreover, given that the empirical evidence in Mato (1989) suggests that Spanish firms' capital formation is significantly constrained by the availability of financial resources,[52] it is critical that the current system of bank credit ceilings be phased out, that the efficiency of banks in the intermediation process be improved, and that long-term bond and stock markets continue to be developed. Undoubtedly, 1992 will increase competition in financial markets. Nevertheless, this must be accompanied by appropriate domestic financial policies.

It is of interest to observe that the internationally high short and long-run Spanish real interest rates, and the existence of credit ceilings – introduced in the summer of 1989 – are both the result of the current policy-mix being pursued in Spain. The very strong growth of private demand together with the lack of flexibility of fiscal policy to moderate inflationary pressures has led the authorities to engineer a relatively contractionary monetary policy and to introduce credit ceilings. As a result, real interest rates have risen, short-run capital inflows have increased, and foreign-exchange controls have been kept to avoid the peseta from going beyond the ± 6% band in the EMS.[53] Only when the policy mix is changed by reducing the expansionary stance of fiscal policy and, therefore, allowing monetary policy to be less contractionary will real interest rates come down and liquidity constraints disappear from credit markets.

In light of the evidence provided earlier in the paper it is also highly desirable that the country continues to attract foreign direct investment to improve the conditions of the productive sector. Available empirical evidence on the determinants of direct foreign investment in Spain seems to suggest that, in addition to the economic and political climate of the country, a significant role is played by infrastructure.[54] However, as shown in Table 7.12, Spain provides public infrastructure less adequately than other EC countries. True enough, since Spain's entry to the EC public investment has gone up from 3.1% of GDP in 1982–85 to 3.7% in 1986–88. However, public spending in infrastructure is budgeted to rise modestly from 1.1% in 1988 to 1.6% in 1989. Consequently, although Spain will continue to receive capital transfers from the EC, it is of strategic importance that a much higher fraction of public purchases of goods and services be allocated to improving Spain's infrastructure. This will allow Spain's economy to become less peripheral,[55] will increase private productivity and contribute to moderating unit labour costs.

The allocation of capital resources will also be significantly influenced by the 1992 liberalization of banking and financial services as the competitiveness of the Spanish financial system is improved through increased competition. Simultaneously, the likely convergence of domestic financial regulations on the most liberal Community standards may have substantial effects on the Spanish budget and, therefore, condition future fiscal policy. In this respect, we have calculated the budgetary effects of moving towards the reserve requirement levels which are expected to prevail in the EC after the completion of financial liberalization. In the hypothetical case where reserve requirements are brought down immediately, there is a net revenue loss in 1990 which amounts to 1.22% of GDP; a figure which corresponds to about 85% of the 1990 Spanish public investment in infrastructure. In steady-state, the net revenue loss is likely to be around 0.7% of GDP according to the calculations, detailed in Mañas (1989).

Our previous analysis of the economic policies that would be required to improve the allocation of labour and capital resources under the new economic conditions imposed by the remaining part of the 'EC cum 1992' shock has profound implications for the budget. On the one hand, additional public spending is required to implement most needed public training programs, and the improvement of infrastructure. On the other hand, there is a net revenue loss coming from the reduction in bank reserve requirements dictated by the international competition of domestic financial policies in 1992. And finally, the changes required in the macroeconomic policy-mix to sustain private investment suggest that a relatively less expansionary fiscal policy is appropriate.

How can the need for higher public spending in certain areas be combined with the reality of future lower tax revenues? One possibility would be to let the budget deficit rise and finance it through money or debt creation. However, this might have inflationary consequences in the first case, and lead to the crowding out of investment or the tradeables sector in the second. A politically more delicate but economically preferable option would be to finance as much as possible of the higher capital spending in some areas with lower current spending in other areas. In this regard, it may also be advisable to bring in the private sector in joint ventures aimed at providing new and better infrastructures (i.e. motorways, railways, telephones, etc. . . .). Moreover, the above strategy may benefit also from continuing with the privatization process started a few years ago.

On the revenue side, there is indisputable evidence of widespread tax-fraud. If the serious fight against fraud already initiated by the government a few years ago is strongly pursued in the future it may give a considerable return in revenues from tax on previously hidden income and wealth, as the recent experience of the introduction of VAT and the disclosure of certain financial operations (operaciones de Seguro de Prima Unica) have vividly shown. Moreover, these additional revenues should be complemented by the official capital transfers from the European Commission which have been established. At the same time, the reduction in nominal and real interest rates brought about by the proposed macro policy-mix may reduce significantly the interest payments on the public debt.

So far, we have not devoted much space to talking about domestic monetary policy. The reasons for this are two-fold. First, because the 'EC cum 1992' shock mostly involves 'real' changes in the structure of goods and financial markets, the appropriate policies are essentially non-monetary in nature. Second, the entrance of the peseta into the EMS[58] in mid-1989 and the future elimination of capital controls will make monetary policy ineffective as a tool for influencing output even temporarily.[59] Consequently, it is desirable that monetary policy be targetted at achieving exchange-rate stability, and consequently low(er) inflation, while tax, budgetary and supply-side policies provide the basis for an adequate sustainable demand and output growth.

4.2   The long run

The policies just described not only help to minimize the adjustment costs associated with the process of integration but also help the economy move in the direction of maximizing its potential long-run benefits. On the one hand, Spain can only benefit from exploiting its labour-cost comparative advantage if labour cost moderation in a socially peaceful environment continues in the future, and if the allocational efficiency of labour and capital markets is improved. On the other hand, the policies directed at sustaining domestic and foreign investment in Spain can contribute significantly to the long-run exploitation of scale and scope economies, and to the improvement of the production technology and productivity of Spain's economy. Larger increases in productivity will help absorb a higher growth of real wages without worsening international competitiveness making it easier to preserve a good climate of industrial relations. This good climate and low unit labour costs will, in turn, help domestic and foreign investment.

There are, no doubt, important uncertainties about the realization of this favourable long-run scenario. Specifically, if wage moderation does not continue, adequate labour market policies are not implemented, the macro policy-mix is not changed, and public expenditure is not significantly reallocated towards capital formation, the long-term potential gains from 1992 will never be realized and the adjustment costs will be economically and socially large. Let us hope that the determination of the Spanish economic authorities in pursuing the appropriate policies makes the 'EC cum 1992' shock a complete success.

5   Conclusions

In the various sections of the paper we have identified and analyzed the main economic issues that are raised by Spain's integration into the EC in 1986 and the creation of the European Internal Market in 1992. Overall, our main conclusion is that the irreversible opening up process started in 1986 and to be completed in 1993 will have important effects on both the real and the financial sides, although the rigidities present in goods and labour markets seem to suggest that problems may be more important in the real sector. It should not be forgotten, however, that given the strong links between banking and industry an unfavourable industrial perform-ance may lead to financial distress.

Among the major rigidities to be removed the most important seem to be associated with the malfunctioning of the labour market, as exempli-fied by Spain's very high past and present rate of unemployment. Another potential source of problems is the insufficient size and low technological level of Spanish industry, which prevent it from moving quickly enough into the more dynamic markets. Moreover, the relatively inefficient financial intermediation process and the lack of well developed long-term capital markets prevent the most efficient allocation of financial resources. Finally, the existence of important rigidities in tax and expen-diture policies further complicates matters both at the micro and macro levels.

From the generally favourable performance of Spain's economy in the 1986–88 period inside the EC it might be thought that our above concerns are unfounded, and therefore that no significant policy measures are needed in the future to reduce those rigidities. However, there are several reasons why a new economic policy strategy based on the simultaneous relaxation of output supply and demand constraints is needed. First, while it is true that the economic adjustment associated with EC integra-tion has so far been satisfactory, this has been due to an important extent to the very favourable world external conditions prevailing as well as to the delayed effect of the internal economic liberalization and growth-promoting policies implemented in recent years. Second, only a fraction of the 'EC cum 1992' shock has so far occurred and – as our simulations have shown – only the first round of its dynamic effects have been felt so far.

It is therefore expected that the remaining part of the 'EC cum 1992' shock will have major aggregate and sectoral economic effects on the Spanish economy, and involve a significant reallocation of labour and capital resources from the contracting to the expanding sectors. While it is true that 1992 will bring itself a number of efficiency-enhancing changes in goods and financial markets, it still needs to be accompanied by appropriate policies starting now. Moreover, these policies need to be even more comprehensive regarding the labour market, due both to its unfavourable workings relative to other markets in Spain, and also to the much smaller beneficial impact resulting from the 1992 reforms relative to those in goods and financial markets in the EC.

For those reasons, it is of paramount importance that an economic policy strategy which combines macro, labour market, tax, budgetary and financial policies in the ways suggested in the paper be implemented as soon as possible. This policy, in turn, should have as its top priorities: the improvement of the allocational efficiency of labour and financial markets within a sustained growth scenario with the aim of minimizing the avoidable and socially costly structural adjustment costs resulting from integration; and the preservation and exploitation of Spain's comparative labour cost advantage and the exploitation of scale economies in production and distribution.

Spain's sound recent economic policies and the pursuit of the economic policy strategy proposed in the paper may decisively contribute to the successful completion of the process of integration of Spain's economy into the EC. However, not all the avoidable adjustment costs can be eliminated through adequate national policies. Consequently, it is necessary that Spain increasingly benefits in the future from the help of the Community in areas such as employment promotion, infrastructure, research and technological development, etc. so that its peripheral status is reduced.[59] This help, in turn, should be designed so as to encourage – not deter – the autonomous incentives of the Spanish private and public sectors in successfully adapting the economy to an internationally more competitive environment.

NOTES

This paper summarizes research carried out by Spain's study group, directed by José Viñals (Banco de España and CEPR), and comprising also by Javier Andrés (Universidad de Valencia), Jaume García (Universidad Autónoma de Barcelona), José Manuel González-Páramo (Universidad Complutense de Madrid y Fundación FIES-CECA), Jordi Gual (Universidad de Navarra and CEPR), Luís Mañas (Repsol, S.A.), Carmela Martín (Fundación Empresa Pública and Universidad Complutense de Madrid), Angel Torres (Ministerio de Economía) and Xavier Vives (Universidad Autónoma de Barcelona and CEPR). The views expressed in the paper are those of the authors, and do not necessarily represent those of the institutions with which they are affiliated.

The paper has benefited from conversations with Javier Ariztegui, Samuel Bentolila, Olivier Blanchard, William Branson, Guillermo de la Dehesa, Michael Emerson, Louka Katseli, Paul Krugman, Jorge Braga de Macedo, César Molinas, José Pérez, André Sapir, Luís Toharia, and Charles Wyplosz. Special thanks are given to John Black, Christopher Bliss, Richard Portes and Alexander Sarris for their many thorough comments and suggestions.

1 The long-run effects of completing the European Internal Market for the Community as a whole are analyzed in Commission of the European Communities (1988a), and also in Baldwin (1989). De la Dehesa *et al.* (1987) provide a detailed account of Spain's long road to trade liberalization since 1959.
2 Measured at current prices and Purchasing-Power-Parity exchange rates.

3 A significant part of this subsection is based on Martín (1989).
4 Data refer to 1985, and nominal protection rates include tariffs, equalization import taxes, and other border duties. The effective protection rate is computed by the Corden criterion. See Martín (1989).
5 The criterion for distinguishing between weak, moderate and strong-demand manufacturing products is defined in Commission of the European Communities (1985), and corresponds to the dynamism of world demand.
6 Since the prices of goods are not available at a very disaggregated level, sectoral industrial analysis has to be done in nominal terms. The data used were originally elaborated using the SITC classification, and have been converted to the NACE-CLIO R-25 nomenclature.
7 These issues have been recently stressed by Krugman (1987), and Richardson (1989) among others.
8 These results are broadly in line with those obtained in Neven (1990).
9 The first index, due to Grubel and Lloyd (1975) is:

$$A_i = 1 - \frac{|X_i - M_i|}{(X_i + M_i)} \times 100$$

where X_i is exports of sector i, M_i is imports of sector i, and i is the ith 5-digit sector from SITC. The index can vary from 0 to 100, and represents the proportion of intra-industry trade in each sector. See Martín (1989) for details.
10 It should be noted that the international comparisons between Spain and other countries are not fully homogeneous. See Neven (1990).
11 See Martín (1989) for details about the calculations.
12 See Martín (1989) for details about the calculations, which are in broad agreement with those in Neven (1990).
13 See Viñals and Bergés (1988) on this point.
14 This section is based on González-Páramo (1989).
15 This section is based on Andrés and García (1989). See also Bentolila and Blanchard (1990) for an alternative analysis.
16 See Rojo (1981). The recession in Western Europe led first to a halt to migration from Spain, and later to negative net migration flows which contributed to increasing the labour supply.
17 The model captures the fact that enough workers were available to work if required to do so. However, it is not detailed enough to determine whether the characteristics of available workers matched those of available jobs.
18 See Bean (1989) for the role of capacity constraints. They are also stressed in the case of Spain by Bentolila and Blanchard (1990).
19 As explained in Emerson (1988) the economic and legal obstacles to the termination of employment contracts and the regulatory constraints on temporary work in Spain are considered to be 'fundamental' by employers' organizations.
20 See Andrés and García (1989) for details of the estimated model. The evidence is consistent also with the results of Dolado and Malo de Molina (1985). The authors estimate Phillips-Curve type equations and derive a measure of real-wage inflexibility that shows that Spain has one of the highest degrees of real-wage inflexibility of the OECD, and that this is a main reason behind the high unemployment rate observed in the country.
21 See Lindbeck and Snower (1989) for an analysis of the role of insiders and outsiders in wage determination.
22 See Andrés and García (1989) for details of the estimated model.

23 See Andrés and García (1989) for details of the empirical results.

24 This subsection is based on Viñals (1989).

25 See, for example, Sachs (1982), Dornbusch (1983), and Svensson and Razin (1983).

26 Edwards (1984) provides a comprehensive survey of the problem.

27 For a general overview of capital controls in Spain at the time of EC entry and now see Ortega (1989).

28 We have taken the 3-month peseta interest rate prevailing in the Madrid interbank market, the 3-month Eurodollar interest rate, and the 3-month forward premium of the dollar *vis-à-vis* the peseta, between January 1982 and December 1985. While the Euromarket and forward premium data correspond to mid-day quotations, the only available Madrid data is a daily weighted average of quotations. Finally, all calculations refer to the last available day of each week.

29 From conversations held with operators, this is the width of the band that seems to correspond to the Spanish market, broadly in line with those quoted in Levi (1983) and other studies.

30 This subsection is based on Mañas (1989). See also Trujillo *et al.* (1988), Cuervo-Arango (1988), and Caminal *et al.* (1989), for recent descriptions of the Spanish financial system.

31 See Commission of the European Communities (1988b).

32 As pointed out by Neven (1989), high profitability seems to have gone hand-in-hand with extensive rent-sharing with labour in the banking sector. This, in turn, suggests low competitive pressure.

33 However, since mid-1989 bank credit ceilings have been introduced as a transitory measure to reduce the overheating of the economy.

34 See Pagano and Roell (1990) for an analysis of European stock markets.

35 See Torres (1989), and Ortega, Salaverría and Viñals (1989).

36 When agricultural products are included in the exercise, the overall effect rises to 30%.

37 See Branson (1990) for a further discussion of the economic significance of external imbalances in EC countries.

38 This subsection is based on Martín (1989), Torres (1989), and Gual *et al.* (1989).

39 See Richardson (1989) on this point.

40 The book by Helpman and Krugman (1985) seems to favour this general type of trade pattern. See also Neven (1990).

41 On this, see Krugman (1987).

42 This subsection is based on Viñals (1989).

43 This analysis might be criticized on the grounds that the computed interest rate differentials are not based on fully simultaneous observations, since the Madrid and London interest rates are not taken at the same time of the day. Also, not distinguishing between bid and offer rates for the domestic, foreign interest rate and exchange rate may have introduced some bias in the calculations. However, as shown in Viñals (1989) these results are confirmed by finer analyses.

44 Specifically, it was not clear how much of the noise came from shifts in the *LM* schedule (financial shocks) and from shifts in the *IS* schedule (real shocks).

45 See Krugman (1990) for a discussion of this issue.

46 This subsection is partially based on Mañas (1989).

47 See Gutiérrez and Campoy (1988) on this point.
48 See Pagano and Roell (1990).
49 In Krugman and Venables (1990) it is recognized that lower wages in peripheral countries may offset the disadvantages of peripherality, and therefore produce a better output outcome in those countries after 1992.
50 This point has been made by Malo de Molina (1983), among others.
51 While Calmfors and Driffill (1988) suggest that, on average, having a very centralized or very decentralized wage-setting process is preferable to being in an intermediate position, their analysis does not deal with intertsectoral shocks, such as the 'EC cum 1992' shock.
52 See also the discussion in Branson (1990).
53 Indeed, the expectations of exchange-rate stability have increased the size of capital inflows triggered by simple interest rate differentials, as indicated in Giavazzi and Spaventa (1990).
54 See the evidence discussed in Torres (1989).
55 See Krugman and Venables (1990) on this point.
56 See Viñals (1990) for an analysis of the peseta's entry to the EMS and its likely effects.
57 Although Branson (1990) suggests that there may be some market segmentation between the 'local' and the 'international' financial sector after 1992 it is not clear if and how this can be exploited by monetary and financial policies.
58 In this respect, see Bliss (1990) and Rodrik (1990).

REFERENCES

Background research papers

Andrés, J. and J. García (1989). 'Main features of the Spanish labour market facing 1992', mimeo, October.
González-Páramo, J.M. (1989). 'The role of the public sector in Spain: structural characteristics and policy adjustment on the road to the EEC Internal Market', mimeo, October.
Gual, J., X. Martínez Giralt, and X. Vives (1989). 'Spain in the EC: the impact of trade liberalization on selected industries', mimeo, October.
Mañas, L. (1989). 'The impact of 1992 financial liberalization on the Spanish financial industry', mimeo, October.
Martín, C. (1989). 'Spain's foreign trade and industrial structure: the effects of EEC membership and the Single European Market of 1992', mimeo, October.
Torres, A. (1989). 'The Spanish experience during the first years of EEC integration', mimeo, October.
Viñals, J. (1989). 'Spain's capital account shock', mimeo, October.

Other references

Andrés, J., J. Dolado, C. Molinas, M. Sebastián, and A. Zabalza (1988). 'The influence of demand and capital constraints in Spanish unemployment', D-88005, Ministerio de Economía y Hacienda.
Baldwin, Robert (1971). 'Determinants of the commodity structure of U.S. trade', *American Economic Review* **61**, 126–46.
Baldwin, Richard (1989). 'The growth effects of 1992' *Economic Policy* No. 9, **4**, 247–81.

Ballarin, E., J. Gual, and J. Ricart (1988). 'Rentabilidad y competitividad en el sector bancario español. Un studio sobre la distribución de servicios financieros en España', Documento de Trabajo 25/1988, FIES.

Bean, C. (1989). 'Capital shortages and persistent unemployment', *Economic Policy* No. 8, **4**, 11–53.

Bentolila, S. and O. Blanchard (1990). 'Spanish unemployment', *Economic Policy* No. 10, **5**, 233–81.

Bliss, C. (1990). 'Adjustment, compensation and faster mobility in an integrated market', this volume.

Branson, W. (1990). 'Financial market integration, macroeconomic policy and the EMS', this volume.

Branson, W. and Junz (1971). 'Trends in U.S. trade and comparative advantage', *Brookings Papers on Economic Activity* **2**, 285–364.

Calmfors, L. and J. Driffill (1988). 'Bargaining structure, corporatism and macroeconomic performance', *Economic Policy* No. 6, **3**, 13–61.

Caminal, R., J. Gual and X. Vives (1989). 'Competition in Spanish banking', Center for Economic Policy Research, Discussion Paper No. 314, July.

Commission of the European Communities (1985). 'La compétitivité de l'industrie européenne: un bilan,' *European Economy*, No. 25, 9–33.

(1988a). 'The Economics of 1992', *European Economy*, No.35.

(1988b). 'Creation of a European Financial Area,' *European Economy*, No. 36.

Cuervo-Arango, C. (1988). 'Financial liberalization: the Spanish perspective', *European Economy*, No. 36, 105–14.

Culem, C. and L. Lundberg (1986). 'The product pattern of intra-industry trade: stability among countries and over time', *Weltwirtschaftliches Archiv* **122**, 113–30.

De la Dehesa, G., J.J. Ruiz and A. Torres (1987). 'The timing and sequencing of trade liberalization: the Spanish case', mimeo, World Bank.

Dolado, J. and J. L. Malo de Molina (1985). 'Desempleo y rigidez del mercado de trabajo en España', *Boletín Económico*, Banco de España, September, 22–40.

Dornbusch, R. (1983). 'Real interest rates, home goods and optimal external borrowing', *Journal of Political Economy* **91**, 141–53.

Drazen, A. (1988). 'Monetary policy, capital controls and seigniorage in an open economy', in M. de Cecco and A. Giovannini (eds.) *A European Central Bank?* Cambridge University Press.

Edwards, S. (1984). 'The order of liberalization of the external sector in developing countries', International Finance Section, Princeton University, Essay No. 156, December.

Emerson, M. (1988). 'Regulation or deregulation of the labour market: policy regimes for the recruitment or dismissal of employees in industrialized countries.' *European Economic Review* **32**, 775–817.

Fariñas, J.C. and C. Martín (1988) 'Determinantes del comercio intra-industrial en España, in J. Velarde et al. (eds.), *El sector exterior de la Economía Española*, Economistas Libros, Madrid.

(1990). 'La ventaja comparativa de España y las exportaciones netas de productos manufacturados', *Investigaciones Económicas*, forthcoming.

Fernández, I. and M. Sebastián (1989). 'El sector exterior y la incorporación de España a la CEE', mimeo, July.

Giavazzi, F. and L. Spaventa (1990). 'The new EMS', forthcoming in P. de Grauwe and L. Papademos (eds.) *The European Monetary System in the 1990s*, Longman.

González-Romero and R. Myro (1989). 'La recuperación de la inversión industrial en España. Sus objetivos y factores determinantes', *Moneda y Crédito*, 188, 17–55.

Grubel, H. and P. Lloyd (1975). *Intraindustry Trade*, London: Macmillan.

Gutiérrez, F. and J.A. Campoy (1988). 'Eficiencia y competencia en el sistéma bancario español', *Boletín Económico*, Banco de España, December, 51–64.

Gutiérrez, F. and R. Segura (1989). 'Los mercados secundarios de acciones: situación y perspectivas', *Boletín Económico*, Banco de España, March, 75–88.

Helpman, E. and P. Krugman (1985). *Market Structure and Foreign Trade*, Cambridge, MA: MIT Press.

Hooper, P. and K. Larin (1988). 'International comparisons of labour costs in manufacturing', International Finance Discussion Paper, No. 330, Federal Reserve Board, August.

Krugman, P. (1987). 'European economic integration: some conceptual issues', in T. Padoa-Schioppa, *Efficiency, Stability, and Equity*, Oxford University Press.
(1990). 'Macroeconomic adjustment and entry into the EC: A note', this volume.

Krugman, P. and A. Venables (1990). 'Integration and the competitiveness of peripheral industry', this volume.

Laborda, A., J.R. Lorente, and F. Prades (1986). 'Los costes laborales unitarios y la competitividad de la economía española', *Economía Industrial*, November.

Lagares, M., R. Alvarez, I. Encabo, J.M. González-Páramo, and J.L. Raymond Bara (1988). 'Niveles de cobertura del gasto público en España', Fundación FIES-CECA, mimeo, July.

Lindbeck, A. and D. Snower (1989). *The Insider-Outsider Theory of Employment and Unemployment*, Cambridge, Mass., MIT Press.

Levi, M. (1983). *International Finance*, McGraw-Hill, New York.

Malo de Molina, J.L. (1983). 'Rigidez y flexibilidad en el mercado de trabajo: la experiencia española durante la crisis'; *Estudios Económicos*, Banco de España, 34.

Mato, G. (1989). 'Inversión, coste del capital y estructura financiera: un estudio empírico', *Moneda y Crédito*, 188, 177–200.

Neven, D. (1989). 'Structural adjustment in European Retail Banking: some views from Industrial Organization', CEPR Discussion Paper No. 311, April.
(1990). 'European integration towards 1992: some distributional aspects', *Economic Policy* No. 10, **5**, 13–62.

Ortega, E. (1989). 'Inversiones de España en el exterior y su comparación con otros países europeos', *Boletín Económico*, Banco de España, February, 29–48.

Ortega, E., Salaverría, J. and J. Viñals (1989). 'La balanza de pagos española en el entorno comunitario', *Boletín Económico*, Banco de España, November, 53–74.

Padoa-Schioppa, T. (1987). *Efficiency, Stability and Equity*, Oxford University Press.

Pagano, M. and A. Roell (1990). 'Trading systems in European Stock Exchanges: Current performance and policy options'. *Economic Policy* No. 10, **5**, 63–115.

Perelman, S. and P. Pestieau (1988). 'Technical performance in public enterprises: A comparative study of railways and postal services', *European Economic Review, Papers and Proceedings* **32**, 432–41.

Raymond-Bara, J.L. and J.M. González-Páramo (1988). 'Déficit, impuestos y crecimiento del gasto público', *Papeles de Economía Española*, **37**, 125–79.

Richardson, J.D. (1989). 'Empirical research on trade liberalization with imperfect competition: a survey', National Bureau of Economic Research, Working Paper No. 2883, March.

Rodrik, D. (1990). 'Soft budgets, hard minds: stray thoughts on the integration process in Greece, Portugal and Spain', this volume.

Rojo, L.A. (1981). 'Desempleo y factores reales', *Papeles de Economía Española* **8**, 124–36.

Sachs, J. (1982). 'Current account in the macroeconomic adjustment process', *Scandinavian Journal of Economics* **84**, 147–59.

Segura, J., C. Martín, L. Rodríguez *et al.* (1989). *La industria española en la crisis: 1978–1984*, Alianza Editorial.

Smith, A. and A. Venables (1988). 'Completing the internal market in the European Community: some industry simulations,' *European Economic Review* **32**, 1501–25.

Sneessens, H. and J. Drèze (1986). 'A discussion of Belgian unemployment combining traditional concepts and disequilibrium econometrics', *Economica* **53**, S89–119.

Steinherr, A. and P.L. Gillibert (1988). 'The impact of freeing trade in financial services and capital movements on the European banking industry', mimeo, August.

Svensson, L. and A. Razin (1983). 'The terms of trade and the current account: the Harberger-Laursen-Metzler effect', *Journal of Political Economy* **91**, 97–125.

Tharakan, P. (1983). *Intraindustry trade: Empirical and Methodological Aspects*, Amsterdam: North Holland.

Torrero, A. (1988). 'El sistéma bancario en los próximos años', mimeo, November.

Trujillo, J., C. Cuervo-Arango, and F. Vargas (1988). *El Sistéma Financiero español*, Ariel, Barcelona.

Viñals, J. (1985). 'El déficit público y sus efectos macroeconómicos: algunas reconsideraciones', *Papeles de Economía Española* **23**, 36–54.

(1990). 'The EMS, Spain and macroeconomic policy', forthcoming in P. de Grauwe and L. Papademos (eds.), *The European Monetary System in the 1990s*, Longman.

Viñals, J. and A. Bergés (1988). 'Financial innovation and investment', in A. Heertje (ed.), *Innovation, Technology, and Finance*, Basil Blackwell.

Weiss, L. (1963). 'Factors in Changing Concentration', *Review of Economics and Statistics* **45**, 70–77.

8 Economic integration in the enlarged European Community: structural adjustment of the Greek economy

LOUKA T. KATSELI

1 Introduction

In 1985–86, a series of decisions were taken to enlarge the Community further to include Spain and Portugal and to deepen the process of economic integration through the creation of an internal market by the year 1992. The measures that were agreed upon involve four broad categories of public policy: (1) the removal of important non-tariff barriers to trade for goods and services including national standards and regulations, government procurement policies, administrative barriers, physical frontier delays and costs, differences in VAT, regulations of freight transport, restrictions in national capital markets, legal impediments etc. (2) the removal of barriers to capital and labour movements and the liberalization of services, especially banking and insurance, (3) the strengthening of European institutions, especially the European Parliament, the European Council and the Commission *vis-à-vis* national governments and (4) the convergence of economic and financial policies as a first step towards a monetary union.

The effects of these decisions at the national level depend not only on initial conditions in each country, which are determined by the structural characteristics of the markets involved, but more importantly by the potential adaptability and adjustment of the political, social and economic systems to changing external conditions. The aim of this study is thus threefold: (a) to identify the existing structural characteristics of the economy that will determine the short-run and medium-term effects of the 1985 decisions, (b) to evaluate the path of structural adjustment that will most likely take place and (c) to consider policy proposals that could lessen the costs that structural adjustment will entail and further the chances of its being politically accepted.

By 1989, Greek trade *vis-à-vis* Community countries had been almost completely liberalized. This is a direct consequence of the progressive integration of the Greek economy into the European economy ever since the Treaty of Association was implemented in 1962 and more importantly after accession to the EC in 1981. Three phases can be distinguished in the process of integration: the first, which coincides with the period of association (1962–81) is characterized by the gradual elimination of tariff barriers coupled with the active use of domestic policy instruments (e.g. differential indirect tax rates on imports) for the selective protection of industrial activity.

The post-entry phase can be divided into two sub-periods. The first, 1981–86, was characterized by faster dismantling of existing trade barriers, especially tariffs and quotas and initial steps towards liberalization of capital markets. These measures were however supplemented by a series of measures aimed at the restructuring of industrial activity and at prolonging the real protection afforded to selected industrial sectors, mainly through the use of non-tariff barriers. A regulatory tax on imports was established in July 1984 which incorporated the protective elements of the indirect tax system. In addition, export subsidies were maintained intact or even increased in the case of small-scale industry and of some important traditional sectors (Maroulis, 1988).

The second sub-period, 1987–89, is characterized by the gradual elimination of export subsidies and by the dismantling of import credit restrictions. In January 1, 1989, the regulatory tax on imports was abolished. By that time, export subsidies accounted for less than 10% of their corresponding level at the end of 1986. They are going to be abolished completely vis-à-vis EC countries at the beginning of 1990. Finally, in recent years there has been considerable progress towards public procurement liberalization, following the EC directives while important steps have been taken towards the liberalization of the domestic financial system and of international transactions in services and international capital flows.

The agreement in 1985 at the European level to speed up the process of market integration thus coincided with the abandonment of any consequent use of industrial or trade policy at the national level. The year of completion of the White Paper, 1985, was thus the first year of a new policy regime that gave highest priority to the liberalization of capital and financial markets and the free play of market forces for the allocation of resources, as opposed to gradual liberalization and adjustment in the context of a national development plan.

In comparing the three 'Southern' countries, it is thus important to note not only differences in the structure of markets but also differences in timing vis-à-vis the process of integration. These factors might also account for differences in perceptions across countries, as to the likely effects of the internal market on potential industrial activity. In the recent survey of European industry's attitudes *vis-á-vis* 1992 (Commission of the EC, 1988a) important differences emerge across countries as to the perceived importance of specific barriers and the chances and risks of the internal market.

Greek industry perceives administrative barriers and physical frontier delays and costs as the major barriers to trade (Ibid., Table 1, p. 6). This is consistent with the structure of national industry and the importance of this type of barrier for the more traditional industrial activities such as textiles, footwear and clothing, paper, printing and publishing, mineral oil refining, metal production etc., as opposed to those barriers (standards, technical regulations, public purchases) which are considered important for the technologically advanced sectors and countries (Ibid., Graph 3, p. 11).

In contrast to all other European countries, Spain and Portugal included, restrictions in the capital markets and exchange controls still rank second in Greece in terms of perceived importance as market barriers. This affects all industrial activity regardless of sector. Similarly, the reduction of banking costs is considered to be the principal component of the expected unit cost reduction as a consequence of the creation of the internal market (Ibid., Table 4, p. 15). These perceptions summarize the important structural differences between Greece and its trading partners within the Community. Thus, the present structure of industry and the structure of capital markets will probably differentiate the process of structural adjustment towards and after 1992 in Greece from that of most other European countries.

The same survey also summarizes the evaluation of industrialists regarding the expected path of structural adjustment, which is the second subject of investigation of this study. The Greek companies interviewed evaluate the creation of the internal market more pessimistically for their own firms than their counterparts in other countries and overall negatively for the whole country (Ibid., Vol. 3, Table 7). This is in sharp contrast with very positive perceptions in both Spain and Portugal. As the report notes, 'Greece is the only member country where it is considered that the risks for the economy as a whole will outweigh the opportunities: these fears predominate among the larger firms with more than 500 employees' (Ibid., p. 35).

Even if we accept the authors' note of caution that in formulating their responses companies might not have all relevant information or do not take into full account the potential changes in the broader, macroeconomic context, these negative attitudes and expectations 'do affect decisions concerning investment, research, product strategy etc. and for that reason are to some extent self-fulfilling' (Ibid., p. 2). It is for this reason that a study that attempts to explain the origins of Euro-pessimism prevalent in Greece today might be useful for the establishment of public policy priorities both at the national and at the Community level.

2   The structure of the Greek economy

The share of the primary sector in total output and employment is considerably higher in Greece than in other European countries. Agriculture in 1988 still accounted for 13% of GDP and 27% of total employment. Developments at the macroeconomic level in the following years will thus depend to a large extent on the evolution of the Common Agricultural Policy and the effects of the internal market on the primary sector of the economy. Despite the importance of agriculture for the overall structural adjustment of the economy, the focus of the present study will be limited to the industrial and service sectors and to those characteristics that will influence the path of structural adjustment as a consequence of the internal market.

2.1   State corporatism and 'soft-budget' constraints

The functioning of markets and their pattern of adjustment to external shocks can hardly be explained in Greece unless one understands the role of the state and the public sector in the regulation of economic activity.

In describing the Greek political and economic model as 'state corporatism' one can paraphrase Katzenstein's definition of neocorporatism (Katzenstein, 1983) as follows: 'State corporatism is the voluntary cooperative regulation of conflicts over economic and social issues through a highly structured and interpenetrated set of political relationships by the state, banks and business augmented at times by unions and political parties . . . Strong corporatist structures have a pervasive ideology of social partnership shared by the leaders of government, banks and business; they rely on the cooperative efforts of relatively centralized institutions representing those interests and they usually lack in worker militancy.'

The historical origins of this model and its consequences for the functioning of democracy and the pattern of industrialization have been analyzed elsewhere (Mouzelis, 1978 and 1986; Tsoukalas 1986; Mallios 1975). The effects however of state corporatism for the functioning of markets, for economic behaviour of individual agents, and for macroeconomic developments have not been adequately studied.

The interlocking set of interests between the state financial institutions and the traditional industrial families has created a thin line between the 'public' and 'private' sectors of the economy. This is manifested not only through the pattern of ownership and management control but also through direct or indirect interventionism of the government in private market activity and of industrial interests in the running of the government.

2.1.1 Public sector ownership, control and duality of markets

In a recent study on the role of the public sector in the Greek economy, Provopoulos (1985) creates a typology of public sector entrepreneurial activity that distinguishes four broad categories of 'state-controlled' enterprises.

The first category consists of public enterprises entirely owned and controlled by the public sector. The sectoral distribution of the 59 enterprises included in this category in 1983 was as follows: 3 were in the energy sector, 14 in transportation-communications, 3 in water-drainage, 11 in manufacturing, 21 in commerce and other services and 7 in banking. Data gathered for 37 of these enterprises show that they employed 155,608 people.

The second category consists of 123 enterprises which are under majority ownership by the state-controlled banks, especially by the National Bank and the Commercial Bank of Greece. Of these enterprises, 76 were in manufacturing, 31 in credit or insurance and 16 in other business. If one excludes 15 firms which were bankrupt in 1983, the others employed 25,581 people.

In the third category, Provopoulos includes those enterprises, 149 in total, for which the state-controlled banks own less than 50% of their stocks. Of these enterprises, 117 were in manufacturing, 11 in credit-insurance and 21 in other activities. Total employment amounted to 56,248 people.

The fourth category consists of the 39 viable but 'overindebted' firms which came under the state-controlled Organisation for the Restructuring of Industry (OAE) in 1983. The majority of these enterprises were in manufacturing (36 out of 390) and employed around 29,544 people. By 1989, only 23 of those enterprises continue to be considered viable, employing around 25,000 people.

Thus, the enterprises under direct or indirect state control employed in 1983 around 267 thousand people. If one adds to that figure employment in central and local government which was approximately 350 thousand, employment in the state-controlled sector exceeds 26% of total wage and salary earners in the non-agricultural sectors of the economy. Similar figures are quoted by Glytsos (1989).

Total assets of state-controlled enterprises reached in 1983, 2,006 billion drs. During that same year, the total assets of the manufacturing sector (including publicly-controlled enterprises) was only 1,819.5 billion drs (Provopoulos, 1985, p. 25).

By 1985, the firms in manufacturing for which the state or its intermediaries controlled at least 20% of their stock accounted for 3.0% of the total number of firms, 20% of total employment and 50% of total fixed assets in manufacturing (Magliveras, 1987, pp. 180–85).

State control over the economy is thus manifested at one level through majority or minority ownership of stocks by the state or by banks, especially by the two largest ones (Commercial Bank of Greece and the National Bank of Greece) which cover around 2/3 of the total banking business (deposits, credits, credit cards etc.).

State control over industrial activity has traditionally been enhanced by the centralized control of the financial sector. Until 1982, the allocation of credit was controlled through the Currency Committee, which was established in 1946.[1]

The Committee controlled the distribution and allocation of credit and was responsible for approving all bank lending, which it did on a monthly, semi-annual, or annual basis. It determined the purpose for which lending was to be undertaken, the sectors towards which credit would flow, the percentages or even sometimes the absolute amounts to be financed by bank lending, the rates of interest to be charged, and the procedures by which loans could be approved (Papandreou, 1988a).

The decision to regulate credit allocation tightly throughout the post-war period through the workings of the Currency Commission and the state-controlled banking sector, influenced the mode of behaviour and institutional developments in the industrial and banking sectors and is largely responsible for the underdevelopment of capital markets.

According to Kouzionis and Georgantelis (1989), the traditional thinness of the capital market can be understood only with reference to the incomplete institutional framework. The Greek stock market still remains exceptionally shallow. Until 1987 only 116 companies were registered, while the amount of capital raised through the stock market represents less than 1% of the total financial flows in the economy. A considerable number of listed shares are totally inactive or thinly traded. Raising capital through issuing bonds has been an exclusive privilege of the state, public utilities and banks, while trading in other important financial instruments (options, futures, commercial paper etc.) has been nonexistent. Other stock exchange-related services such as portfolio management and advisory services, underwriting etc., have also been underdeveloped.

The total dependence of the private sector on the state-administered banking sector for both long-run and short-run working capital under conditions of credit rationing, intensified the need for 'cooperative', i.e. 'political resolutions of conflicts' with important consequences for the structure of the private sector itself.

The presence of tightly family-run firms can be interpreted as a manifestation of the state-corporatist environment: negotiations still have to be conducted in closed circles and extensive bargaining is required. This explains why concentration of management in family hands is a characteristic mainly of 'large' firms, i.e. firms which were able to expand their size and secure access to credit after extensive negotiations (see Section 2.3). This can be seen more clearly if one analyzes the ownership and management structure of the 'overindebted' or 'problematic' firms which are now registered with OAE under the restructuring plan of 1983. These were the traditionally family-run companies with strong political affiliations and easy access to subsidized credit. The absence of entrepreneurship and of new entrants into the industrial class during the period 1950–80 is another manifestation of the effects of state corporatism on the workings of the private sector.

Finally, this environment condoned and fostered the development of 'dual' institutional structures in all the relevant markets. In the commodity, credit or labour markets there still exists on the one hand an 'official' sector[2] which can be either public or private in its ownership structure, but which possesses 'command–economy' characteristics in resource allocation and decision-making. The rules and commands pertaining to the effectiveness of regulations, to pricing, to taxation or subsidization, to protection from competition, to hiring and firing, to credit extention etc. have traditionally been negotiated bilaterally, usually between the enterprise and the relevant decision-making authority and more seldom through representative bodies (Federation of Greek Industrialists etc.). On the other hand, there exists an extensive 'unofficial' sector which consists largely of small-scale industrial or commercial enterprises that possess no negotiating power but instead exhibit more competitive behaviour in all relevant markets, often operating in the 'underground' economy.

Evidence is cursory for the operations of this sector. The existence of an informal market for credit largely for small- and medium-sized enterprises can be evidenced by the increasing share of post-dated and bad cheques to sight deposits. According to Kouzionis and Georgantelis (1989) the ratio of the number of bad cheques to the total number of cheques issued in Greece has recently reached the high level of 5%, as opposed to 0.61% in Denmark. From preliminary evidence it seems that the number of post-dated cheques is a multiple of the number of bad cheques. According to a recent study, the underground economy measured as the percentage of economic activity not recorded in the national income accounts is highest in the service sector, especially in housing, in construction and in trade, i.e. sectors which had limited access to the banking system and thus faced high costs of production (Pavlopoulos, 1987, p. 176). According to the same author, the manufacturing sector, i.e. the sector which absorbed by bulk of new credit through the banking system, has had the lowest contribution to the underground economy.

The dual nature of institutional arrangements is also prevalent in the labour markets. Wages, employment policy and social policy in general are determined within the 'official' sector. The key players are the government, public-sector unions and employers of large firms in manufacturing and the service sector. The 'unofficial' sector is instead a price-taker with much greater flexibility in hiring and firing practices.

The pattern of ownership and control identified with state corporatism and the dual institutional structures that have evolved were directly challenged by the integration of the economy in the European Communities in 1981 which coincided with internal political change that gave high priority to financial reform and the 'socialization' of the state. They are challenged even more fundamentally by the 1985 decisions, especially those pertaining to the liberalization of capital markets. The prolonged life of 'state corporatism' as the prevalent model of social organization has given rise however to specific structural rigidities in all markets. These evolved over time as a consequence of specific policies that are briefly reviewed in Section 2.1.2.

2.1.2 Patterns of control and 'soft-budget' constraints

The principal means of control exercised by the government on industrial activity, in the context of the institutional framework described in Section 2.1.1, is the selective application of rules or exemptions from rules for the conduct of business. The multiplicity of laws and regulations still existing for investment activity, for financing, for production or trade has created a nexus of differentiated market conditions for the different sectors of economic activity, often reflecting special underlying interests at the enterprise level. Price controls and selective protection coupled with credit rationing and subsidies on the cost of capital have been the most commonly used regulatory instruments.

Price controls have been in operation since the late 1940s. Originally, these controls only covered a small number of products and were intended to curb high prices of essentials, chiefly foodstuffs. The controls were extended in the 1960s and 1970s as inflation rose and are presently monitored by a branch of the police known as the 'market police' and decided upon by the Ministry of Commerce.

According to the 'Market-Law Code', based on Bavarian laws from the 1830s, products fall into one of three categories:

(i) 'essential and in short supply'
(ii) 'essential and not in short supply'
(iii) 'non-essential'

The first category of goods contains basic consumer goods, chiefly foodstuffs, for which, in most cases, a maximum price is set. For some goods in this category and for all goods in the second category that includes other consumer products such as clothes, books, paper etc., the Greek Ministry of Commerce sets a maximum allowable mark-up over average unit costs. The third category includes goods that are essentially exempt from controls (Lalonde and Papandreou, 1984; Katseli , 1986). In 1984, of the commodities included in the CPI, 25.5% were commodities in category (i), 27.6% in category (ii) and 32.5% in the category (iii). The remaining 14.4% of the commodities were services provided by the public sector.

The behaviour of product prices and hence of the aggregate sectoral indices and profits are thus affected by the Ministry's actions in adjusting the price ceiling or the allowable mark-up after extensive negotiations with firm representatives. It is only in the last five years that some of the product categories have been removed from categories (i) and (ii) and their price is now market-determined.

The evolution of sectoral protection over time also reflects the discriminatory application of domestic fiscal instruments to counter the trend towards overall trade liberalization. Until 1981, these included an array of *ad valorem* and specific taxes such as the turnover tax, luxury and consumption taxes, stamp fees, wage bill taxes, specific import taxes etc. Only the turnover tax was at the same fixed *ad valorem* rate for all products. The others differed by product categories. Imports were selectively discriminated against either explicitly through nominal rate differentiation or implicitly through notional changes of the tax base (Georgakopoulos, 1989).

A breakdown by Sarris (1988) of the average *ex-post* border tax rates for dutiable imports by 2-digit SITC categories for 1983 shows that 'the rates differ widely among product classes from zero up to 94%' (Sarris, 1988, p. 336). The selective application of domestic production taxes and subsidies at the sectoral level is evident by the evolution of the Nominal Effective Protection Rate (NEP) in individual manufacturing sectors.[3] According to Sarris's calculations (1988) while in most industrial sectors the NEP declined between 1970 and 1980, protection increased for wood and cork, refinery products and non-metallic minerals and remained high for beverages, textiles and yarn, rubber and plastics, furnitures and metal products.

The sector for which the NEP rose the most, namely refinery products, is one of the most highly concentrated sectors, where in 1984 the largest 15 firms out of a total of 212 owned virtually 100% of the total assets at the two-digit industry level (Papandreou, 1988a). The concentration rate is also high (over 70%) in the beverages, wood and cork, furniture, non-metallic minerals, basic metallurgy and metal product sectors all of which have enjoyed high levels of nominal and effective protection over the 1970–80 period. The benefits of this protection were shared by few traditional industrial firms that were operating in the 'official' sector of the economy.

Selective protection was extended to individual industrial firms not only through fiscal instruments but also through the operations of the banking system and the control of credit provision. The availability of credit has been significantly restricted since 1972, forcing the market to operate under rationing regimes (Haritakis, 1981).

Access to the banking system and the provision of credit was limited to individual firms in the 'official' industrial sector with no clear observance of market signals. Commercial firms for example have traditionally had limited access to credit even though the rate of return in commerce defined as net profits to total assets, has been positive and rising, as opposed to negative rates in manufacturing. Even though needs for credit in commerce may well be less than those in the manufacturing sector (Dutta and Polemarchakis, 1988), it is still surprising that the credit to output ratio in commerce remains extremely low (average for period 1980–87 is 3%) in relation to manufacturing (average ratio 17%), given that the commercial firms' output represents between 80–90% of the value of manufacturing output (Kouzionis and Georgantelis, 1989).

The selective promotion of credit to manufacturing was also pursued against market trends in investment activity. Whereas the bulk of private investment during the 1960–84 period was directed towards the service sector, especially housing, lending was extremely limited in those sectors (Papandreou, 1988a). Instead, the ratio of credit to output has remained above average in the same sectors which have enjoyed high levels of nominal and effective protection, namely in the paper, beverages, textiles, non-metallic mineral and basic metallurgy sectors, despite large negative returns on equity for these sectors.

The post-1981 integration of the economy into the world economy and the ensuing liberalization of trade has posed a serious threat to the long-protected 'official' industrial sector. It has posed an even more serious threat to the workings of 'state-corporatism' as a viable model of social organization and to 'soft-budgeting' as its principal mode of operation.

According to Kornai (1986) a firm's budget constraint is soft when the strict relationship between expenditure and earnings has been relaxed, because excess expenditure over earnings will be paid by some other institution, typically by the State (Kornai, 1986, p. 4). Kornai identifies four conditions each one of which is sufficient to render the firm's budget constraint 'soft': (a) price-making by firms where firms can influence the prices that are formally determined by the administrative price authorities as a consequence of influence over the authority's decision; (b) softness of the tax system when tax rules are influenced by firms, exemptions or postponements are granted as individual favours and taxes are not strictly collected; (c) the provision of state grants such as contributions to investment expenditure without repayment obligations and of *ad hoc* subsidies in compensation for losses; (d) softness of the credit system when firms are granted credit even if there is no full guarantee of their ability to repay and terms are arbitrarily negotiable.

The workings of price controls, the arbitrary provision of effective protection and of credit to individual firms through the state-controlled institutions with no legally sanctioned commitments as to performance or repayments have created a 'soft-budget' environment for private firms in the 'official' sector and for most public-sector enterprises including banks.

'Softness' has also characterized the budget constraint of households in the official sector through counter-cyclical public sector employment and incomes policies. Given life-long job security and high fringe benefits in public sector employment, the preference for public sector employment is strong, resulting in excess supply of labour at the prevailing wage and labour rationing in the 'official' labour market. The composite growth rate of public sector employment has been 44% higher than that of the private sector (Vavouras, *et al.*, 1989). Public sector employment has grown rapidly in periods of low growth and more moderately in periods of high growth. The income elasticity of public sector employment with respect to income changes is thus negative (Glytsos, 1989). Real wages, on the other hand, largely set by the public sector, have exhibited a large variance relative to the rest of Europe as the government has frequently changed the rules to accommodate conflicting interests (Glytsos, 1989).

The 'softness of the budget constraint' has had profound implications for economic behaviour, for the structure of economic activity and for attitudes and perceptions as to behavioural norms for the government, for firms and for state-controlled institutions such as banks. These effects are analyzed in Sections 2.2–2.5 of the paper.

Years	Goods and Services		Public investment		Transfer payments		Total expenditure
	% Expend.	% GNP	% Expend.	% GNP	% Expend.	% GNP	% GNP
58–66	47.5	11.3	24.0	5.7	28.4	6.7	23.8
67–73	42.5	12.2	24.3	7.0	33.2	9.5	28.7
74–81	46.7	15.3	16.6	5.5	37.7	12.8	33.7
82–87	41.0	19.3	14.5	6.9	44.5	21.0	47.2
82	42.9	17.9	14.0	5.8	43.1	17.9	41.7
83	42.0	18.6	15.6	6.9	42.4	18.8	44.3
84	41.4	19.5	15.9	7.5	42.7	20.1	47.1
85	39.6	20.6	15.8	8.2	44.6	23.1	51.8
86	39.9	19.6	14.2	7.0	45.9	22.6	49.2
87	40.3	19.7	11.6	5.7	48.1	23.5	48.9

Table 8.1. The structure of Greek public expenditure, 1958–87
Source: National Accounts of Greece.

2.2   Structural characteristics of public sector activity

The public sector's structural characteristics reflect the traditional role of the government in the context of the state corporatist model. The public sector includes the central government, the local authorities and the legal entities of Public Law, mainly social insurance and other public funds. Its size has grown considerably in terms of GDP.

2.2.1 The structure of expenditure

Public expenditure, which includes current expenditures on goods and services, transfer payments and investment expenditure, rose from 21% of GNP in 1958 to 49% in 1987 (Table 8.1). The changes in the composition of public expenditures demonstrate the redistributive role of the public sector in the economy and its main function as an arbiter of conflicting social claims rather than as a provider of public goods.

After the first oil crisis, as stagflation set in, the share of public investment in public expenditure dropped significantly, while the share of transfer payments increased. The share of expenditures on goods and services in GNP rose steadily from an average of 12.2% in 1967–73 to 19.3% in 1982–87. The corresponding share for transfer payments rose from 9.5% to 21%. The opposite paths of transfer payments and investment as a share in total public expenditure, reveals the government's preference for present rather than future consumption, and for the selective protection of targeted groups such as pensioners, farmers or exporters.

Wages and salaries constitute about half of total public expenditure of goods and services. The wage bill (for both civil and military personnnel) rose as a share of GNP from 9% in 1967–73 to almost 13% in 1982–86 (Table 8.2). From 1975 up to 1985, the share of civil wages in GNP increased steadily by an average annual growth rate of 5% (Karavitis *et al.*, 1989). The percentage participation of civil purchases of goods and services in total expenditure remained stable throughout the period except for those years when military expenses augmented. The expansion of military expenditure was thus realized through cuts in civil purchases of goods and services and not in the wage bill.

The sectoral composition of public expenditures on goods and services reveals that about one-third of total expenditures and around half of civil expenditures is absorbed by public administration (Ibid., 1989). Expenditures on human–capital formation, research and technology or health remain relatively low in the whole period with the exception of the period 1981–85 when their share in total expenditures rose drastically. The large weight of wages and salaries in current public expenditures reflects the active use of income policies as a counter-cyclical policy tool especially in the 1980s.

Transfer payments to the private sector include net transfers to households, subsidies and interest on public debt. Net transfers to households, consisting of pensions, unemployment compensation, sickness and other benefits or allowances, have constituted in the 1970s and 1980s over 60% of total transfer payments (Ibid., 1989). Their share in GNP rose rapidly in the 1980s as the new government in 1981 increased pensions. Thus net transfers to households amounted to 13.5% of GNP in 1982–87 against 7–8% in the period 1973–80.

On the other hand subsidies, that is once-and-for-all payments to the private sector, including subsidies to farmers, to industry and rebates on export financing costs, were subject to cyclical variations. The peaks correspond to general election years (1974, 1978, 1981, 1985) reflecting the effect of the political cycle on the structure of expenditures.

Interest on public debt increased throughout the period as a proportion of total transfer payments and as a proportion of GNP. After 1978 and especially after 1983 the interest paid on public debt rose sharply as a result of three contributing factors: (a) the rise in overall public debt, (b) the rise in interest rates as a consequence of monetary reform and (c) changes in the method of financing, largely through the sale of short-run maturity Treasury Bills to the non-bank public. In 1985 TBs sold to the

Years	Civil sector			Military sector			Total expenditure on goods and services (1)+(2)+(3)+(4)
	Wages and salaries (1)	Other purchases (2)	Total (1)+(2)	Wages and salaries (3)	Military equipment and construction (4)	Total (3)+(4)	
(% of total expenditure)							
1958–66	47.5	17.8	65.3	26.0	8.6	34.7	
1967–73	49.1	15.0	64.0	24.3	11.0	36.0	
1974–81	47.2	12.4	59.6	20.0	20.4	40.4	
1982–86	50.2	17.3	67.7	17.9	14.7	32.6	
1982	49.9	14.8	64.7	19.4	15.9	35.3	
1983	50.3	15.9	66.2	18.4	15.4	33.8	
1984	50.2	16.8	67.0	17.8	15.2	33.0	
1985	52.0	17.2	69.2	16.8	14.0	30.8	
1986	48.6	21.6	70.2	17.0	12.8	29.8	
(% of GNP)							
1958–66	5.4	2.0	7.4	3.0	1.0	4.0	11.3
1967–73	6.0	1.9	7.8	3.0	1.4	4.4	12.2
1974–81	7.3	1.9	9.2	3.0	3.1	6.2	15.4
1982–86	9.7	3.3	13.0	3.4	2.8	6.2	
1982–87							19.3
1982	8.9	2.6	11.6	3.5	2.8	6.3	17.9
1983	9.4	3.0	12.3	3.4	2.9	6.3	18.6
1984	9.8	3.3	13.0	3.5	3.0	6.5	19.5
1985	10.7	3.5	14.2	3.5	3.9	6.3	20.6
1986	9.5	4.3	13.8	3.3	2.5	5.8	19.6
1987							19.7

Table 8.2. Greece: the structure of government expenditure on goods and services, 1958–86

Source: National Accounts of Greece.

non-bank public financed 1.1% of the Public Sector Borrowing Requirement (PSBR). In 1988 this figure reached 28.1% and it is expected to climb to 40% in 1989 (Karavitis, *et al.*, 1989, Table 4).

Finally, with the exception of the 1982–85 period, public investment has always played a residual-factor role in the structure of expenditures. The share of public investment in GNP declined steadily during 1973–82 and again after 1985, both as a share in total public expenditure and a share of GNP. There does not appear, historically at least, to be any medium-term strategy for public investment expenditures consistent with development prospects and targets. Periods of contraction or expansion are associated with either fast or low growth of investment. It is only in the early 1980s that the modernization of economic and social infrastructure was considered a top policy priority and an effort was made to restructure expenditures towards investment and away from consumption. After 1985, when contractionary fiscal policy was attempted, once again the burden of adjustment fell on public investment as opposed to other categories of expenditures (Karavitis *et al.*, 1989).

2.2.2 The structure of public revenues

Contrary to the average European experience, indirect taxes have traditionally provided over half of total public revenues. In the period 1982–87 the share of direct taxes on households was roughly equal to the share of indirect taxes in total public revenues (Table 8.3). As a percentage of GNP, tax revenue increased from an average of 24% in 1967–73 to 32.5% in 1982–87. This rise came predominantly from higher direct taxes on households. Given the significant exemptions from taxation from agricultural income, it can be concluded that growth in the public sector's income came from wage earners and pensioners of the urban sector. Thus, on the one hand, the public sector expands the income of urban households through direct employment or transfers and on the other, it is obliged to expand direct taxation to raise revenue.

In a recent study Provopoulos and Zambaras (1988) analyzes the statistical properties of the two time-series in an effort to determine the statistical exogeneity of government expenditures relative to taxes. He concludes that expenditures appear to be statistically exogenous to taxes in accordance with a political-cycle model of government behaviour.

2.2.3 The public sector deficit and public debt

The public sector deficit (PSD), equal to the difference between total public expenditures and revenues, amounted to 12.9% of GNP during the 1982–87 period compared to 4.6% in 1974–80. The rise in the PSD

Years	Direct taxes on		Total (1)+(2) = (3)	Indirect taxes (4)	Total taxes (3)+(4) = (5)	Income from property (6)	Transfers from the rest of the world (7)	Total public revenue
	Households (1)	Corporations (2)						
(% of total revenue)								
1958–66	34.0	2.5	36.0	55.5	91.5	7.6	0.9	
1967–73	36.2	2.5	38.7	54.5	93.2	6.8	0.0	
1974–81	39.1	4.5	43.6	49.0	92.6	9.2	0.0	
1982–87	45.2	3.6	48.8	45.8	94.6	5.4	0.0	
1982	46.2	4.0	50.2	44.5	94.7	5.3	0.0	
1983	46.3	2.9	49.2	45.6	94.8	5.2	0.0	
1984	46.5	3.3	49.8	44.4	94.2	5.7	0.0	
1985	46.3	3.2	49.5	44.6	94.1	5.9	0.0	
1986	43.4	4.2	47.6	46.9	94.5	5.5	0.0	
1987	42.4	4.1	46.5	48.5	95.0	5.0	0.0	
(Public revenue as % of GNP)								
1958–66	7.4	0.4	7.8	12.2	20.0	1.7	0.2	21.9
1967–73	9.2	0.6	9.8	13.9	23.7	1.8	0.0	25.5
1974–81	11.0	1.3	12.3	13.8	26.1	2.0	0.0	28.1
1982–87	16.0	1.3	17.3	15.7	33.0	1.9	0.0	34.9
1982	14.5	1.2	15.7	13.9	29.6	1.6	0.0	31.2
1983	15.2	1.0	16.2	15.0	31.2	1.7	0.0	32.9
1984	16.0	1.0	17.0	15.2	32.2	2.0	0.0	34.2
1985	16.0	1.1	17.1	15.4	32.5	2.0	0.0	34.5
1986	15.5	1.5	17.0	16.8	33.8	2.0	0.0	35.8
1987	15.9	1.5	17.2	18.1	35.3	1.9	0.0	37.2

Table 8.3. Greece: the structure of public revenues, 1958–87

Source: National Income Accounts of Greece.

stemmed from the faster growth of expenditures relative to public revenues and followed a political cycle, increasing sharply during years
corresponding to general elections. The accumulating deficits of the
public sector have raised the central government's total debt to GNP ratio
from 32.7% in 1981 to 58.0% in 1985 and 63.3% in 1987.

The corresponding figure for the total public sector debt including public
enterprises rose from 47.2% in 1981 to 84.1% in 1985 and is projected to rise
to 104% in 1989 (Karavitis *et al.*, 1989). In 1981, 72% of the total public
sector debt was domestic. By 1985 the corresponding ratio fell to 58%, as an
increasing share was financed from abroad. The issue of Treasury Bills to
the non-bank public in 1986 and 1987 following the 1985–87 'stabilization'
plan changed the composition of financing in favour of domestic resources.
The ratio of domestic financing in 1988 rose to 95.5% of the net PSBR as
opposed to 67.4% three years earier (Ibid., 1989, Table 4).

2.2.4 Structural rigidities in public sector activity
The analysis of the structure of public expenditures and revenues reveals
major rigidities emanating from public sector activity that have important
implications not only for the structural adjustment of the economy as
integration proceeds but also for the conduct of macroeconomic policy.
These rigidities which have their root in the 'state corporatist' model can
be summarized as follows:

(a) Rigidities in the restructuring of public expenditures due to past
public sector employment policies that have raised inordinately the share
of the wage bill. Growing demands for public goods can be satisfied only
at the expense of transfers or at the expense of the overall deficit unless tax
reform is initiated.

Severe bottlenecks have already appeared in the functioning of private
markets due to the lack of economic and social infrastructure, especially
in the rural areas. It should be noted that the marginal efficiency of
private sector investment as measured by the elasticity of output to
investment appears extremely low in all Southern Countries (Padoa-
Schioppa *et al.*, 1987, p. 167), largely due to the lack of 'social' capital.

(b) Rigidities in the functioning of labour markets due to wage-setting
behaviour in the public sector at large that acts as a price-leader for the
economy as a whole. As a result of past public-sector employment
policies, the only effectively organized unions operate in the public sector
especially in public enterprises. Nominal wage contracts are negotiated
annually between the government and public sector unions and are
incorporated in the 'Incomes Policy' package that is announced at the
beginning of each year. The incomes policy announced stipulates norms
for private sector contracts that are often legally enforced.

Wage-setting behaviour on the part of the public sector has traditionally resulted in an excess supply of unskilled labour in the private
sector, that then exercises pressures for its absorption into the public
sector.[4] Entry into the public sector is negotiable and subject to bargaining, lobbying etc., i.e. 'soft' (Appendix 1). Unemployment appears then as
a residual.

(c) Allocative and X-inefficiency in public sector operations. There is
by now substantial evidence to indicate that one of the main problems of
government expenditure is 'low quality'. The relative price for public
sector services relative to the GDP deflator has risen consistently from an
average of 0.959 in the 1965–73 period to 1.084 in 1974–80 and to 1.215 in
1981–88 (Karavitis et al., 1989). The increase in the relative price of
government services is attributed to a widening real wage gap between the
public and private sectors as well as to rising relative demand for government services. While the average real wage rate in the public and private
sectors rose by comparable rates between 1958 and 1986 (3.19 times in the
public sector as opposed to 3.13 times in the private sector), the average
annual growth rate of the labour productivity differential moved 2.9%
against the public sector. The relatively slow productivity growth in the
public sector is attributed not only to faster employment growth[5] but also
to outdated capital and inefficient modes of operation and management.

While the public sector appears to be relatively more capital-intensive
than the private sector, the capital stock is underutilized and usually of an
older and worse vintage than that of the private sector (Vavouras et al.,
1989).

The bureaucratic and heavily politicized mode of operation has led to a
rigid type of planning with minimum controls regarding the expediency,
feasibility and implementation of the various programmes, or the quality
and quantity of public purchases. This has given rise to substantial
allocative inefficiencies, i.e. to levels of production that are higher or
lower than the socially optimum ones and to X-inefficiencies, i.e. to
higher than minimum-cost methods of production (Vavouras et al., 1989;
Karavitis et al., 1989).

(d) Rigidities in revenue collection. The structure of employment and
past policy priorities that excluded the agricultural sector from any
considerable tax burden has created a limited tax base that is confined to
urban dwellers, especially wage-earners. The presence of an underground
economy largely in the service sector has limited the tax base even further
to wage-earners in industry or the public sector. In addition, the presence
of 'soft taxation' where rules are unclear and negotiable and where the
fulfillment of tax obligations is not strictly enforced, has meant that the
progressivity of the tax system is influenced by the political cycle,

Year	Policy	% Change in Public Investment	% Change in GDP at 1970 prices	% Change in GDP deflator	Deficit/ GDP (%)
1959	Expand	23.9	4.0	0.1	3.82
1960	Contract	18.7	3.1	3.8	3.44
1961	Contract	19.0	11.3	1.1	3.04
1962	Expand	1.5	0.6	5.1	3.08
1963	Contract	−4.0	10.1	1.1	2.37
1964	Expand	10.3	7.5	4.4	2.88
1965	Expand	10.4	9.2	4.3	4.23
1966	Contract	0.2	5.3	5.1	3.33
1967	Expand	10.7	4.7	3.0	4.91
1968	Contract	7.0	5.7	1.8	4.41
1969	Contract	24.4	9.3	3.4	3.88
1970	Contract	−3.1	8.3	4.0	3.68
1971	Expand	27.7	8.0	3.2	5.74
1972	Contract	13.4	9.1	5.2	5.45
1973	Contract	−3.3	8.3	19.8	4.87
1974	Expand	−20.1	−1.8	20.7	6.29
1975	Contract	−6.0	5.1	11.2	6.76
1976	Contract	2.0	6.1	15.8	5.38
1977	Expand	−10.2	2.9	12.6	6.07
1978	Expand	6.8	6.4	13.1	6.83
1979	Contract	10.9	3.6	18.2	5.83
1980	Expand	−2.2	2.1	19.9	6.58
1981	Expand	0.1	0.2	21.8	14.39
1982	Contract	6.9	0.6	23.5	12.96
1983	Expand	13.4	0.4	17.8	13.07
1984	Expand	10.1	2.9	19.5	13.88
1985	Expand	10.0	3.4	19.0	17.85
1986	Contract	−18.1	1.3	16.9	13.84
1987	Contract	−21.0	−0.4	13.6	11.15
1988	Expand	10.2	3.5	12.8	17.50

Table 8.4. Greece: structural deficits and fiscal impulses, 1959–88

Source: Karavitis *et al.* (1989).

exacerbating the effects of expansionary fiscal policy on the government deficit prior to elections.

(e) Rigidities in public sector deficits and public debt. Public-sector deficits (PSD) in Greece are 'structural', in the sense that they would persist even if the economy were at a 'normal' level of GDP, i.e. neither in a boom nor a depression. Calculations of the structural budget deficit

	1982–87	1987	1988[1]
Greece[2]	51.1	63.3	72.3
Portugal	60.5	72.0	—
Spain[2]	41.1	48.1	48.2
Italy	80.1	92.7	94.5
Ireland	116.6	137.2	—
Belgium	119.5	132.5	135.5
France[2]	43.6	43.9	43.5
Germany	41.7	43.6	44.6
Netherlands	66.8	76.9	80.2
Denmark[2]	60.8	57.2	56.1
UK	52.9	50.0	45.0

Table 8.5. Central government gross public debt, 1982–88 (% of GNP)

Source: OECD, *Economic Outlook*, June 1989. For Portugal, *Eurostat, Money and Finance*.

Notes:
1. OECD estimates.
2. Does not exclude public sector mutual indebtedness.

(Karavitis *et al.*, 1989) indicate that the combined effects of government policies and structural changes have not been on average linked to underlying economic conditions as described by the growth of output and the change of its deflator (Table 8.4).

The central government debt has growth rapidly to reach 72.3% of GDP in 1988 (Table 8.5), placing Greece at the higher end of the public indebtedness distribution for European countries. The expansion of the PSD and the abrupt switch towards domestic borrowing has led to increases in nominal and real interest rates, exacerbating the burden of interest payments on the outstanding public debt. By 1988, net debt interest payments had reached 17% of total expenditure (Table 8.6).

Thus the traditional role of the state as an 'overall insurance company (Kornai, 1986, p. 10) has narrowed the capacity of the state to modernize itself and to restructure its expenditures in order to serve effectively the process of development.

2.3   Structural rigidities in private sector activity and the ineffectiveness of market signals

Before analyzing the effects of soft-budgeting on private sector activity, some of the characteristics of the economic environment should be noted.

	1982–87	1987	1988
Greece	10.7	15.9	16.8
Spain	4.4	7.0	6.9
Italy	14.7	14.9	15.1
Ireland	12.1	13.2	12.0
Belgium	16.8	18.4	18.2
France	3.6	4.0	4.0
Germany	4.1	5.1	4.9
Netherlands	8.3	8.7	9.0
Denmark	1.7	1.7	1.7
UK	7.1	6.7	6.3

Table 8.6. General government net debt interest payments, 1982–88 (% of total expenditure[1])

Source: OECD, *Economic Outlook*, June 1989.

Note:
1. Total expenditure defined as current expenditure minus net lending.

2.3.1 Market signals, the cost of information and the duality of markets
The presence of a ponderous state bureaucracy, limited entry into the 'official' sector and protracted negotiations between agents have contributed to relatively high transaction costs for all those engaged in economic activity (Papandreou, 1988a). These have in turn created incentives for joining the underground economy, an economy estimated to be as high as 30% of GNP (Pavlopoulos, 1987).

State corporatism is also responsible for the absence of a strong flow of relatively accurate information within the economy and the prevalence of 'low quality' information on price and quality, on the value of firms, on the riskiness of projects or on actual rates of return. As a result transaction costs are high for all economic units, while valuable signals are indistinguishable from noise.

Even when the signals are correctly diagnosed, 'soft budgeting' implies that the response elasticity of agents is lowered, since adjustment can be postponed by pleading with the state for protection. 'The attention of the firms' leaders is distracted from the shop floor and from the market to the office of the bureaucracy where they may apply for help in case of financial trouble' (Kornai, 1986, p. 10).

It is not coincidental that institutions that depend on accurate information, such as the stock market, have not been developed in Greece. The chief reason cited by most observers is that the Greek entrepreneur wants to keep control of the firm and in particular to keep the firm in family hands so that he can negotiate effectively with the state or the banking bureaucracy. While the high degree of family control keeps information concerning profitability, taxation and investment plan 'all in the family', it does not contribute to a flow of reliable information (Papandreou, 1989).

Information flows are finally disrupted by the presence of fragmented local markets, by the small size of most Greek firms and by the absence of standardized procedures in accounting and recording.

Apart from the existence of low-quality information, the other major effect of 'state corporatism' is the duality of markets. Preferential treatment granted by the public sector to a selected sub-sample of industry has meant that barriers to entry have been erected. These have taken the form of legal barriers, sector-specific regulations and limited access to investment subsidies and to bank credit.

The 'official' manufacturing sector that had access to rationed capital under subsidized, negative real rates, often borrowed in excess of productive needs in order to extend credit at higher rates to the 'unofficial' sector of the economy, leading effectively to bank disintermediation. For instance in the car market and in other commercial activities the interest rate offered in the 'parallel' market was above 3% per month, that is double the prime rate offered in the official market (Kouzionis and Georgantelis, 1989, p. 8). Despite regulations that until recently required banks to lend a minimum quota of 10% of total deposits to small firms at preferential rates, this figure has never been exceeded, due to the high banking costs involved in small loans. Thus, the 'official' sector rapidly became overcapitalized and eventually overindebted as real rates rose in the 1980s, while the unofficial sector remained undercapitalized and small. The outcome of this policy pattern has been the segmentation of market.

Each industry is dominated by a few large firms. Less than three hundred firms own 70% of total industrial assets (Table 8.7). Thus we have strong industrial concentration as most assets are held by a few firms with considerable market power, while there exists a large constellation of small firms that operate in their product vicinity. Forty percent of employment in industry is generated by units of less than 10 individuals (Papandreou, 1989). In contrast to the large firms, the number of small firms in the economy seems to grow with the working population. Though there are over 200,000 more employees in the manufacturing sector of the economy in 1986 than there were in 1968, 20 years ago, the number of establishments has grown from 120,000 to approximately 130,000, so that the average size of the enterprise has remained the same, between 4 and 5 employees.

The small-scale, family-run unit possesses limited knowledge and

Table 8.7. Greece: number of firms, employment and concentration ratios by industrial sector, 1984–86

CCCN code	Sector	Number 1984	%	Employment 1984	%	Average employment/ firm 1984	Concentration ratios[1] (%) 1986
20	Food	19,708	13.6	99,715	14.3	5	36
21	Beverages	2,268	1.6	14,063	2.0	6	77
22	Tobacco	142	0.1	10,223	1.5	72	100
23	Textiles, yarns	4,625	3.2	65,435	9.4	14	49
24	Shoes, clothing	21,788	15.1	98,763	14.1	5	31
25	Wood and cork	13,769	9.5	33,484	4.8	2	83
26	Furniture	11,249	7.8	31,781	4.5	3	62
27	Paper products	575	0.4	10,845	1.6	19	77
28	Printing & publishing	3,105	2.1	17,762	2.5	6	53
29	Leather goods	4,701	3.2	17,116	2.4	4	96
30	Rubber and plastics	3,022	2.1	20,297	2.9	7	58
31	Chemicals	1,296	0.9	27,637	4.0	21	55
32	Refinery products	212	0.1	5,843	0.8	28	100
33	Non-metallic minerals	6,020	4.2	39,288	5.6	7	71
34	Basic metallurgy	114	0.1	11,288	1.6	99	99
35	Products of metal	15,634	10.8	52,911	7.6	3	67
36	Non-electrical machinery	5,222	3.6	24,905	3.6	5	57
37	Electrical machinery	6,945	4.8	29,112	4.2	4	55
38	Transport equipment	19,811	13.7	75,919	19.9	4	95
39	Other	4,536	3.1	12,257	1.7	3	71
	Total industry	144,742	100.0	698,644	100.0	5	70

Sources: National Statistical Service of Greece, Survey of Industry, 1984. ICAP, Financial Directory of Companies, 1988.

Note:
1. Fifteen largest firms as share of total assets.

Year	Large[1]	Small	Overindebted[2]	Total
1980	3.2	2.8	− 2.8	2.4
1981	2.6	1.9	− 7.5	1.3
1982	− 0.3	0.5	− 10.0	− 0.8
1983	0.3	1.5	− 14.2	− 0.4
1984	− 0.4	2.1	− 21.3	− 1.0
1985	− 1.0	3.4	− 27.3	− 1.7
1986	0.2	6.1	− 19.2	0.1

Table 8.8. Rates of return in Greek industry, by large, small and overindebted firms, 1980–86 (%)

Source: Commercial Bank of Greece.

Notes:
1. Large firm: member of top 100 largest in terms of assets.
2. Overindebted: unable to repay loans to banks.

information concerning potential markets. This contributes further to the segmentation of markets and to inefficient operation. Contrary to the case of large firms however, the market is relatively competitive in that there exists free entry, relocation and quick exit from specific activities. This is reflected in the number of firms that enter and exit industries year by year. Between the years 1969–78 20,904 enterprises 'exited' and 25,537 'entered' industry. This large movement does not reflect bankruptcy, since there are less than 4,000 formally registered bankruptcies each year (Papandreou, 1988a) but relocation and extension into other branches which appear more profitable. This enormous movement and change in the small units can be treated both as a sign of dynamism and of backwardness. It reveals a high degree of capital mobility as the owners of these firms are sensitive to market pressures. In the more liberalized environment of the 1980s, rates of return for 'small' industrial firms became consistently higher than those for the large ones (Table 8.8). On the other hand, the fact that so many firms can so easily shift into other activities reflects the small firm's low level of specialization (Papandreou, 1988a). Many small firms are 'multi-product' firms. This does not relfect the 'economies of scope' attributed to large and modern firms, but the inability of small firms to survive on the production of any one product alone.

2.3.2 Soft budgeting and firm behaviour
Soft budgeting by the corporatist state to protect a selected sub-sample of firms from competition took many forms. According to Kornai (1980,

1986) with soft budget constraints, costs of production do not become a matter of life and death; the firm is less responsive to price competition and less concerned about its own strategy. The firm responds to competitive pressures not in the traditional, neo-classical sense, (i.e. cost reduction efforts) but by trying to influence the relevant ministry, tax authority, or bank, by spending time and money on lobbying efforts. And finally, the soft budget constraint implies that the firm can shift risks onto the entity providing support.

At the firm level, evidence of the soft budget constraint appears in many guises. The implicit subsidies from negative real interest rates accounted for 46% of total announced profits for the period 1975–85 (Giannitsis, 1982, pp. 105–11 and Papandreou, 1988a).

The continual support of loss-making firms through loan extension and rescheduling burdened firms with large debt–equity ratios. As the profitability of industry fell from 8% in 1979 (net return on equity) to -11.7% in 1985, the debt–equity ratio rose from 2.7 to 6.9 (Table 8.9).

The soft-credit constraints, as well as the multitude of rules and regulations surrounding lending procedures, contributed to an internal financial structure for firms which seems irrational from an orthodox point of view, but rational within the artificial world of credit rationing (Trangakis, 1980). Fixed assets are often increased by borrowing short-term capital while working capital is frequently supplied through long-term loans (Papandreou, 1988b). In the soft drink industry, for example, an examination of firms' accounts for the years 1973–80 revealed that the sources for increases in long-term investment (fixed assets) were: 8% self-finance, 30% long-term borrowing, 38% increases in share capital (equity) and the remaining 24% short-term loans, at relatively high interest rates. Thus investment was and continues to be financed by relatively high-cost short-term loans. This is because in the rationed world of credit, firms take credit where they can get it.

That firms continue to have access to outside financing despite poor economic performance shows either that such performance does not result in automatic exit from the industry or that it is perceived to be temporary and reversible. The continuation of this state of affairs for more than a decade lends support to the first hypothesis.

Exit by loss-making firms has been traditionally pre-empted through extention of subsidies and protection. While loss-making firms accounted for 40% of all firms for the period 1979–86, the number of firms declaring bankruptcy remained relatively small, at 7%. These bankruptices reflect shutdowns not by the large loss-making firms, but by small firms. The asset value of the firms declaring bankruptcy (1980–87) is on average no greater than 2 million drachmae – approximately $20,000. Large firms are

Financial indicators	1979	1980	1981	1982	1983	1984	1985	1986
1. Profitability								
% of Loss-Making Firms	37.0	37.0	37.0	45.0	42.0	40.0	36.0	31.0
% Bankruptcies	7.0	7.0	6.0	6.0	7.0	8.0	7.0	4.0
Return on equity (%)	8.0	7.0	5.4	-4.7	-3.5	-13.6	-11.7	-0.4
Net Income (Index)	100.0	110.0	92.0	-116.0	-89.0	-294.0	-235.0	-12.0
2. Financial costs								
Financial Expenses (index)	100.0	118.0	136.0	139.0	144.0	160.0	173.0	153.0
Financial Expenses as:								
share of total costs (%)	24.0	27.0	28.0	23.0	28.0	30.0	33.0	33.0
share of total debt (%)	6.2	6.8	7.5	7.7	8.0	7.6	8.3	8.3
3. Borrowed to Own Capital								
as a share (%)[1]	37.0	31.0	30.0	36.0	31.0	19.0	14.5	17.0
as a ratio	2.7	3.3	3.4	2.8	3.3	5.4	6.9	5.8
Number of Firms in Sample	2,680	2,860	3,074	3,176	3,157	3,113	3,166	3,263
WPI (1979) = 100)[2]	100	124	153	182	220	264	314	396

Table 8.9. Profitability and debt-equity ratios for Greek industry, 1979–86

Source: Greek Business Federation, *1987 Yearbook.*

Notes:
1. Owed capital as a share of borrowed.
2. Wholesale price index.

This table is constructed from surveys conducted by the Greek Federation of Business and includes large and relatively modern firms which have an average of 1 to 3 million dollars (1986) in working capital.

Year	Capacity utilization
	%
1969	43.2
1970	40.6
1971	44.8
1972	51.1
1973	65.0
1974	49.3
1975	48.0
1976	61.0
1977	54.3
1978	63.3
1979	69.1
1980	59.7

Table 8.10. Greek capacity utilization rates, all industries, 1969–80
Source: Papandreou (1988a).

rarely allowed to close down and fire their employees (Papandreou, 1988a).

Besides distortions at the firm level, the existence of a protected environment has had effects at the industry level by creating inefficient industrial configurations. The banks promoted investments and supported entry into certain industries, and at the same time supported unprofitable firms which would otherwise have existed. This combination of excess entry without subsequent exit led to industries clogged by too many firms, all operating at too small a scale. Fixed costs, including the heavy financial burden, could not be covered, since they were not spread across high levels of output (Papandreou, 1988a).

One first and obvious result of this 'entry-without-exit' phenomenon is the persistence of excess capacity in Greek industry throughout the 1970s and 1980s. The overcapitalization of firms in the 'official' sector in the 1970s when overall demand was declining has resulted today in plants with huge unused capacity. Though firm capacity figures are hard to come by, Table 8.10 indicates the capacity utilization rates in industry during the 1970s. Capacity utilization rates are low for all years and reach their peak in 1979, where the rate reaches 69%. Relative to other countries, where capacity utilization rates range between 75% to 95% in normal economic conditions, capacity utilization in Greece must be considered low. The average for the period 1969–80 is 54%, with a minimum as low as 40.6% in 1970.

Industry (Standard Industrial Code)	Number of firms in sample and industry	Market share[1]	Actual to optimal[2] unit cost	Cost savings in $ millions ($ 1973)[3]
Inefficient industries:		%		
Dairy (202)	4/13	40	2.85	44.0
Food processing (203)	11/19	65	2.50	13.0
Textiles (231)	14/20	50	4.00	40.0
Textiles (232)	17/22	50	2.17	90.0
Leather (291)	5/5	100	1.50	0.5
Total	51/79		2.60	187.5
Efficient industries:				
Flour million (205)	9/11	80	1.00	0.0
Cigarettes (222)	4/4	100	1.00	0.0
Cement	4/4	100	1.00	0.0
Total	17/19		1.00	0.0

Table 8.11. Degree of industrial inefficiency in selected Greek industries, 1973–80

Source: Papandreou (1986), pp. 99–100.

Notes:
1. Sample output value relative to total industry, for the years 1973–80.
2. Measures how much greater actual average (unit) costs are than average costs at optimal scale of production. A value of unity implies that there is no statistically significant difference between actual and optimal average cost.
3. This is a dollar measure of the waste incurred from inefficient operation of the industry. It compares the total costs of operation of the industry to the costs that would be incurred if the firms in the industry were operating at the optimal size.

In keeping with the 'soft budget constraint' argument, it is perhaps no accident that the textile and fruit juice industries, whose capacity utilization rates declined between 1973–80 and 1980–87, have received the lion's share of all export subsidies, or about 32% of the total (Papandreou, 1989).

The presence or underutilized capacity at the same time that import penetration is increasing implies that the problem of Greek industry is one of structural competitiveness. The inefficient industrial structure results in high-cost production and diminishing competitiveness as integration proceeds.

A better measure for industrial inefficiency than capacity utilization is an estimate of how close firms are to the 'minimum efficient scale' on the average cost curve. Table 8.11 compares actual costs to estimated 'optimal' costs, defined as the lowest possible costs of production, given output and technology, for 8 Greek industries during the 1973–80 period (Papandreou, 1989).

Five of the eight industries can be considered as being inefficiently configured. In all cases save one, those industries possessing many firms (not just in the sample but industry-wide), are those which reveal the largest potential cost savings. Actual costs are about 3 times higher than optimal for the dairy industry, 2.5 times higher for food processing, 4 times higher for yarns and fabrics, 2 times higher for ginned cotton, and about 1.5 times higher for the leather industry. On the other hand, those industries with few firms appear to be far better configured. Actual costs are close to optimal costs for cigarette manufacturers, cement producers, and flour-milling companies.

Total cost savings available from better industry structure approach $186.5 million ($1973), or 35% of the total value of production. Cost savings available from those industries with few firms are marginal. Conversely, the cost savings in those industries inhabited by many firms are high.

If one were to draw an average cost curve for the inefficient industries, it would show that most firms are located to the left of the minimum efficient scale. For the textile industry (232), which reveals the greatest disparity between the smallest and the largest firms, small-firm unit costs are nearly 6 times greater than the larger firms in the industry (Papandreou, 1989). These results are indicative and support the contention that certain Greek industries are 'overpopulated'.

The coexistence side by side of firms with such large differences in cost, is partly the result of the protective umbrella under which inefficient firms operate. Even firms which are not overtly dependent on outside support cannot escape the effects of the soft budget constraints, since they are confronted with competitors who cannot be dislodged even through aggressive pricing strategies. Thus, the costs of the inefficient firms are shared by the industry as a whole.

In conclusion, soft budgeting has removed those characteristics of the market economy which are responsible for its dynamic nature: prices are distorted, negotiable competition is no longer a central determinant of firm behaviour, and efficiency is not the main determinant of survival (Gilpin, 1987, p. 19).

2.4   Structural characteristics of capital and financial markets

The effects of state corporatism on the financial markets are reflected on the asset and liabilities of the financial institutions (i.e. Commercial Banks, Special Credit Institutions and the Bank of Greece).

The commercial banking system in Greece is still an effective oligopoly with two banks (Commercial Bank of Greece and the National Bank of Greece) covering around 2/3 of total banking business (deposits, credits, credit cards, etc.) and holding 74.5% of the total assets of commercial banks. Therefore competition has been limited, although in the last few years it has been increasing as can be seen from the considerable changes in the market shares of the banks (Kouzionis and Georgantelis, 1989), in the number of new branches opened, in advertising campaigns to attract new customers, etc. Examination of the consolidated balance sheets of the monetary system for the period 1970–88 reveals the following (Table 8.12).

On the asset side the dominant items are loans and advances to the private sector but with a remarkable decline of their contribution during the period in consideration, from 52% in 1970, to 42% in 1980 and 24.0% in 1988. Claims on the Government (Treasury Bills) increased from 8.9% in 1970 to 16.5% in 1988, whereas advances to public enterprises, bonds, etc. have remained rather steady.

On the liabilities side, the contribution of M1 (currency in circulation and sight deposits) to total liabilities shows a decreasing pattern (24.7% in 1970 to 9.2% in 1988), while the share of private deposits to total liabilities of the monetary system remains high (around 43%). There is a remarkable increase in the share of foreign-exchange liabilities from 3.6% in 1970 to 12.8% in 1988 and in the share of other liabilities.

Examination of the consolidated balance sheets of the Commercial banks for the same period reveals that in 1988 total deposits constituted 86.8% of total liabilities and that deposits in foreign exchange rose sharply from 4.2% in 1970 to 19.3% in 1988. On the asset side, the share of loans and advances fell from 61.8% in 1970 to 32.3% in 1988 and was replaced by Treasury Bills, whose share rose from 15.2% to 30.5% during the same period (Ibid., 1989, p. 1).

The consolidated balance sheets of the monetary sector and of the Commercial banks reflect the most important structural characteristics of the financial market. These can be summarized as follows:

(a)   Exclusive concentration of banking activities, in 'traditional' activities, largely loans and advances and operation in the Treasury Bill market. Around 90% of gross profits of the public banks has been accrued in traditional banking activities.

	1970	%	1980	%	1988	%
Assets (total)[1]	219.9	(100.00)	1,973.0	(100.00)	13,064.4	(100.00)
Claims in foreign exchange	14.7	(6.68)	126.0	(6.38)	1,080.0	(8.27)
Claims on Government	50.5	(22.94)	494.2	(25.05)	4,378.2	(33.51)
Treasury bills	19.5	(8.88)	245.7	(12.46)	2,162.0	(16.54)
Loans and advances	25.6	(11.66)	238.3	(12.08)	773.9	(5.92)
Claims on public entities and enterprises	17.3	(7.84)	131.7	(6.67)	1,337.7	(10.24)
Claims on private sector	116.1	(52.79)	862.4	(43.71)	3,474.7	(26.60)
Loans and advances	113.3	(51.50)	828.1	(41.97)	3,176.3	(24.31)
Other assets	17.6	(7.98)	336.5	(17.05)	2,793.9	(21.39)
Liabilities (total)[2]	219.9	(100.00)	1,973.0	(100.00)	13,064.4	(100.00)
Money supply	54.3	(24.70)	313.1	(15.86)	1,202.5	(9.20)
Private deposits	91.7	(41.67)	782.1	(39.64)	5,573.9	(42.67)
savings	69.6	(31.65)	541.2	(27.43)	3,849.8	(29.47)
time	15.4	(6.99)	212.8	(10.78)	1,634.8	(12.51)
Public entity deposits	17.1	(7.72)	99.7	(5.05)	2,775.0	(2.12)
Liabilities to the Government	64.5	(2.94)	44.6	(2.26)	127.5	(0.98)
Liabilities in foreign exchange	8.0	(3.63)	249.7	(12.66)	1,673.4	(12.81)
Bank bonds	—		17.1	(0.87)	384.7	(2.94)
Capital and reserves	15.4	(7.00)	92.0	(4.66)	517.7	(3.96)
Other liabilities	23.2	(10.76)	356.4	(18.06)	3,307.1	(25.31)

Table 8.12. Consolidated balance sheet of the Greek monetary system: end-of-period balances, 1970–88 (billion drs)

Source: Monthly Statistical Bulletin of the Bank of Greece (series).

Notes:
1. Excludes bank premises and equipment, so they do not add-up to 100%.
2. Excludes deposits by international organizations, so they do not add-up to 100%.

(b)   Underdevelopment of capital markets.

(c)   Large and rising allocation of resources to the Treasury Bill market as a consequence of the increase in the public sector's borrowing requirements (PSBR) and of the rising credit risk of large and 'problematic' firms in the official sector.

(d)   Limited, relatively to OECD standards, international exposure to net foreign assets with adverse implications for the exchange risk position of the banks.

Finally,

(e)   Limited competition in financial services expressed by a large, even though declining share of the public banks, especially of the two largest ones, in total assets and liabilities.

Apart from these characteristics one should note rigidities in the internal labour market and the provision of capital which significantly raise the cost of intermediation. In a survey on current banking practices by Levegue (1987), Southern European banks consider themselves overstaffed and are the least influenced by industry-wide trends in pay scales.

In Greece, the average rate of increase of employment in the commercial banks and Special Credit Institutions in the period 1980–87 has been 4%, a high rate compared with employment trends in the European banking sector. The number of people employed was around 49,000 people at the end of 1987, approximately 1.25% of total employment. The salary system is characterized by non-substantial differences among functional categories and between starting and ending salaries of employees (Ibid., 1989). The Greek banking system has thus followed the same incomes policy as the rest of the public sector and is presently facing similar structural rigidities in its internal labour market, namely wage rigidities and limited mobility. It should be noted that the Greek banking system is characterized by the highest share of staff costs to total operational expenses among the OECD countries, that is around 80% compared to 66% for the OECD. As wages and salaries are among the most inflexible elements of operational expenditure, the large share of the wage bill limits the opportunities for significant cost reduction, and for the effective modernization of the banking system.

Wage costs are not the only source of inefficiency. The cost of capital and of intermediation is also high and rising. The cost of deposits for the commercial banks in the period 1980–87, estimated as the weighted average interest rate on nine different types of deposits, has increased from 12.69% in 1980 to 14.44% in 1987 as a consequence of the overall increase of interest rates and the increasing share of time deposits (Ibid., 1989).

On the asset side, the estimation of the effective return on loans had to take into account, till January 1989 when it was abolished, the complex system of regulations, name of blockings, designed to affect the direction of credit towards specific activities (mainly manufacturing) and away from others (mostly trade). According to Kouzionis and Georgantelis (1989), this system of blockings and deblockings has significantly raised banking operation costs and weakened the effectiveness of monetary policy. For instance an increase of the nominal interest rate charged for a specific category of loans by 2.5% resulted in only a 0.72% increase in the actual interest rate received by banks. This increase was so small that it reduced the banks' incentives to provide further funds, and distorted the effects of monetary policy.

The determination of revenue after taking into account the restrictions imposed by the monetary authorities is a difficult task because of the many changes of these restrictions. Today the main restrictions refer to the reserve requirements on deposits which are channelled to Treasury Bills (38%), compulsory deposits at the Bank of Greece (7.5%), compulsory financing of public enterprises and entities (10.5%), and of handicrafts (10.0%) totalling 66% of total deposits. A year ago the above restrictions were almost 80% of total deposits.

Under some hypotheses concerning the distribution of deposits and credits of a 'typical' commercial bank in 1987, the return on credit derived from the above system of restrictions was around 16.5%. Taking into account that the cost of deposits in drs was around 14.4% in 1978 this provides an interest margin of 2.0% (Ibid., 1989, p. 21). The mean value of net interest income to average total assets of the Greek Banks in the period 1980–84 was 2.05% (OECD, 1987). This value is considered slightly below that enjoyed by competitive EC countries (Spain 4.41%, Italy 3.25%, U.K. 3.40%, France 2.71%, Belgium 1.76%, Portugal 2.28%, Germany 2.37%).

The profitability indicators of Greek banks in general are among the lowest in Europe. Only three Greek banks are listed among the 300 top European banks and they are in very low ranking positions (*The Banker*, October 1988). Their average pre-tax profits to assets ratio is 0.33% compared to a mean value of 0.59% of all top 300 European banks in 16 countries while their average capital/asset ratio is the lowest (2.13% against an average 4.47%).

The low profits–asset ratio of the Greek banks is a consequence not only of the structural characteristics of the banking system but of its principal modes of operation in a state corporatist environment. The subsidization of credit through the application of negative real interest rates throughout the 1970s, the extension of new credit to inefficient firms that eventually became overindebted, the continuous absorption of labour as part of the employment policy of the public sector at large, and the absence of internal financial management largely as a consequence of the omnipotence of the Currency Committee in all financial decisions, has promoted a large, risk-averse and largely inefficient banking system.

In the 1980s a quiet revolution has taken place for the modernization of the banking sector and for monetary reform. In the period 1982–85, measures such as the rationalization of the interest rate structure, simplification of credit rules, introduction of new products etc. prepared the ground for more changes to come. During 1985–88 all interest rates except saving deposit rates were liberalized. CD's were introduced and interest rates on loans were allowed to be freely negotiated by banks. These measures were followed by the abolition of the blocking–deblocking system in January 1989. Today around 70–75% of commercial bank loans are freely negotiated. On the deposit side all interest rates are market determined with the only exception the savings deposit rate which is fixed by the Central Bank. Short and long lending rates are mostly market determined; only loan interest rates to handicrafts, agriculture and public corporations are still set by the Central Bank.

There still exists however a vast web of bureaucratic restrictions determined largely by inertia, built-in risk aversion and the need to finance the public sector's deficit.

The interbank market among commercial banks and other Special Credit Institutions (SCI) which is in existence since 1980 continues to be extremely thin. Most of the transactions are done on an overnight or weekly basis and only a few on a monthly or quarterly basis. Recently, commercial banks and SCI have also been using rediscounting of Treasury Bills.

The relative small volume of transactions carried out daily (around 10 billion drs per day on average) is one of the main causes of the large variance in the interbank rate. For example, in the period Jan. 1986–Sept. 1988, interest rates fluctuated from 2% to over 23%, whereas all other nominal interest rates were nearly steady. The large variation of the interbank interest rate also reflects the continuous changes of the institutional financial framework, such as the abolition of the system of blockings and deblockings, which significantly influence the liquidity of the banks. Finally, it reflects the inability of banks to accurately forecast their exact obligations towards the Bank of Greece. The observed differences between their forecasts and the actual values, regarding deposits, credits, etc., give rise either to excess liquidity or to immediate borrowing requirements that are needed to avoid the high penalty rates imposed by the Bank of Greece. These differences can reach almost 26%.

The interbank market rate could potentially act as an important market-signal for financial management. Available time series evidence (Kouzionis and Georgantelis, 1989) suggests that there is still substantial sluggishness in market clearing probably due to informational rigidities. As a result, the monthly interbank market rate does not behave as a typical asset-market price in the sense that this month's rate is not an unbiased predictor for next month's rate. Instead, substantial lags are evidenced.

Apart from informational rigidities, the existing regulations and controls on banking activity have considerably slowed down the process of securitization and the adoption of new financial instruments by Greek banks. A legal framework for leasing, factoring and forfaiting services by banks has been introduced only in the last two years. Lack of information, of appropriate training and management, and of an adequate institutional framework, places the traditional Greek banks in an adverse position relative to their foreign competitors.

This is augmented by the fragile capital structure of most Greek banks. Ownership of companies in distress by the banks themselves and the overindebtedness of these companies to these same banks which are unwilling to bear the burden of adjustment for restructuring, have resulted in a proliferation of the vicious circle of indebtedness – bad performance – higher protection. Though exact figures on the total amount of non-performing and bad loans are not available, it is roughly estimated that the liabilities to banks of firms which declared bankruptcy during the last decade amount to over 30 billion drs (Ibid., 1989, p. 12). At the end of 1986, the total liabilities of problematic firms were approaching 300 billion drs with over 70% of total liabilities extended to banks. All loans to 'problematic' firms have been non-performing after the official registration with the OAE. Furthermore as most of the firms registered with OAE have not yet improved their performance significantly, the greatest part of equity that loans were converted into as a result of the restructuring plan (around 62 billion drs) can be considered as non-performing (Ibid., 1989, p. 13).

Thus banks which have a large share of their capital invested in problematic companies (foremost the largest Greek bank – the National Bank of Greece), face serious portfolio problems.

Financial liberalization and the internal market for financial services thus challenge directly the privileged position of Greek banks in the home market and their central role in the state corporatist model. The outside pressure for rapid modernization and capital restructuring has given rise to increasing friction between the central government and the banking system in the 1980s as each of the traditional partners has attempted to shift the burden of adjustment onto the other: banks by requesting government support and subsidies to cover losses that have their origin in past financial decisions that were largely endorsed by the state; the government by refusing to burden the budget excessively in order to rescue the banks from what is considered to be financial mismanagement of public funds.

The resolution of this conflict has been long and painful both in economic and political terms and is continuing unabated. As with the international debt problem, issues of liquidity, confidence and adjustment are involved that can be resolved only through a negotiated settlement between the different players in a way that is consistent with the longer-term goals of efficiency and development.

2.5   Structural characteristics of the labour markets

The analysis so far of the structure of public and private sector activity provides an insight into the peculiarities of the Greek labour market which differs substantially from that of the other EC countries.

The agricultural labour force is almost four times higher than the EC-10 average (about 28% against 7%). The proportion of self-employed and family members is very high not only in agriculture but also in the non-agricultural sector. It should be noted that in 1986, self-employment accounted for more than 50% and family members 15%, whereas paid employment was only 49% of total employment, against 82% in the EC area as a whole.

The high percentage of employment in agriculture and in the public sector, as well as the very high percentage of self-employed in the agricultural and service sectors (Table 8.13) imply that the 'organized' labour market consisting of wage-earners in the private sector is relatively small and insignificant in determining labour-market conditions.

Labour-market conditions have been characterized by the continuous increase in the labour force, which reached 9.5% during 1971–81 and 5.8% during 1981–85 largely due to the inflow of repatriated migrants and to increases in the female participation rate. The latter increased from 29.8% in 1981 to 34.1% in 1986 but is still lower than the EC-10 average (39.3%). The rate of increase of the labour force concentrated in the urban areas whereas the rural labour force continued to decline over time (Glytsos, 1989). The pattern of employment has continued to change in favour of urban employment especially in services.

Given the structure of employment opportunities indices of total open unemployment are not satisfactory indices of total excess supply in the labour market especially in times of recession. Farmers or the

ISIC industries code and sectors	Employment shares						Average annual growth rates 1983–87				
	Total employment		Wage and salary earners		Self-employed		Total employment	Wage and salary earners	Self-employed	Wage and salary earners, (% in each industry)	
	1983	1987	1983	1987	1983	1987				1983	1987
Agriculture	29.9	27.0	2.6	2.1	55.6	51.7	−2.0	−3.3	−1.9	4.1	3.9
Secondary	28.6	28.0	42.1	39.7	15.9	16.3	−3.0	−0.1	0.5	71.2	70.7
Utilities	0.8	1.0	1.7	1.9	0.0	0.0	5.1	5.3	−24.0	98.9	99.7
Construction	7.8	6.4	11.4	9.1	4.4	3.9	−3.9	−4.2	−3.4	70.8	70.0
Manufacturing	19.3	19.9	27.5	27.4	11.5	12.4	1.5	1.4	1.8	69.2	68.8
Tertiary	41.5	45.0	55.3	58.1	28.5	32.0	2.7	2.6	2.8	64.5	64.4
Total	100.0	100.0	100.0	100.0	100.0	100.0	0.6	1.4	−0.1	48.4	49.8

Table 8.13. Employment shares and growth rates in the Greek economy, by occupational status and industry, 1983–87

Source: Greek National Statistical Service, *Labour Force Survey*, 1983, 1987.

self-employed appear as working persons even if they are underemployed to a considerable extent.

Whereas in most EC countries registered unemployment is almost identical with total unemployment, in Greece it covers only about 1/3 of total unemployment (Vassilakopoulos, 1986). A better indication of the existing slack in labour-market activity is youth or female unemployment as the market for these two groups is more flexible and more accurately depicts the underlying economic conditions. While total open unemployment has not exceeded 8% of the total labour force during the period 1980–86, total youth unemployment has risen from 13.8% in 1981 to 24% in 1986 and total female unemployment from 5.7% to 11.6% (Table 8.14). Long-term unemployment (over 12 months) accounted for about 43% of total unemployment in 1986, against 21% in 1983 and concerned primarily young persons under the age of 30. The average duration of unemployment has also expanded from 5.2 months in 1981 to 7.9 months in 1986.

Apart from increases in the open unemployment of these sub-groups of the total labour force there exists indirect evidence of increasing excess supply in the labour markets. Total hours paid per week has decreased considerably in the 1980s partly as a result of the reduction in legal weekly working time from 48 hours in 1975 to 40 hours in 1984, but also as a result of the decline in real economic activity. The percentage of employees working less than 35 hours per week, a usual index of underemployment has risen from 6.0% for males and 11.8% for females in 1974 to 19.8% and 31.5% respectively in 1984 (Glytsos, 1989).

In a recent report, Vassilakopoulos constructs two separate indices for underemployment: (a) the so-called 'conservative' index based on a full-time equivalent rate and (b) the 'enlarged composite index' of labour slack which includes besides part-time employment and unemployment, passive unemployment and visible underemployment. The two indices reveal much higher rates that those for open unemployment exceeding 10.5% in 1985 (Vassilakopoulos, 1986, p. 17). As was expected, overt or passive unemployment is concentrated in the major urban areas, especially Athens and Salonica, whereas visible underemployment has increased in the agricultural regions of the country.

Relatively to other European countries, part-time work in industry, defined as average hours worked per week has been considerably higher in Greece (29.0 hours on average in 1983 as against 21.8 hours on average for ten European countries (Glytsos, 1989).

Among those who have a job but are actively seeking another for various reasons, 22% cite as the primary reason the risk of losing their present job and 59.4% that they are seeking better conditions. The

Unemployment rate (%)

Age bracket	1981 M	1981 F	1981 All	1986 M	1986 F	1986 All
14–24	10.5	17.8	13.8	15.9	34.1	24.0
25–44	3.3	4.4	3.6	4.8	9.9	6.6
45–64	1.8	1.6	1.7	2.6	3.1	2.7
65+	0.3	0.2	0.3	0.5	0.2	0.4
All ages	3.3	5.7	4.0			

Unemployment structure (%)

Age bracket	1981 M	1981 F	1981 All	1986 M	1986 F	1986 All
14–24	32.8	56.5	43.4	35.9	49.9	43.7
25–44	45.8	43.2	40.7	44.4	41.6	42.8
45–64	20.9	9.1	15.6	19.3	8.4	13.2
65+	0.5	0.2	0.3	0.4	0.1	0.3
All ages	100.0	100.0	100.0	100.0	100.0	100.0

Average duration of unemployment (months)

Age bracket	1981 M	1981 F	1981 All	1986 M	1986 F	1986 All
14–24	4.6	6.5	5.7	6.6	8.8	8.0
24–55	4.9	5.7	5.2	7.0	8.9	8.0
45–66	5.2	6.5	5.5	6.3	6.5	7.0
65+	5.5	4.0	5.1	4.3	—	5.6
All ages	4.9	6.2	5.2	6.7	8.8	7.9

% of long-term unemployment (over 12 months)

Age bracket	1981 M	1981 F	1981 All	1986 M	1986 F	1986 All
14–24	15.2	30.3	24.1	28.7	51.4	43.2
24–55	14.4	25.3	18.5	35.3	55.2	46.2
45–66	14.6	34.4	19.5	28.4	48.5	35.3
65+	5.6					16.7
All ages	7.9	14.6	28.8	31.5	52.8	43.4

Table 8.14. Greek unemployment: rate, structure and duration, by age and sex, 1981–86.

Source: Greek National Statistical Service, *Labour Force Survey*, 1981 and 1986.

corresponding ratios on average for the 10 European countries are 17.4% and 39.6% (Glytsos, 1989). Slackness in the Greek labour market is manifested not only by underemployment, overt unemployment for young and female workers and by increased uncertainty as to future employment but by the low productivity of labour in all the relevant markets.

This has been intensified in the late 1970s and 1980s as growth was substantially lowered. The cyclical nature of labour productivity is evidenced by the strong positive association between average labour productivity and output growth in manufacturing especially after 1978 when fluctuations in output growth explain a large proportion of variations in average productivity growth round a declining trend (Ibid., 1989).

The pattern of employment, unemployment and underemployment reflects the structure of economic activity. Rigidities in the labour market thus correspond to the rigidities in the functioning of public and private sector markets. These can be summarized as follows:

(a) Segmentation of the labour market between rural and urban and between 'official' and 'unofficial' labour markets with important barriers to entry and limited mobility especially between the latter two.

The application of quotas, of selective educational qualifications and of a complex system of selection criteria constitute the bulk of entry barriers into the public sector where employment is guaranteed. Strict regulations about employment policy and firing limit the possibilities of exit from the organized private sector especially in manufacturing. According to current legislation, firms employing between 20–50 workers cannot dismiss more than 5 workers per month unless special permission is granted by the Ministry of Labour. The corresponding ratio for firms employing more than 51 workers is 2–3% of total employment. Finally, the lack of social infrastructure and the asymmetric distribution between public and private sector services between the urban and rural areas constitute effective barriers to rural employment especially for young workers.

(b) Wage-setting behaviour on the part of the public sector that provides guidelines for private sector settlements regardless of labour-market conditions at the industry or enterprise level. Wage-setting behaviour concerns not only minimum wage legislation and total or partial wage indexation depending on the relevant income bracket, but also stipulations as to real wage increases decided either on the basis of wage bargaining or by arbitration, a practice very often resorted to in Greece. The minimum wage level is set annually by the General Collective Agreement which follows the announcement of the incomes policy guidelines at the beginning of each year. The ratio of average to minimum wages has

	Standard deviation of real weekly wages (%)			Coefficient of determination of real hourly wage across two-digit manufacturing industries
	Males	Females	Both sexes	
1970	18.9	72.6	—	
1971	48.2	29.2	—	
1972	26.9	31.4	30.9	1.00
1973	34.4	28.1	25.3	0.93
1974	46.9	23.7	49.8	0.94
1975	26.9	27.2	38.1	0.94
1976	30.8	23.7	27.7	0.94
1977	39.6	19.0	47.0	0.88
1978	24.3	20.8	33.4	0.91
1979	28.0	19.7	23.3	0.92
1980	40.6	21.8	45.2	0.91
1981	29.7	27.8	42.7	0.86
1982	33.2	23.7	36.1	0.88
1983	15.9	9.9	19.8	0.43
1984	16.3	10.5	19.8	0.48
1985	6.1	3.4	7.0	0.81
1986	6.5	4.0	7.8	0.82

Table 8.15. Wage flexibility in the Greek labour market, 1970–86

Sources: Bank of Greece, *The Greek Economy*, 1982: Greek National Statistical Service, Annual *Labour Statistics* and *Statistical Yearbooks*.

changed little in the period 1974–79, and has decreased after 1981 as a result of the post-1981 increases in minimum wages (Glytsos, 1989).

Wage setting by the public sector affects mostly the organized labour market. The standard deviation of real weekly wages across manufacturing sectors (weighted by average hourly wages) has decreased from 45.2% in 1980 to 19.8% in 1983 to 7.0% in 1985 (Ibid., 1989). Similarly, the coefficient of determination of real hourly wages obtained by regressing wages by industry in each year with the corresponding wages at the base year (1972) does not show important changes in the rank of industrial wages (Table 8.15).

The prevalence of wage-setting thus limits inter-industry wage flexibility, a trend which is confirmed by regression analysis across the 19 two-digit manufacturing industries (Ibid., 1989). The percentage annual average change of hourly wages is not found to depend in any systematic way on changes in average productivity, in the value of sales or in the composition of employment. This suggests that wages are determined exogenously, mainly by macroeconomic and institutional factors.

This is confirmed by dynamic time-series analysis of the average real wage series which indicates that the real wage rate can be effectively described as a random walk with the one-lag coefficient not significantly different from unity. Statistical exogeneity tests between the real wage and the employment series also suggest that the real wage can be considered statistically exogenous in the determination of employment (Ibid., 1989).

The exogenous determination of real wages and the presence of restrictions on employment policy give rise to a loose relationship between real wages and employment in Greek manufacturing, especially for the organized labour market which consists of male employment as confirmed by the very low correlation coefficients between male employment and wages for the period 1979–85 (average for the period = 0.0457).

(c) Job-mismatch distortions due to wage-setting and employment policies and educational rigidities. Wage-setting by the public sector has created serious disincentives for hiring unskilled labour for unskilled jobs in the private sector. Between 1982–86 minimum salaries increased by 2.7 times, average earnings by about 2.1 times and earnings for skilled labour by 1.6 times. The ratio between high and low earnings was thus reduced from 533% in 1981 to 308% in 1986. Minimum wages in 1982 alone were raised by 46% while unit labour costs increased by 37.6%. Workers with one to six years of elementary education constituted in 1981 63.8% of the total number employed. This ratio dropped to 60.3% by 1986 (Ibid., 1989).

At the other end of the educational spectrum there exists excess demand for qualified personnel that cannot necessarily be satisfied by Greek university graduates who do not always possess the necessary qualifications as a result of the anachronistic educational system. The unemployment rate for university graduates has risen to 8.4% in 1986 despite the presence of vacancies and high real wages in the private sector. In response to these developments, the public sector ends up erecting selective barriers to public-sector entry by creating job qualifications that do not correspond to the requirements of the jobs but which disqualify unskilled or semi-skilled workers in favour of university graduates. The public sector has thus become the largest employer of university graduates at the cost of pervasive job dissatisfaction. At the same time there exists excess demand for qualified personnel in the private sector.

Market segmentation with limited mobility, wage-setting and job-mismatch distortions are the major structural features of the Greek labour market that give rise to both classical and structural unemployment

CCCN code	1981	1982	1983	1984	1985	1986
20	18.58	18.62	22.68	20.46	18.74	18.79
21	1.01	0.96	1.10	0.98	1.42	1.47
22	4.83	5.32	5.23	4.58	4.40	4.74
23	12.51	11.46	11.90	12.38	11.73	11.49
24	14.47	15.44	16.56	17.71	19.33	26.44
25	0.40	0.46	0.52	0.43	0.39	0.40
26	0.11	0.10	0.10	0.07	0.06	0.07
27	1.31	1.23	0.62	0.64	0.76	0.68
28	0.32	0.29	0.22	0.23	0.25	0.24
29	2.02	2.05	2.12	1.86	1.86	2.67
30	0.00	0.00	0.00	0.00	0.00	0.00
31	6.03	6.29	6.29	5.83	5.25	5.71
32	11.06	12.75	8.17	10.50	12.08	5.83
33	7.92	8.25	7.91	6.23	5.96	5.24
34	9.49	7.83	8.83	11.72	11.37	10.06
35	3.35	2.37	2.65	2.14	1.98	1.73
36	1.08	1.53	1.00	0.94	0.73	0.79
37	3.02	2.49	1.94	1.55	1.94	1.76
38	1.44	1.43	1.17	0.57	0.84	0.74
39	1.02	1.07	0.96	1.12	1.21	1.10
Total	100.00	100.00	100.00	100.00	100.00	100.00

Table 8.16. Structure of Greek manufacturing exports by two-digit industrial classification, 1981–86 (%)

Source: Greek National Statistical Service, *Statistical Yearbooks.*

in the economy. These structural characteristics can be attributed to the workings of the state corporatist model.

The pattern of public sector interventions and the 'cooperative regulation of conflicts' between the state, the banks and some industrial interests has produced a heavily regulated dual labour market characterized by no clear structure of incentives and low productivity.

2.6   Structural rigidities in the balance of payments

The presence of structural rigidities in production and in the functioning of capital and labour markets is reflected in the relative pattern of trade. Agricultural exports account for more than 24% of total exports while industrial exports are concentrated in few traditional industrial sectors. Food, textiles and yarns, shoes and clothing, chemicals, refinery products

CCCN Code	Net fixed assets in industry over total employment							Average 1980–86
	1980	1981	1982	1983	1984	1985	1986	
20	660	630	710	650	680	670	606	660
21	1,410	1,480	1,980	1,560	1,360	1,400	1,030	1,460
22	450	410	570	520	470	490	400	470
23	690	700	940	710	600	590	630	690
24	190	190	280	220	200	190	210	210
25	1,030	930	1,080	900	760	620	590	840
26	420	400	610	590	460	420	490	480
27	1,840	1,570	1,530	1,430	1,270	1,090	810	1,360
28	450	450	680	620	630	580	640	580
29	400	490	880	620	500	460	350	530
30	720	690	790	180	690	690	590	620
31	830	870	1,100	1,010	1,030	1,040	840	960
32	3,220	3,230	3,240	3,630	4,180	4,300	5,510	3,900
33	1,370	1,440	2,020	1,840	1,660	1,520	1,300	1,590
34	2,210	3,290	4,180	3,350	3,400	3,400	2,570	3,200
35	690	640	800	700	510	460	750	650
36	470	470	600	610	450	450	420	490
37	580	500	660	600	490	440	560	550
38	1,500	1,500	2,170	2,410	2,590	1,190	2,490	1,980
39	870	730	1,250	580	510	620	610	740
Average	1,000	1,030	1,300	1,140	1,120	1,030	1,070	1,100
Number of firms in sample	2,860	3,074	3,176	3,157	3,113	3,166	3,264	

Table 8.17. Greece: capital–labour ratio by two-digit industry, 1980–86[1] (thousand 1980 drs per employee)

Source: Commercial Bank of Greece, National Statistical Service of Greece.

Note:
1. Capital is defined as net fixed assets deflated by the wholesale price index.

and basic metallurgy accounted for over 75% of total exports in 1980 and 78% of total exports in 1986 (Table 8.16). No significant export diversification has taken place in the 1980s.

The nominal devaluation of the currency and the extensive subsidization of exports have been necessary conditions for export promotion as the export-competing sectors have not based their competitiveness on relatively lower costs of production. The overcapitalization of those sectors that had access to the banking system and the preferential

SITC	LDCs	ACP	MED	ARAB	MAG	C & S AMER
0	32	17	66	57	59	27
1	70	76	97	45	45	60
2	42	34	41	45	17	46
4	14	28	55	86	89	37
5	46	24	41	44	22	36
6	39	11	47	54	41	37
7	41	31	48	54	52	36
8	53	47	68	55	60	40

Table 8.18. Similarity of EC imports from Greece and various groups of developing countries, 1986 (Finger–Kreinin index[1])

Source: Computed from data in *Eurostat*: Analytical Tables of Foreign Trade (SITC).

Note:
1. The value of the Finger–Kreinin index is bounded below by 0, indicating complete dissimilarity and from above by 100 indicating perfect similarity.

treatment of export-oriented industries in the past by the public sector, have raised inordinately the capital–labour ratios in those sectors relative to others. Thus, as can be seen in Table 8.17, the capital–labour ratio is higher in the traditional export industries relative to the import-competing ones, contrary to what one would expect given relative natural endowments.

Greece's trade pattern resembles that of any other typical developing country. Greek exports to the EC are in fact quite similar in structure to EC imports from other LDCs especially the Mediterranean and Arab countries (Table 8.18). Intra-industry trade between Greece and its trading partners is limited to traditional manufacturing while inter-industry trade predominates at the aggregate level (Average Trade Overlap Coefficient, $TO = 0.48$). These results are similar to those of Neven (1990) who finds that both Portugal and Greece deviate from the rest of the Community in terms of their trade pattern by having much less intra-industry trade than the other countries. Intra-industry specialization ($TO \geq 0.70$) predominates in food, beverages, textiles and yarns, printing and publishing, refinery products and basic metallurgy while it is limited to ($TO \leq 0.30$) in wood and cork, paper and paper articles, plastics and rubber, machinery and appliances, electrical equipment, transportation or miscellaneous (Table 8.19). When compared with the EC-9's global trade in manufacturing, where four-fifths of trade overlaps

CCNN Code	80	81	82	83	84	85	86	Average 80–86
20	93	92	83	82	91	81	79	87
21	70	61	91	84	85	86	78	79
22	21	28	33	08	37	41	39	30
23	94	99	100	94	94	96	88	95
24	37	29	29	29	27	26	26	29
25	33	34	36	40	37	30	30	34
26	46	42	28	43	40	32	32	38
27	33	37	31	19	20	22	21	26
28	40	80	79	74	71	73	71	70
29	95	39	43	44	49	45	51	52
30	40	00	01	00	01	02	04	07
31	50	37	42	43	41	35	34	40
32	41	47	44	80	88	17	98	59
33	71	53	53	49	56	61	68	59
34	73	86	78	77	99	90	84	84
35	75	66	55	65	59	57	50	61
36	04	09	12	08	08	07	07	08
37	26	42	36	31	28	29	23	31
38	09	16	13	14	08	10	09	11
39	20	29	27	26	32	29	26	27

Table 8.19. Trade overlap coefficients[1] between Greek exports and imports, 1980–86

Source: Greek National Statistical Service, *Statistical Yearbooks.*

Note:

1. Calculated as follows:

$$TO = \frac{200(\text{Min}(X_i, M_i))}{X_i + M_i}$$

where Min defines the magnitude of the total manufactured trade which overlaps in dollar value terms. The closer TO comes to 100, the more intra-industry specialization predominates.

(Donges *et al.*, 1982, p. 87), the limited trade overlap between exports and imports indicates that Greek trade can be analytically considered as distorted Heckscher–Ohlin trade, distorted in the sense that domestic price and credit-market distortions have led to the relative overcapitalization of the export industry relative to the import-competing ones. The impact of credit-market distortions on the pattern of trade helps explain Neven's (1990) observation that 'Portugal and Greece do not appear to have a comparative disadvantage in industries which are highly capital-intensive' (Neven, 1990, p. 19).

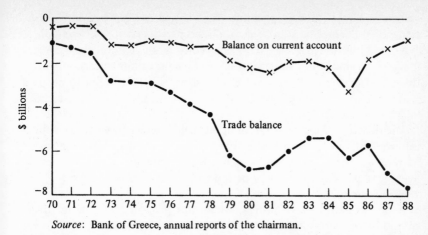

Source: Bank of Greece, annual reports of the chairman.

Figure 8.1 Greek trade and current account deficits, 1970–88

The widening structural trade deficit during most of the 1970s and 1980s (Figure 8.1) has been largely financed by invisible receipts, which are highly covariate (tourism, emigrant and shipping remittances, including transfers from the EC) as well as from capital inflows both from private and official sources.

As can be seen in Figure 8.2, the surplus in the invisible account as a ratio of the trade deficit has fluctuated, largely dependent on domestic interest and exchange-rate policies, on the world economic cycle, on the energy crisis and on EC transfers which have grown rapidly in the past

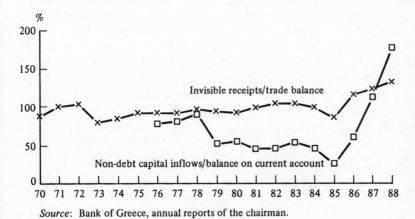

Source: Bank of Greece, annual reports of the chairman.

Figure 8.2 Greece: ratios of surplus on invisibles to trade deficit and of non-debt financing to the current account, 1970–88

few years. Largely due to the inflow of EC funds and the decline in energy prices, the current account deficit has been reduced to $957 million in 1988, that is to 1.8% of GDP. The considerably more expansionary macroeconomic policy stance in 1989 and the prevailing uncertainty prior to and after the two national elections are likely to contribute to a worsening of the current account deficit which is projected to rise above $2.5 billion for this year.

The deficit in the current account has been financed by private capital inflows and foreign borrowing. The ratio of non-debt financing to the current account deficit has also exhibited wide fluctuations from an average of 90% in the 1975–79 period to 51% in 1979–84 and to 111% in 1987 (Figure 6.2).

If one excludes EC transfers, which are projected to rise relatively smoothly, the dependence on highly volatile sources of financing to cover a widening structural trade deficit, increases uncertainty regarding future borrowing needs and the appropriate conduct of policy.

3   Effects of trade and capital market liberalization on the Greek economy

Integration into the European Community in 1981, which coincided with the beginning of a period of progressive liberalization and institutional reform at the domestic level, and the subsequent 1985 decisions for the creation of an Internal Market by 1992, have challenged directly the fundamentals of state corporatism (a) through the opening up of the official sector to outside competition, (b) through the liberalization of capital markets and (c) through the exercise of pressures for greater decentralization, openness and efficiency in public-sector activities.

Three types of shocks can be readily identified as a consequence of these decisions with important implications for the structure of production and the workings of the labour market: (1) a considerable reduction in the profitability of the internationally traded-goods sector due to the abolition of import protective measures and export subsidies, (2) changes in the price of capital and credit terms for the official and unofficial sectors of the economy as the capital market is integrated and liberalized and (3) the pursuit of restrictive fiscal and monetary policies to ease the internal and external imbalances and thus facilitate entry into the European Monetary System.

3.1   Trade liberalization and its effects

By 1985 the average nominal protection rate for all 20 industrial sectors reached 33.6%, down from 45% ten years earlier (Giannitsis, 1988).

Category	1974	1980	1985	% change 1980/1974	% change 1985/1980
Consumer goods	36.8	30.6	24.8	−16.8	−19.0
Intermediate	25.1	21.8	25.7	−13.1	17.9
Capital goods	22.4	23.3	41.5	4.0	78.1
Traditional (13 sectors)[1]	54.6	38.8	33.6	−28.9	−13.4
Modern (7 sectors)	27.2	24.5	33.5	−9.9	36.7

Table 8.20. Greek nominal protection rates by broad categories, 1974–85 (%)

Source: Giannitsis (1988).

Note:
1. Sectors 20–29, 32–34.

As can be seen in Table 8.20, however, trade liberalization has not taken place with equal force in all industrial sectors. Whereas the nominal protection rates declined continuously throughout the decade for imports in traditional sectors and for consumer goods, nominal protection increased during the 1980–85 period for the import-competing capital-good sectors.

If domestic production taxes and subsidies are also taken into account in the calculation of total protection afforded to industrial sectors, it appears that in the first part of the 1980s effective protection has in fact increased substantially for intermediate goods and manufacturing equipment and declined only slightly for manufactured consumer goods (Table 8.21). Thus, at least till recently, the decline of nominal tariff protection for imports from the EC countries was largely offset by domestic subsidies and the imposition of domestic taxation.

The removal of the regulatory tax on imports in January 1989, the elimination of all remaining trade barriers, the harmonization of taxation and the projected elimination of all export subsidies by 1990 is likely to lower the drachma price of most tradables and lower the profitability of the internationally traded-good sector of the economy with adverse effects on output and employment. The reduction in the price of tradables relative to non-tradables is likely to shift domestic consumption patterns towards tradables thus leading to a worsening of trade competitiveness and a deterioration of the trade deficit.

Over the medium run, if the creation of the European Internal Market succeeds in producing competitive gains in fast-growing sectors, so that economies of scale are exploited and production costs are systematically

Sector	1970	1975	1980	1981	1982
Agricultural, forestry and fishery products	29	20	28	42	29
Fuel & power products	−21	−17	−12	−9	−11
Manufactured consumer goods	15	15	11	10	9
Manufactured equipment	11	7	9	15	15
Manufactured intermediate goods	16	13	11	15	17

Table 8.21. Nominal effective protection[1] in Greece as a percentage of import prices, 1970–82

Sources: Katsos and Spanakis (1983), Sarris (1988).

Note:

$$NEP = \left(\frac{1+t}{1+(\varphi - s)} - 1\right)100$$

where: t = the tariff and border tax rate on sector i
 φ = the rate of taxes levied on production of sector i
 s = the rate of production subsidies on sector i

reduced (Commission of the EC, 1988b), then the cost of Greek imports is likely to be reduced further, leading to an improvement in the industrial terms of trade. This hypothesis is consistent with industry's perceptions that the Internal Market will in fact lower the cost of intermediate goods (Commission of the EC, 1988a, Table 4). The magnitude of terms-of-trade improvement will depend *inter alia* on the evolution of export prices in traditional industrial activities which in turn depends on competition from the non-EC developing countries and the Common External Tariff Policy of the EC.

A slight terms of trade improvement is in fact evident in the 1981–88 period, as compared with the period prior to official entry (Table 8.22). The distinguishing characteristic of developments in the post-entry period however, is the increased volatility of the price of tradables and of the terms of trade largely due to shifts in policy regimes as indicated earlier.

The projected improvement of the terms of trade over the medium run is expected to shift resources towards exportables, i.e. towards the traditional manufacturing sector and away from the more modern, R&D-intensive import-competing sector. According to a typical three-goods, two-factors Heckscher–Ohlin model, the movement of the prices of exportables and importables determines unequivocally the changes in rewards of both capital and labour. These in turn determine the effects on the price of non-tradables and the real exchange rate. In a typical small

	1973–81		19891–89		1973–89	
	Mean	Standard deviation	Mean	Standard deviation	Mean	Standard deviation
$\dfrac{P_x}{P_m}$	86	0.049	88	0.055	87	0.050
P_x	218	0.830	691	2.152	445	2.967
P_m	254	0.990	793	2.778	512	3.507

Table 8.22. Greece: industrial terms of trade, 1973–89 (1970 = 100)

Sources: Greek National Statistical Service, *Statistical Yearbooks.*

country where exportables are more labour-intensive than importables, trade liberalization is expected to lead to an increase in real wages, a reduction in the price of capital and an increase in the price of non-tradables if exportables are more capital-intensive than home goods (Edwards and Van Wijnbergen, 1987, p. 460).

These results have to be amended if distortions have led to overcapitalization of exportables relative to both non-tradables and importables (Table 8.17). In that case, trade liberalization is expected to lead to a reduction in wages, an increase in the price of capital and a reduction in the price of non-tradables. The effects on the real exchange rate are ambiguous and depend on the downward movement of tradables relative to non-tradable prices. If wages and the price of non-tradables exhibit downward rigidity, then the real exchange rate will appreciate and unemployment will ensue (Ibid., p. 462). The results are not expected to be different if one of the factors, namely capital is in the short run sector-specific. In that case, trade liberalization will lead to excess supply for non-traded goods as resources shift into non-tradables and consumption shifts away from them, leading again to a reduction in their price. This might be mitigated somewhat by an increase in income and expenditure as the distortionary costs of tariffs are reduced. In either case however, the real exchange rate is likely to appreciate especially if downward price rigidity is manifested.

Given the structural characteristics of the economy that have been described in Section 2, trade liberalization is apt to lead to unemployment at least in the short run as production in importables declines and the official exportable sector, already overindebted, faces a rising cost of capital and a downward rigid real wage. The excess supply in the labour

	Traditional	Modern
1960–70	10	50
1970–80	9	47
1981–82	10	42
1983–84	13	45
1985–86	16	51

Table 8.23. Greece: average import penetration,[1] 1960–86

Sources: Greek National Statistical Service, *Statistical Yearbooks.*

Note:

1 $IP_i = \dfrac{M_i}{GP_i + M_i - X_i}$

where M_i = imports, GP_i = gross domestic production and X_i = exports of sector i.

The 2-digit sectors were classified for all periods into two categories according to their import penetration ratios. Those that exhibit a penetration of less than 30% are identified as 'traditional', the rest as 'modern'. According to this definition, throughout the 1980s, sectors 29, 31, 34, 36, 37, 38 and 39 are 'modern' sectors.

market will not be easily absorbed into the public sector, as financial constraints become binding. It is thus highly likely that part of employment will be diverted towards construction and the service sector where demand is projected to rise, especially in view of the increasing volume of sales of underpriced assets, most notably land, to foreigners.

The diversion of consumption towards importables is likely to increase import penetration and the trade deficit, thus augmenting the need to secure a continuous and steady flow of resources from abroad to avoid solvency problems.

In the light of this discussion and the likely short-term and medium-term effects that have been described, it is interesting to observe the post-1981 developments in terms of overall and sectoral trade patterns and competitiveness.

Import penetration, defined as the ratio of imports to total domestic consumption has increased rapidly in the 'traditional' sectors, which faced a reduction in the nominal protection rate (Table 8.23). For the modern sectors, the import penetration ratio increased after 1985 as trade became liberalized in those sectors as well.

With the exception of sector 24 (shoes and clothing) that expanded rapidly into the export market after 1981, the export propensity as

Sector	1981	1982	1983	1984	1985	1986
20	14	14	19	18	15	15
21	5	5	6	6	8	7
22	32	32	35	39	34	41
23	15	15	17	19	17	16
24	32	35	45	53	56	78
25	2	3	4	4	4	4
26	1	1	1	1	1	1
27	7	6	3	3	4	3
28	3	2	2	2	2	2
29	12	13	14	14	14	16
30	0	0	0	0	0	0
31	9	10	11	22	8	9
32	13	17	11	15	16	8
33	19	21	25	22	22	18
34	18	17	18	26	23	23
35	7	5	7	6	6	5
36	3	4	3	3	2	3
37	8	7	6	6	6	5
38	3	2	3	1	2	2
39	10	9	9	11	2	9

Table 8.24. Greece: export propensity ratios,[1] 1981–86

Source: Greek National Statistical Service, *Statistical Yearbooks.*

Note:

1 $XP_i = \dfrac{X_i}{GP_i + M_i}$

where X_i = exports, GP_i = gross domestic production and M_i = imports of sector i.

measured by the ratio of exports to total supply has deteriorated as expected in the more technologically advanced sectors (36–39), and has increased in the traditional export sectors as resources have shifted slightly in favour of the more traditional export sectors (Table 8.24).

Sectoral trade competitiveness as measured by the Balassa index, that refers to net sectoral trade $|X_i - M_i|$ with the EC as a ratio of total trade $(X_i + M_i)$, has deteriorated in all traditional sectors except in tobacco (22) and paper and printing (27). Competitiveness has increased slightly in the modern sectors (chemicals, machinery, electrical appliances and transport equipment) and in minerals, i.e. in sectors where protection has increased.

Deterioration of trade competitiveness in the 1980s immediately after entry, reverses the trends prevailing in the 1970s for all categories of

Sectors	Third countries			EC countries		
	1974–77	1978–80	1981–86	1974–77	1978–80	1980–86
20	0.32	0.68	0.75	0.04	−0.004	−0.10
21	0.85	0.93	0.79	0.51	0.35	0.10
22	0.28	−0.55	0.17	−0.90	−0.99	−0.70
23	0.20	0.35	0.24	0.50	0.58	0.42
24	0.64	0.36	0.39	0.82	0.76	0.54
25	−0.06	−0.06	−0.14	0.63	0.26	−0.45
26	0.60	0.42	0.12	−0.95	−0.95	−0.97
27	−0.85	0.09	−0.46	−0.95	−0.88	−0.96
28	0.03	0.02	0.48	−0.82	−0.87	−0.73
29	−0.07	0.13	0.26	0.20	0.12	−0.14
30	0.00	−0.05	−0.06	−0.80	−0.76	−0.73
31	−0.19	−0.05	−0.27	−0.79	−0.79	−0.83
32	0.17	0.06	0.38	0.17	0.52	0.18
33	0.84	0.83	0.83	−0.66	−0.79	−0.73
34	0.07	−0.02	0.33	−0.05	−0.04	−0.25
35	0.32	0.27	0.33	−0.81	−0.81	−0.83
36	−0.89	−0.84	−0.81	−0.99	−0.99	−0.97
37	−0.37	−0.45	−0.52	−0.87	−0.82	−0.77
38	−0.58	−0.84	−0.78	−0.95	−1.00	−0.99
39	−0.54	−0.69	−0.54	−0.79	−0.87	−0.84
Sum	−0.078	0.072	0.044	−0.396	−0.339	−0.393
Consumer goods	−0.001	0.0304	0.182	0.217	0.228	0.040
Intermediate goods	0.178	0.399	0.256	−0.562	−0.442	−0.659
Capital goods	0.037	−0.065	0.070	−0.756	−0.724	−0.737

Table 8.25. Greece: trade competitiveness[1] by sector and period, 1974–86 (%)

Source: Giannitsis (1988), p. 185.

Note:

1 Balassa index.

goods (consumer goods, intermediate goods and capital goods) especially for commodities traded with the EC countries (Table 8.25). Trade liberalization has thus exposed all industrial sectors, traditional and more modern alike, to increasing competition with negative effects on output, employment and overall trade competitiveness.

The overall trade deficit which declined between 1981 and 1984 from $6,697 million to $5,351 million grew rapidly in the following years to reach $7,631 million in 1988.

Independent variables	Dependent variables			
	$\ln L_{it}$	$\ln L_{it}$	$\ln L_{it}$	$\ln(W/P)_{it}$
c	-0.555	-0.158	-0.035	-0.137
	(0.9)	(0.9)	(0.3)	(1.1)
$\ln C_i$	0.749			0.027
	(13.8)			(1.5)
$\ln(X_i/P_{xi})$	-0.136		0.011^{1}	-0.003
	(5.8)		(1.8)	(0.6)
$\ln(M_i/c_i)$	-0.305		-0.012^{1}	-0.007
	(10.9)		(1.4)	(0.8)
$\ln(VA/P_i)$			0.0172	
			(0.9)	
$\ln(W/P)_i$	-0.433	-0.018	-0.21	
	(1.1)	(0.2)	(0.2)	
$\ln(W/P)_{i,t-1}$	-0.168	0.002	0.027	0.905
	(0.4)	(0.03)	(0.3)	(28.3)
$\ln L_{it-1}$		1.0	0.975	-0.019
		(94.5)	(51.2)	(1.1)
$\ln P_{xi}$		0.073		
		(2.1)		
$\ln P_{mi}$		-0.048		
		(1.4)		
$\bar{R}^{-2}$	0.70	0.984	0.984	0.867
DW	0.44	2.32	2.21	2.0

Table 8.26. Estimated trade effects on employment and real wages in Greek industry, 1976–84

Source: Glytsos (1989).

Note:
1. Independent variables lagged once.

Trade liberalization has also reduced the existing intra-industry specialization. Thus as protection has been reduced in the consumer goods industries, the trade overlap coefficient has decreased (Table 6.19). In the intermediate and capital-good sectors, where effective protection has increased, intra-industry specialization has increased. Thus, the inter-industry pattern of specialization and trade will predominate as trade liberalization proceeds.

Following Abowd and Lemieux's (1987) analysis for Canada, Glytsos (1989) estimates the effects of trade expansion and the terms of trade on employment and real wages in industry. Table 8.26 presents the empirical estimates of inter-industry regressions constructed by pooling together one-digit cross-industry data for the period 1976–84. Employment by industry expands as export promotion and domestic consumption increase and contracts as import penetration increases. Movements in the terms of trade also seem to affect employment.

Increases in exort prices appear to have affected positively employment by industry while movements in import prices do not appear to have a significant impact on employment. This partial evidence seems to support the hypothesis that trade liberalization and import penetration will tend to reduce employment at the industry level.

Glytsos also estimates the impact of trade on real wages using the same pooling of 19 industries for the period 1976–84. Only past real wages seem to affect current real wages while there is a negative even though statistically insignificant relationship between real exports and real wages that is consistent with the theoretical hypotheses described above in light of the overcapitalization of the export sector.

Despite the short-run negative effects of trade liberalization on employment and the trade balance, the reduction in effective protection will produce competitive gains, will increase efficiency of operations and will promote the restructuring of industry.

Protection from foreign competition has allowed large firms to exercise monopolistic power in the domestic market. The largest 300 firms that control over 70% of all assets have maintained in the past substantial price–cost mark-ups as they have been sheltered from competition. Using pooled cross-section, time-series data for 100 firms for the period 1973–80, Papandreou (1989) estimates that the price–cost margin maintained by large firms is positively related to the firm's domestic market share and inversely related to the share of sales directed to the international market (Table 8.27). Thus, increased competition due to integration will force Greek firms to lower their price–cost margins significantly. Given the presence of excess capacity and the evidence that many firms operate to the left of the minimum point on their average cost curves, one effective way to lower costs, or the price–cost margin, is to exploit scale economies more fully. Given that the domestic market is small and will be facing increased competition, moving down the average cost curve implies expanding operations into other markets and restructuring production into new competitive areas. This is a major challenge for Greek firms given the historical attitudes and practices of entrepreneurs who have been used to work in a protected environment.

It is highly likely that in the short run entrepreneurs will find it easier and more profitable to sell companies to foreigners rather than meet the task of industrial restructuring, of upgrading quality and product scale and of modernization of production and organizational methods. There is ample evidence that mergers and acquisitions by foreigners have increased very rapidly in the last two years especially in the traditional sectors of the economy. After a long tradition of 'soft-budgeting' and of contractual operations in the context of a state-corporatist environment, the development of entrepreneurship will take time and effort. It can be facilitated by internal institutional reforms, by structural assistance and by the promotion of joint ventures between European and Greek firms.

3.2   Capital-market liberalization and its effects

The 1980s have been characterized by the progressive liberalization of the domestic capital and foreign exchange markets (Kouzionis and Georgantelis, 1989). The establishment of the interbank market, the abolition of the system of blockings and deblockings, the introduction of new banking services (leasing, factoring, forfaiting etc.) and the opening up of the Greek banking system to external competition have drastically changed the environment within which Greek banks have to operate. In order to compete effectively however in an integrated market for financial services, the Greek banking system will need to modernize itself much further within a very short period of time, and more importantly to alter its capital structure.

According to the EC's Second Directive, recently submitted by the Council of Ministers, banks are not allowed to place more than 60% of their own capital funds in special capital participation. The largest Greek bank, that is the National Bank of Greece, in 1987 had over 70% of its own funds in special capital participation. The Second Directive also stipulates that no more than 15% of own bank funds can be placed in any individual non-financial institution. This limit is often exceeded in the case of Greek banks (Table 8.28). This problem is magnified if insurance companies are included in the sample of non-financial institutions. It becomes serious for the largest banks, especially the National Bank of Greece, which has more than 60% of its own capital invested in problematic companies and faces serious portfolio problems.

Thus in the next few years the state-owned banks, especially the two largest ones, will be forced to restructure their portfolios, to modernize their operations, to promote new products and to guarantee sufficient liquidity for the internal market.

There is evidence that the liberalization of the banking system in the last few years has led to a voluntary restriction of credit flows to manufacturing as banks became more cautious in their lending practices. The flow of new credit to output ratio for manufacturing has declined dramatically

| | Independent variables | | |
Key variables	Industry price-cost margin intercepts	Year	Year cross export/sales
Domestic Share 0.1303[1] (0.0404)	334 (Cement) 0.4177[1] (0.0579)	1973	-0.1540[1] (0.070)
Exports to Sales —	301 (Tires) 0.1484 (0.0554)	1974	-0.0625[1] (0.0714)
Subsidies to Sales -0.5877[1] (0.0499)	291 (Leather) 0.1128[2] (0.0571)	1975	-0.1592[1] (0.0749)
Advertise to Sales 0.8496[1] (0.1243)	233 (Textiles 3) 0.1821[1] (0.0570)	1976	-0.1114[1] (0.0748)
Residual Avg. Var. Cost -0.0183[1] (0.0039)	232 (Textiles 2) 0.1720[2] (0.0574)	1977	-0.1038[1] (0.0460)
Debt/Assets -0.0120[2] (0.0076)	231 (Textiles 1) 0.1293[1] (0.0576)	1978	-0.1132[1] (0.0576)
Constant 0.0030 (0.0618)	222 (Cigarettes) 0.1010[2] (0.0560)	1979	-0.1470[1] (0.0560)
	214 (Soft drinks) 0.1556[1] (0.0557)	1980	-0.0494 (0.0477)
	213 (Beer) 0.1239[1] (0.0574)		(0.0466)
	212 (Wine) 0.1959[1] (0.0567)		
	211 (Alcohol) 0.1277[1] (0.0562)		
	205 (Flour mill) 0.0993 (0.0575)		

R^2	0.4909	203 (Food processing)	0.1576[1]
			(0.0574)
$\bar{R}^2$	0.4670	202 (Dairy products)	0.0919
			(0.0556)
		201 (Meat products)	0.0947
			(0.0571)
No. of observations	780		
Degrees of freedom	745		

Table 8.27. Determinants of Greek price–cost margins, 1973–80

Source: Papandreou (1989).

Notes: Standard errors in parentheses.
1. Significant at the 5% level.
2. Significant at the 10% level.
Regression excludes Industry 207 (Sugar Monopoly), includes year dummies, 1973–1980, excluding 1976).

		More than 10% participation based on own bank's capital (%)		More than 50% participation based on own bank's capital (%)	
National Bank	Piraiki–Patraiki	(23)*	72.71		(75.44)
Commercial Bank	Elefsis Shipyard	(19.79)	26.19		(33.62)
ETEVA	Henninger	(17.60)	52.99		(55.17)
	Hercules Cement	(16.50)*			
	Athenian Paper	(15.76)*			
Ionian Bank	Ionian Hotel Enterprises	(12.80)	22.87		(22.87)

Table 8.28. Participation by major Greek banks in commercial business exceeding limits imposed by the EC's Second Directive, 1987 (1987 data)

Source: Kouzionis and Georgantelis (1989).

Notes: Asterisk indicates company classified as problematic. Numbers in parentheses take into account special participation in insurance companies.

from 25% in 1980 to 0.5% in 1987 as a result of changes in both supply and demand conditions[6] (Dutta and Polemarchakis, 1988).

The decline of credit to manufacturing was matched by its reallocation towards the public sector. The ratio of total bank credit extended by commercial, investment banks and Specialized Credit Institutions to the public sector at large has expanded from 14.7% in 1980 to 24.2% in 1986 (Kouzionis and Georgantelis, 1989). Thus the expansionary stance of fiscal policy (Table 8.4) coupled with an increase in the risk premia for lending to the manufacturing sector as a consequence of liberalization have led to substantial increases in both short-run and long-run real rates. The weighted average real interest rate on credits to manufacturing has increased from -3.25% in 1981 to 3.70% in 1987. The increases in the real rates of interest in the 1980s are finally attributed to the contractionary monetary policy pursued by the Bank of Greece in an effort to finance the growing public sector deficit and attract foreign saving to meet the external imbalances.

Figure 8.3 presents the estimated deviations from covered interest parity in the 1980s. From 1982 onwards, the deviations (D)[7] become positive and exceed 6% in 1988 (Table 8.29). The maintenance of large positive deviations largely through increases in the regulated domestic deposit rates provided incentives for investors to borrow abroad, convert foreign exchange into drachmas, deposit it in domestic savings accounts or in the Treasury Bill market, where rates are even higher, and make

	1980	1981	1982	1983	1984	1985	1986	1987	1988
Average	−0.2	−0.5	−0.2	0.3	0	0.3	0.3	4	5
Std. Dev.	0.03	0.03	0.02	0.04	0.02	0.03	0.02	0.02	0.02

	1980–81		1982–83		1984–85		1986–88	
Average	−0.35		0.08		0.15		3.8	
Std. Dev.	0.035		0.041		0.029		0.019	

Table 8.29. Deviations of Greek interest rates from covered interest-rate parity, 1980–88 (3-month deposits, January 1980–April 1988)

Source: Own calculations, based on Bank of Greece data.

forward transactions to cover risk and repay their foreign-exchange loans. The substantial rise of net short-term private capital flows after 1986, largely reflects the profitable opportunities for banks and other private investors from investing in the domestic TB or money market (Figure 8.4).

The maintenance of artificially high nominal and real interest rates to

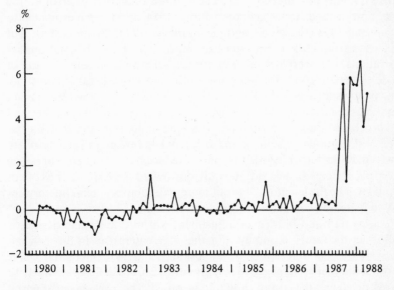

Source: Own calculations.

Figure 8.3   Deviations of Greek interest rates from covered interest parity, 1980–88

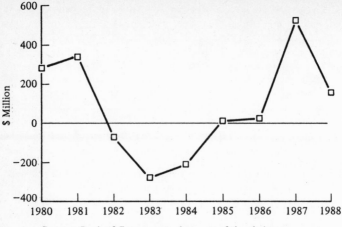

Source: Bank of Greece, annual reports of the chairman.

Figure 8.4   Greece: net private short-term capital inflows, 1980–88

attract foreign financial capital for balance-of-payments purposes has meant that, in the absence of effective means to sterilize reserve accumulation, the short-run capital inflows increased M3 and contributed to excess liquidity into the economy. The mean value of forecast error for the total flow of funds in the economy during 1984–86 has been estimated to be around 18% (Kouzionis and Georgantelis, 1989). To the extent that this excess liquidity is not sterilized effectively through open-market operations, it exacerbates inflationary pressures and the deterioration of trade competitiveness. Despite these adverse effects, the restrictive monetary policy stance is not likely to be reversed as long as the trade deficit continues to increase due to the structural problems described earlier and the process of trade liberalization. The level of nominal and real interest rates will continue to be high and rising unless foreign interest rates are lowered or the domestic PSBR is sharply reduced. In the absence of policy reversals at home or abroad, the only downward pressure on the cost of capital will be the lowering of profit margins of domestic banking services due to increased competition from foreign banks.

The pattern and burden of adjustment will not be symmetric across sectors in the Greek economy. For the large enterprises in the 'official' sector of the economy, which were subsidized and had preferential access to the credit market at negative real interest rates, credit flows are likely to be restricted and the cost of capital to be raised. The increase in the rental price–wage rate ratio would postpone the necessary investment in new equipment and will worsen the burden of overindebtedness that many of

Independent variables	Dependent variables		
	$\ln L_t$	$\ln K_t$	$\ln K_t$
c	2.746	5.150	4.151
	(6.4)	(11.1)	(17.6)
$\ln Y_t$	0.095	0.549	0.531
	(2.2)	(11.5)	(8.2)
$r - \dot{P}$	−0.006	−0.001	−0.005
	(3.4)	(0.6)	(2.0)
$\ln W/P$	0.380	−0.172	0.376
	(2.9)	(0.2)	(6.1)
t	−0.006	0.036	
	(0.7)	(4.2)	
$\bar{R}^2$	0.974	0.995	0.991
DW	0.78	1.01	0.88

Table 8.30. Effects of interest rate and wage rate movements on Greek employment and capital accumulation, 1962–85

Source: Glytsos (1989).

Note: Based on aggregate manufacturing data, 1962–85.

these firms already face. At the same time the presence of labour-market rigidities would prevent the expansion of employment. Some of these enterprises will be forced to exit as the profitability of operations will be questioned. For those enterprises that did not have access to cheap credit but had to rely on expensive credit provided in parallel markets, the cost of capital is likely to be lowered and the capital–labour ratio to be raised.

Capital accumulation is thus likely to increase much faster than employment in response to changes in factor prices. This is confirmed by preliminary empirical evidence provided by Glytsos (1989). Using time-series data for manufacturing during the period 1962–85, he examined the impact of real interest rate and real wage rate fluctuations on the capital stock and on employment. He finds that increases in the real interest rate lower not only the capital stock but also employment (Table 8.30). Increases in the real wage rate also lower employment.

In conclusion, if the liberalization of both the trade and the capital accounts would tend to increase the cost of capital especially for the traditional export-competing sector of the economy, then the likely macroeconomic effects of integration would be unemployment and a widening trade deficit.

In this transition period, however, especially if the public sector ceases to absorb the excess labour shed from the import-competing sectors, unemployment will be rising faster for skilled labour and for university graduates who used to be absorbed in the public sector and who will compete fiercely for managerial positions in the limited higher paid jobs of the private sector. The long-run effects on employment will depend *inter alia* on the speed of adjustment that the more flexible, relatively small-scale enterprises would exhibit and the entrepreneurship that will be developed as competition increases and the credit market becomes more open and flexible. If this process is slowed down, then it is highly likely that there will be a new wave of emigration – this time a brain and skill drain – that would adversely affect long-run growth prospects. It is these costs that policy should seek to minimize.

4   The policy challenge in the 1990s

4.1   A programme for development: priorities for policy-making

The presence of structural rigidities inherited from a long tradition of state-corporatist practices and the need to address urgently but effectively existing internal and external imbalances pose a serious challenge for policy-making. The liberalization of commodity and factor markets inherent in the Internal Market exercise is going to reduce domestic market distortions and weaken the 'network of implicit entitlements that cut through various layers of society' (Rodrik, 1990, p. 2). The thrust of the policy challenge for the 1990s is to redress major imbalances and to design and implement a sustainable program for development (PROD) where there is structural adjustment with growth.

The strategic objective of PROD would be to expand and upgrade the productive base of the economy in a competitive but socially acceptable way in order to exploit the opportunities provided by the creation of the internal market and to promote social cohesion within a unified Europe.

The design of such a programme has to take into consideration not only the existing structural rigidities, and the costs of economic adjustment that the process of liberalization would bring about, but also the pattern and speed of adjustment of the political and social system to a changing environment. It is only proper regard to these conditions that would guarantee 'credibility' of the programme, a necessary condition for its success.

Credibility will be greatly enhanced if important aspects of PROD are discussed and agreed upon by the major political parties and by social partners. In a period of transition and of profound changes in the economic and social mode of organization away from 'state corporatism', political parties that will probably be called upon to form coalition governments will have to set some clear and internally-consistent policy guidelines and priorities that go beyond the time limits of a volatile political cycle. Credibility is not achieved however by mere consensus if a programme is not internally consistent and its implications are not clearly spelled out. It is not useful for example for political parties, for successive governments or even for international organizations to call for a reduction of public deficits without a clear indication as to how this will be done in the presence of inelastic expenditures and structural rigidities in public sector operations, as to who will bear the burden of adjustment, as to what kind of compensation schemes will be envisaged and more importantly as to what are the implications of such action for public investment and long-term growth. Announcements of intentions that are not credible increase uncertainty further and worsen the existing imbalances as consumers, investors or producers attempt to insure themselves against an expected costly adjustment. The more ill-defined the proposals, the greater the imbalances that would be created, as people strive to secure employment, to raise wages and mark-ups or to protect foreign-exchange earnings from an imminent devaluation. In an economy with underdeveloped forward markets to hedge risk, the reduction of uncertainty as to future employment and income prospects, as to the prevailing investment rules and business climate and as to the stance of policy becomes a top priority both for a smooth adjustment and the reduction of internal and external imbalances.

In addition to the reduction of uncertainty, policy for smooth adjustment should integrate structural adjustment policies with macroeconomic policies. The failure of the 1985–87 stabilization plan can be attributed to the one-sided application of restrictive income and monetary policies cum devaluation with no proper understanding of the source of inefficiencies, especially in industry. The widening trade deficits for example cannot be attributed solely to a transitional loss of price competitiveness but is closely linked to the problems of overcapitalization and overindebtedness of the long-protected traditional industries which are suddenly exposed to competition and to higher costs of capital. The external imbalance problem will not be resolved unless one addresses at the same time the problems of industrial inefficiency.

A third priority for policy-making should be the active promotion of entrepreneurship. Attitudes and modes of behaviour in both the public and private sectors have adapted to the workings and requirements of a state-corporatist environment. Risk-taking, the gathering and use of market information or of modern services and organizational techniques for production and marketing, the efficient use of resources, the capacity to organize teams for particular tasks and finally the efficient execution of

specific programmes are not necessary prerequisites for operation under
'soft-budgeting' conditions. When hard budgets are suddenly imposed in
a competitive environment, the lack of entrepreneurship can be extremely
costly. It can only be promoted through learning by doing but this
requires time, assistance and concerted effort.

Finally, an issue that is often downplayed but critical for the process of
adjustment is the appropriate selection of development agents in an
individual or institutional sense. According to A. Hirschman the major
bottleneck for development is not the shortage of capital, of skilled labour
or of foreign exchange but the capacity of the society to organize itself for
development. This is especially true for a country like Greece where the
centralization of authority and the workings of state corporatism have
weakened initiatives at the local or regional level and have hindered the
development of independent and autonomous institutions. Even when
institutions were created for the purpose of breaking this vicious circle,
sooner or later due to lack of funds, technical support of other reasons
they had to streamline their operations and conform their practices to
those of other units in the official sector. One of the central tasks of
PROD therefore is to create a network of institutions, agencies or
mechanisms to instigate and support development at the national,
regional and local levels. Such emphasis is consistent with recent directives on the part of the Commission regarding the conduct of regional
policy, which emphasize the need for creation of intermediate regional
organizations for the support of local development initiatives and for the
disbursement of 'total grants'.

4.2 Structural adjustment policies

Given the strategic objective of PROD, the thrust of structural adjustment policies in Greece should be to support efforts and initiatives
towards industrial restructuring that would include *inter alia* (a) the
upgrading of production (quality, standardization, new product development etc.) in traditional-sector activities such as food processing, beverages, textiles etc. in order to increase competitiveness in the European and
world market, (b) the upgrading of quality and price competitiveness in
traditional services (e.g. tourism, shipping, cultural services, banking
etc.), (c) the support of development initiatives and joint ventures in

Table 8.31. Greece: real effective exchange rates, calculated from relative
consumer price indices (REER1) and unit labour costs (REER2), 1981–
89

Source: Centre of Planning and Economic Research, Athens.

Year		NEER	REER1	REER2
1981	Q1	100.0	100.0	100.0
	Q2	104.1	98.7	94.8
	Q3	106.6	96.1	96.4
	Q4	105.1	102.7	97.3
1981		103.9	99.5	97.3
1982	Q1	108.7	102.6	105.6
	Q2	113.9	101.9	113.1
	Q3	119.3	96.9	110.8
	Q4	120.7	100.2	108.3
1982		115.7	100.2	109.8
1983	Q1	141.3	98.5	101.8
	Q2	140.7	94.4	106.8
	Q3	142.6	92.6	104.5
	Q4	153.5	89.9	101.7
1983		144.8	91.4	103.7
1984	Q1	162.2	87.3	97.4
	Q2	169.7	87.4	107.8
	Q3	175.6	85.1	106.4
	Q4	185.3	84.0	102.8
1984		172.6	86.2	106.8
1985	Q1	191.3	84.0	111.9
	Q2	199.1	83.1	107.8
	Q3	203.9	82.8	106.9
	Q4	241.3	76.2	85.6
1985		208.9	81.2	102.0
1986	Q1	248.4	78.1	96.6
	Q2	248.0	81.4	93.3
	Q3	250.1	82.2	95.3
	Q4	258.3	83.9	92.7
1986		250.8	81.5	94.6
1987	Q1	264.6	83.8	98.1
	Q2	268.7	86.3	94.9
	Q3	275.4	84.1	96.9
	Q4	277.3	87.3	93.5
1987		271.5	85.4	95.8
1988	Q1	281.8	86.8	106.7
	Q2	285.4	88.7	108.4
	Q3	295.2	86.6	107.3
	Q4	298.6	89.4	104.0
1988		294.0	87.9	106.6
1989	Q1	307.0	87.0	—
	Q2	—	—	—
	Q3	—	—	—
	Q4	—	—	—
1989		—	—	—

selective human capital-intensive modern-sector activities (biotechnology, information technology, marine biology, machinery and tools etc.) where Greece could have a comparative advantage due to climatic conditions, costs and quality of human resources, proximity to markets etc.

These three directions of industrial policy orientation should be complemented by drastic action on two fronts: (a) the restructuring of public administration according to modern organizational and management techniques and (b) the development of capital markets and the modernization of banking sector activities and infrastructure.

The pursuit of these policy guidelines necessitate the development of a coordinated programme of action agreed upon by ministries, by local or regional agencies and by the Commission partly under its structural fund programmes. It implies a major reorientation of adjustment compensation away from general transfers towards support for structural adjustment compensation schemes. These could include Community incentives for the promotion of joint industrial ventures and for European plant diversification and extension in the least developed regions of the Community or national incentives for the promotion of local entrepreneurship, i.e. incentive for the use of information networks, for increasing the use of R&D in industrial production, for upgrading management and organizational techniques or for promoting training programmes.

The implementation of the policy guidelines described above also necessitates a sizeable increase in public investment towards the modernization of social and economic infrastructure. In that case, public investment expenditures cannot and should not be used as a fiscal policy instrument for demand-management purposes, but rather as an instrument for the promotion of structural adjustment and development. Furthermore, industrial restructuring will be facilitated if the cost of capital is substantially reduced. This however requires a different policy mix and highlights the interdependence between structural adjustment and macroeconomic policies.

4.3   Macroeconomic policy

The deterioration of the internal and external balances in the last few years, most notably of the public sector deficit, the trade deficit and inflation can be attributed (a) to a substantial increase in uncertainty caused by the expected change in policy regimes and by the volatility of policies actually pursued, (b) to the deterioration of trade competitiveness as a consequence of trade liberalization and the structural inefficiencies of the traditional exportable sector and (c) to the policy-mix. The pursuit of expansionary fiscal and contractionary monetary policies in combination with an appreciation of the real exchange rate (Table 8.31) has resulted in high interest rates, widening budget and trade deficits and an acceleration of inflationary pressures. While the absolute level of the Central Government's debt to output ratio is not among the largest in Europe (Karavitis *et al.*, 1989, p. 22), its accelerating rate of growth, the increasing burden of interest payments and its short maturity structure are causes for serious concern. The reversal of these trends requires a reduction of the primary deficits and the PSBR. Measures in that direction include the reduction of current civil and military expenditures, where feasible, the reduction of explicit or implicit subsidies such as delays of necessary price adjustment for public services, the gradual reduction of public sector employment and the reduction of transfer outlays. These measures have to be supplemented by the introduction of modern budgeting techniques and the reorganization of public administration in an effort to increase the government sector's productivity and efficiency of operations.

The brunt of adjustment however has to be on the revenue side since total revenues cover only 60% of government expenditures in 1988, down from 87% in 1970 and 79% in 1980 (Karavitis *et al.*, 1989). Tax reform should involve (a) major changes in the regulatory and tax-collection system especially as it affects the self-employed categories with the objective to reduce tax evasion which is estimated to be between 300–500 billion drachmae, (b) rationalization of the social contribution tax rate structure and increases in the relevant rates where necessary and (c) expansion of the tax base to include property and agricultural income which is not subject to taxation. The gradual reduction in the budget deficit would permit a progressive reduction in nominal and real interest rates that would reduce the burden of debt accumulation taking advantage of the 'seigniorage' tax. According to recent estimates (Ibid., 1989), returns from seigniorage amount to between 2–3% of GDP on an annual basis. The maintenance of positive growth rates would also ease the burden of adjustment as opposed to rapid deflation.

The need for a credible gradual adjustment to reduce the debt–GDP ratio to sustainable levels would also argue against early entry into the EMS on public finance grounds. The counter-argument (Gros, 1989) that entry into the EMS would diminish the government's incentives to use surprise inflation to lower the burden of outstanding debt does not hold given the short-term nature of the outstanding debt (over 95% of debt is short-term) and its effective indexation. Strategic arguments are however more important than public finance arguments in tilting the balance in favour of postponement of EMS-entry. The creation of the internal market and the liberalization of the trade and capital accounts have asymmetric effects in Greece relative to other European countries largely due to the structural rigidities described earlier. In that case, imposing a common monetary policy and limiting the use of the exchange rate as a policy instrument would give rise to inefficiencies (Cohen and Wyplosz, 1989). In the presence of these asymmetries, the use of the real exchange would permit a smoother internal adjustment as well. Even on more traditional grounds, in the absence of an integrated tax and transfer system at the European level, exchange-rate fixity would enhance regional disparities.

Early entry into the EMS is finally advocated on discipline grounds. If the cost of exchange-rate adjustment is high, then the government will be forced to adjust fiscal policy. A counter-argument could be that whenever this has happened and the evidence is not clear (De Grauwe, 1989), governments have shifted the burden of adjustment onto future generations by lowering investment as opposed to consumption expenditures. Furthermore, in the presence of structural rigidities, especially in the traditional export sector, the abrupt removal of the implicit subsidy from the exchange-rate movement would further worsen profitability in those sectors and aggravate the short-run costs of adjustment in terms of employment and export performance.

If, despite these arguments, entry into the EMS is decided for political or other strategic reasons, then adjustment would be facilitated and its acceptance would be enhanced, if some form of voluntary guideposts for prices, wages and the interest rate were negotiated among social partners and with the Commission to reduce uncertainty and stabilize expectations over the medium run. A similar effort, however short-lived, in July 1985 proved to be extremely useful. Part of the package for negotiations could include incentives for structural adjustment initiatives and medium-term financial assistance for investment promotion and regional development.

If the success of the internal market in terms of effectiveness and acceptability depends on the degree of integration of the least developed regions into the rest of the Community, then a concerted effort should be made to promote a consistent and credible programme for development of the Greek economy. If in turn, some minimum consensus on policy priorities and guidelines is a prerequisite for the successful implementation of such a programme, then the reality of the internal market could enforce a major reorientation of political platforms and practices and the modernization of political life. The presence of an 'external constraint' reflected by 1992 can thus create incentives for economic and political modernization that transcend the narrow bounds of economic integration.

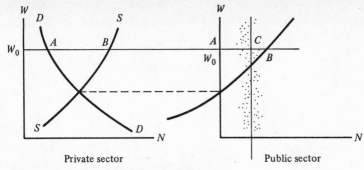

Figure 8A.1   The determination of employment

Appendix: Labour market adjustment

The workings of the labour markets can be described by Figure 8A.1.

The nominal wage, W, is set in the public sector as an outcome of negotiations between the government and unions that take into account private sector employment conditions. At the nominal wage W_0, the excess supply created, AB, in the private market seeks public sector employment. The number actually employed in the public sector AC is determined through the imposition of a 'soft constraint' derived from the overall deficit constraint and the political cycle. The unemployment rate appears as the residual, CB.

If w^p and w^g are the real wages for the private and public sector respectively that are exogenously determined through wage-setting, the excess labour supply that is directed to the public sector is a positive function of w^p and a negative function of productivity (v_p/E_p) in the private sector.

If we assume that the quota applied by the government is a negative function of w^g and of a budget constraint, defined here as the ratio of government expenditures to taxes, then, the share of public sector employment to total employment is expected to be a positive function of w^p and E^p and a negative function of y^p, w^g and G/T. Table 8A.1 below presents preliminary econometric evidence regarding, the fraction of public sector employment (Glytsos, 1989).

The results are consistent with the hypotheses outlined above.

NOTES

This paper is based on research that was conducted by N. Glytsos, N. Floros, N. Karavitis, N. Kosteletou, D. Kouzionis, N. Papandreou and A. Sarris, coordinated by the author. The author however has sole responsibility for the methodology

Dependent variable	c'	w^g	w^P	y^P	$\log w^g$	$\log w^P$	$\log y^P$	$\log \frac{G}{T}$	$\log E'$	$\log E^g_{t-1}$ $D0$	$D1$	$D2$	R^2	DW
1.1 E^g/E	0.155 (6.821)	−3.281 (3.451)	7.129 (2.679)	−0.0000004 (1.892)							−0.002 (0.431)	−0.009 (−1.615)	0.830	0.90
1.2 E^g/E	0.157 (6.563)	−3.668 (3.759)	8.187 (2.991)	−0.0000005 (1.904)						−0.001 (0.375)			0.809	0.92
1.3 $\log(E^g/E)$	−2.180 (2.970)				−0.223 (9.861)		−0.085 (1.306)	−0.241 (1.712)			0.006 (0.212)	−0.053 (1.291)	0.958	1.93
1.4 $\log(E^g/E)$	−6.416 (1.506)				−0.234 (8.533)		−0.241 (0.971)	−0.438 (3.667)	0.408 (0.854)	0.298 (1.458)			0.963	2.38
1.5 $\log(E^g/E)$	−4.880 (3.234)				−0.804 (5.465)	0.739 (4.311)	−0.050 (0.735)	−0.039 (0.373)		0.304 (1.677)			0.982	2.34

Table 8A.1. Econometric evidence regarding employment of permanent civil servants (E^g) as a fraction of total wage employment (E), 1970–87.

Source: Greek National Statistical Service, Labour Force Surveys and *Statistical Yearbooks*.

Notes:
t values in parentheses
$D0$: dummy with value 1 for 1979, 1981, 1985; zero otherwise
$D1$: dummy with value 1 for 1979; zero otherwise
$D2$: dummy with value 1 in 1981; zero otherwise

pursued, the structure and conclusions of the paper and the policy implications. Research assistance by S. Zographakis and M. Vasalou as well as helpful
comments from the editors, and from M. Emerson, D. Maroulis and R. Portes are
very gratefully acknowledged.

1 This Committee was similar in composition to the Italian Committee on Credit;
however it was vested with far greater powers. Initially it was comprised of two
ministers (Coordination and Finance), the Governor of the Central Bank, and
two foreign members (one British and one American). Later, the two foreign
members were replaced by three Ministers (Agriculture, Commerce, and
Industry).

2 This terminology is preferred to the more traditional distinction between
'formal' and 'informal' sectors as it applies to behavioural characteristics that
do not necessarily involve unregistered, unorganized or illegally conducted
activities.

3 NEP is calculated by Sarris as follows:
NEP $= ((1 + t)/(1 + (\varphi - s)) - 1) 100$ where $t = $ the tariff and border tax rate on
sector i, $\varphi = $ the rate of taxes levied on production of sector i and $s = $ the rate of
production subsidies on sector i.

4 Emigration provided another outlet till 1977.

5 The composite growth of public sector employment is 44% higher than that of
the private sector (Vavouras et al., 1989).

6 The increase in retained earnings after 1985 as a result of the 1985–87 stabilization programme and the substantial increase in real interest rates have also
lowered the demand for credit.

7 $D = (1 + i) - (1 + i^*)f/e$ where i and i^* are the 3-month domestic deposit rate
and the Eurodollar deposit rate respectively, f is the three-month drachma–
dollar forward rate and e is the corresponding spot rate.

REFERENCES

Economic integration in the enlarged European Community: structural adjustment in the Greek economy – Background research papers

Glytsos, N. (1989). 'Economic Integration and Its Implications for the Greek
Labour Market', unpublished.

Karavitis, N., N. Kosteletou and N. Floros (1989). 'Fiscal Inefficiencies and
Structural Rigidities in the Greek Public Sector', unpublished.

Kouzionis, D. and S. Georgantelis (1989). 'Structural Characteristics in the
Capital and Financial Markets', unpublished.

Papandreou, N. (1989). 'Market Power, Soft Budgets and State Subsidies in
Greek Industry', unpublished.

Sarris, A. (1989). 'Rigidities and Macroeconomic Adjustment under Market
Opening: Greece and 1992', unpublished.

Other references

Abowd, J., and T. Lemieux (1987). 'The Effects of International Trade on
Collective Bargaining Agreements: Evidence from Canada', unpublished.

Cohen, D. and C. Wyplosz (1989). 'The European Monetary Union: An Agnostic
Evaluation', CEPR Discussion Paper, No. 306, April.

Commission of the European Communities (1988a). Research on the 'Cost of

Non-Europe', *The Completion of the Internal Market: A Survey of European Industry's Perception of the Likely Effects*, Volume 3.

(1988b). *European Economy: the Economics of 1992*.

De Grauwe, Paul (1989). 'The Cost of Disinflation and the European Monetary System', CEPR Discussion Paper No. 326, July.

Donges, J.B. *et al*. (1982). *The Second Enlargement of the European Community: Adjustment Requirements and Challenges for Policy Reform*. Tubingen: J.C. Mohr (Paul Siebeck).

Dutta, J. and H. Polemarchakis (1988). 'Credit Constraints and Investment Finance: Some Evidence From Greece', Discussion Paper, Columbia University, Barnard College, January.

Edwards, S. and S. Van Wijnbergben (1987). 'Tariffs, the Real Exchange Rate and the Terms of Trade: On Two Popular Propositions in International Economics', *Oxford Economic Papers* **39**, 458–64.

Georgakopoulos, Th.A. (1989). 'Trade and Welfare Effects of Common Market Membership: Greece', Paper presented at the 9th World Congress of the International Economic Association in Athens, unpublished.

Giannitsis, T. (1982). *Greek Industry: Development and Crisis*. Athens: Gutenberg.

(1988). 'Entry into the European Community and Effects on Industry and International Trade', (in Greek) Centre for Mediterranean Studies, Athens.

Gilpin, R. (1987). *The Political Economy of International Relations*, Princeton University Press.

Gros, D. (1989). 'Seignorage and EMS Discipline', unpublished.

Haritakis, N. (1981). 'The Disequilibrium Estimation of the Credit Market in Greece', Chapter VII of Ph.D. Dissertation.

Katseli, L. (1986). 'Discrete Devaluation as a Signal to Price Setters: Suggested Evidence from Greece' in S. Edwards and L. Ahamed (eds), *Economic Adjustment and Exchange Rates in Developing Countries*, University of Chicago Press, pp. 295–326.

Katsos, G. and N.I. Spanakis (1983). *Industrial Protection and Integration*, Center of Planning and Economic Research (KEPE), Athens.

Katzenstein, P. (1983). 'The Smaller European States in the International Economy: Economic Dependence and Corporatist Policies' in J.G. Roggie (ed.), *The Antinomies of Interdependence*, New York: Columbia University Press, 91–130.

Kornai, J. (1980). 'Hard and Soft Budget Constraint', *Acta Oeconomica* **25**, 231–45.

(1986). 'The Soft Budget Constraint', *Kyklos* **39**, 3–30.

Lalonde, R. and N. Papandreou (1984). 'An Appraisal of Price Controls in Greece: Past, present, future', KEPE, Athens, mimeo.

Levegue, J.M. (1987). 'Banking is Changing . . . But what about Men?', Institut International d'Etudes Bancaires, Athens.

Magliveras, S. (1987). *The State Sector in the Greek Economy and the Crisis*, Modern Times, Athens (in Greek).

Mallios, N. (1975). *The Present Stage of Capitalist Development in Greece*. Athens: Synchroni Epochi (in Greek).

Maroulis, D.K. (1988). 'Problems, Pre-Conditions and Prospects for the Development of Greek Exports', KEPE, unpublished (in Greek).

Mouzelis, N. (1978). *Modern Greece; Facets of Underdevelopment*. London: Macmillan.

(1986). *Early Parliamentarism and Late Industrialisation in the Balkans and Latin America*. London: Macmillan.

Neven, D. (1990). 'EEC integration towards 1992: some distributional aspects', *Economic Policy* No. 10, **5**, 13–62.

OECD (1987). *Bank Profitability*, Paris.

Padoa-Schioppa, T. *et al.* (1987). *Efficiency, Stability and Equity*. London: Oxford University Press.

Papandreou, N. (1986). 'Price Controls and Industry Structure: A Theoretical and Empirical Analysis', Princeton University, Ph.D. Dissertation.

(1988a). 'Credit Policy and Industry Structure: The Case of Greece', unpublished.

(1988b). *Flow of Funds in Greek Industry*, 1973–1980, unpublished.

Pavlopoulos, P. (1987). 'The Underground Economy in Greece', *Special Studies*, Institute of Economic and Industrial Research (IOBE), Athens.

Provopoulos, G. (1985). *The Public Sector in the Greek Economy: Recent Trends and Economic Impact.* Athens: IOBE.

Provopoulos, G. and T. Zambaras (1988). 'From Government Spending to Taxation or from Taxation to Spending?', IOBE, Athens, unpublished.

Rodrik, D. (1990). 'Soft Budgets, Hard Minds: Stray Thoughts on the Integration Process in Greece, Portugal and Spain', this volume.

Sarris, A. (1988). 'Greek Accession and EC Commercial Policy Toward the South', in L.B.M. Mennes and J. Kol (eds), *European Trade Policies and the Developing World*, Croom Helm.

Trangakis, G.E. (1980). 'Greek Banking Law and Practice', Federation of Greek Banks (in Greek).

Tsoukalas, K. (1986). *State, Society, Labor in Post-War Greece*. Athens: Thelemio (in Greek).

Vassilakopoulos, D. (1986). Underemployment in Greece', Report for EC, DG IV, unpublished.

Vavouras, I., N. Karavitis and A.K. Tsouchlou (1989). 'The Productive Process in the Public Sector and the Rise of Government Expenditures: The Case of Greece', Athens (in Greek), unpublished.

9 External liberalization with ambiguous public response: the experience of Portugal

JORGE BRAGA de MACEDO

1 Introduction

Integration with the rest of Europe has become quite evident in Portuguese society only four years after the country joined the European Community. The government regards the deadline for completing the internal market by the end of 1992 as a major political challenge. This stance departs from a tradition of ambiguous policy towards European integration which has shared some features with the British position. Once before, in 1975, there was an attempt to break with this tradition, but on that occasion the new departure was in the opposite direction, when the revolutionary leaders sought to reject the West in favour of central planning along the lines of Eastern Europe. Although it was soon aborted, the attempt had the effect of keeping the public sector frozen until 1989, which muted the economic effects of accession to the European Community in 1986. The market is still heavily influenced by the state, and economic liberalization lacks domestic political credentials. This applies to Portugal even more than to historically dirigiste countries, such as, until recently, France. Yet Portugal's case may be of far-reaching interest. The experience of a country that is undergoing transition from widespread nationalization to privatization within a democratic set-up may be useful to countries in Eastern Europe striving to achieve political democracy and to reform their economies at the same time.

In this paper the tradition of ambiguous response of the Portuguese government is explained as revenue-seeking by the state. The paper views administrative· regulation in financial markets as implicit taxation and argues that the confusion that has resulted from this disguise has not served Portugal well. Regulation in product and labour markets has had comparable effects. It has resulted in a dual structure, comprising competitive and rigid segments, which generates efficiency losses. This dualism is of long standing. In the 1960s, trade liberalization uncovered previously

310

ignored export potential in manufactures, but at the same time industrial and financial regulation produced conglomerates whose activities spread to the African colonies: they were soon to become state-owned and uncompetitive.

After the revolution of April 1974 the public sector was enlarged through widespread nationalizations and then frozen by an article of the new constitution that made these nationalizations irreversible. At the same time state intervention in the rest of the economy was extended. In some areas, such as the labour market and some parts of industry, the private sector has circumvented or overcome intervention. In recent years the government has begun to dismantle some of the measures taken in the early post-revolutionary years, for example, by providing for greater flexibility in the labour market, by allowing new banks to enter the financial sector and by initiating the privatization of some of the nationalized banks. Privatization necessitated a constitutional amendment to repeal the irreversibility of the nationalizations. The way is now open to unfreezing the public sector.

Much of the impetus to free the economy has been generated by Portugal's increasing integration with the European Community. With accession to the Community in 1986 Portugal entered a period of transition towards full integration with the Community by 1996. The pressures this has generated for liberalizing the economy have since been reinforced by the agreement of the twelve member states to remove all remaining barriers to trade and to factor mobility by the end of 1992. Yet much has still to be accomplished if Portugal is, in the words of the government's slogan, 'to win 1992'. Unless state intervention is reduced, Portuguese firms will have great trouble preparing for the single market. Furthermore, if the economy fails to catch up with the rest of the Community, the government may feel unable to make the commitment to Economic and Monetary Union.

Help from the Community is coming in the form of increased funds for structural programmes. The structural funds will reach 4.5% of GDP in 1993, from 2.7% in 1989 and will provide for about one-third of investment over the period. Programs aimed at providing the country with an adequate infrastructure and training are included in the Regional Development Plan (PDR) of 1989. There are also specific programmes aimed at modernizing agriculture and industry, respectively the PEDAP of 1986 and the PEDIP of 1989. The Community may also delay until 1996 the deadline for Portugal's financial integration, which will entail the freezing of all capital movements. This paper argues that a precondition for the success of European integration is transparent fiscal policy. Even if Portugal's reported budget deficits continue to fall, hidden deficits may persist – and the tradition of ambiguous public response will be perpe-tuated.

The remainder of the paper is in six sections. To set the stage, Section 2 establishes the tradition of ambiguous response. It asserts that ambiguity in Portuguese policy towards European integration is not simply the result of the absence of political democracy from 1926 to 1974. In particular, the country's neutral stance during World War II and the enduring colonial ties with Africa made it as averse as Great Britain to the federalist enthusiasm of the late 1940s. A combination of external shocks and domestic policies steered Portugal into a process of catching up with the European Community which is still continuing.

Next some economic features relevant to the development process are discussed. Employment, emigration and the causes and effects of real wage flexibility are taken up in Section 3. Section 4 presents evidence of the trade effects of accession to the European Community. The ease with which industry has adapted since 1986 is noted. Simulation of some of the trade effects of the single market programme shows that the full impact of external competition has not yet been felt, either on traditional labour-intensive exports or on prospects for intra-industry trade. The role of foreign direct investment and of more open financial markets is stressed.

The following sections attempt to reveal the root of the ambiguous public response to external liberalization. Revenue-seeking regulation of industry and finance is found side by side with trade liberalization. Section 5 points to the trade-off between regulation and competition in banking: it confirms that the propensity towards rationing schemes and the process of European integration have been equally durable. In Section 6 attention is turned to the constraints on fiscal adjustment implied by a public sector which includes banks and was frozen by constitutional law between 1976 and 1989.

Section 7 shows how a frozen banking sector and a disguised fiscal policy constrain monetary and exchange-rate policy. Trends in competi-tiveness are assessed, and the growing ineffectiveness of the crawling peg regime introduced in 1977 is documented. Displaying the intention of joining the European Monetary System (EMS), as the government has done, is not enough. A credible peg requires convergence of nominal values with those of the EMS partners. But this necessitates disinflation, which cannot last without some restriction of demand. This in turn is predicated on the credibility of fiscal adjustment.

The sequencing discussed in Section 8 with the objective of EMU in mind requires a programme implemented over several years, much like the Programme to Correct External Imbalances and Unemployment (known as PCEDED) approved in 1987 and revised in 1989 to incorporate the effect of Community structural funds. But a multi-annual fiscal adjustment strategy – which may be called MAFAS – appropriate to 1992 needs to be more ambitious. The share of public expenditure in GDP must be reduced, and taxes must be made more transparent and less susceptible to avoidance and evasion. The paper concludes by suggesting that such a medium-term orientation be made evident in the government's handling of the budget for 1990, which remains too high a percentage of GDP (8%, the same deficit as the initial 1989 budget).

2   Domestic constraints on integration policy

Accession to the EC in 1986 and preparation for the completion of the internal market have provided a renewed opportunity for and impulse towards modernization, which entails liberalizing those aspects of the economy where intervention remains excessive. The government has identified meeting the 1992 deadline as the major challenge facing the nation. The objective of EC economic and social cohesion is seen as requiring Portugal to meet this challenge. Partly as a result of government pronouncements and advertising efforts, the business community is becoming increasingly aware of the need to compete with firms elsewhere in Europe after 1992. Strategies are mapped out with this objective in mind, and fears of failure are prompting a surge of lobbying aimed at delaying integration or at limiting its scope.

Such apprehension exists even though the first years of membership of the EC have been a major success in terms of export expansion and the response of firms, as well as macroeconomic performance. Doubts as to whether these advances can be maintained reflect concern that public sector reform has been far from adequate. The introduction of income tax, the partial privatization of public enterprises and other 'structural' reforms have been too slow to provide the underpinnings for further progress. Furthermore, the inefficiency and uncompetitiveness of the large public sector have made the challenge of preparing for 1992 that much greater for the economy as a whole. Nevertheless, that there is now less ambiguity towards integration is a major departure from previous experience of external liberalization.

The ambiguous response to the challenge of European integration dates back to the 1940s. Then Portugal accepted Marshall aid and so took up the challenge of catching up with the rest of Europe. Yet at the same time the government was determined to hold on to the African possessions, which were turned from colonies into provinces in the 1951 revision of the Constitution. The idea of 'fortress Portugal' was accentuated in the 1960s. In 1974 the revolution maintained the fortress mentality but the domestic

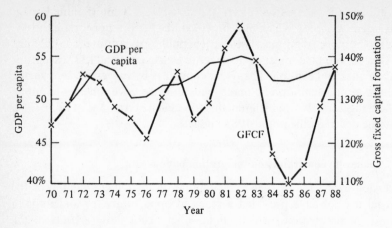

Source: DG II, Commisssion of the EC.

Figure 9.1   Portugal and EC: investment and catching up, 1970–88

objective constraining European integration changed: colonialism was replaced by socialism. Both were understood to be strictly domestic objectives rather than manifestations of international trends.

Before and after the revolution the economy displayed a dual structure with elements both of liberalization and of intervention. In the early post-war period control over public spending and the accumulation of foreign exchange were the keys to defending the currency and securing the financial independence of the state. This implied strong supervision by the central bank. Barriers to foreign competition were part of a regulatory environment that also featured investment licensing in many industrial sectors. Economic exchanges with the colonies were also regulated despite the fortress idea, expressed as an objective of 'national economic integration'. Yet competition prevailed, fortunately, in sectors where in the late 1950s trade was liberalized in the framework of the British-led European Free Trade Association (EFTA). Export growth was so pronounced in clothing that Portugal was sometimes labelled as a 'pyjama republic'.

Thanks to sizeable migrants' remittances, tourism and growing foreign investment, gold reserves piled up during the 1960s. Against the background of the first enlargement of the Community to include former EFTA partners Denmark, Ireland and the United Kingdom, Portugal signed a free trade agreement with the EC in 1972. This crowned a successful decade of export-led growth, which was followed by a stock market boom. Existing exchange controls were unable to prevent growing financial interdependence.[1]

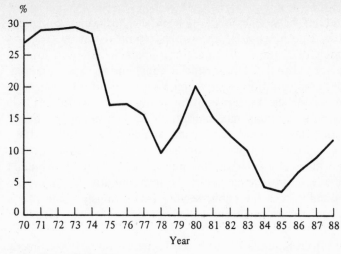

Source: as Figure 9.1

Figure 9.2   The Portuguese incremental output-capital ratio, 1970–88

The rate at which the Portuguese economy has been catching up with the EC over the past two decades can be seen in Figures 9.1 and 9.2. Figure 9.1 plots two ratios of Portugal to EC12 variables from 1970 to 1988: on the left hand scale, gross domestic product per capita at current prices and purchasing power standards; on the right hand scale, the share of gross fixed capital formation in gross domestic product. Figure 9.2 plots the incremental output–capital ratio, given by the growth rate of output divided by the output share of gross fixed capital formation; the variable provides a rough estimate of trends in the marginal efficiency of capital in Portugal during the same period. The figure suggest that the main reason underlying the catching up was either that investment was a significantly larger share of output in Portugal than the average of the 12 EC countries or that it was much more productive.

As Figure 9.1 shows, after catching up rapidly with the European Community in the early 1970s, the Portuguese economy suffered a relative decline. In late 1973 the first oil shock hit Portugal with particular severity. Moreover, the political situation disintegrated to the point where the fifty-year-old authoritarian regime fell without resistance on 25 April 1974. A military junta took power and vowed to 'democratize, decolonize and develop' in the name of the people. Democracy and development soon became equated with an 'original' brand of socialism, but the originality was constrained by the combined influence of the armed forces and of the Communists. The Common Market was seen as a capitalist and imperialist threat. Economic solidarity with the Eastern bloc and the Third World was proposed as a superior development strategy.

On 11 March 1975, under the threat of a military take-over, firms in protected sectors, especially the financial conglomerates, were nationalized without compensation to shareholders.[2] To ensure the transition to socialism, an article of the political constitution passed in 1976 froze the post-revolutionary nationalizations as 'irreversible conquests of the working classes' until the second amendment, voted in 1989, overturned this irreversibility. Nationalization without compensation had the effect of greatly enlarging the public sector virtually overnight with no side-effects on revenue, while the irreversibility of the nationalizations basically froze the public sector. This seriously hindered the process of economic restructuring called for by the global shocks of the 1970s.

It is evident from Figure 9.1 that the Portuguese economy was already beginning to catch up again in 1977, when the application for EC membership was lodged and agreement was reached on the first stabilization plan involving the International Monetary Fund (IMF). It is worth noting that the combined expectation of trade liberalization and of microeconomic stabilization did not appear to hamper the process of catching up. Flexibility in the economy was such that exporting firms and workers adjusted sufficiently to compensate for the downward rigidity of public expenditure.

The relentless expansion of public debt that resulted from the enlarged public sector made private firms the residual borrowers from credit enterprises. The private sector was subject to recurrent squeezes because of stop-go macroeconomic policies. These were in part politically motivated cycles which occurred even when a government was succeeded by another of the same coalition of parties. Thus Portugal's business cycles were often more pronounced than those of its main trading partners, especially the EC, as Table 9.1 shows. The first government led by the social democrats stabilized inflation in 1980, and the second government of the same coalition expanded during the world recession of 1981–82. A coalition government of socialists and social democrats stabilized during the world boom in 1983–85, a stabilization that involved a belated increase in domestic interest rates. We see from Figure 9.1 that relative income per capita fell in 1983. Thus the second liberalization-stabilization package, unlike the first, reversed the catching-up process. This time the consequences of the frozen public sector were too strong to be offset by a fall in real wages. The effect was exacerbated because the Portuguese economy was out of phase with the EC economies, a feature that will

	Real GDP		GDP deflator	
	P	EC	P	EC
1970–73	9	5	6	7
1974–75	−2	0	18	14
1976–77	6	4	21	12
1978–79	5	3	20	11
1980–82	3	1	20	11
1983–85	0	2	23	7
1986–88	4	3	15	5
1989–90*	5	3	12	5

Table 9.1. Growth cycles in Portugal and the twelve, 1970–90 (annual % rates of growth)

Source: Eurostat, rounded to nearest percent.

*Forecast from *European Economy*, Oct. 89.

continue to be a problem as long as fiscal policy is determined by the need to finance too large a public sector borrowing requirement.

That the public sector remained frozen for so long was indicative of the ambiguity of public response towards European integration. Politically it was important to balance European integration against constitutional socialism. Throughout the eight years of negotiations with the EC, conflict between the commitment to EC membership and the commitment to socialism was associated with personal rivalries between the Prime Minister and the President of the Republic. Yet the ambiguity of integration policy in the years after the revolution stemmed from the constitutional system of government as much as from personalities. Because the executive system favoured in the constitution was semi-presidential or bipolar, rivalry between the two poles of the executive was hard to avoid. The objective of EC membership was repeatedly emphasized by the socialist leader, Mario Soares, who was Prime Minister from 1976 to 1978 and again in 1983–85, whereas the objective of a socialist economy was defended by the military leaders from the African wars gathered in the Revolutionary Council chaired by General Eanes, the President of the Republic from 1976 to 1985. Furthermore, until the first constitutional amendment abolished the Revolutionary Council in 1982, the loyalty of the President was divided between the electorate who had voted him into office and the army, represented by the Revolutionary Council.

Before 1982 the rivalry between the two poles of the executive was particularly crippling. Despite the efforts of a social democratic government in 1980, the economic consequences were progressive expansion of the public sector without any attempt at reform and continuous squeezing of the private sector. Mounting public sector deficits were an inevitable corollary. By the time the Revolutionary Council was abolished and the powers of the President of the Republic were reduced, the problems had become too great to be easily resolved. A succession of coalition governments proved incapable of bringing order to public finances. The process of debt accumulation was becoming explosive, and the rate of inflation reached over 20%.

An anti-inflationary programme, coupled with the first steps towards fiscal adjustment, was adopted late in 1985, with the election of another reformist government of the social democratic party led by Cavaco Silva – the minister of finance in the 1980 endeavour. Even though the government's candidate for the Presidency lost, the rivalry between the two poles of the executive subsided shortly afterwards, when Mario Soares became President in February 1986. The popularity of the reformist strategy was strikingly confirmed by the landslide victory of the government in the elections of July 1987.

The government made known during the electoral campaign its intention to revise the constitution and unfreeze the public sector. Its victory set the stage for the second constitutional amendment. This took two years to achieve, however, because to reach the two-thirds majority required to pass an amendment, some kind of arrangement had to be reached with the socialists. Perhaps anticipating the difficulty of such agreement, the government decided in November 1987 to sell 49% of the capital of state-owned enterprises to private investors without waiting for the amendment to the constitution. In attempting to divorce ownership from control, the decision made the privatization process more complex but not necessarily faster. The very gradual nature of the privatization process can be viewed as another reflection of the ambiguity of integration policy.

All political parties except the Communists now acknowledge that generalized state intervention was a failure. Yet liberalization has not been accepted easily by any major political force, and the social democrats are anxious to avoid being branded as pro-business. Their preference for some form of social pact was evident in efforts to accommodate the objectives of the non-communist trade union – the General Workers' Union (UGT) – in the disinflation process initiated in 1985. The employers' confederations – especially the Confederaçao da Industria Portuguesa – also agreed to base wage increases on expected inflation in 1986, but the agreement broke down in 1988 when the inflation outturn was almost twice as high as the target.

Since EC accession the catching-up process has resumed. In 1989 Portugal was forecast to reach a level of GDP per capita sightly higher than Greece. Measured at current market prices and purchasing power standards, Portugal scored 54.4 and Greece 54.1 as a share of the EC average. This was heralded as showing that the country was no longer 'at the tail of Europe'. Yet 'to win 1992' requires structural adjustment as well as faster growth, and both have been hindered by the frozen public sector. The commitment of the government to the single market objective serves as a reminder of the electoral promise to reform the public sector.

The results of the anti-inflationary programme initiated with accession should be seen in this light. The government managed to cut the rate of increase of the GDP deflator from 23% in 1983–85 to 15% in 1986–88, while replacing stagnation by a 4% growth rate over the same period. The forecasts of the European Commission reported in Table 9.1 indicate that the performance in 1989–90 will be even brighter, with growth 1 percentage point faster and inflation 3 percentage points slower.

The improvement in inflation was matched by a reduction of the public sector deficit from 11% to 7% of GDP, as shown in the first panel of Table 9.2. The improvement is less remarkable, however, if net unrequited official transfers (mostly from the EC) are excluded from foreign savings, so that capital transfers from the public to the private sector are included in private investment. This approach (which seems to be favoured by the IMF) is followed in the second panel of Table 9.2. Conversely, the third panel shows a drastic improvement if state-owned enterprises are included in the accounts of the public sector. This reflects the stringent control that has been exerted on the deficits of these companies. By all three criteria there remains substantial room for improvement. Awareness is growing that the sizeable public deficit, coupled with the high public debt, rekindled inflation in 1988, requiring a credit squeeze in early 1989. Unless public finances are reformed, a resumption of stop-go macroeconomic policies will be unavoidable.[3]

3   Wage flexibility and labour mobility

The labour market has undergone substantial change in recent decades. During 1965–73 more than 100,000 people emigrated to the then six member states of the European Community, but with the change in the immigration policies of the destination countries in 1973–74 Portuguese international migration came to a virtual stop. Moreover, there was massive return migration from the former colonies, amounting to some one million people, equivalent to about one-tenth of the population. At the same time, agricultural employment began a steep decline which

	Private savings − investment	Gen. govt budget balance	Current account balance
1970–73	5	−2	3
1974–75	−3	−3	−6
1976–77	−3	−6	−9
1978–79	5	−9	−4
1980–82	0	−11	−11
1983–85	7	−10	−3
1986–88	8	−7	1
1989–90*	3	−6	−3
Excluding official transfers from current account			
1980–82	−2	−8	−10
1983–85	6	−9	−3
1986–88	6	−6	0
Including state-owned firms in public sector			
1980–82	12	−22	−10
1983–85	14	−17	−3
1986–88	11	−10	1

Table 9.2. Portugal: sectoral financial balances, 1970–90 (% of GDP)
Source: Table 9.1 and IMF.
Note: *Forecast.

amounted to 30% during 1974–88, though at 21% of total employment it still represents a higher share than in the rest of the Community. The decline in agricultural employment has been compensated by increased employment in manufacturing (21% over the same period) and even more so in services (58%), while employment in public administration grew by 42% during 1981–88. These sectoral shifts have been associated with substantial migration from rural to urban areas.

The activity rate in Portugal (about 44% in 1986) is slightly higher than in the EC overall. The proportion of women in the civilian labour force grew slowly through 1983–88 to reach over 43%, a higher level than the EC average. Paid, registered part-time jobs, however, accounted for only 4% of employees in Portugal in 1986, compared with 12% in the Community as a whole. The proportion of self-employed workers is very high in Portugal, standing at more than 30% in 1988. The figure for average hours worked each week is also higher than the EC average (40 hours against 37.6 in 1986).

Employment has risen in Portugal in every year except 1978, 1982, 1984 and 1985, and unemployment has not been a problem since the late 1950s.[4] The rate did jump up in 1974 and peaked at 8.5% in 1985, then declined to 5.6% in 1988, about half the average for the Community. For new entrants into the labour force Portugal's performance has been closer to that of the rest of the EC, with youth unemployment of 19% during 1984–88 compared with 23% for the EC as a whole. Furthermore, 'underemployment' may be widespread because of the highly bureaucratic public (and private) administration and because of the high cost of adjusting manpower. If the organization of the economy changes, there will be a large potential for workers to be released to undertake new activities. These workers, however, are generally poorly trained and lack special qualifications. Comparatively low wages may attract investment in new industries, which may increase the demand for labour.

During most of the post-revolutionary period real wages have been quite flexible. In the wake of the revolution trade unions and other workers' organizations, which had been docile under the corporatist regime, became very strong and engineered steep real wage increases. Rivalries between the communist and the non-communist union (UGT), however, undermined their bargaining power. At the same time, because they had become accustomed to a stable exchange rate, workers were unaware of the erosion in real wages that currency depreciation was now causing. This allowed the stop-go policies of the various governments to result in falling real wages during most of the post-revolutionary period.

To assess the amount of real wage adjustment and the contribution of devaluation, measures of wage gaps are sometimes used. Such measures provide only a rough approximation, but given the size of the shocks that the Portuguese economy has encountered they can shed useful light. An index of the actual labour share with base 1973 = 100 is presented in Figure 9.3, together with one measure of the 'warranted' share based on the observed consumption real wage, an elasticity of substitition between labour and capital of one half and the small country assumption, that is to say infinite trade elasticities. The Figure shows the gap closing during the two stabilization episodes. The lack of response of nominal wages to exchange-rate devaluation was essential to the process of closing the gap, whereas the initial success of the 1985–87 anti-inflationary programme induced wage moderation afterwards.[5]

Making internal and external balance a function of the wage gap and the output gap, roughly measured as the deviations of output from trend, we can divide the space of the two gaps into four 'zones of economic

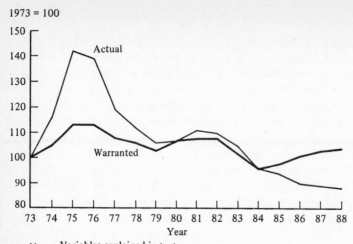

Note: Variables explained in text.
Source: Freitas and Macedo (1990).

Figure 9.3   Portugal: labour share, 1973–88

unhappiness,' which feature different combinations of internal and external imbalances. In Figure 9.4 the locus of internal balance coincides with the vertical axis and the locus of external balance is downward-sloping: from a point on it a greater output gap (arising, say, from excess demand) requires a smaller wage gap (arising, say, from wage moderation). For one measure of the wage and output gaps, Figure 9.4 plots the observed combinations, so as to elucidate the nature of the adjustment process. The measure of the output gap is given by the deviations from a 2.8% trend growth over the 1973–88 period. The wage gap reported in Figure 9.4 does not make assumptions about trade elasticities. It simply computes the labour share allowing for changes in the terms of trade assuming that the share of non-traded goods in the consumer price index is one-fourth. The base year of 1973 is taken as a position of internal and external balance. The combination of an external deficit and unemployment in 1974–75 is followed by deficit and accelerating inflation in 1976–77 and surplus with inflation after the stabilization of 1978–79. The renewed expansion of 1980–82 turns the surplus into deficit until the stabilization of 1983–85. The expansion of 1986–88, initially characterized by a surplus and disinflation, is now turning towards inflation and deficit.[6] The plots in Figure 9.4 do not exactly follow the observed sequence but demonstrate wide variations in the wages and output gaps, suggesting an adjustment process where real wages bore the brunt of adjustment as the public sector continued to expand.

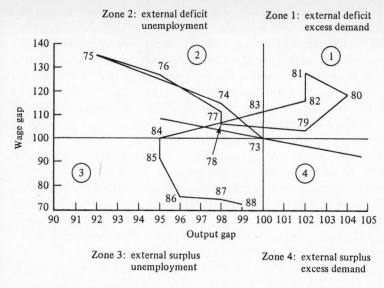

Figure 9.4   Portugal: wage and output adjustment, 1973–88

A degree of flexibility has been maintained in the labour market despite the 1976 law which confined lay-offs to the most extreme cases. Employers have outflanked the law by hiring employees on renewable short-term contracts (usually 6 months). These employees accounted for an average of 12% of total employment in the period 1983–88. Short-term contracts enable employers to adjust to changes in economic performance, and their existence means that the labour market is not so much rigid as segmented. The announcement in 1987 of the intention to replace the 1976 law by an allegedly more flexible one did not prevent short-term contracts from increasing in 1988.

The impact of the completion of the internal market on the labour market will depend on how long wage levels in Portugal remain significantly below those elsewhere in the Community and on how fully freedom of movement of labour is applied. Portuguese emigration shows a very high elasticity to foreign per capita income. Since the differential between incomes in Portugal and in the developed EC countries is still large, completion of the single market is likely to be followed by emigration. The pattern of emigration in the long run depends on how workers perceive the evolution of wages in the home country, since expected higher future home wages lower the emigration rate. If workers believe that home wages will not approach the levels of other EC countries for some time, they will emigrate and perhaps return after wages have adjusted.

With total freedom of labour to move where it likes, new (domestic and foreign) investment will not go to industries that can survive only on the basis of cheap labour, because investors will expect that by the time the investments mature the cost of labour will have risen relative to alternative locations for these industries. If the EC partner countries, however, maintain their present immigration policies beyond the single market deadline, investment in industries that gain from the use of cheap unskilled labour is to be expected. The period for recouping the investment will be shorter the faster wages converge on EC levels.

Pressure in the labour market for qualified workers is going to be significant even if there is no free mobility, because the level of qualification of the labour force is very low compared with the other countries of the EC and the educational system has been slow to upgrade. Immigration at the top levels of skills is thus likely.

4   Trade liberalization and competitiveness

The world recession induced by the second oil shock in 1979, the strong dollar and the Third World debt crisis did not interrupt Portugal's catching up with the EC until 1983. Between 1980 and 1982 Portugal grew at an annual rate of 3% while the EC stagnated. Yet the fall in the terms of trade was 3% a year between 1980 and 1984, and it was compounded by the rise in world interest rates. The belated adjustment to these two adverse shocks was carried out in a second stabilization package with the IMF, in 1983–84. Then, between 1985 and 1988, Portugal's merchandise terms of trade rose by 22% or 5.8% a year. This improvement, which was due to the falling dollar as well as to the decline in oil prices, was shared by other EC countries, but, because of Portugal's great openness, it had a stronger effect. It allowed the government to pursue an expansionary policy without sacrificing its anti-inflation stance, at least in 1986 and 1987.

This fast-growth policy fuelled an investment boom which turned out to be much greater than the forecasts in the PCEDED. The public sector behaved as planned so the current account was worse than forecast in 1987. Yet the external consequences remained under control because of the good behaviour of exports and sizeable inflows of capital. The favourable trend in competitiveness since 1976 is evident from Figure 9.5. In terms of relative unit labour costs (labelled *RULC*) it was reversed in 1981 and has deteriorated slightly since accession. The indicator based on unit costs (named *RUC*), which allows for changes in the relative user cost

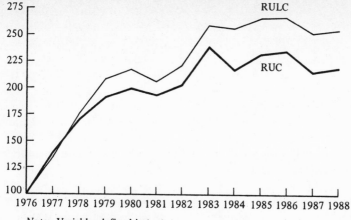

Note: Variables defined in text.
Source: Macedo (1985), updated.

Figure 9.5   Portugal: indices of competitiveness, 1976–88

of capital, shows a decline from the 1983 peak. This shows that the policy of low real interest rates that was pursued because of the high public debt burden did not manage to lower the user cost of capital relative to the main trading partners. Indeed, capital costs are likely to be higher for private firms, which do not have favoured access to credit from nationalized banks. Since accession, the major explanation for the good export performance has been not exchange-rate policy but the response of traditional export sectors to a stable macroeconomic environment.

This was also the case before the revolution, when the escudo was pegged to the dollar. Even though it appreciated in nominal terms relative to the pound and the franc and inflation picked up after 1967, exports to EC and EFTA markets remained competitive. Indeed, the relative neglect of the colonial markets in Africa was already visible in the 1960s on both the export and the import side. Since then the EC and, in particular, neighbouring Spain have become even more dominant export and import markets (Table 9.3). As the colonial issue became more overwhelming politically, it was losing economic importance. While free trade with the African colonies rose in political and declined in economic significance, European integration became of more economic but less political importance.

The divergence between political objectives and economic imperatives helped to perpetuate the ambiguous response to external liberalization. It was exacerbated after the revolution. State-owned enterprises remained long after their external competitiveness had been eliminated in favour of

	1970		1983		1985	
	Imports	Exports	Imports	Exports	Imports	Exports
EC9	48	42	39	58	52	62
Spain	5	2	7	4	12	9
EFTA	9	12	6	11	7	11
Total	62	56	52	73	71	82

Table 9.3. Portugal: direction of trade, 1970–85 (% of total merchandise)
Source: Data from Mexia (1989).

private exporters. This dual structure reappears in different guises throughout the period. Thus manufacturing is dominated by textiles – particularly cotton – and oil-refining, each a good example of the two distinct segments of manufactures. The first is labour-intensive and oriented to exports and the domestic market; the second is more capital-intensive and import-substituting. These characteristics are evident in the sample of industries (identified by their NACE Code as well as by name) reported in Table 9.4.[7]

The first segment, which began as an export enclave in the 1960s, includes cotton (NACE Code 432), knitwear (436), clothing (453) and footwear (451), metal products, small tools and equipment (316), pulp and paper (471), glass (247), ceramics (248) and cork products (466). Textile exports represent 25% to 30% of total exports. Except for pulp, economies of scale internal to the firm are small. The average value of production per firm is less than or equal to the UK or Italy but larger than Spain. In the textile industry, however, Portugal and Spain have a dualistic structure with a large number of very small family-run firms and a few large, more competitive and more export-oriented firms.

The firms nationalized after the revolution belonged to the second segment. Import-substituting, state-owned firms are either monopolies or had significant market power in the domestic market in 1983. For these industries the average size of firm, in terms of output and employment per firm, is greater than or equal to the average size of firms in the UK, Italy or Spain. Such is the case for oil-refining (140) and cement (242). The iron and steel industry presents smaller firm size. Before EC entry these industries were protected from international competition through several devices, including quantitative restrictions such as those on oil products. They were also favoured in terms of government procurement. Foreign investment was restricted or even forbidden. As a result industries in the second segment were heavily concentrated.

NACE code	Name	1983 share of industrial		Concentration H High M Medium L Low	Ownership G State P Private F Foreign
		Output %	Employment %		
140	oil-refining	13.0	0.3	H	G
242	cement	1.5	0.4	H	G
257	pharmaceuticals	1.0	1.1	M	P/F
260	man-made fibres	0.6	0.4	H	P
316	metal tools	2.4	4.6	L	P
345	electronic appl.	2.2	2.2	M	P/F
432	cotton	5.9	10.3	L	P
471	pulp paper	2.7	1.7	H	G/F
Sum		29.3	21.0		
221	iron and steel	2.1	1.0	H	G
247	glass	0.7	1.3	L	P
248	ceramics	0.8	1.9	L	P
350	motor vehic.	3.0	2.3	H	F/P
436	knitwear	2.1	4.5	L	P
451	footwear	1.2	2.8	L	P
453	clothing	2.5	6.1	L	P
466	cork	1.1	2.0	L	P
Sum		13.5	21.9		

Table 9.4. Portugal: industry characteristics, 1983
Source: Adapted from Corado (1989), Tables A1-2, 3, 4.

In spite of this dual structure, simulations which apply different versions of the single market programme to the eight industries listed in the top panel of Table 9.4 indicate that social welfare in Portugal would tend to rise because consumers' gains would more than offset producers' losses. To interpret the results reported in the left hand panel of Table 9.5, note that the experiments involve 'tariff equivalent' reductions which reduce direct trade costs, and increase intra-EC trade flows. If the number of firms is fixed (short-run), an increase in imports will increase competition and lower prices, so consumers will gain. If the fall in profits offsets this, welfare falls. In the long run, profits are restored to base values through the exit of firms from the industry. Firm scale is increased and average costs decline, but a greater concentration brings higher prices so that consumer surplus falls. This experiment underestimates what is involved in the transition to EC membership combined with the completion of the single market, because the major effect of 1992 is to replace

NACE code	Name	Segmented markets		Integrated markets	
		Short-run	Long-run	Short-run	Long-run
140	oil-refining	0.5	n.a.	8.9	n.a.
242	cement	−0.9	0.0	2.1	n.a.
257	pharmaceuticals	1.4	0.2	5.8	4.8
260	man-made fibres	−0.5	0.3	8.6	13.9
316	metal tools	1.5	0.6	1.8	0.9
345	electronic appl.	0.5	0.6	3.8	4.6
432	cotton	−0.3	0.2	0.9	3.7
471	pulp paper	2.0	2.1	17.9	n.a.

Table 9.5. Portugal: simulated welfare gains from the Single Market (% 1983 consumption)

Source: Adapted from Corado (1989), Table 3.

segmented national markets by an integrated one. In that case, referred to in the right panel of Table 9.5, firms must charge the same producer price, although consumer prices might still diverge because of differences in trade costs. The same difference between short-run and long-run welfare effects is present here. Since firms will reallocate sales towards the domestic market (where they previously charged a higher price), production rises in net-importing countries. But since the (common) price–cost margin is reduced, prices are lower and therefore welfare effects are larger if firms cannot price discriminate. As a percentage of base consumption, welfare gains in Portugal are larger than in Spain, which in turn tend to be close to those for the entire EC.[8]

The positive results in Table 9.5 hide substantial losses in output and profits. More detailed case studies of textiles and clothing, the success story of EFTA phase, provide grounds for cautious optimism. The first industry accounted for 25% of manufacturing employment in 1985. Even though it is only a negligible export, it produces a major input for clothing, which in turn accounted for 22% of manufacturing employment and 17% of exports in 1985. This export share rose from 13% in 1981 to 22% in 1987. The predominance of small-scale firms in these two industries is clear from the total number, respectively 684 and 1,467 in 1985. However, their evolution has been different. In the input sector, concentration has been increasing together with investment in machinery. Labour costs have become less overwhelming and labour productivity in 1985 was about 40% higher than in 1977. Price trends suggest an upgrading from low- to high-grade fabrics. In the output sector, concentration has been falling, investment has been modest and labour productivity increased by only 20% between 1976 and 1985. Even though manual work predominates, the low cost of labour enabled textiles and clothing to achieve a very substantial improvement in their shares of the EC market between 1980 and 1985, respectively from 1 to 2% and from 2 to 4%.

Yet, although Portugal already exported (and re-exported) 102% of output in 1985, the improvement in market shares for clothing were even more impressive for Turkey which may have replaced Portugal as a 'pyjama republic'. Moreover, evidence of quality upgrading for Portugal comes from comparison of unit prices which are twice as large as Turkey's but only about two-thirds of Italy's. Wages per man hour in 1986, on the other hand, were 2 US dollars, about the same as in Hong Kong, half those of Spain and one-fifth those of Italy. If the transition to higher grades is fast enough, this trend will not be threatened by competition from outside the EC.[9]

Is the fact that comparative advantage has been strongly at work, despite the adverse fiscal environment, another example of market forces overcoming the consequences of ambiguous public response to external liberalization? Up to a point. The optimism must be qualified when a more aggregative view is taken, grouping sectors according to the growth of demand (measured by apparent consumption) in the EC, the US and Japan. So-called 'strong-demand' sectors such as office and data-processing machines, electrical and electronic goods, and chemicals and pharmaceuticals have been growing at over 5% p.a. since the 1960s. Growth of about 3% p.a. identifies 'moderate-demand' sectors, such as rubber and plastics, transport equipment, food, beverages and tobacco, paper and printing products and industrial and agricultural machinery. Finally, so-called 'weak-demand' sectors, such as metal products, miscellaneous manufactures, ferrous and non-ferrous ores, textiles, leather and clothing, and construction materials have experienced a growth rate of less than 2% p.a. in recent decades. These groupings have been thought robust enough to explain the strength of Germany's export performance and to predict the costs of adjusting to 1992. To the extent that inter-industry trade is associated with weak-demand sectors, the single market will imply falling profits in labour-abundant countries.

Portugal's industrial structure according to these criteria is presented in Tables 9.6–9.9. Higher and growing output shares for weak-demand sectors, especially in the very dynamic trade with Spain and the other EC countries, the declining index of intra-industry specialization in strong-demand sectors, and rising employment and investment in weak-demand

	1977			1986	
Demand	P	EC		P	EC
Strong	11	20		12	23
Moderate	42	46		37	46
Weak	47	34		51	31

Table 9.6. Structure of value added in Portugal and the EC, 1977–86 (% of total)

Source: Data from Mexia (1989).

	Imports			Exports		
Demand	EC10	Spain	Other	EC10	Spain	Other
Strong	82	112	54	18	165	− 10
Moderate	143	162	41	68	196	5
Weak	127	227	68	117	433	58
Total	121	167	49	82	251	34
World		95			65	

Table 9.7. Direction of Portuguese trade in manufactures, 1985–87 (% volume increase from 1985 to 1987)

Source: Data from Gama (1989).

	World		EC	
Demand	1983	1987	1983	1987
Strong	37	33	31	32
Moderate	21	26	23	27
Weak	18	24	17	25
Total	23	26	22	27

Table 9.8. Intra-industry specialization in Portugal's total trade, 1983–87 (% total trade)

Source: Data from Gama (1989).

Demand	77–79	80–82	83–85	1986
Imports = 100				
Strong	28	28	31	29
Moderate	45	45	43	43
Weak	27	27	26	28
Export = 100				
Strong	15	15	19	16
Moderate	30	30	27	26
Weak	55	55	54	58
Employment = 100				
Strong	7	8	8	8
Moderate	30	29	30	29
Weak	63	63	62	63
Investment = 100				
Strong	n.a.	21	16	10
Moderate	n.a.	34	38	39
Weak	n.a.	45	46	51

Table 9.9. Portuguese trade and industrial structure, 1977–86 (% of total)
Source: Data from Gama (1989).

sectors, all seem to indicate that significant adjustment costs are to be expected from the necessary restructuring of Portuguese industry. If firms do not invest in differentiated products, export upgrading will be too slow and the industrial structure will remain fragile.

The same message emerges from the recent acceleration of foreign direct investment in Portugal. The accumulated rate of increase from the 1980–85 average to 1986–88 was 153% (79% for manufacturing) and the share of the EC partners rose from 48% to 67% during the same period. Although foreign direct investment is likely to be a major force in Portugal's industrial restructuring, the level is still below the Community average. Table 9.10 shows that foreign direct investment is mostly directed to weak-demand sectors. Table 9.11 reveals the changing composition in terms of sectors and type of operations: the attractiveness of services (financial or otherwise, including real estate) and of existing firms is quite pronounced.

Trade and investment opportunities are thus being exploited, but fundamental policy choices are being postponed, perhaps until the external environment – and in particular the common external tariff – are not quite as favourable to Portuguese exports to other EC markets. The

	80–82	83–85	86–88	1988
Manuf. share of total	61	49	35	33
Of which weak-demand	67	63	78	75
Share of GDP (%)	n.a.	1	1.4	2.3

Table 9.10. Foreign direct investment in Portugal, 1980–88 (% increase)
Source: Data from Mexia (1989).

	1985	1988
Commerce, tourism		
Construction (1)	18	48
Import substitution (2)	13	15
Textiles, clothing, footwear	3	3
Resources-based exports (3)	30	4
Financial services (4)	21	18
Chemicals and base metals (4)	11	7
New firms/subsidiaries	25	21
Existing firms	60	48
Other	15	31

Table 9.11. Structure of foreign direct investment in Portugal, 1985–88 (% of total)

Notes:
1. including real estate
2. food, beverages, tobacco
3. pulp and mining
4. formerly restricted sectors

Source: Adapted from Corado and Leite (1989).

pattern of trade competitiveness shows features of both inter-industry and intra-industry specialization, so that the economy's response to the 1992 challenge remains as ambiguous as public policy.[10] Eventually a better domestic environment will be needed to contend with the effects of continued worldwide trade liberalization.

5   Banking regulation and competition

A better domestic environment requires a strong financial market. This implies not only less interference on the part of the government but also a clearer notion of what the public sector is. Moreover, the major obstacle to a more transparent fiscal policy – revenue-seeking – will be eroded by the increased factor mobility that the single market will entail.[11]

In highly competitive and unregulated markets, banks tend to avoid the financing of medium- and long-term investment and to concentrate instead on short-term operations. Where control of corporate behaviour through mergers or take-overs is restricted (and banks are more regulated), firms tend to be committed to their group's commercial bank, which in turn adopts a more flexible approach and a longer-term view. In Portugal the creation of industrial groups which were able to provide their own finance was a consequence of the excessive financial regulation of the 1960s. Tight regulation of credit – with ceilings established on an individual bank basis – made it essential for an emerging industrial and financial group to avail itself of a commercial bank. Most of the seven 'family' groups were indeed called by the name of their respective commercial bank. Because of the close links of these groups with the government, the competitive fringe of new conglomerates did not manage to bring about industrial and financial restructuring.

Had this fringe been successful, thriving firms might have been able to shop around for more attractive sources of funding, but the financing of the export enclave of small manufacturing firms did not operate in this competitive way. Most firms outside groups, deprived also of the option of borrowing abroad, had to finance their long-term investment through their own resources or through revolving short-term loans. The oligopoly situation of the seven groups, together with the comfortable external position, explains why non-monetary financial intermediaries failed to develop. Excessive regulation was not limited to commercial banks.[12]

Because of their diversified earnings, large industrial and financial groups, such as those identified with the 'seven families', do not require a financial market for investment. In the 1960s the managers of the commercial banks at the core of these conglomerates were nurtured in a type of financial intermediation where most of the operations were internal to the group. As the groups could do without a financial market, after the nationalizations of 1975 they probably took the same view of the nationalized sector as a whole. The closing down of the stock market, shortly after the revolution, reinforced this perception. At the same time, the abnormally high levels of gold and foreign exchange reserves changed its nature. Urged by politicians to put banks 'at the service of the people', the managers saw those reserves as collateral against which the nationalized enterprises were borrowing. It can be shown that when there is imperfect monitoring of projects by banks, a rise in collateral makes borrowers more likely to default. To compensate for this decline in the expected return of a loan, the bank selects riskier borrowers and projects, which cause expected bank returns to fall. To avoid a fall in profitability, the bank will prefer to ration credit, even if there are no macroeconomic disturbances.

Credit rationing in equilibrium is exacerbated in a disequilibrium situation characterized by binding credit ceilings on private firms. In an inflationary environment, where every borrower, especially the government, faces negative real interest rates, the disequilibrium effect may be very strong. Financial repression made private firms more dependent on bank credit at a time when retained earnings were low and there was no substitute in the stock or bond markets. The heavy dependence of firms on bank credit made the financial system more fragile because some of the debts were not expected to be repaid to the banks. This reinforced the lack of incentives for creditors to monitor borrowers. It is thus no surprise that after the stock market was revived in 1987 it attracted mostly firms with insufficient retained earnings and with low collateral.

During the expansion of 1981–82, with high wage inflation and controlled prices, profits and retained earnings fell. When interest rates were raised in 1982, the adverse selection effect towards riskier borrowers (who are less reluctant to pay higher rates) was probably offset by a less binding constraint on credit ceilings. This allowed banks a better mix of borrowers and projects. But, in so far as deposit rates were administratively fixed, higher lending rates increased the intermediation margin and reduced the profitability of nationalized banks. Arrears and bad debts accumulated, peaking at 15% of credit to non-financial enterprises and individuals in 1986. At the time non-performing loans were three times as large as the equity of commercial banks. The system is effectively bankrupt: bad debts fell to about 11% of credit in early 1989, but the figure in Spain is 4%. The figures would be much higher for the nationalized banks, which are also saddled with the need to provide for the pensions of their numerous staff.[13]

Paradoxically, the role of nationalized banks in collecting hidden taxes may have helped stabilize the system. The hidden taxes were collected through their excessively wide intermediation margins and passed on through their forced purchases of public debt. Since nationalized banks were acting as collectors of implicit taxes, depositors could be confident that the state would bail them out.[14]

Ten years after the great nationalizations the government finally authorized new entrants, both domestic and foreign, into the banking sector, even though some of them were direct competitors of the nationalized commercial banks. The combined share of the eight nationalized commercial banks in total commercial bank credit fell from 98% in 1979 to 94% in 1985, on account of the rise in the share of foreign banks from 2% to 6%. The share of the eight fell again to 91% in 1987 because of the rise in the share of private domestic banks from zero to 3%. In terms of total assets the new commercial banks were then equivalent to an increase in the total number by one more bank of equal size: in other words, the number equivalent Herfindahl index rose from 8 to 9 between 1985 and 1987.

The new banks avoided holding public debt instruments other than Treasury bills, which had only been introduced in 1984. They were also reluctant to lend to the troubled state-owned enterprises. This meant that they were less exposed to bad debts and suggested a contrast between 'clean' and 'tainted' banks that might prompt depositors' runs on the allegedly riskier banks. The share of private commercia! banks is still small, especially on the liabilities side, but their spectacular growth has had a strong demonstration effect on banking competition, stronger than the mere increase in the number of players.

Instead of attacking the debt overhang of nationalized banks, however, the government decided to impose further regulation on the new banks through a ceiling on deposit rates and a (retroactive!) increase in equity requirements. Because the criterion for establishing credit ceilings was related to a bank's capital, there were significant incentives to overcomply, so that the initial negative reaction to the retroactive capital requirements subsided. The only long-term solution is purification of the 'tainted' banks rather than contagion of the 'clean' ones. On the eve of privatization, however, the government announced a series of mergers within the nationalized banking sector, whereby 'clean' (mostly investment) banks were saddled with 'tainted' commercial banks. This procedure, comparable to the engineered mergers of the nationalization period, met with resistance from managers of the well-run nationalized banks. As a result the government has withdrawn the proposal and has said that the state will buy the bad debts of nationalized banks. To the extent that depositors believed that ultimately the state would bail out the nationalized banks, this was indeed the appropriate measure. The consequent increase in public debt will in part be offset by the proceeds from the privatization of most of the state-owned enterprises that were nationalized in 1975, now that the Constitution has been amended to allow it.

Once again, in the light of the single market objective, the process of catching up needs to be coupled with economic restructuring. The banking sector, through privatization or other means, will have to absorb the overhang of inefficiency. This is unlikely to be completed before 1992, though a faster readjustment cannot be ruled out. As with trade and industry, the pressure for financial readjustment is coming more and more from outside – and it is visible in the booming Spanish financial market. No excessive regulation in Portugal is likely to last without severe damage to financial development, because business will go across the border to Spain. Against the slow evolution of Portuguese nationalized banks, financial restructuring in Spain began several years ago and continues, in the form of mergers among large banks, often encouraged by the monetary authorities.

6   Fiscal adjustment in a frozen public sector

Credit ceilings have been the major instrument of monetary control. In their present form they date from 1978, the time of the first stabilization package. Not surprisingly the allocation of credit to the private sector has been squeezed because of the debt behaviour of the enlarged public sector. Since the demand for credit exceeds what can be afforded by a responsible monetary policy, the potential excess liquidity ends up in the banking system. The rational response on the part of the commercial banks would be to turn down deposits that cannot find their way into loans. To pre-empt this response the Central Bank has created interbank securities markets, where through repurchase agreements, banks invest in securities that are part of the Central Bank's portfolio. The rate of remuneration of the banks' excess liquidity has been determined through an auction system which makes it a kind of 'market' interest rate. Since liquidity purchases have been increasing rapidly – in part because of capital inflows from abroad – new instruments have been created and a more active interest rate policy has been pursued in the interbank market. Yet, in 1988, the net effective interest rate on the public debt held by the Central Bank turned negative.

Restrictive measures were introduced in March 1989 which relied mostly on tighter credit ceilings (including much higher reserve requirements) and avoided the large increases in interest rates that would be required to cool off demand.[15] The real interest rate on domestic public debt rose from −9% in 1980–82 to −3% in 1986–88, but the difference with the rate of growth remains negative and large, as shown in Table 9.12, column 5. Although a further rise in interest rates would increase the burden of public debt, and lower the profits of the Central Bank, it might also reduce the scope for implicit taxation, as argued below.

In July 1989 the Portuguese government approved a revised version of

Years	Change in debt/Y (1)	Implicit nominal int. rate (2)	Change in nominal income (3)	Debt/Y (4)	Interest growth factor (5)	Implied deficit (6)	Reported deficit (7)	Residual deficit (8)
70–73	− 1	3	15	20	− 2	1	− 1	2
74–75	4	3	14	20	− 2	6	2	4
76–77	4	5	25	31	− 6	10	4	6
78–79	4	8	23	38	− 6	10	6	4
80–82	1	11	21	45	− 4	7	1	6
83–85	6	13	22	60	− 5	11	5	7
86–88	2	12	18	71	− 4	6	0	6

Table 9.12. Portugal: decomposition of changes in the total debt–income ratio, 1970–88 (%)

Notes:
(5) = [(2) − (3)] × (4)
(6) = (1) − (5) = (7) + (8).

Source: Macedo (1989b).

the Programme to Correct External Imbalances and Unemployment (PCEDED): reduction in consumption and transfers, increases in taxes, and privatization of public enterprises, including banks, should generate primary surpluses sufficient to stabilize the total debt to output ratio before 1992. This revision had been expected since late 1988 and the objective is not very ambitious. To judge from the 1990 budget, however, whether the required fiscal restraint can be enforced is open to question. One prerequisite for any fiscal adjustment strategy which is lacking is reliable public finance data. The planned size of the yearly adjustment must be credible, but in the absence of data there is no way to monitor the progress of the adjustment effort. Moreover, because some debt is held involuntarily the interest burden calculated by dividing interest payments by the nominal value of the debt is overstated. This is another reason why the PCEDED should be more ambitious. A consolidation at the market rate would imply a substantially lower value of public debt.

Available figures on Portuguese public finances show debt standing at over three-quarters of GDP in 1988, which is already quite large by EC standards. The debt to GDP ratio rises to 100% when 'guarantees' provided by the general government for loans to public enterprises are taken into account (the debt of the electricity company alone was about 20% of GDP in 1987). To the extent that these loans will never be repaid, the existence of these 'guarantees' justifies the notion of a frozen public sector that includes the general government and also state-owned enterprises, including both financial and non-financial enterprises. The so-called 'enlarged' or 'administrative and entrepreneurial' public sector definition was used in the third panel of Table 9.2. Unfortunately its borrowing requirement is difficult to reconcile with debt figures and the reported government deficit.

The accounting framework used here is based on the debt to income ratio rather than on the debt itself. In broad terms this ratio should as a rule be stable in a steady state. In high public debt countries it should probably decline. If interest rates on debt exceed growth rates, the public debt ratio would rise without limit. In such a situation bondholders, fearing that the authorities will try to wipe out the value of the debt through inflation or repudiation, would precipitate a financial collapse. Using such a basis for sustainability calculations implies that bondholders' fears are so strong that they induce the government to announce and enforce a multiannual fiscal adjustment strategy (MAFAS). This is simply a plan to stabilize the accumulation of public debt through increases in revenue and decreases in expenditure such that, excluding interest payments, there is a budget surplus.[16] This rule of thumb provides a useful benchmark, as long as the underlying assumptions are kept in mind.

Calculations based on the debt to income ratio indicate an implied, or actual, deficit that has often been much larger than the reported deficit, suggesting the presence of a sizeable hidden deficit. Table 9.12 decomposes public debt as a share of gross domestic product since 1970. The broader measure of public debt used shows an unsustainable situation, with a ratio increasing at 4% a year for over ten years, despite high growth and negative real interest rates. The difference between the implied deficit – the change in the debt to income ratio net of the interest and growth factor – and the reported deficit is in part due to deficient data, but largely reflects disguised fiscal policy.

Unreported lending operations by the Treasury and debt take-over operations by the government (to the benefit of autonomous funds as well as of public enterprises) are acknowledged sources of discrepancy. They make the decomposition of stock accumulation into well defined flows difficult to interpret on a year-to-year basis but facilitate future fiscal management. Before the revolution the reported surplus was hiding a deficit, except in 1972 when the reported deficit was hiding a surplus. Between 1977 and 1985 – leaving out 1980 because of the debt write-off operation – the implied deficit was on average double the reported deficit,

Years	Chg debt held by: (1)	Interest rate (2)	Tax rate (3)	Tax base/Y (4)	Tax revenue/Y (5)
	%	%	%	%	%
Central Bank					
76–77	67	6	61	15	9
78–79	34	5	29	23	7
80–82	14	4	10	20	2
83–85	29	6	23	25	6
86–88	−2	−3	1	21	0
Central bank and nationalized banks					
76–77	39	6	34	26	9
78–79	30	9	21	30	6
80–82	23	11	12	34	4
83–85	29	15	14	38	5
86–88	16	13	3	41	1

Table 9.13. Portugal: seigniorage tax revenue, 1976–88

Notes: (3)=(1)−(2), (5)=(3)×(4).

Source: Updated from Macedo and Sebastiao (1989) and Beleza and Macedo (1988).

though there were substantial year-to-year variations. This is the same as saying that on top of the reported deficit there was a hidden deficit of equal size. In 1986–88, however, while the reported primary budget deficit was about zero, there was a hidden deficit of 6%.

In Tables 9.13 and 9.14, to interpret better this trend in the total debt to income ratio, public debt is decomposed into domestic and foreign and the domestic into privately and publicly held debt. Total debt accumulation accounts for foreign borrowing by the state and distinguishes the voluntary from the forced holding of public debt. The former is restricted to Treasury bills; all other holdings of public debt count as seigniorage, which is an implicit tax. The reason for using this definition rather than the monetary base is precisely the focus on revenue-seeking by the state. Seigniorage revenue from the foreign counterpart of the monetary base accrues to the foreign state. The interest and growth factor is correspondingly retricted to the debt voluntarily held.[17]

In Table 9.13 the revenue from seigniorage is given by the net accumulation of non-privately held debt (the tax rate) times the non-privately held debt to income ratio (the tax base). Although the revenue has been falling, the pattern is more erratic than the averages in Table 9.13 suggest.

Years	Change debt/Y (1)	Interest growth factor (2)	Implied deficit (3)	Reported deficit (4)	Net foreign borrowing (5)	Seigniorage revenue/Y (6)	Residual deficit (7)
	%	%	%	%	%	%	%
Excluding Central Bank debt							
76–77	−2	−2	0	4	1	9	6
78–79	0	0	0	6	3	7	3
80–82	2	0	2	1	3	2	5
83–85	2	1	1	5	4	6	6
86–88	8	2	6	0	0	0	6
1986	7.3	2.2	5.1	−0.7	0.1	1.8	7.6
1987	8.7	2.4	6.3	−0.3	−0.3	0.2	6.5
1988	6.7	1.5	5.2	−0.2	0.6	−0.8	5.2
Excluding nationalized and Central Bank debt							
76–77	0	0	0	4	1	9	6
78–79	0	0	0	6	3	6	3
80–82	0	0	0	1	3	4	5
83–85	1	0	1	5	4	5	6
86–88	4	0	5	0	0	1	6
1986	7.1	−0.6	7.7	−0.7	0.1	−0.8	7.6
1987	4.1	−0.3	4.4	−0.3	−0.3	2.0	6.5
1988	1.6	−0.4	2.0	−0.2	0.6	2.4	5.2

Table 9.14. Portugal: decomposition of the change in the domestic debt–income ratio, 1976–88

Notes:
$(3) = (1) - (2) = (4) - (5) + (7)$

Source: Same as Table 9.13.

In 1981 and in 1984 revenue from the central bank was 7% and 8% respectively, and in 1981 and 1985 revenue from the nationalized banking system, including the central bank, reached 9% and 10% respectively. The table shows that the tax base and rate differ substantially depending on what is treated as being in the public or the private sector. The different base and rate for the seigniorage tax reflect the distribution between debt privately and publicly held, since in both cases net foreign borrowing remains the same. If nationalized banks are aggregated with the private sector, the tax base remains at about 20% throughout the past decade, but the tax rate falls from 10% in 1980–92 to 1% in 1986–88. Conversely, if only Treasury bills are taken to be privately held, the rate still falls, from 12% to 3%, but the base actually rises from 34% to 41%. Here only the domestic counterpart of the monetary base is included in the definition of seigniorage. When the change in the monetary base is used, there is a much smaller decline in tax revenue from seigniorage. The difference is related to the strong external position in 1986–87.[18]

The existence of implicit taxes and hidden deficits is central to the pattern of macroeconomic adjustment observed in Portugal since the revolution. The adjustment process has largely spared government expenditure. The absence of restrictions on public spending implies larger increases in revenue and resorting to hidden forms of taxation. The accounting framework introduced above was able to uncover disguised fiscal policy. In the same way, taxation analysis cannot neglect the economic incidence of all forms of taxes. To understand fiscal adjustment correctly necessitates going beyond overt incidence.[19]

This approach shows the taxation of financial intermediation to be far different from what is prescribed in the tax code. There is an implicit intermediation tax imposed on borrowers and depositors in the banking system. The rate of implicit intermediation tax depends on the spread between the loan rate and the deposit rate net of an assumed intermediation margin, since both borrowers and lenders suffer from excessively large interest margins. The implicit intermediation tax base depends on the slopes of demand for and supply of credit and deposits. These are in turn related to the alternatives offered to residents. In general seigniorage and other concealed taxes will be collected not only from borrowers and depositors but also from bank shareholders. If the binding constraint is the existence of credit ceilings of private borrowers, the tax base is the corresponding stock of loans. Here this is assumed to be the case, even though private depositors may occasionally have been constrained.

To compute the implicit intermedition tax rate, an average rate on deposits can be calculated from the figures for the stock of total deposits and the interest bill paid by banks. The loan rate for the 91- to 180-day maturity (which was administered until September 1988) can be used as the representative rate for loans extended by commercial banks during the sample period. Credit ceilings imply that these loans are a relatively small share of the total assets of banks. Estimates of the excess burden are shown in Table 9.15 for the case where a reasonable intermediation margin is assumed to be 3%. If the tax base is private credit, then the hypothetical implicit intermediation tax 'revenue' is sizeable. It peaks at almost 10% of GDP in 1982, falling to close to 4% in 1987.

The pressure of the single market deadline was not strong enough to affect the design of the 1988 Tax Act.[20] The most important effect of the introduction of comprehensive income taxation in 1989 may be an

	Deposit rate D	Annualized loan rate L	Private credit/GDP	Tax rate L−I−D	Tax revenue/GDP
78–79	9	20	59	8	5
80–82	12	24	74	9	6
83–85	18	34	63	13	8
86–88	11	21	49	7	4
1986	13.7	22.6	51.6	5.9	3.0
1987	10.1	21.3	48.8	8.2	4.0
1988	8.9	19.7	46.6	7.8	3.7

Table 9.15. Portugal: estimated revenue from implicit intermediation tax, 1978–88 (%)

Note: I=intermediation rate, assumed to be 3%.

Source: Updated from Beleza and de Macedo (1988).

increase in the credibility of a future tax reform in which concealed taxation is reduced to a level consistent with external financial liberalization. Then the government, through a multi-annual fiscal adjustment strategy, will be able to commit itself to restoring control over public finances. This commitment is all the more necessary since the doubling of Community structural funds cannot be expected to continue forever after. Moreover, such a large increase is bound to bring additional pressure on public investment expenditure, because of the requirement that recipient countries match these funds to an equal amount.

7   Monetary and exchange-rate policy

Disguised fiscal policy ends up determining monetary and exchange-rate policy as well. But the effectiveness of capital controls needs also to be taken into account. International capital mobility and free trade in financial services, by greatly increasing the competition among banks, is bound to make Portuguese banks unwilling and unable to finance the deficits of the public sector at rates substantially below comparable borrowers. The conflict between banking competition and constitutional socialism affects public sector reform and the process of catching up in various ways. The most immediate is probably the increased cost of collecting the implicit intermediation tax from depositors, borrowers and shareholders. The new behaviour began in 1985 with the new banks and is likely to become stronger with the banks privatized in 1989. At the same

	Bias	$r-r^*$	$fd-e$	$e+p^*-p$	$i-i^*-fd$	$i-i^*-fd$ peseta
	(1)	(2)	(3)	(4)	(5)	(6)
1984	3.6	−1.1	−10.1	11.9	−2.9	0.2
1985	−3.8	8.8	40.8	−25.2	−6.8	0.1
1986	3.3	4.4	24.4	−15.2	−4.8	0.1
1987	0.7	3.1	11.8	−8.2	−0.5	1.7
1988	0.8	−1.5	−5.5	4.0	0.0	0.8

Table 9.16. Effective crawl bias and real interest differentials, 1984–88 (%)

Notes:
Bias: expected vs realized change in effective exchange rate,
r (r^*) real interest rate,
i (i^*) nominal interest rate,
p (p^*) consumer price inflation,
fd forward rate against the dollar in London,
e realized depreciation against the dollar.

Source: Adapted from Macedo and Torres (1989). Data (1) from *Bank of Portugal Monthly Bulletin.*

time, even if the liberalization of capital movements on a Europe-wide scale is delayed, it is difficult to believe that barriers against the movement of capital between Portugal and neighbouring Spain will be effective. As barriers to trade in goods are being dismantled in accordance with the transition agreement with the EC, capital controls are becoming less effective.

Most EC member countries have retained some restrictions on international capital movements and so have been placed in a group characterized as having a semi-open capital market.[21] Greece and Portugal, like several developing countries, were in the group with closed capital markets. Exchange controls kept interest rates in Portugal artificially low, indicating that as barriers to capital outflows they operated very stringently. Table 9.16 shows in columns 5 and 6 that the average covered interest differential against the dollar between 1984 and 1988 was 0.6% in Spain and about −3.0% in Portugal. If more recent observations are introduced and the early period ignored, the difference between the two neighbouring countries is maintained but Portugal emerges as much less closed.

In view of the opening up of domestic capital markets required by the single market objective, the public finance situation in Portugal is threatening the sustainability of external liberalization. This is also the case in

	Rate of crawl actual	Rate of crawl implied	Nominal effective exch. rate	Relative cons. prices	Relative unit lab. costs	Relative adjust. factor	Relative unit costs
1970–73	0	0	0	−1	4	0	5
1974–75	0	0	2	−7	−4	4	0
1976–77	2	2	18	4	19	0	19
1978–79	14	15	22	8	24	−5	18
1980–82	8	9	10	0	0	0	0
1983–85	12	14	20	1	9	−2	7
1986–88	6	5	5	−3	−2	0	−2

Table 9.17. Portugal: indices of competitiveness, 1970–88 (% per annum)

Notes: Implied rate of crawl has same weights as effective exchange rates; actual rate of crawl has undisclosed weights used by Bank of Portugal.

Source: Updated from Macedo (1985).

other EC countries with a high public debt, such as Greece and Italy. Temporarily to maintain a closed domestic capital market may be justified as a transitory protection of inflation tax revenues. Hence it has been suggested that high-inflation EC countries might together pursue financial repression in a 'soft currency club'. These soft currencies would crawl relative to the EMS, so as to stabilize relative prices throughout the EC. It would be difficult to organize a special arrangement of this sort, however, and the case for such a half-way house is not convincing. Tables 9.16 and 9.17 point to some of the limitations of this approach by suggesting that a passive crawl like the one followed by Portugal since 1977 not only may have ceased to alter relative prices, but has also introduced a significant bias in the system.

The crawl bias shown in the first column of Table 8.16 is obtained by subtracting the nominal interest differential relative to the basket peg using the rate of crawl from the realized interest differential. A positive bias implies that the domestic currency turned out to be less attractive than expected. The size of the bias is related to the variance–covariance matrix of exchange rate changes relative to the numeraire, and it falls from 1986 largely because of the greater fixity of exchange rates after the January 1987 realignment within the EMS.

Like Table 9.17, Figure 9.6 suggests that the crawling peg is no longer altering relative prices. The rate of crawl (*icrawl*) is compared with the change in an effective exchange rate (*NEF*) in which roughly equal weight

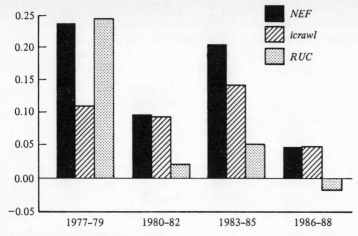

Note: Variables defined in text.
Source: As Figure 9.5

Figure 9.6   Portugal: erosion of the crawling peg, 1977–88

is given to the dollar, the pound, the DM and the French franc. It can be seen that the change in cost competitiveness (relative unit costs including cost of capital, as in Figure 9.5 above) is mostly due to the discrete devaluations of the 1978–79 and 1983–85 periods.

The effect on the Portuguese stock markets of the Wall Street crash of October 1987 was certainly stronger and more lasting than would have been expected in a fairly closed market. This observation confirms the importance of financial development as the output shares of insurance, banking and the marketing of securities grow strongly in EC countries, including the less developed. Table 9.16 shows that the capital market has become much more open since EC entry, with the average negative covered interest parity relative to the dollar falling from close to 6.8% in 1985 to zero in 1987 and 1988. The same pattern can be observed in the case of real interest rates, where a positive differential of almost 9% in 1985 becomes a negative differential of 1.5% in 1988, as well as in the decrease in the expected change in the real exchange rate, related to imperfect integration of goods markets. These developments are in line with the substantial capital inflows observed during and after EC entry and the successful anti-inflationary strategy of 1985–86.

Credit ceilings are a feature of closed capital markets, and in Portugal they have proved quite effective during periods of stabilization. In spite of recent rises, interest rates tend to be kept low so as to alleviate the burden of public debt. This shows again how the political element creeps into financial discipline. The only credible measure to end the direct financing of the Treasury by the banks in EC countries with a high public debt may be an agreement among the central bank, the ministry of finance and the spending ministries on a plan of deficit reduction involving both expenditure and revenue, and perhaps including tax reform. This is the essence of a multi-annual fiscal adjustment strategy (MAFAS).

Because of exchange controls, monetary policy will remain much more passive than in the current members of the EMS or in the UK. True, the government's diminished scope for collecting the implicit intermediation tax led the Treasury to announce that it would cease to have automatic access to the central bank with effect from 1989.[22] Even if this 'divorce' lasts in the 1990s, it is not clear how far the independence of the central bank will be circumscribed by the incomes policy programme, which tends to be agreed between the government and the mostly socialist trade union, the UGT.

For the Portuguese central bank to follow the policies of the German central bank would be an important institutional change. How well the operation of monetary policy adapts in preparation for this change greatly affects the assessment of the costs and benefits of joining the EMS. The divorce between the bank and the Treasury needs to be consolidated and monetary policy needs to learn to operate without the strictures of implicit taxes. The announcement in 1989 of the intention to introduce indirect monetary control needs to be implemented soon if it is to be believed. The decision to subject credit to the public sector to the same ceilings as credit to private firms, with effect from 1 July 1989, is a welcome change in the direction of eliminating the privileges of public-sector borrowing. But it is no substitute for a (credible) MAFAS.

With respect to exchange rate arrangements, the experience of the United Kingdom outside the exchange-rate mechanism of the EMS seems to suggest the advantage for Portugal of exploring forms of association which will enhance the credibility of domestic macroeconomic management without excessive reliance on the policies of the Bundesbank. To experiment with some form of wider band, as in Italy and Spain, seems unavoidable. Indeed, the pressure on the United Kingdom brought about by Spain's joining the EMS and the gathering momentum towards economic and monetary union make earlier membership of the system more likely.

The effect of joining the EMS is simulated in Table 9.18 by fixing the escudo to the DM and comparing the real effective exchange rate obtained, with and without price adjustment. Except in 1988, the real appreciation that has occurred since 1985 would have been exacerbated

	Nominal exchange rate		Rel. cons. prices	Real exchange rate		
	actual	nominal fix		actual	real fix	nominal fix
Bilateral with respect to D mark						
1986	119	100	112	106	100	95
1987	136	100	121	112	100	93
1988	140	100	132	107	100	81
Effective with weights US = UK = 24%; D = 28%; F = 23%[a]						
1986	103	87	108	95	90	80
1987	109	80	116	94	84	70
1988	115	82	124	93	87	66

Table 9.18. Simulating the escudo fixed to the D-mark, 1986–88 (1985 = 100)

Note:
[a]Weight rounded.

Source: Data from Table 9.17.

by pegging to the DM. This is because the escudo depreciation relative to the DM was less than the dollar, franc and pound depreciation in 1986 and 1987. Had prices remained fixed, the real appreciation would have been even stronger, reaching 44% in 1988 relative to 1985. Moreover, it would have continued in 1988. These two experiments provide upper and lower bounds for the effect of exchange-rate policy during the 1985–86 disinflation process. Without a passive crawling peg, the real appreciation would have been excessive, yet inflation was partly fuelled by depreciation. These very crude measures suggest therefore that disinflation cannot last without prior control over the level of expenditure, which is impossible without fiscal adjustment. Joining the EMS with largely open capital markets will not reverse inflationary expectations and thus will not be credible unless reductions in the public sector borrowing requirement are expected.[23]

For a time in 1987 the pound sterling followed the EMS informally, but demand expansion made this a short-lived strategy. Were Portugal to make a similar attempt it would require a greater degree of monetary and fiscal restriction than in the PCEDED. A shadow exchange-rate arrangement would be less rigid than membership of the EMS, which would tie the central bank's hands. If the MAFAS is so gradual that the public sector remains essentially frozen, shadowing the EMS may be the only feasible alternative consistent with opening the capital markets before 1996. In short, for the immediate future experimentation with an informal peg may be more credible than either keeping the crawling peg or joining the EMS with a wide band, though as time passes shadowing will become a less satisfactory solution. Should the MAFAS not materialize beyond the existing PCEDED, such extra credibility would quickly disappear. The argument for shadowing has been made more pressing by Spain's decision to join the EMS. The great acceleration of trade between the two neighbours is exerting pressure for their financial markets to be integrated as well. This makes it harder for Portugal to pursue an independent monetary policy, even before the beginning of stage one of the Economic and Monetary Union.

8   Conclusions

Portugal's experience makes clear that the expectation of external liberalization does not by itself secure a change in the domestic regime. This was true for labour, trade and industry as well as for finance. Ensuring the durability of the change in policy regime hinges essentially on the credibility attached to the multi-annual fiscal adjustment strategy. Since the existing programme for debt stabilization is not explicit about the means to achieve the objective, its credibility may be questioned. Immediate steps should include improving knowledge of the debt situation of the enlarged public sector and, perhaps, rethinking exchange-rate policy, in the direction of shadowing the EMS.

The order in which trade protection and financial protection are removed does matter. It would be preferable for domestic real liberalization to precede external financial liberalization.[24]

This suggests that the removal of financial protection requires domestic financial liberalization, namely, the recognition of the implicit taxes and administrative controls that are designed to favour borrowing by the Treasury. The ability to bring about an irreversible monetary reform without external pressure may be limited in countries with a high public debt. By requiring the implementation of a multi-annual fiscal adjustment strategy designed to control durably public expenditure, external financial liberalization may be a way of neutralizing the efforts of those groups close to the public sector who lobby for deficit financing and for implicit taxation because these require less adjustment on their part.

The financial regime in Portugal has changed a great deal since private commercial banks began to operate in 1985. Nevertheless, domestic seigniorage and other implicit taxes remain significant burdens on the economy, let alone sizeable sources of government revenue. The pressure of 1992 has not been sufficient to affect the design of the comprehensive income tax introduced in January 1989, but it is raising awareness of the need for a credible multi-annual fiscal adjustment strategy that will go beyond the recently revised Programme to Correct External Imbalances and Unemployment (PCEDED). The agreement of the EC to double structural funds by 1992 is having the same effect, both because it cannot be expected to continue forever and because it requires additional public investment.

When the disinflationary process was reversed in 1988, inflation was still substantially higher than the Community average. At the same time, the financial sector is facing a serious overhang of bad debts. Under these conditions, shadowing the EMS seems to be the appropriate signal that the objective of economic and monetary union will not fail in Portugal because of the burden of a frozen public sector. The burden is evident in commercial banks that are providers of grants disguised as loans paid for by the collection of taxes disguised as margins. In Portugal fiscal adjustment is a prerequisite for financial development. More than that, it is a prerequisite for sustained economic growth and structural change. The longer public sector reform is delayed, the faster it must proceed to meet the single market deadline. Even if financial liberalization is as remote as 1996, its impact will combine with the efforts to move towards economic and monetary union and is likely to be felt much earlier. The tradition of ambiguous public response to external liberalization is not an attractive feature of Portugal. The government should abandon it by embedding the 1990 budget in a multi-annual fiscal adjustment strategy which will meet the 1992 challenges and bring about the desired economic and social cohesion of the European Community.

NOTES

This country study for the CEPR project on 'Economic Integration in the Enlarged European Community' draws on nine background papers identified in the references. Financial support from the Institute of Portuguese Foreign Trade (ICEP) and criticism from project participants are gratefully acknowledged. Joan Pearce was responsible for substantially reducing ambiguity in the analysis and in the text. Special thanks go also to Bill Branson, for his comment, and to Odete da Cunha, who typed the manuscript countless times. The views expressed are personal. They should not be interpreted as those of the Directorate General for Economic and Financial Affairs of the Commission of the European Communities (DGII), where the author is Director of National Economies.

 1 The channels of structural interdependence are analyzed in Macedo (1981) and the EFTA phase is discussed in Macedo, Corado and Porto (1989). See also Macedo (1989a), whose Annex contains a discussion of the recurrence of

liberalization-cum-stabilization packages between 1977 and 1985, drawing on Corado and Macedo (1989).

2 Government bonds were promised a few years later, but this compensation was regarded by former shareholders as grossly inadequate. The issue became entangled with the legal nature of nationalization and has remained unresolved. The constitutional obstacles to modernization are addressed in Macedo (1984).

3 Freitas (1989) contains further evidence on financial balances and the PCEDED objectives and realizations in 1987–90. Thus annual growth in private consumption was 4.9% rather than 2.9%, public consumption 2.6% rather than 1% and investment 13.7% rather than 7.9%. The 3% difference between actual and forecast domestic demand growth was made up by net imports, so output growth was only 0.5% higher than forecast. Inflation however was almost twice as high 10.5% rather than 5.6%.

4 This was particularly remarkable in 1974–75 when output fell by more than in the EC but employment rose, thanks to a 20% increase in public-sector employment. The model of Barosa and Pereira (1989) tracks well emigration, activity and employment from 1959 to 1985, with a structural break in 1974. Caveats about the data abound.

5 The magnitudes are very approximate because of the unreliability of the data (especially employment data before 1983) and because of the 'wage gap' methodology. The alternatives are explained in Freitas and Macedo (1990).

6 This is the modification of the well-known Swan diagram proposed in Krugman and Macedo (1979). The interaction between the phases of the macroeconomic adjustment process and the gains from trade and factor mobility are taken up in Macedo (1984).

7 According to Leao, Ramada and Reis (1989), the export concentration in EC markets leaves Portugal vulnerable to a loss of competitiveness relative to the newly industrialized countries of the Far East or the emerging market economies of Eastern Europe. While both product differentiation and market diversification are desirable, the pursuit of comparative advantage is difficult to criticize – except insofar as it has been based on subsidies such as the ones included in the PEDIP. If the upgrading called for in Macedo (1984) continues the concentration is not likely to be a serious problem. But the evidence of Leao *et al.* (1989) is very scanty.

8 Corado (1989) compares the two Iberian countries with each other as well as with Italy and the UK. The Spanish country study emphasizes the 'EEC cum 1992 shock'. Corado and Leite (1989) extend the analysis in Corado (1989) and consider the case where Portugal does not remove protection. The welfare gains are somewhat larger than in the segmented market case but smaller than in an integrated market. The sectors covered are only NACE 316, 345, 350 and 471.

9 See note 7 above. Neven (1990) identifies Portugal and Greece as the EC members relying more heavily on comparative advantage based on labour-intensive goods. Unlike Greece, however, Portugal displays comparative advantage in natural resource-based goods – such as paper pulp (NACE 471). This highly concentrated industry is the third case study in Leao *et al.* (1989). There are 3–4 firms but over 70% of output is exported and investment per worker has increased tenfold and labour productivity has doubled since 1977. The predominant export is eucalyptus, which has sometimes been seen as

ecologically unsound. (See D. Smith 'An eucalyptus success story', *Financial Times*, 11 October. 1989.) Similar evidence of export dynamism can be gleaned from other industries, especially telephonic equipment, cereals and biscuits, as well as railway equipment. Buigues and Ilzkovitz (1988) propose a methodology which is applied by Goncalves (1989) to these and other 'sensitive' industries.

10 This goes back to our discussion of the effects of inter- and intra-industry trade, in the context of Portugal's accession to the EC. The notion in Macedo (1984) was that differentiated products and foreign direct investment from outside Europe could replace emigration. Krugman and Venables in this volume show how a small country's comparative advantage in labour-intensive manufacturing may be overwhelmed by market access and size at both high and low levels of trade barriers. They also claim that labour mobility reinforces centripetal forces and may thus hurt the periphery. See Mexia (1989) for a statement of Portugal's industrial and trade strategy after accession: differentiated products and diversified markets.

11 The importance of the revenue-seeking motive was already noted in Macedo, Corado and Porto (1989) in connection with the introduction of the 1985 sales tax – which was supposed to compensate for the loss in tariff revenues. See also note 20 below.

12 If only commercial banks were too tightly regulated, there would be incentives for other financial institutions to create money. Note that when commercial banks are not regulated enough, they become prone to panics and disasters. Corbett (1989) draws this lesson with Eastern Europe in mind.

13 Branson (1986) suggests that the outcome could have been either a collapse or a stable solution. He cites interviews giving much higher figures than the ones from Banco de Portugal, *Boletim Trimestral*, Marh 1986 reported in the text. Many bad debts are not listed as non-performing loans, and there is no disaggregated data available from the banks' reports. During the stabilization episode of 1977–79 bad debts were kept outside the credit ceilings, so that there was a perverse incentive running against the adverse selection effect. These points are elaborated upon in his contribution to this volume and in his comment on this paper.

14 The proposed implementation in Portugal of a scheme such as the Federal Deposit Insurance Corporation in the US could only exacerbate the bias towards bad loans, even on the part of heavily exposed banks. There is already an excess of insurance against bank failures, based on the gold reserves of the Banco de Portugal as well as on an implicit guarantee by the taxpayer.

15 According to Silva (1968), prime minister since 1985, the bias was already present in 1966. Freitas (1989) discusses the growing ineffectiveness of credit ceilings and the increase in reserve requirements in March 1989 (from an average rate of 6% to a single rate of 17%), together with the recent measures to eliminate the privileges of the public sector as a borrower.

16 The original version of the PCEDED approved in 1987 did not include a MAFAS. The current version compares the base case with a 'no adjustment' scenario. The first yearly Plan for Public Debt (PDP) was also approved in 1989.

17 The revenue perspective followed here suggests this definition, but at the cost of preventing comparability with Table 9.12. If income growth were spread over the entire debt (including the debt involuntarily held), the interest and growth factor would remain the same. See Gaspar and Macedo (1989). Tables

9.12 and 9.14 are not directly comparable but it is clear that excluding foreign borrowing and debt not held in the nationalized banks makes a substantial difference. Also the average implied deficit is the same for both criteria, and the interest factor is negligible for Treasury bills. Since the reported deficit has a mostly political content, it is interesting to note that it is only slightly larger on average than foreign borrowing.

18   In his comment on this paper, Branson provides the following reader's guide to Tables 9.12–15: 'The expression for the growth rate of the ratio of debt to income (*db*) is given in equation (3) of my paper, repeated here for reference:

(1) $db = (r - n)b + d - s.$

Here *r* is the real borrowing rate, *n* is the real growth rate, *b* is the ratio of debt to GNP, *d* is the ratio of the non-interest deficit to GNP, and *s* is the ratio of seigniorage to GNP. Equation (1) can be rewritten as an expression for the implicit deficit, as

(2) $d = db - (r - n)b + s.$

In Table 9.12, the implied deficit in column (6) is calculated as the change in the debt–income ratio, our *db*, in column (1) less the interest–growth factor, our $(r - n)b$, in column (5). This is the implicit deficit net of seigniorage, $(d - s)$. For example, in 1980–82, the implicit deficit in Table 9.12 is 7 percent of GNP, compared with a reported deficit of 1 percent. To obtain the total implicit deficit, inclusive of seigniorage finance, we add central bank seigniorage tax revenue/*Y* from Table 9.13, 2 percent in 1980–82, for a total 9 percent. The financing of this deficit can be obtained from column (5) of Table 9.14, which gives the IIT component. For example, in 1980–82, the foreign component was 3 percent of GNP, and the IIT was 6 percent.'

19   Gomulka (1989) identifies a 'hidden interest rate subsidy' which rose to 25% of GDP during the hyperinflation of June/December 1989. Hillman (1989) dwells on 'soft budget constraints' in Hungary, a point emphasized in the Greek country study and by Rodrik in this volume.

20   The modernization of the tax system began with the introduction of a value added tax in 1986, was follows by the introduction of a comprehensive income tax on 1 January 1989 and is to be completed by the reform of capital taxation. Without the abatement of concealed taxation fiscal adjustment would be incomplete on the revenue side. The importance of simplicity is evident in the proposal for tax reform of Macedo and Gaspar (1989), which involves a single marginal tax rate.

21   The interpretation uses the approach of Jeffrey Frankel as discussed in Macedo (1990). A complete set of data is in Macedo and Torres (1989).

22   The accounting framework used in Section 6 was originally applied to Italy, where the situation was similar before the so-called 'divorce' between the central bank and the treasury in 1981. See Macedo and Sebastiao (1989) and Beleza and Macedo (1988) on the Portuguese experience. Klein and Neumann (1989) discuss the German and UK experience of central bank seigniorage.

23   The real appreciation resulting from joining the EMS is dealt with by Branson and by Krugman in this volume. See also Gaspar's comment and Gaspar and Macedo (1989).

24   The argument is made in connection with Greece, Spain and Portugal in Macedo (1990), where further references are cited.

REFERENCES

Background papers

Barosa, J.P. and P.T. Pereira (1989). 'Labour Supply in an Environment with Emigration: An Empirical Study of the Portuguese Case', August.

Corado, C. (1989). 'Portuguese Industry and the Effects of EC Membership', August.

Freitas, M.L. (1989). 'Portugal Perante o Mercado Unico: As Reformas Macro-economicas no Processo de Ajustamento', September.

Freitas, M.L. and J.B. Macedo (1990). 'The Portuguese Wage Gap Revisited', January.

Gama, A.C. (1989). 'Vantagens Comparativas para Portugal', August.

Leao, E., P. Ramada and A.B. Reis (1989). 'Evolucao Recente e Perspectivas Futuras do Sector Exportador Portugues de Tecidos, Vestuario e Pasta de Papal', August.

Macedo, J.B. (1989a). 'The Political Economy of Portugal's European Integration 1949/88', August.

(1989b). 'Financial Integration and Disguised Fiscal Policy in Portugal', August.

Mexia, A. (1989). 'Conclusoes', September.

Other references

Beleza, L.M. and J.B. Macedo (1988). 'Implicit Taxes and Credit Ceilings: The Treasury and the Banks in Portugal', Working Paper No. 106, New University of Lisbon, December.

Branson, W. (1986). 'Portugal's Entry into the European Communities: Challenges and Opportunities', draft paper of a World Bank Report.

Buigues, P. and F. Ilzkovitz (1988). 'The Sectoral Impact of the Internal Market', draft paper, Commission of the European Communities, DGII, July.

Corado, C. and A.N. Leite (1989). 'Industrial Location and Foreign Investment in the Iberian Peninsula', draft paper presented at the Second European Research Workshop on International Trade, Bergen, June.

Corado, C. and J.B. Macedo (1989). 'Competitiveness under Liberalization cum Stabilization Packages (LCSP): the Experience of Portugal 1977–1985', *Nova Economia em Portugal (Barbosa Festschrift)*, New University of Lisbon, pp. 541–58.

Corbett, J. (1989). 'Policy Issues in the Design of Banking and Financial Systems for Industrial Finance', draft paper presented at DGII, Commission of the European Communities, Seminar on Poland and Hungary.

Gaspar, V. and J.B. Macedo (1989). 'The Case for Budgetary Restraint in Portugal: Short-Run and Long-Run Arguments', draft paper written at Conference on 'Economic Integration in an Enlarged European Community', October, Delphi.

Gomulka, S. (1989). 'Monetary Policies in Poland 1989–90', draft paper presented at DGII, Commission of the European Communities, Seminar on Poland and Hungary.

Goncalves, P. (1989). 'Les Enjeux Sectoriels du Marche Interieur pour l'Industrie Portugaise', draft paper for the Commission of the European Communities, DGII-V project on the Internal Market, Associacao Industrial Portuguesa, October.

Hillman, A. (1989). 'Macroeconomic Policy in Hungary and its Microeconomic Implications', draft paper presented at DGII, Commission of the European Communities, Seminar on Poland and Hungary.

Klein, M. and M. Neumann (1989). 'Seigniorage: What Is It and Who Gets It?', Institut für Internazionale Wirtschaftspolitik, Universität Bonn, Discussion Paper No. B-124.

Krugman, P. and J.B. Macedo (1979). 'The Economic Consequences of the April 25th, 1974 Revolution', *Economia* 3, 455–83, reprinted as Economic Growth Centre Paper No. 299, Yale University, 1981.

Macedo, J.B. (1981). 'Portugal and Europe: The Channels of Structural Inter-dependence', in J.B. Macedo and S. Serfaty (eds), *Portugal since the Revolution: Economic and Political Perspectives*. Boulder, Colorado: Westview Press.

(1984). 'Portugal and Europe: Dilemmas of Integration'. In T. Bruneau *et al.* (eds.) *Portugal in Development: Emigration, Industrialization, the European Community*, University of Ottawa Press.

(1985). 'Integracao Europeia: Fim do Principio ou Principio do Fim?', *Economia* 9, 515–29.

(1990). 'Financial Liberalization and Exchange Rate Policy in the Newly Integrating Countries of the European Community', forthcoming in Bergamo Conference on 10th Anniversary of EMS, edited by P. Ferri: Macmillan.

Macedo, J.B., C. Corado and M.L. Porto (1989). 'The Timing and Sequencing of Trade Liberalization Episodes in Portugal', Working Paper No. 109, New University of Lisbon, January.

Macedo, J.B. and V. Gaspar (1989). 'Uma Reforma Fiscal para 1992: Imposto Liner Unico sobre o Rendimento', *Nova Economia em Portugal (Barbosa Festschrift)*, New University of Lisbon, pp. 381–402.

Macedo, J.B. and M. Sebastiao (1989). 'Implicit Taxes and Public Debt: the Portuguese Experience', *European Economic Review* 33, 573–79.

Macedo, J.B. and F. Torres (1989). 'Interest Differentials, Financial Integration and EMS Shadowing: Portugal and a Comparison to Spain', draft paper presented at Conference on Portugal and the Internal Market of the EEC, Lisbon, October.

Neven, D. (1990). 'EEC integration towards 1992: some distributional aspects.' *Economic Policy* No. 10, 5, 13–62.

Silva, A.C. (1968). *O Mercado Financeiro Portugues em 1966*, Lisbon: Gulbenkian Institute of Science.

10 Soft budgets, hard minds[1]: stray thoughts on the integration process in Greece, Portugal and Spain

DANI RODRIK

As economists, we are culturally predisposed towards markets. Therefore, when we analyze the consequences of economic integration into the European Community, as the country studies in this volume do so well, we naturally focus on its effects on the workings of specific markets. The most important markets being those for goods, labour and capital, the analysis turns on questions of the following sort: how will integration affect trade performance and current account balances? What will be the consequences for the domestic allocation and availability of credit and capital, and how about the outlook for unemployment?

Yet in their own different ways, the three country studies also highlight another kind of influence rising from European integration, one that is perhaps ultimately of greater consequence for eventual economic performance: the impact on established modes of public sector behaviour and state–society relations. The importance of this channel rises from its obvious role in determining the setting in which the aforementioned markets operate. The terminology may differ – Louka Katseli talks of state corporatism, Jorge de Macedo of the frozen public sector, and José Viñals of the need to bring the private sector into new alliances with the government – but the realization that the public sector's role will have to be refashioned is common. Arguably, it is in this domain that the integration shock will be felt most severely.

In all three countries, the public sector has built a network of implicit entitlements that cut through various layers of society. In Portugal, both the colonial and the more recent socialist experience help explain the continuing 'ambiguity' of the government to liberalization. In post-Franco Spain, democratization and expanded regional autonomy account for the new demands put on the public sector and the upward pressure on transfers and subsidies. And in Greece, a protected, 'official' sector has long been intertwined with the public sector along corporatist lines, to the detriment of the 'unofficial' sectors. It is these attitudes and patterns of behaviour that are threatened by the competitive pressures brought by integration with the rest of Europe.

To know where we are going, it helps to know where we are. Is there a common malady of the public sector in these Southern European countries? Louka Katseli uses the 'soft budget constraint', borrowed from Janos Kornai (1986), as an overarching theme in explaining how the government interacts with different markets in Greece. Many of the same arguments would apply to the other two countries as well. Put simply, the idea is that selected groups in society (labour unions, large firms and banks, perhaps some farmers' organizations) have traditionally had easy access to the government's resources, and therefore do not face a 'hard' budget constraint as in textbooks. Key weaknesses in the economy's performance are then attributed to the presence of such soft budgets.

Soft budgetism is an interesting concept, but needs to be distinguished at the outset from other structural features equally common in other countries. At one level, we have the general phenomenon of underdevelopment, which the Southern European countries share to varying extents with developing countries. The presence of fragmented markets, sizeable transaction costs, poor information flows, and socio-economic dualism are all features of underdevelopment, as is the generalized tendency to rely on the state for developmental leadership (as highlighted by Alexander Gerschenkron, 1962, a long time ago). At another level, we have the generalized problem, shared equally with industrial countries, of the dynamic inconsistency of government policy. Unlike our textbook model of policy-making, governments all too frequently are Stackelberg followers rather than leaders in setting policy. They generally have the incentive to subsidize and insure agents against their mistakes *ex post*. The notion of 'a responsive government' is based precisely on this expectation (see the discussion in Rodrik and Zeckhauser, 1988). The problem is that this leads individuals and organized groups to take advantage of the government by anticipating such responsiveness.

What independent mileage can we get from the concept of soft budgets then? If individuals and firms can relax their budget constraints by undertaking certain activities, isn't this simply an additional margin over which they optimize? If so, what is so special about behaviour under soft budget constraints?

One way of making the concept analytically interesting is to place it squarely within the familiar rational-choice paradigm, and then ask: what are the ways in which a soft-budget society differs from a hard-budget one, and do these differences help us interpret the Southern European experience? Abstracting from specific markets, then, let us think of a certain action ('a') that individuals (or groups) in the private sector are selecting optimally and which yields utility $u(a)$. This action has costs, given by $c(a)$, which cannot exceed the available budget, b. We write the budget as $b = b(e, \theta)$ to take into account that under soft budgets the constraints may be relaxed by undertaking a certain amount of effort, e (time spent in the ministry's corridors, for example). We presume that a hard budget society would be one where $b(.)$ cannot be relaxed in such a manner ($b_e = 0$). The parameter θ represents an exogenous shock to individuals, which will allow us to carry out comparative statics later on. In turn, there is a certain amount of disutility associated with e, which we can write as $v(e)$. Agents maximize their utility by selecting a and e optimally. The associated Lagrangean is given by:

$$\mathcal{L} = u(a) - v(e) + \lambda[b(e, \theta) - c(a)]$$

Given what we have said so far, derivatives are signed as follows: $u' > 0$, $v' > 0$, $b_e > 0$, $c' > 0$, and if increases in θ are associated with negative shocks, $b_\theta < 0$. Under the usual assumptions regarding rising marginal costs and diminishing marginal utilities, we also have $u'' < 0$, $v'' > 0$, $b_{ee} < 0$, $c'' > 0$.

The three first-order conditions for this optimization are:

$$\mathcal{L}_a = u' - \lambda c' = 0 \tag{1}$$

$$\mathcal{L}_e = -v' + \lambda b_e = 0 \tag{2}$$

$$\mathcal{L}_\lambda = b - c = 0 \tag{3}$$

where I asume that a strictly positive level of effort will be chosen so that (2) holds as an equality. Substituting for λ from (2) into (1), we have the comparative-statics system:

$$\begin{bmatrix} v'c'' - b_e u'' & c'v'' - u'b_{ee} \\ c' & -b_e \end{bmatrix} \begin{bmatrix} da \\ de \end{bmatrix} = \begin{bmatrix} u'b_{e\theta}d\theta \\ b_\theta d\theta \end{bmatrix}$$

with the determinant $\Delta < 0$.

We can now ask how behaviour under soft budget constraints (S) differs from behaviour under hard budget constraints (H). First note that under a hard budget constraint ($b_e = b_{ee} = 0$), the individual's response to a negative shock can be found directly from his budget constraint:

$$(da/d\theta)|_H = b_\theta/c' < 0 \tag{4}$$

The activity has to be reduced sufficiently to make ends meet under the new, reduced budget. The corresponding expression under soft budget is

$$(da/d\theta)|_S = b_\theta/c' + (b_e/c')(de/d\theta) \tag{5}$$
$$\quad\quad (-) \quad\ (+)\ \ (?)$$

whose sign is indeterminate. The second term here comes from the induced effect on e as the budget shifts inward. We can solve for $de/d\theta$ from the above system to get:

$$de/d\theta = -\Delta^{-1}\{b_\theta(b_e u'' - v'c'') + c'u' b_{e\theta}\}$$
$$\quad\quad (+)\quad\quad\quad\quad (+)\quad\quad\ (?) \tag{6}$$

The cross-partial $b_{e\theta}$ captures the differential responsiveness of the government in 'bad' and 'good' states of the world. Now it makes sense to think that the government will be more sympathetic to agents' pleas for assistance when the latter are facing hard times (unless, perhaps, these shocks are strongly correlated across agents). That implies $b_{e\theta} > 0$, which in turn makes equation (6) unambiguously positive: individuals will spend more time in ministry corridors when they get hit by negative shocks.

Going back to equation (5), the important implication from the perspective of economic performance is that the response elasticity of individuals will now be *lower*. Some of the loss in income will be made up by transfers from the government, reducing the need to adjust. In a soft-budget economy, then, consumers, workers, and entrepreneurs will adjust only partially to changes in their external environment. In fact, if $b_{e\theta}$ is large enough the adjustment to shocks could be entirely perverse: it is possible that $da/d\theta > 0$.

An immediate objection to the above is that in general equilibrium somebody *must* face a hard budget constraint. In practice, of course, governments can borrow from abroad, and when they can't, they collect the inflation tax. In either case, the recipients of government largesse do pay for it one way or the other – either immediately, as in the case of the inflation tax, or eventually, as in the case of foreign borrowing. But the uncoordinated pursuit of self-interest by each individual recipient can make a soft-budget equilibrium both possible and, once it exists, sustainable.

When the government can resort neither to foreign borrowing nor to the inflation tax, the consequences may add to the perversity. Now the public sector has to extract additional resources from the unprotected, unofficial sectors of the economy to mobilize the resources needed for the transfers. These latter sectors then operate under double jeopardy: not only do they bear the full cost of negative shocks that hit them; on top they have to pay for the consequences of the shocks that the protected sectors face and manage to pass on. This outcome perhaps becomes more likely as integration proceeds: governments may well be tempted to push the burden of adjustment that the traded sectors will necessarily feel onto the non-traded or residual sectors with less organizational strength and fewer corporatist ties to the state. This may further solidify dualistic structures in these countries. As we see in many countries ranging from Japan and Italy to Turkey, unorganized and unprotected sectors frequently have a functional role to play as the dual (in both the mathematical and structural senses) of the external competitiveness of traded sectors. They serve this role by providing a pool of cheap labour, cheap intermediate inputs, and implicit or explicit taxes.

Soft-budgetism, then, can shed some light on a number of features observed in Southern European economies. It can explain a certain amount of inertia, structural rigidity, and lack of adjustment to changing circumstances. It can explain overly risk-taking activities, where such exist. It can explain the functional role of dualism: we need the unofficial sector for the official sector to be reliably protected from its mistakes. It can explain lower response elasticities throughout. Finally, it may explain the presence of a certain amount of slack or x-inefficiency in enterprises, which is the necessary counterpart to the time spent by managers bending politicians' ears.

But there are a certain number of things that cannot be pinned as easily on soft-budgetism. It is hard to see how soft budgets would lead to a *cumulative* deterioration of performance over time, unless we happen to be observing an uninterrupted string of negative shocks. It cannot explain a growing technology or productivity gap, unless we posit that the state acts asymmetrically.[2] Nor can it explain the presence of excess capacity, high price–cost margins, overcapitalization, and real wage rigidity – all features which are blamed on soft-budgetism in the case of Greece. It is also not quite clear how much qualitative, as opposed to quantitative, change in behaviour is involved.

Understanding the analytics of how the government and the economy interact is not of purely academic interest. We would like to know how integration will affect the working of these economies, and, as I have been arguing, much of the answer lies in what integration will do to this interaction. We want to know which of the observed features are truly 'structural', and which are likely to change under the influence of integration.

In terms of the above model, we can hypothesize that integration could have two effects, quite contradictory to each other. First, integration may facilitate the making of binding commitments by governments that are so inclined. Bureaucrats and ministers may find it easier to say 'no' to supplicants, citing international agreements or EC rules and directives. Many of the forms in which protection would have been provided (e.g. import restrictions) may no longer be available. All this corresponds to a reduction in the magnitudes of b_e and $b_{e\theta}$, and would improve the performance of the economy. The second influence will go in the opposite direction. We can expect a certain amount of central EC funds to be reserved for the purpose of assisting and/or compensating poorer countries and regions. The enlarged resources would then threaten a magnification of soft-budgetism. This is likely to be a real problem, as the *demand* for such resources will no doubt also be magnified (as the above model suggests) by the intensified competitive pressures coming from integration.

To sum up, in economies as highly politicized as those of Greece, Spain, and Portugal, integration is likely to have an impact that goes beyond the economic arbitrage imposed by trade in goods and assets. There will be a second type of arbitrage, between political institutions in the centre and the periphery. Mismanaging the latter shock may result in much greater dislocations. But, as the above suggests, the shock also presents an opportunity for policymakers to design and improve institutions in a manner conducive to successful economic performance.

NOTES

1 With apologies to Alan Blinder and thanks to Bill Branson.
2 Once the agent is hit by a negative shock the additional transfers made by the government may become the new benchmark for future assistance. When the agent's environment improves, the transfers are not reduced and the budget remains bloated. Over time, the effects of negative shocks become cumulative. This possibility is suggested in a criticism of the soft-budget paradigm by Bajt (n.d.). I am grateful to Richard Portes for showing me this paper.

REFERENCES

Bajt, Aleksander (n.d.). 'Soft budget constraint in socialist economies: Dichtung und Wahrheit', unpublished paper.
Gerschenkron, Alexander (1962). *Economic Backwardness in Historical Perspective*, Cambridge, MA, Harvard University Press.
Kornai, Janos (1986). 'The soft budget constraint', *Kyklos* **39**, 3–30.
Rodrik, Dani and Richard Zeckhauser (1988). 'The dilemma of government responsiveness', *Journal of Policy Analysis and Management*, Fall, 601–20.

Index